Moral Fictionalism and
Religious Fictionalism

Moral Fictionalism and Religious Fictionalism

Edited by
RICHARD JOYCE AND STUART BROCK

Great Clarendon Street, Oxford, OX2 6DP,
United Kingdom

Oxford University Press is a department of the University of Oxford.
It furthers the University's objective of excellence in research, scholarship,
and education by publishing worldwide. Oxford is a registered trade mark of
Oxford University Press in the UK and in certain other countries

© the several contributors 2023

The moral rights of the authors have been asserted

All rights reserved. No part of this publication may be reproduced, stored in
a retrieval system, or transmitted, in any form or by any means, without the
prior permission in writing of Oxford University Press, or as expressly permitted
by law, by licence or under terms agreed with the appropriate reprographics
rights organization. Enquiries concerning reproduction outside the scope of the
above should be sent to the Rights Department, Oxford University Press, at the
address above

You must not circulate this work in any other form
and you must impose this same condition on any acquirer

Published in the United States of America by Oxford University Press
198 Madison Avenue, New York, NY 10016, United States of America

British Library Cataloguing in Publication Data
Data available

Library of Congress Control Number: 2023908811

ISBN 978–0–19–888186–5

DOI: 10.1093/oso/9780198881865.001.0001

Printed and bound in the UK by
Clays Ltd, Elcograf S.p.A.

Links to third party websites are provided by Oxford in good faith and
for information only. Oxford disclaims any responsibility for the materials
contained in any third party website referenced in this work.

Contents

Acknowledgments vii
List of Contributors ix

Introduction: Fictionalism—Moral, Religious, Hermeneutic, Revolutionary 1
Richard Joyce

1. Reasons for Pretending and Pretend Reasons 21
   James Lenman

2. Should Moral Error Theorists Make Do with Make-Believe? 40
   Jessica Isserow

3. Moral Fictionalism: How and Why? 64
   Victor Moberger and Jonas Olson

4. Moral Fictionalism and Misleading Analogies 86
   François Jaquet

5. Religious Fictionalism 107
   Graham Oppy

6. The Pretensions of Religious Fictionalism 127
   Bradley Armour-Garb and Frederick Kroon

7. Is the Pope Catholic? Religious Fictionalism and the Hazards of Belief 148
   Mary Leng

8. Religious Fictionalism: Strategies and Obstacles 167
   Michael Scott

9. The Contours of Religious Fictionalism 184
   Natalja Deng

10. Should Moral Fictionalists be Religious Fictionalists (or Vice Versa)? 203
    Robin Le Poidevin

11. Do We Have Reason to Adopt Religious Fictionalism or Moral Fictionalism? 219
    Seahwa Kim

12. Revolutionary Moral Fictionalism and the Problem of
    Imaginative Failure   234
    Stuart Brock

13. Yes to Moral Fictionalism; No to Religious Fictionalism   256
    Richard Joyce

Index   277

Acknowledgments

Many of the papers in this collection grew out of a workshop on moral and religious fictionalism, hosted by Victoria University of Wellington in September 2021. This workshop and published collection were components of a broader research project carried out by the two editors, which was generously supported by a grant from the Marsden Fund Council, managed by Royal Society Te Apārangi.

List of Contributors

Bradley Armour-Garb, Professor of Philosophy, University at Albany-SUNY

Stuart Brock, Professor of Philosophy, Victoria University of Wellington

Natalja Deng, Associate Professor of Philosophy, Yonsei University

Jessica Isserow, Associate Professor in Moral and Political Philosophy, University of Leeds

François Jaquet, Assistant Professor, University of Strasbourg

Richard Joyce, Professor of Philosophy, Victoria University of Wellington

Seahwa Kim, Professor of Philosophy, Ewha Womans University

Frederick Kroon, Professor of Philosophy (emeritus), University of Auckland

Mary Leng, Professor of Philosophy, University of York

James Lenman, Professor of Philosophy, University of Sheffield

Robin Le Poidevin, Professor of Metaphysics (emeritus), University of Leeds

Victor Moberger, Associate Professor of Philosophy, Umeå University

Jonas Olson, Professor of Practical Philosophy, Stockholm University

Graham Oppy, Professor of Philosophy, Monash University

Michael Scott, Reader in Philosophy, University of Manchester

Introduction
Fictionalism—Moral, Religious, Hermeneutic, Revolutionary

Richard Joyce

1. What is Fictionalism?

Much philosophical activity is born of an anxiety that the ontological commitments of ordinary thought and language exceed what the world has to offer. Though we ordinarily talk readily about all the things that we "know," for example, we can also be brought to worry, in epistemologically reflective moments, that perhaps we don't really know anything at all. Though we speak breezily about some actions being "freely chosen," it is not hard to motivate the suspicion, after some metaphysical rumination, that maybe none of our actions are really freely chosen. And so on.

One response to such worries is to embrace skepticism: to accept that some or many of the things to which we ordinarily commit ourselves (knowledge, freedom, etc.) simply do not exist. This skeptical view sees ordinary thinkers and speakers as making the *error* of believing and asserting things that are not true. Such a skeptical response, by its very nature, runs counter to common sense.

By contrast, non-skeptical responses to such worries will generally fall into one of two camps. Some non-skeptics re-examine the commitments of ordinary thought and language, and come to the conclusion that these commitments do not, after all, require anything that the world does not provide. Perhaps, for example, the concept of *knowledge* can be clarified or tweaked or revised in such a way that we turn out to know all sorts of things. Other non-skeptics re-examine the ontology of the world, and come to the conclusion that, when properly understood, the world does, after all, contain whatever entities are required to satisfy our commitments. Either way, the non-skeptical view sees ordinary thinkers and speakers as not falling systematically into error when they hold beliefs and make assertions about the topic in question (though still, of course, *sometimes* making errors).

Regarding some topics, the existence of debate between the skeptic and the non-skeptic is well-known and has been on the public record for centuries.

Richard Joyce, *Introduction: Fictionalism—Moral, Religious, Hermeneutic, Revolutionary* In: *Moral Fictionalism and Religious Fictionalism*. Edited by: Richard Joyce and Stuart Brock, Oxford University Press. © Richard Joyce 2023.
DOI: 10.1093/oso/9780198881865.003.0001

Arguments over the existence of God, for example, have a history that stretches back millennia, and ordinary folk are aware that the general debate exists, even if they are a bit vague when it comes to recounting, say, the details of Anselm's ontological argument. Ordinary language even has names for the basic positions of this debate: "theism," "atheism," "agnosticism." Regarding other topics, however, ordinary folk, untutored in philosophy, might be surprised to learn that there is serious debate to be had. The skeptical hypothesis that *colors* do not exist, for example, is not well-known (despite the fact that even Newton espoused the view),[1] and we have no common label for this view or for the person who holds it. Similarly, the skeptical stance on *morality* is not well-known outside the circles of academic philosophy. Ordinary people are, of course, entirely familiar with ethical debates that occur *within* morality—over euthanasia, vaccination mandates, etc.—but the proposal that *nobody* is correct in such debates, because there is nothing to be correct about, because there's no such thing as *moral goodness* or *moral rightness*, etc., is not a viewpoint that one would expect to hear espoused in popular discussion. Even the well-known villains of Hollywood fictions are usually presented as having a distorted or mistaken view of morality rather than denying its existence altogether. The label for this skeptical view—"moral error theory"—is one that students typically encounter for the first time when studying ethics.

This book investigates two such debates: over religion and morality. The debate over the first is, as noted, ancient and famous. By contrast, the debate over morality (again: not debates *within* morality, but the debate over whether any moral claim at all is ever true) is considerably less familiar. These are not two arbitrarily chosen topics placed side by side for comparison; clearly, these two subject matters have a long history of entwinement. Indeed, it is not an unusual view that morality depends on religion, such that a skeptical attitude to religion *entails* moral skepticism. This entailment might well be taken as a reason to resist atheism and agnosticism, inasmuch as these views would leave humans without a moral compass: free to pursue wanton impulses; lacking reason or motivation to be kind, cooperative, or honest; and undermining the very foundations of human civilization. (Or so the more apocalyptic version of the worry goes.)

Those who have doubts about the existence of gods, then, but who aren't so keen on undermining morality, will be motivated to deny this entailment. And, indeed, this has been the dominant thread of Western moral philosophy since the Enlightenment: to find a place for moral truths in the naturalistic world, without the need of any backing from supernatural forces. At the level of public

---

[1] "[I]f at any time I speak of Light and Rays as coloured or endued with Colours, I would be understood to speak not philosophically and properly, but grossly, and accordingly to such conceptions as vulgar People in seeing all these Experiments would be apt to frame. For the Rays to speak properly are not coloured" (Newton 1704: 90).

acceptance, this project has been a resounding success; of the many people who now wholeheartedly embrace atheism, very few harbor serious doubts about morality. Atheists will still usually maintain that torturing innocent people is morally wrong, that being kind to those in need is a moral virtue, that one morally ought to repay borrowed money, and so on. That moral discourse continues, confidently and extensively, beyond the influence of religion, is a fact that cannot be denied.

But whether such a naturalized morality is *defensible* is another matter. The moral error theorist maintains that moral properties like moral goodness, moral virtue, moral responsibility (etc.) fare no better, ontologically speaking, than gods, miracles, and the eternal afterlife. Just as the atheist may have a range of arguments in favor of disbelief (and some atheists may be persuaded by arguments that leave other atheists unmoved), so too the error theorist has a range of arguments—empirical, metaphysical, epistemological—to the conclusion that there are no moral truths. (For arguments advocating moral error theory, see Mackie 1977; Joyce 2001; Olson 2014.) Generally, though, the error theorist will still be keen to deny that this moral skepticism leads to the nasty practical consequences mentioned earlier. Just as the atheist typically thinks that one doesn't need religion in order to have good reason to be kind, cooperative, honest (etc.), so too the moral error theorist typically thinks that one doesn't need *morality* in order to have good reason to be kind, cooperative, honest (etc.).

This book focuses on a particular type of theory that appears in contemporary philosophical debates over both religion and morality: *fictionalism*. The possibility of fictionalism arises whenever the possibility of skepticism arises: so not only for religion and for morality, but also for knowledge, free will, colors, numbers, scientific entities, truth and meaning, mathematics, abstract objects, biological information, musical works, etc., etc. Regarding all these topics, doubts can be raised as to whether our ontological commitments are satisfied by the world, and so the possibility arises that we are simply in error when we talk about such things. Fictionalism is proposed as a way of avoiding that error.

The language of fiction is of philosophical interest because it allows us to speak of things that we don't believe in but without making any *error*, for the reason that the fictional context nullifies ontological commitment. If, for example, I introduce a game of make-believe with some children by saying "Let's pretend to be unicorns," I do not thereby commit myself to the existence of unicorns. If, while playing the game, I say "I'm a purple unicorn!" I again do not commit myself to the existence of unicorns, for although I've uttered a false sentence, I haven't *asserted* that sentence. If, after the game, I say "In our game, we pretended to be unicorns," again, I make no error. In this last case, my utterance *is* an assertion—an assertion about the content of the game—but while I do thereby commit myself to the existence of a game, I do not commit myself to the existence of unicorns. Thus we find in familiar talk surrounding fiction—even simple fictions like pretending to be a unicorn—a variety of linguistic mechanisms that allow us to talk and think about non-existent things without any kind of confusion or mistake.

When faced with a seemingly-problematic subject matter (e.g., religion or morality) the fictionalist proposes to model our talk and thought about that topic on one of these error-free ways that we already talk and think about familiar fictions. In order to count as a fictionalist, one must liken the target discourse to fictional discourse *in some obvious respect*, but, as we have just seen, familiar fictional discourse employs a variety of quite different commitment-nullifying devices, allowing different fictionalists to make different analogies.

What does it take for a discourse to be like fictional discourse "in some obvious respect"? Rather than being stipulative, it is probably preferable for a general characterization of fictionalism to leave matters in this purposely vague state. Doing so has the advantage of accurately reflecting the way that the term "fictionalism" is actually used in the philosophical literature, though brings the disadvantage of leaving plenty of room for disagreement over whether a given proposal does or does not count as an instance of "fictionalism." Given that a more precise definition of "fictionalism" would itself inevitably prompt disagreement, as well as exclude certain theories whose advocates consider themselves "fictionalists," the prospects of avoiding the latter disadvantage seem slim. It is better to err on the side of ecumenicism, albeit leaving the question of whether a borderline theory should or should not count as "fictionalism" to be, sometimes, a matter of philosophical instinct. In this, it should be noted, the term "fictionalism" is left no worse off than its likely rivals in a given debate: "realism," "constructivism," "noncognitivism," etc.

It is important to bear in mind that the fictionalist's interest in the analogy with fictional language and thought has a restricted purpose: generally, all they want and need from the analogy is the removal of the offending ontological commitment. There are also *non*-fictionalist proposals that aim to remove potentially troublesome ontological commitments from our language and thought. For example, A. J. Ayer (1936) famously maintained that when one says "Stealing money is wrong" one does not assert anything—not even an assertion about one's own state of mind—but, rather, merely *expresses* a certain negative sentiment that one has toward stealing. However, although Ayer's noncognitivist proposal may be seen as motivated by the same worries that give rise to forms of moral fictionalism—that is, the desire to strip morality of any commitment to potentially troublesome moral properties (in this case, moral wrongness)—his interpretation of moral discourse does not deem it similar to fictional discourse in any obvious manner, and therefore Ayer is no moral fictionalist.

By contrast, any proposal that attempts to avoid ontological commitment by likening moral judgment to *make-believe* will generally be counted as a form of moral fictionalism. Make-believe is central to many of the familiar ways we engage with fiction (reading novels, watching movies, acting, etc.) and also, clearly, nullifies commitment. An actor, for example, is not committed to the existence of the things that she mentions while on stage, for the simple reason that an actor does not *assert* the things she says (many of which are false)—rather, she *pretends to assert* them, just as she pretends to be angry, pretends to be a queen, etc. As we have already seen, though, there are other possibilities for moral fictionalism that would not involve any make-believe at all.

However it is that the fictionalist chooses to model their target discourse on fictional discourse, the analogy must be treated with care. There will be features of familiar fictional engagement (other than commitment nullification) that the fictionalist will likely consider unwelcome distractions. For example, one common feature of familiar acts of make-believe is a disposition to drop the fiction when the practical stakes are raised. (The actor ends the pretense the moment that someone at the back of the theater yells "Fire!") But in all probability the fictionalist—whether religious, moral, or otherwise—has little interest in importing *that* aspect of the analogy. Or, to consider a different example: if a disagreement arises over whether there are unicorns in Narnia, then there are canonical texts that can be consulted to settle the matter. But, again, in all probability the fictionalist does not think that there are any analogous texts that could be consulted to settle, say, moral disputes. Or to take one more example: when engaged in a game like playing with the children, we generally remain fairly aware throughout that "it's just a game"; the activity has a certain phenomenology that sets it apart from things that we genuinely believe. But, once more, the fictionalist may want to eschew this aspect of the analogy altogether.

In short, since different fictionalists focus on different aspects of the analogy (or, if you like, focus on different analogies), the opportunities for confusion are many. Those engaged in debate over any fictionalist proposal must be aware of which aspects of the analogy the fictionalist is intending to exploit and which they are not—and the fictionalist should try to be explicit about this. Of course, on occasion there will be room for a critic to argue that in embracing one aspect of the analogy the fictionalist *must* embrace another—that the desirable element that the fictionalist seeks *entails* an undesirable element that the fictionalist cannot avoid. But any such criticism requires an argument to establish the entailment, not merely the observation that familiar fictional engagement often includes both elements.

One basic division among fictionalists is between the *hermeneutic* and *revolutionary* projects.

Let us consider, first, religious fictionalism. The hermeneutic religious fictionalist interprets the thought and talk of those engaged with religion as *already* similar in the relevant ways to familiar fictions. Religious discourse, according to this type of fictionalist, is not systematically in error and never was, since, although religious discourse does involve false propositions (e.g., "God exists"), when we engage in this discourse we are not really *asserting* or *believing* these propositions. (We may be not making assertions at all, or we may be asserting something else.)

A different kind of religious fictionalist maintains that our current engagement with religion *does* involve systematic error: when religious people engage in this discourse they do assert and believe false things (as the typical atheist maintains). According to this fictionalist, though, we could *alter* our practice so as to remove from it these ontological commitments and thus eliminate the error. This is a form of *revolutionary* fictionalism, since it recommends a change from erroneous belief and assertion to something more like fictional engagement (without error).

Moral fictionalism also comes in hermeneutic and revolutionary forms. According to the former view, people already treat their moral judgments as something a bit like a fiction; according to the latter view, people should come to treat their moral judgments as something a bit like a fiction. Revolutionary moral fictionalists are moral error theorists about our current moral discourse, but offer a way of escaping error theory. Hermeneutic moral fictionalists are not moral error theorists—rather, they offer an interpretation of moral discourse that allows us to construe it as error-free. Thus both hermeneutic and revolutionary fictionalism can be seen as motivated by a desire to avoid error theory, but one proposes to achieve this via an *interpretation* of our moral judgments, and the other via a *change* in our moral judgments.

Hermeneutic fictionalism and revolutionary fictionalism are very different types of theory, and must be assessed quite differently. Hermeneutic fictionalism purports to be *true*, and thus in order for it to be assessed it is reasonable to seek evidence that supports or counts against the theory. Revolutionary fictionalism, by contrast, does not claim to be true as an account of current practice, but rather is put forward as *advice*, thus in order for it to be assessed we must ask whether it would be good advice or poor advice. What counts as a consideration either for or against one form of fictionalism might be entirely irrelevant if raised regarding the other. Hence in what follows they shall be treated separately, in turn.

2. Hermeneutic Fictionalism

What evidence might lead one to conclude that a form of hermeneutic fictionalism is true? Imagine if before making any pronouncement of the form "x is P" speakers were seen to consult a particular fictional text (*F*). Then we might conclude that their pronouncements were really elliptical assertions of "According to *F*, x is P." Or imagine if speakers said things of the form "x is P" when in everyday circumstances, but were observed to back off and say "No, x is not P" when pressed in a more serious tone ("What, *seriously*?"). Then we might conclude that they didn't really believe that x is P. When, however, it comes to serious hermeneutic fictionalist proposals—such as regarding religion or morality—no such obvious evidence leaps forth; whatever evidence there is must be much more subtle than this. (It is true that the consultation of canonical texts often plays an important role in religion, but those who do so do not consider these texts to be works of fiction.)

Regarding morality, for example, Mark Kalderon (2005) defends a hermeneutic form of fictionalism by attempting to show that the norms that govern moral discourse differ from those that govern assertion and belief. When one believes something, Kalderon claims, then upon encountering an epistemic peer who firmly disagrees, one has a "lax obligation" to examine one's reasons for believing as one does. Kalderon calls this "noncomplacency." However, he argues, the norms surrounding morality permit complacency: we feel no embarrassment in steadfastly maintaining our moral views in the face of disagreement from epistemic peers. According to Kalderon, then, the attitude that we take toward moral facts should be classed as one of "acceptance" rather than belief, and when we express this attitude in public language, the speech act we perform is not assertion.[2]

Regarding religion, various types of evidence might be gathered to show that people who appear to be robustly engaged in religion do not really believe what they're saying. Georges Rey (2007), for example, musters support for a view that he calls "meta-atheism": that although people believe that they believe in God (etc.), in fact many of them are, at some level, self-deceived, and they don't really believe in God at all. For instance, Rey argues that observation of people's attitudes toward petitionary prayer should lead one to conclude that they do not really believe that it works:

> Indeed, if petitionary prayer were a matter of serious belief, then why aren't those who engage in it disposed to have the National Institutes of Health do a (non-intrusive) demographic study, say, of the different sorts of prayers, as they would were they interested in the claim that soy beans prevent cancer? And why do none of them expect prayer to cure wooden legs? Or bring Lazarus back after two thousand years? I suggest that there are obvious limits to people's self-deception, and they know full well that God couldn't really intervene in such obviously impossible ways.   (Rey 2007: 261)

Though Rey mentions how attitudes toward religion have a certain similarity to our attitude toward fiction (e.g., we no more inquire into the details of how God created the universe than we do into what Hamlet ate for breakfast), he does not

---

[2] Whether Kalderon's analysis would leave moral discourse sufficiently similar to familiar fictional discourse to warrant the label "fictionalism" might be disputed (though probably not very fruitfully). He does introduce the terminology of "pretense" into his description of the situation, but he says that it is "not terribly central" to his account (Kalderon 2008: 34), and he uses it more as a term of art than anything comparable to the kind of activity that the word "pretense" might typically bring to mind.

explicitly present his view as a version of hermeneutic fictionalism. It is, however, easy enough to see how a hermeneutic religious fictionalist might be tempted to draw support from the kind of evidence that Rey puts forward. Nevertheless, there are a couple of complications that should be highlighted, especially if we are to better understand the nature of the general claim that the hermeneutic fictionalist makes.

First, note that Rey is not making a universal claim about *all* religious people; he is merely describing a kind of self-deception that, he maintains, is more widespread than is usually thought, especially among those who have been "exposed to standard science" (2007: 245). In this, Rey's view of religion differs from Kalderon's view of moral discourse—the latter of which (presumably) involves a claim about *all* moral speakers. This comparison brings into the light a question that must be put to any hermeneutic fictionalist proposal, concerning its scope: Is the fictionalist analysis offered as a description of just some current users of the target discourse, or is it supposed to capture the stance of *everyone* who engages with the discourse? If the latter, then it will be tempting to conclude that the fictionalist analysis is not put forward merely as a contingent matter, but that it aims to capture the inherent nature of engagement with this discourse.

Kalderon's theory appears to aim for this latter stronger claim when he focuses on the "norms" that govern moral engagement. The norms in question are not the kind of thing that an individual can unilaterally determine; rather, these norms require a community of people to reach some kind of shared understanding (whether explicitly or implicitly) of how moral judgments work. When, for example, Kalderon claims that the norms surrounding moral language are different from those that govern assertion, he is talking about conventions accepted by both the speaker and the audience. This is a feature of speech acts in general, and warrants bearing in mind in discussions of fictionalism; thus it is a point worth pausing on.

Consider the speech act of promising. If I say to you "I promise to pay you $5" (in a serious tone of voice, in circumstances where this wouldn't be a completely bizarre thing for me to say, etc.), then I have made a promise to you. This remains true even if, all along, my promise was utterly insincere and I never had any intention of paying you a cent. If you later demand the $5, I could not reasonably retort "No, it wasn't a real promise, because I secretly had no intention of repaying you." The revelation that I never had that intention would show that I promised *insincerely*, not that I never promised at all. Whether or not I promised is not just a matter of my intentions; it's determined by the conventions, understood by both speaker and audience, that governed my utterance in the circumstances. Suppose I say to my dog "I promise to take you for a walk later." I haven't really succeeded in making a promise, since this audience (my dog) cannot grasp the norms surrounding the speech act. Again: my intentions to make a promise are not sufficient to determine that I have succeeded in doing so; which speech act

I have performed, if any, is determined in part by how my audience takes my utterance. In the case of a canine audience, even though dogs can make associations between words and objects/activities (e.g., "biscuit," "sit"), there can be no question of any speech acts being successfully performed.

When, therefore, Kalderon maintains that moral judgments are neither beliefs nor assertions, it is important to see that these are two very different claims. The question of whether an individual *believes* that stealing is wrong (say) might be taken to depend on what's going on in that person's head. Even if everyone thinks that Amy believes that stealing is wrong, it doesn't follow that Amy does believe that stealing is wrong. By contrast, the question of whether an individual *asserts* that stealing is wrong depends on the shared conventions between individual and audience. If Amy goes round saying "Stealing is morally wrong," and everyone takes her to be asserting this, and Amy does nothing to indicate that she isn't asserting this (e.g., by explaining herself, or by adding "Just kidding!"), then she *is* asserting that stealing is morally wrong, regardless of whether she believes it or whether she even intends to assert it.

These observations raise a second complication for those who would interpret evidence like Rey's as providing support for hermeneutic religious fictionalism. Since Rey is claiming that only *some* religious people are self-deceived about their own religious beliefs, then although this might be taken as evidence that these individuals do not really *believe* religious propositions, it could not be taken as evidence that these individuals do not really *assert* religious propositions. In order for this latter claim to be made, one would have to argue that religious people know, at some level, that they and other religious speakers are self-deceived and that none of them really have religious beliefs, and that this shared knowledge is reflected in the norms that govern their religious speech acts. But such an argument would surely have little plausibility to it, not least because of the obvious tension in the claim "We all know, deep down, that we're self-deceived about X."

Instead of attempting to establish hermeneutic fictionalism via bringing forth positive evidence that users engage with the target subject in some sort of fictional manner, one might offer the theory as a charitable interpretation of the discourse, especially if the only other resort is to ascribe massive and ubiquitous error. This, it might be thought, is the kind of thing that we already do. Consider, for example, how the ancients thought the Earth to be a stationary object at the center of the universe—a belief that allowed them to speak of things "moving" in an absolute sense. We now know that nothing moves in an absolute sense—all motion is relative. Now consider an assertion made by a past speaker concerning something moving: say, "The chariot moved along the street." If we ascribe to this speaker a reference to *absolute* motion, then we'd have to conclude that they believed and said something false. But we evidently don't do this. Rather, we charitably interpret them as speaking of *relative* motion—even though this is certainly not what the speaker had in mind, nor even something they would assent to if asked.

Gilbert Harman uses such an argument to support a form of moral *relativism* (Harman & Thomson 1996). He argues that there are no such things as absolute moral truths, but there are such things as relativistic moral truths (in other words, the sentence "Stealing is morally wrong *period*" might be false while the sentence "Stealing is morally wrong from the point of view of my culture" remains true). In this case, Harman thinks, we should interpret people's moral judgments as referring to the latter, even though this is not what speakers *intend* to refer to when they make a moral claim. To insist on interpreting speakers' moral judgments in an absolutist sense, and thus as false, would be "mean-spirited," says Harman (Harman & Thomson 1996: 4). It is not the business of this introduction to assess the prospects of moral relativism; let us suppose (as the moral error theorist will maintain) that relativistic moral facts ultimately prove to be just as non-existent as absolutist moral facts. One can then imagine the hermeneutic moral fictionalist, confronted by such a circumstance, trying to pull a similar ostensibly charitable move: rather than adopting the mean-spirited approach of ascribing massive error, they suggest that we could interpret speakers as not really believing and not really asserting their moral claims. (And, of course, the same kind of move would be available for the hermeneutic *religious* fictionalist.)

There are at least two reasons to be wary of this latter kind of strategy for establishing hermeneutic fictionalism.

First, the move seems entirely too easy. If such a strategy were viable, then whenever the threat of error arose, it could be easily sidestepped by simply interpreting speakers as not really believing or asserting the claims in question, thus not being ontologically committed to the entities they speak of, and thus not in error. Shall we, however, do this with ancient Greek talk of their Olympian gods?—with medieval talk of bodily humors?—with 18th-century scientists' talk of phlogiston? The point of raising these examples is to draw attention to the fact that we often don't *want* to rescue a discourse from error, and, even if we *were* to want to, doing so shouldn't be so easy as a click of the fictionalist's fingers.

Second, it remains questionable just how "charitable" the fictionalist interpretation really is. We'll stick with the example of moral fictionalism to illustrate the general point. If there are no moral properties, then anyone who asserts "x is morally wrong" has made an error; so if we interpret such speakers' utterances not as assertions but as, say, make-believe assertions (or as "quasi-assertions") then the error evaporates. But any such exercise in error-avoidance has really succeeded only in pushing the error elsewhere. Imagine the fictionalist informing ordinary speakers that it has been decided that henceforth their moral judgments will be interpreted as a form of make-believe. (We are, recall, currently assuming that this fictionalist lacks any positive linguistic or psychological evidence to back this up; it's just how they've decided these utterances should be construed.) It is easy to imagine that this will meet with indignant denial: "Of course I *believe* that genocide is morally wrong!" it will be protested, "I'm not just *pretending*!" Thus, despite the hermeneutic fictionalist's aim of avoiding ascribing to people false moral beliefs, they are instead going to have to interpret people's higher-order beliefs—such as their belief that they believe that genocide is morally wrong—as false. And faced with this option of *where* to ascribe the massive error to people, one might well think that the moral error theorist's option is the preferable one. The error theorist, after all, thinks that people are mistaken about the nature of reality—a perfectly familiar phenomenon—whereas the hermeneutic fictionalist thinks that people are massively mistaken about the nature of their own mental states and speech acts (see Liggins 2020: 89–90).

In sum, hermeneutic fictionalists appear to be on more solid ground if they can produce some positive evidence that users of the target discourse engage with it in a way that does not involve belief or assertion. We have also seen that hermeneutic fictionalists must answer a question about the scope of their view: is it being put forward as a contingent claim about just some users or as a universal claim about the very nature of the engagement in question? If the former, in particular, then the conjunction "belief and assertion" cannot be treated in a casual manner. Put simply: when considering users of a certain discourse (e.g., religion or morality) the claim "Some of them believe what they're saying and some of them don't" is uncomplicated in a way that the claim "Some of them are asserting what they're saying and some of them aren't" is not.

3. Revolutionary Fictionalism

In some ways revolutionary fictionalists have it easier than their hermeneutic cousins. The former don't need to establish that any actual current discourse, such as morality or religion, is anything remotely like any fictional discourse. The revolutionary fictionalist maintains that their target discourse currently involves straightforward belief and assertion (as, it may be assumed, it appears to) but that these beliefs and assertions systematically fail to be true. The revolutionary fictionalist's characteristic claim is that we should, therefore, alter our practice to bring it in line, in some obvious respect, with fictional discourse, so as to remove the erroneous ontological commitments. (In the case of moral fictionalism, the "should" in the previous sentence obviously cannot be understood in a moral sense.) But the revolutionary fictionalist's project of offering practical advice brings its own set of challenges.

All fictionalists must offer an account of why participating in the target discourse is useful. In the case of religion, for instance, one might point to the benefits of being part of a supportive religious community, of having a sense of existential purpose, of having one's fear of death assuaged, and so on. In the case of morality, one might also point to the benefits of being committed to shared social values, while also underlining the role that moral valuing plays in helping individuals avoid various kinds of practical self-sabotage, such as short-sighted selfishness or weakness of will. (These are just gestures towards answers; in reality the benefits of religion and morality are presumably extremely complex and varied.)

The revolutionary fictionalist—whether religious or moral—looks upon such benefits and is anxious about their loss. They acknowledge that the discourse in question is massively mistaken in ontological terms, but also believe that its flat-out abolition is likely to lead to practical harms. But the revolutionary fictionalist faces a fundamental challenge: all these "traditional benefits" accrued in pre-revolutionary times, when the discourse was truth-oriented; therefore the worry naturally emerges that the useful role that the discourse has historically played depended on its being *believed*. It is, for example, one thing to claim that moral beliefs can help people strengthen their motivational resolve in various ways, but it's quite another to claim that something other than belief (e.g., make-believe) could play that same pragmatic role. A particular challenge for the revolutionary fictionalist, then, is to show that usefulness can survive the revolution.

In assessing whether the revolutionary fictionalist can meet this challenge, it is vital to understand what meeting the challenge would require. The revolutionary fictionalist does not have to establish that the post-revolutionary fictionalized discourse would be *just as useful* as the pre-revolutionary believed discourse. The revolutionary fictionalist's principal two opponents here are, first, the *abolitionist*—someone who thinks that the discourse is on balance harmful and therefore should be abolished (in much the same way as we largely abolished talk of bodily humors and witchcraft)—and, second, the *conservationist*—someone who thinks that we should retain our false beliefs in everyday settings because they are useful, even while acknowledging (when in reflective settings) that they are false.[3] Against the abolitionist the fictionalist might argue that whatever harms the discourse has historically begotten were the result of its being *believed* and *asserted*; but once we shift to some kind of nondoxastic and nonassertoric stance toward the subject, those harms can be mitigated. Against the conservationist the fictionalist might argue that carrying on believing something that you know, at some level, to be false (a.k.a. irrationality) is itself likely to be a harmful and undesirable practice. However those arguments turn out, the important thing to note is that in no case do the benefits of continuing with the false discourse (in the manner recommended by the revolutionary fictionalist) need to match the pre-revolutionary benefits of straightforward *belief* and *assertion*. The benefits

---

[3] The labels "abolitionism" and "conservationism" are used in the debate over morality, but can be extended in obvious ways to cover the analogous debate over religion, or to views that rival other kinds of fictionalism too.

promised by the fictionalist stance might be only 50 percent of the pre-revolutionary usage (or 20 percent, or 5 percent), and the fictionalist's advice might nevertheless still be pragmatically better than that offered by the abolitionist or the conservationist.

There are several other complicating features concerning the nature of the revolutionary fictionalist's advice, which will be run through briefly in turn.

First, because the revolutionary fictionalist's recommendation amounts to a piece of advice, questions arise regarding *to whom* the advice is offered. Consider the *moral* fictionalist's recommendation, which we'll simplify to "Make a fiction of morality." This advice might be directed at individual moral error theorists. Or it might be aimed specifically at moral error theorists who were once moral believers. Or it might be meant for individual moral error theorists in certain circumstances (e.g., if surrounded by people who are moral believers). Or it might be intended not as advice for individuals at all, but rather as advice to a *group* of moral error theorists. Or it might be offered as advice for humans in general, whether or not they are moral error theorists (see Jay 2020). Or it might be suggested as advice for humans *now*, but not necessary for future humans (see Burgess 2020). And so on. Ideally, of course, the fictionalist should endeavor to clarify the target and nature of their advice, but it should also be borne in mind that these kind of indeterminacies surround practical advice-giving in general. "Eat plenty of leafy green vegetables" can be considered sound advice, but it doesn't necessarily mean *everyone* (for some people are allergic to certain vegetables), and nor does it mean *under any circumstances*. Just as there may be certain situations where eating vegetables would be inappropriate (e.g., while bouncing on a trampoline), so too there may be certain circumstances where the fictionalist's advice "Make a fiction of morality" should definitely not be followed. This possibility would not show it to be poor advice generally.

A second indeterminacy of advice-giving in general—and therefore an expected feature of the revolutionary fictionalist's advice—is that is often difficult to say *precisely* what practical ends the following of the advice is supposed to serve. Will eating leafy green vegetables afford you more pleasure, or will it satisfy your preferences, or will it fulfil certain objective human values? The fact that there is a philosophical literature that tussles over these questions (much of it concerning the general nature of *human well-being*) does not imply that we should all abstain from ever offering any practical advice until these arguments are settled. The fictionalist's recommendation should not be held to a higher standard in this regard than we hold ordinary advice; the fictionalist might not have anything very special to say about the precise nature of the well-being that their advice is intended to serve.

A third question that can be raised about the revolutionary fictionalist's advice is its intended modal strength. An ambitious revolutionary fictionalism might claim that following their advice is (for people with certain ends) *rationally obligatory*, in the sense that complying with the recommendation is the only, or by far the best, means of achieving those ends. A more modest revolutionary fictionalism might claim that following the advice is *permissible*, in the sense that it is one reasonable means of achieving those ends, possibly among others. (See Deng 2015.)

Fourth and finally, there is the question regarding what activity the revolutionary fictionalist is recommending that we adjust: our language, our thoughts, or both? Either element can be ontologically committed: our language is committed when it is asserted; our thoughts are committed when they are believed. The motivation for fictionalism, recall, is to remove these offending commitments, and so it is worth teasing apart the revolutionary fictionalist's recommendation into two separate pieces of advice. Regarding language, the fictionalist recommends what might be called *nonassertoric affirmation* (as opposed to assertion); and regarding mental states, the fictionalist recommends what might be called *nondoxastic acceptance* (as opposed to belief). These are intended to be generic labels, so different fictionalists may have substantively different accounts of what they consist in (e.g., some fictionalists may take nondoxastic acceptance to involve *make-believe*; others may not). They are also terms of art, so allow a degree of stipulation.

One aspect of the stipulation is worth highlighting. Consider the kind of fictionalism that suggests that claims of the target discourse be modeled on talk *about* a fiction (e.g., "In the Narnia books, there is a unicorn"). A revolutionary fictionalist of this kind would recommend that we introduce a "story operator" into our discourse—so "x is morally wrong," for example, becomes something of the form "According to fiction F, x is morally wrong" (the former, we're assuming, being false; the latter true). A group of speakers following this advice would still be engaged in *assertion* and *belief*—it's just that they would now be asserting and believing the more complex proposition that includes the story operator. One might now stipulate the following: (i) if S asserts "According to F, x is P," then S nonassertorically affirms "x is P"; and (ii) if S believes that according to F, x is P, then S nondoxastically accepts that x is P. In this way, one could say that this kind of revolutionary fictionalist still recommends nonassertoric affirmation and nondoxastic acceptance. The rejection of this stipulation would not spell any substantive problems for the revolutionary fictionalist; it would just call for a more complicated and disjunctive account of how to characterize the theory in general terms. Nevertheless, there are further complications enough.

We earlier noted an important difference between *belief* and *assertion*, inasmuch as "Keep thinking that x is P but don't believe it" is advice that an individual could follow privately, as it were, whereas "Keep saying 'x is P' but don't assert it" is not, since the question of which speech act a speaker performs (if any) involves audience participation. Of course, there is a range of familiar devices that we can use to show to our audience that we are not asserting the thing that we're saying. We can, for example, be entirely explicit: "I don't really believe the following, but I'm just being the devil's advocate…" Or sometimes it's more subtle than that—when, for instance, we indicate that we're just kidding about something via tone or facial expression. So if the revolutionary fictionalist's advice to cultivate nonassertoric affirmation is directed at an individual, it must be accompanied with the understanding that the individual somehow indicates to their audience (and the audience must understand this) that the attitude taken toward the thing being said is one of nondoxastic acceptance rather than belief.

Consider the example of revolutionary religious fictionalism. Let us suppose that an individual, Bob, is an atheist who is trying to follow the revolutionary fictionalist's advice, so as to retain some of the benefits that religious engagement has traditionally brought. Bob doesn't believe in God, but perhaps he finds that thinking about God is comforting, and he find prayer therapeutic, and so on, and so he nondoxastically accepts God. Now suppose that Bob is involved in a conversation with some religious believers. It would be reasonable to expect Bob's nondoxastic acceptance of God to be reflected in his speech, so he finds himself saying things like "Yes, God loves you." Bob could, of course, at this point start to explain himself, thereby removing the assertoric force from his claim. But suppose that he does not. Then he has—albeit perhaps unwittingly—made an assertion. The problem with this, from the fictionalist's point of view, is that even though Bob's mental states may not be ontologically committed to the existence of God, his public language remains so.

This ties in to the earlier point concerning *to whom* the revolutionary fictionalist advice is offered. If the advice concerns what mental state to take toward the problematic subject (i.e., nondoxastic acceptance) then it is reasonable to offer this advice to an individual. And maybe that's all a revolutionary fictionalist's advice need involve; maybe if following their advice gets us to stop *believing* false things then their job is done. But if the advice also extends to what kind of speech act to employ when discussing the problematic subject (i.e., recommending nonassertoric affirmation)—if, in other words, the fictionalist aspires to get us to stop *asserting* false things—then it doesn't make much sense for this advice to be offered to an individual—not unless the advice includes the suggestion that the individual always lets their audience know what's going on. Ultimately, then, the revolutionary fictionalist runs into the same complication that we saw faced the hermeneutic fictionalist. If "textbook" revolutionary fictionalism is taken to recommend both nondoxastic acceptance and nonassertoric affirmation, then the natural recipient of such advice is a *group* of skeptics, rather than an individual skeptic.

4. The Purpose and Structure of This Book

This is a collection of thirteen chapters on moral fictionalism and religious fictionalism. Over the past couple of decades these two types of fictionalism have been critically assessed largely in different places: moral fictionalism within the metaethical literature, and religious fictionalism within the philosophy of religion literature. The motivation for this project is the hope that seeing two forms of fictionalism discussed together may help to elucidate both theories, and also fictionalism more generally. Perhaps, for example, one form of fictionalism faces special problems that the other doesn't; or perhaps one has selling points that the other lacks. Maybe what is said for or against one form of fictionalism will have implications for what one is likely to say, or is logically required to say, regarding the other. When discussion of a particular type of fictionalism takes place in relative isolation—as is generally the case—it can be difficult to discern which features of the debate pertain to that particular type of fictionalism and which pertain to fictionalism more generally.

Some such benefits of clarification could, in principle, be gained by considering *any* two forms of fictionalism side by side—say, fictionalism about musical works and fictionalism about biological information—but, obviously, the decision to discuss morality and religion together was not an arbitrary one. These two areas of debate have a long, rich, and to some extent *shared* backstory—to such an extent that it remains a live suspicion, both in popular thought and among certain academics, that they stand or fall together. It is not within the scope of this collection to answer *that* old question, but the question of whether moral *fictionalism* and religious *fictionalism* stand or fall together is something on which some light may be shed.

Some of the chapters are concentrated exclusively on one form of fictionalism, some on the other, and some on both. The collection is roughly structured in this way: it begins with some chapters that focus largely on only moral fictionalism, then some chapters that focus largely on only religious fictionalism, and finally some chapters that discuss the relation between the two forms of fictionalism.

The first grouping, on moral fictionalism, consists of three chapters that are critical of the theory, and one that defends and advocates it.

In Chapter 1, James Lenman argues against revolutionary moral fictionalism, though his real target is the moral error theory that motivates the fictionalist proposal in the first place. If the revolutionary fictionalist allows that there are norms concerning what we "should" do—in answering the question "If moral error theory is true, then what should we do with our erroneous moral discourse?"—then, Lenman argues, this just shows that morality was never really founded on an error in the first place. This so-called "what next? question," Lenman thinks, cannot be treated as a purely non-moral "practical" matter, as the revolutionary moral fictionalist proposes.

In Chapter 2, Jessica Isserow presents a dilemma for any revolutionary moral fictionalist who focuses on *make-believe* as the proposed attitude to take toward our erroneous moral discourse. Isserow cannot see a way that this proposal could supply the benefits that the fictionalist touts. Either this "moral make-believe" will involve exhausting psychological running costs—in which case it brings additional harms—or the very features that distinguish it from moral belief will also ensure that moral make-believe cannot supply the same practical advantages of moral belief.

In Chapter 3, co-authors Victor Moberger and Jonas Olson agree with much of Isserow's case against any moral fictionalism that recommends make-believe (they call it "narrationist fictionalism"), but they go on to discuss a rather different type of revolutionary moral fictionalism: one which proposes that we model moral discourse on metaphorical language. Like make-believe, metaphor is a familiar phenomenon whereby we can discuss non-existent things (e.g., raining cats and dogs) but without any ontological commitment. Moberger and Olson present a number of objections that aim to show that metaphorist fictionalism ultimately fares no better than make-believe fictionalism.

In Chapter 4, François Jaquet mounts a defense of revolutionary moral fictionalism—and, in particular, of the kind that proposes an attitude of make-believe. Jaquet focuses on three criticisms of this kind of fictionalism: that a fictionalized morality could not accommodate deductive inferences, that it could not provide the motivational force that we want of moral engagement, and that it leaves no place for moral disagreement. Jaquet rejects these criticisms, arguing that they are often based on the fictionalist's critic having a limited view of what "moral make-believe" might involve.

The second grouping of the collection is focused on religious fictionalism. Again, much of the discussion is critical, though we eventually get to more sympathetic treatments.

In Chapter 5, Graham Oppy makes a distinction between *original* and *parasitic* religious fictionalism. According to the former, none of the followers of a religion really believe it and none of them ever have, but they nevertheless gain certain practical benefits from participation; according to the latter, some followers of a religion might not really believe it, and the practical benefits that they gain from participation depend on there being a significant body of sincere believers. Either way, Oppy finds the religious fictionalist's claim doubtful. He considers some of the kinds of benefits that engaging with religion plausibly brings (e.g., relieving existential anxiety), and expresses pessimism that an attitude other than belief could bring comparable benefits.

In Chapter 6, co-authors Brad Armour-Garb and Fred Kroon argue against both hermeneutic and revolutionary forms of religious fictionalism. They worry, first, that in application to religion the term "fictionalism" has been used to cover such an array of vastly different attitudes that it has become a shallow and relatively uninformative label. They find revolutionary fictionalism has more initial promise than hermeneutic, but ultimately they have doubts (along similar lines to Oppy's) that any religious institution as we know it could survive the wholesale movement away from belief. They argue that moral fictionalism does not face these particular challenges.

In Chapter 7, Mary Leng begins by wondering whether engaging with religion in a fictionalist manner might be morally dubious (e.g., dishonest) if one knows that other religious speakers are sincere believers. She presents Kant's "moral hazard argument," according to which sincere belief in religion is actually morally *worse* than nondoxastic acceptance, since the former threatens to corrupt one's motivation with selfish anticipation of divine reward. Leng then discusses a long-standing criticism of fictionalism: that if one's "acceptance" is to all intents and purposes indistinguishable from belief, then it *is* just belief. She turns the tables on this reasoning, arguing that certain features of religious "belief" (e.g., anxiety about death) seem more indicative of a nondoxastic attitude, and thus she suggests that hermeneutic religious fictionalism might be true of at least some followers of religion.

In Chapter 8, Michael Scott raises certain challenges to revolutionary religious fictionalism that seem unique to this form of fictionalism. One problem is how the fictionalist proposes to negotiate the inferential connections between religious propositions, which are merely "accepted," and non-religious propositions (e.g., "Our universe started with the Big Bang") for which *belief* seems the appropriate attitude. This problem is exacerbated by the fact that religion has more ubiquitous concrete ontological implications than, say, morality or mathematics. Scott suggests that the would-be revolutionary fictionalist would be well-advised to select a religion for which such ontological implications are minimal—but if there were such a religion then it would be amenable to a hermeneutic fictionalist analysis. Scott ends with a discussion of the theological tradition of apophaticism, and how it might serve as an instance of a kind of localized revolutionary religious fictionalism.

The third and final group of chapters are those where both moral and religious fictionalism are discussed, and the focus is more squarely on the relation between them.

In Chapter 9, Natalja Deng distinguishes between *thoroughgoing* and *lightweight* fictionalism, applying the distinction to both religious and moral domains. Thoroughgoing fictionalism involves a more complete "immersion" in the fiction, where the fictionalist's proposed "acceptance" aims to mimic sincere belief—the difference between them emerging only in critical contexts. Lightweight fictionalism is less immersive, such that the individual may remain aware that they are engaged in a fictional manner and retains more choice over which fiction to adopt. Deng expresses skepticism that the kind of nondoxastic acceptance involved in thoroughgoing fictionalism can withstand critical scrutiny, but she is considerably more optimistic about religious fictionalism down the lightweight end of the spectrum. She describes a kind of fictionalist religious engagement that is permissible (rather than rationally obligatory) for an individual to adopt, where they may choose freely among different religious traditions to find a combination that suits their pragmatic purposes.

In Chapter 10, Robin Le Poidevin expresses neither a positive nor negative attitude toward either moral or religious fictionalism; rather, he is concerned with investigating the logical relations between the two views. He first considers the prospects of combining religious realism with moral fictionalism, and then the prospects of combining religious fictionalism with moral realism. Either combination leads to odd consequences, mostly surrounding the fact that God is generally ascribed moral qualities. For example, would someone who believes in a real God ascribe only fictional goodness to God? Le Poidevin explores the peculiarities of these consequences, ultimately speaking in favor of a position that combines fictionalism about both domains, wherein a fictional God is viewed as the source of fictional moral values.

In Chapter 11, Seahwa Kim provides three conditions that an erroneous discourse might satisfy that would speak in favor of retaining the discourse in a fictionalist manner rather than eliminating it. If the discourse is extremely widespread (the Ubiquity Condition), if it is necessary for certain practical purposes (the Indispensability Condition), and if the abandonment of the discourse would require major changes to behavior (the Business As Usual Condition), then there are pro tanto reasons for retaining the discourse. Kim argues that religion satisfies none of these conditions, and therefore she is, to that extent, opposed to religious fictionalism. By contrast, she argues that moral discourse satisfies two of these conditions, and therefore moral error theorists have a pro tanto reason to adopt some form of moral fictionalism.

In Chapter 12, Stuart Brock presents the moral fictionalist with a challenge based on the so-called "problem of imaginative resistance." The problem goes back to Hume's essay "Of a standard of taste" (1757), where Hume observes our reluctance or inability to enter imaginatively into fictional worlds where the moral status of things is markedly at odds with what we take it to be. This poses a problem for revolutionary fictionalists, for they recommend that we do exactly that: pretend that things in the world have moral status which we believe them not to have. Because this problem arises concerning how *morality* figures in our imaginative acts, it does not seem to arise for the religious fictionalist.

In Chapter 13, Richard Joyce develops and defends an account of moral fictionalism, based on the thought that sometimes in order to achieve our goals we must distract ourselves from their true nature. This is the basis of both Coleridge's "suspension of disbelief" in response to implausible artworks, and Mill's solution to the paradox of happiness. When we distract ourselves from what we really believe in this manner, it can be classed as a kind of nondoxastic acceptance. Joyce argues that in order to achieve our Humean *non-moral* ends (which are not particularly metaphysically or epistemologically fishy) we must sometimes dress those ends up in the guise of objective Kantian *moral* norms (which renders our evaluations false). He then discusses whether an analogous argument for religious fictionalism would be plausible, and presents a couple of reasons for thinking it would face particular problems.

References

Ayer, A. J. 1936. *Language, Truth, and Logic*. Victor Gollancz.

Burgess, J. 2020. "Fictionalism as a phase (to be grown out of)." In B. Armour-Garb & F. Kroon (eds.), *Fictionalism in Philosophy*. Oxford University Press. 48–60.

Deng, N. 2015. "Religion for naturalists." *International Journal for Philosophy of Religion* 78: 195–214.

Harman, G. & Thomson, J. J. 1996. *Moral Relativism and Moral Objectivity*. Blackwell.

Jay, C. 2020. "A realist-friendly argument for moral fictionalism: Perhaps you'd better not believe it." In J. Falguera & C. Martínez-Vidal (eds.), *Abstract Objects*. Synthese Library 422. Springer. 339–56.

Joyce, 2001. *The Myth of Morality*. Cambridge University Press.

Kalderon, M. 2005. *Moral Fictionalism*. Oxford University Press.

Kalderon, M. 2008. "The trouble with terminology." *Philosophical Books* 49: 33–41.

Liggins, D. 2020. "Against hermeneutic fictionalism." In B. Armour-Garb & F. Kroon (eds.), *Fictionalism in Philosophy*. Oxford University Press. 81–102.

Mackie, J. L. 1977. *Ethics: Inventing Right and Wrong*. Penguin.

Newton, I. 1704. *Opticks*. Smith and Walford.

Olson, J. 2014. *Moral Error Theory: History, Critique, Defence*. Oxford University Press.

Rey, G. 2007. "Meta-atheism: Religious avowal and self-deception." In L. Antony (ed.), *Philosophers without Gods: Meditations on Atheism and the Secular Life*. Oxford University Press. 243–65.

1

Reasons for Pretending and Pretend Reasons

James Lenman

1. The Dao

In our house we do not call one another "scrote," "pig-face," "arsemonger," "slag," "wanker," or "prick." We are polite and civil and abhor such coarse and unparliamentary language. We always aim, in general, to be friendly and kind to our housemates as well as to anyone who may come visiting. We have each our private spaces, our rooms, and we can control who can enter or leave those spaces as well as our private things which others cannot consume or use without our consent.

Fighting or any sort of violence is not allowed. Domestic chores we aim to share out fairly, where there is quite a complicated story to be told about our understanding of just what "fairly" entails and how it has evolved over the years. Some of us form friendships with each other and we have particular shared understandings of what friends should expect of each other. Some of us become lovers, and we have more shared norms to govern that aspect of life. In short, we have a rich and complex body of rules and standards, shared normative understandings, and normative expectations that shape our lives together. For the sake of calling it something, call it the *Dao*.

We did not make these rules and shared normative understandings up. This house has been here with people living in it long before we came along and they have always had a Dao. It has slowly taken shape over a long time to meet the needs and fit the natures of the creatures who live here. It is deeply embedded in our shared lives, woven into our literature, our poems and our songs, our rituals and manners, the very conceptual water in which we swim. It has changed a little bit down the centuries and it will certainly change some more in centuries to come. Many of us are critical of some aspects of it and would like to change it. We have regular meetings where these things are discussed.

The Dao is deeply expressive of our biological, animal nature. We are mortal creatures who last some eighty years plus or minus twenty when spared premature ill health or accident. We are sexually differentiated and reproduce sexually. In reproductive strategy we are like other mammals and unlike, say, salmon: we are *K*s and not *r*s (where *r*s have huge numbers of offspring and invest almost

James Lenman, *Reasons for Pretending and Pretend Reasons* In: *Moral Fictionalism and Religious Fictionalism*. Edited by: Richard Joyce and Stuart Brock, Oxford University Press. © James Lenman 2023.
DOI: 10.1093/oso/9780198881865.003.0002

nothing in their survival while *K*s have very few offspring and invest a lot). We are social animals given to forming familial groups and larger political communities. We live in the circumstances of justice: dependent on scarce resources and altruistic within limits. The Dao is not determined by these deep but contingent facts about us but it is shaped by and expresses them and would, we may be confident, certainly have been very different had any or all of them been different. But while it expresses our animal natures, it also civilizes and domesticates them in the light of ideas of duty to and respect for each other shaped by many millennia of human cultural evolution.

The Dao is very important to us and we take it pretty seriously. Because of it, we live together in a community that is more or less peaceful, orderly, and secure, where people cooperate successfully on terms that are acceptable to (almost) all of us, where we treat each other with civility and respect. (At least on a good day. I idealize a little.) Because of this, the Dao is something we value immensely, cling to, cherish, and protect. We appreciate how big a deal it is that we have achieved a stable, harmonious community. We have heard of other houses that have not achieved this so well and life there sounds just awful. So, even though we often want to criticize it, we rejoice in our Dao, embrace it, and identify ourselves with it.

We love the Dao because we think it enriches and improves our lives and it would be a catastrophic loss to be deprived of it. Because the Dao encompasses so large a part of our normative lives, we should not think of the reasons that we love it and would hate to lose it as reasons external to and independent of it. The Dao itself inescapably supplies the reasons that we value the Dao. There is no place outside it where normative thought can happen for us. That is okay. In normative thought we engage in piecemeal Neurathian boat repair, scrutinizing and repairing small piece by small piece. The Dao is not some small inessential corner that we can expect temporarily to decommission for inspection and reconstruction without sinking the whole ship.

I say we love and respect the Dao, but not everyone does. Some people are disaffected, unreasonable, not really on board with the project of making a flourishing community together. These people are a problem, but it is very clear that the rules of the Dao still apply to them. They apply to everybody. Is that fair and reasonable? Well, that is itself a question internal to the Dao, and the Dao has things to say about when and why it is sometimes okay to insist that people conform to rules they may not accept.

2. Error?

So here we all are living lives shaped by the Dao, and one day something weird happens. Some skeptical philosophers show up and tell us,

Listen, this Dao thing you make so much fuss about—we've been thinking and we have decided, basically, that it is junk; it's garbage, a tissue of untruths.
Golly (we think), *really? What can you mean, how can that be right?*
Well (they reply), *like we said, we've been thinking and we have come to the conclusion that the whole edifice rests on a ROPEY METAPHYSICAL PRESUPPOSITION—RMP—and we are sorry to tell you that the RMP is false.*

Not everybody of course thinks the Dao is junk. Others think it is in perfectly good order. Some of these others however *agree* that it makes sense *only* if we buy into the RMP, but one person's *tollens* is another's *ponens*, and this crowd, the *Heavy Duty Realists*, seek to rescue the Dao from oblivion by doing just that.

Then there is my gang, the *Deflationary Realists*, you might call us. We are quite a miscellaneous ragbag of expressivists, constructivists, and others, but we are united against both skeptics and Heavy Duty Realists. The Dao, we say, makes excellent sense and we don't need any RMPs to make sense of it.

The structure of the issue here is a bit like what we find with responsibility and free will, with some people insisting that our moral practice makes sense only if we see it as propped up with what Strawson (1974: 25) famously denigrated as "obscure and panicky metaphysics" which they proceed to embrace, others accepting the dependency claim but jumping the other way into skepticism about responsibility and free will, while others fight a war on two fronts against both of the first two groups who are united (we think), despite their disagreement, by the very same deep and fundamental mistake.

What is the RMP? Some contend that the Dao presupposes the existence of categorical imperatives, demands that apply not just to actual people but to any conceivable rational creature, without needing to speak to their contingent desires and purposes and that they are condemned for failing to obey. Others offer a narrative of a strange *sui generis* domain of non-natural facts.

Of course, no English-speaking philosophers talk about "the Dao"[1]—rather, people talk about "morality." Richard Joyce, whose 2001 book *The Myth of Morality* set the agenda for contemporary error theory, argues that we should convict morality of error on just such grounds of ropey presupposition. When he says this, he is not, he makes clear, following Bernard Williams (1985: chapter 10) in seeing "morality" quite narrowly as a "peculiar institution" cooked up by people like Kant in relatively recent times. Rather, Joyce claims:

I do not think that this kind of desire/interest-ignoring condemnation is a particularly modern or Western phenomenon. Despite the fact that it required an eighteenth-century Prussian to label categorical imperatives, I am confident that

---

[1] The only exception I know of is C. S. Lewis (1943).

they have been with us for a long time. Did, say, ancient Chinese people retract condemnation of their own moral monsters upon discovering their unusual desires? I doubt it.   (Joyce 2001: 43)[2]

So, yes, we really are talking about the Dao! Not only is categorical morality old, it is pervasive:

> Let us suppose that…moral discourse consists largely of untrue assertions. Those arguments have primarily targeted deontological notions like obligation and prohibition. One might object that even if these arguments were faultless, all they show is that a certain proper subset of our moral discourse is flawed, but there is a rich and robust moral language that remains untouched. However, it is my contention that moral concepts are to a large degree holistically connected, such that a persuasive attack on categorical imperatives will, one way or another, count as a persuasive attack on a great deal more besides.
>
> If there are no inescapable moral obligations, for instance, then there will be no inviolable claim rights (and claim rights are the central currency of ordinary rights-based moral discourse). Similarly, talk of virtues and vices generally implies the existence of obligations. Virtues are often thought of as character traits that one is obligated to cultivate. Or even if not that, a virtuous agent is taken to be one who is, inter alia, sensitive to, and acts in accordance with, her moral obligations.   (2001: 175)

Everything must go. Only it turns out that not really. Indeed, it turns out—and this is the rum thing here—that nothing much need change. Here there is a difference between Heavy Duty Realists and many skeptics. Heavy Duty Realists tend to talk up the extent to which, as they see it, without the Dao and the RMPs that they think prop it up, utter catastrophe beckons and all is lost. Some contemporary error theorists, by contrast, mostly talk this down. They are, after all—at least the ones I know—remarkably nice individuals, not at all given to people-trafficking or selling contaminated medicine to children's hospitals. They espouse error theory but are not out to frighten us for, on the contrary, they think that their skepticism can be tamed and domesticated. J. L. Mackie, as we will see, having, as he supposes, refuted morality, proceeds to moralize at some length. And here is how Joyce presents his own skepticism:

> There is a vague but deep-rooted concern that moral skepticism might corrupt the youth, or, more generally, leave people believing that "everything is permissible,"

---

[2] This insistence by Joyce that his skepticism reaches to such remote cultural places is, incidentally, part of my motivation for talking about "the Dao." Nothing much should hang here on the terminological specificity of the word "morality."

with potentially destructive effect. A moral error theory is...seen not merely as counter-intuitive, but as genuinely threatening. If this concern is shown to be unjustified—as the possibility of moral fictionalism suggests it may be—then perhaps the motivation for resisting a moral error theory is in need of re-examination. (2001: 231)

I am, as will become apparent, unconvinced by this.

3. Practical Reason

Interestingly there is a normative category that Joyce thinks escapes this corrosive holism. There has to be if his argument for moral fictionalism is to get off the ground. That is the category of our talk of reasons. This is pretty important. If normative reason gets sucked into the holistic whirlpool then we can surely forget about a domesticated skepticism.[3]

Joyce espouses a roughly Humean, subjectivist view inspired by Williams' reasons-internalism. I have reasons to do things that will advance my purposes and desires—or, rather, the purposes and desires of a version of me that has been somewhat idealized (where of course we need to understand "idealized" in some way that builds in nothing moral).

We could question this, of course. Williams talks of the case of a man who is not very nice to his wife and has no purposes or desires to which being nicer to his wife would speak, and nor would sound deliberation on his part produce any such. Nonetheless, the friend of "external reasons"—reasons that lack any such anchorage in the agent's desiderative profile—will insist that the man has a reason to be nicer to his wife. Williams writes:

> There are of course many things that a speaker may say to one who is not disposed to do something when the speaker thinks that he should be, such as that he is inconsiderate, or cruel, or selfish, or imprudent; or that things, and he, would be a lot nicer if he were so motivated. Any of these can be sensible things to say. But one who makes a great deal out of putting the criticism in the form of an external reason statement seems concerned to say that what is particularly wrong with the agent is that he is irrational. It is this theorist who particularly needs to make this charge precise: in particular, because he wants any rational agent, as such, to acknowledge the requirement to do the thing in question. (1981: 110)

---

[3] Bart Streumer (2017) defends a global normative skepticism. Happily for us all, however, Streumer professes not to believe his own view. I discuss Streumer's position in *The Possibility of Moral Community*.

T. M. Scanlon considers this passage and the criticisms that Williams is happy to let us level at this man (that he is inconsiderate, etc.):

> These criticisms do involve accusing him of a kind of deficiency, namely a failure to be moved by certain considerations that we regard as reasons. (What else is it to be inconsiderate, cruel, insensitive, and so on?) If it is a deficiency for the man to fail to see these considerations as reasons, it would seem that they must be reasons for him (If they are not, how can it be a deficiency for him to fail to recognize them?) Why not conclude, then, that the man has reason to treat his wife better? (1998: 367)

Scanlon's thought seems to be that it appears odd to say that we think it a deficiency on someone's part to fail to see the force of some considerations as reasons but that we do not think they are indeed reasons, and reasons for him. So what will count as a reason cannot readily be insulated from the rest of the normative landscape, including the moral part. The sphere of practical reasons is not a proper part of the normative domain. It is the sphere of everything we might credibly say after a "Because" in answer to a "Why?"

Williams' famous example is of an unkind husband. A pivotal and central example for Joyce is the unrepentant gangster.

> Suppose we have caught a criminal who stands before us in the dock. There is no question about his guilt—he admits it freely. What is curious about this criminal is that he is utterly unrepentant: he tells us that he desired to kill the person, and that the killing did not frustrate any of his desires (we imagine that he even wanted to be caught and punished). Such criminals with such desires may be statistically rare, but they are surely possible. Imagine that the criminal is quite convincing in relating all this to us. Are we in any way moved to retract our judgment that the criminal did something that he morally ought not to have done? Of course not. (2001: 32)

This—what Joyce calls the *inescapability* of moral judgment—does not attach, he thinks, to judgments about normative reasons. The latter, unlike the former, do depend on the desires and purposes of the agent who is the object of the judgment. It is just this inescapability that Joyce thinks is ropey, so motivating his embrace of error theory.

So Felon—let us call him—is a cold-hearted killer. We will suppose that none of the circumstances that may be argued sometimes to make killing permissible obtain: he has done murder. Well, I do indeed think that Felon's killing is morally wrong, and I think that it is wrong even if Felon is unrepentant in the way Joyce describes. But in thinking Felon has done something morally wrong I do not fall into error.

What am I doing when I say that what Felon did was morally wrong? I may be doing a number of things. One is to *avow* a certain normative stance. I am signaling my acceptance of a moral code that prohibits extreme violence as a response to (we'll suppose) a trivial perceived slight. In doing this, I let you know that you should rely on me not to conduct myself that way, and, if I do, you can hold me to account for having violated a norm that I myself avow and embrace. I am also ordinarily doing something else: making a *demand*. I'm signaling a *normative expectation* toward you, my conversational partner and audience. You must not conduct yourself in such a way, and I will hold you accountable if you do. It makes abundant sense for me to do both these things, however unrepentant Felon may or may not be.

That sounds familiar: "I approve of this! Do so as well!"[4]—but not quite. In fact, this well-known Stevensonian formula is way too individualistic. For I speak (ordinarily) as a member of a normative community, a space of shared understandings and agreed rules, and as such I invoke the Dao. After all, a world of reciprocal normative expectations, of accountability, had better be a world of shared and agreed norms or it won't work. So I take my avowal not just as an expression of the passions in my soul but as an expression of the values and requirements that we all (and, a fortiori, we both) accept. You can expect this of me and I will expect it of you because it is part of this big important thing that we agree about. We approve of this! Do so as well![5]

I may say this even when it may not be obvious to you that we agree about any such thing. Someone might have stood up in the House of Commons 200 years ago and said that women should be accorded the same political rights to vote and stand for public office as enjoyed by men (or, more precisely, back then, *some* men). Likely no one else present would have recognized *that* as part of the Dao that they agreed about, but the speaker may well have supposed it was. "Listen," we may think of him as suggesting, "if you think carefully and hard about what certain core moral values and principles we all share really commit us to, you will end up agreeing with me on this." (To them, this may have seemed quite mad. To many of us, I guess, it now seems entirely credible.)

When we belong to the same moral community under the Dao, some such supposition is ordinarily in play. I have called it the *optimistic implicature*, based on the maxim of conversation that *what one is saying is not pointless*.[6] If we have so little shared normative understanding, so little common ground that I am certain

---

[4] Stevenson 1944: chapter 2.
[5] In *The Possibility of Moral Community*, I defend this picture at length.
[6] Lenman 2013: 402. This is of course a much weaker claim than the moral rationalist's claim that morality presupposes the ideal convergence of all rational agents. For critical discussion of the latter see Lenman 1999. The optimistic implicature makes no reference to the vast space of possible rational beings. It is a matter of claiming what Gibbard calls "contextual authority" (1990: 174ff.) grounded in contingent commonalities of shared moral understanding that, it is hoped, furnish us as fellow members of a community of judgment with enough common ground to continue talking fruitfully.

nothing I ever say will get any motivational purchase (and in real life this is surely almost never the case), then moral condemnation addressed to you does start to look, in many contexts, like browbeating—or, as Williams has it, "bluff" (1981: 111). Maybe not all. Telling the morally unreachable what we think of them sometimes has a point, if we wish to explain to them why we are locking them away or why we do not want to be their friends. Or of course there are cases where one's addressee is not the whole of one's audience. Debating on TV with Fred the Fascist, I may well hold out little hope of changing Fred's mind; it's the audience I am really hoping to influence and persuade. And of course when the judge, in passing sentence, says to Felon, "Felon, you are very wicked," she is addressing not only Felon himself but the whole community whose laws it is her job to uphold.

I say then that what Felon does is morally wrong. In doing this I avow my embrace of an interpretation of the Dao, my community's shared moral code, as prohibiting murder, and I encourage you, as members of my community, to do likewise. I may even encourage Felon himself to do likewise, but I may accept that I would be wasting my breath and not bother. I see no error here.

And there are many other things I can say about him. That we act rightly in punishing him, that his actions bring shame on his family, that he is not a moral exemplar, that he is not a good person to choose as a friend, a spouse, a teacher, a government official, or many of the other roles we choose people to fill. I can say that if a king habitually acted like this we might quite properly depose him—as the founder of the Zhou Dynasty is said to have deposed the depraved last king of the Shang, back in the day. (It was often just such things as these that ancient Chinese people were given to saying about moral monsters.)

Does Felon himself have a reason to repent his crime and change his ways even when, as we might suppose, Felon+, his ideally coherent counterpart, recognizes no such thing? We Deflationary Realists don't all say the same thing here. Non-expressivist constructivists like Bernard Williams and Sharon Street will say no. Of an "ideally coherent Caligula" Street writes:

> it is important to remember all the things an attitude-dependent theorist can say about them and regard herself as speaking truly. For instance, we can say that we loathe the ideally coherent Caligula; that it's awful, from our point of view, that he and his normative reasons are like this; and that the rest of us who do care about morality have every normative reason to lock him up, defend ourselves against him, and to try to change him if we can. (2009: 293)

She nevertheless maintains that on her view the ideally coherent Caligula has no normative reason to change his ways. This acknowledgement, she argues, is important for her metaphysical take on what morality is. But it is hardly a reason to think morality is garbage.

The expressivist wing of Deflationary Realism doesn't concede even this. Thus Allan Gibbard in *Wise Choices, Apt Feelings* (1990) proposes that to call something—say, the needless distress caused to Felon's victim and their family—"a reason" to do or refrain from something is to express acceptance of a system of norms that treats it as weighing in favor of so doing or refraining. Like Simon Blackburn, Gibbard thinks that there is space here for mind-independence: for the embrace of norms that tell me, as a substantive normative matter, that I should abstain from pointless and gratuitous violence *even in a world where I see nothing wrong with it*.[7] Expressivists make sense of attitude-independent, external reason talk with no ropey presupposition required.

There are further questions about Felon. Is he morally responsible for his wrongdoing? Can we blame him for it? Does he deserve his punishment or should we think of ourselves as just caging him as we might a dangerous animal, fearful of the danger he poses but without resentment? But these are questions—important and interesting questions—that we ask *within* morality. Nothing conceptually non-negotiable for morality is plausibly at stake here.

4. What Next? Mackie

I was, I now confess, being unfair when I said the error theorists say that morality is garbage. To say something is garbage is ordinarily to recommend that we bin it as it is of no value. But in fact many error theorists do not think that morality is of no value and that we should bin it accordingly. Some, it is true, *do* recommend the bin. For abolitionists like Ian Hinckfuss, Richard Garner, and Joel Marks the bin is where it belongs. They argue that morality is a social evil that does terrible harm so we should get rid of it.[8] Others disagree. Thus, for Joyce, morality is "precious and consequential" (2001: x). Joyce and others think that there are important benefits to keeping morality in play, despite its being a massive tissue of falsehoods. Some, reformers, think we should tinker with it to free it from error.[9] Others think we should contrive to make-believe that it is true. There are two versions of this latter claim. The first, usually called "fictionalism," has it that we should merely make-believe this and not actually believe it for real.[10] Then there is the stronger version, conservationism, which invites us to a more thoroughgoing pretence where we will seek to actively embrace a state of illusion and contrive to

---

[7] Blackburn 1984: 217–20. Cf. Gibbard 1990: 160–6.
[8] Hinckfuss 1987; Garner 1994; Marks 2013. I discuss abolitionism in Lenman 2013 and *The Possibility of Moral Community*.
[9] For an interesting proposal along these lines see Lutz 2014.
[10] Defended by Joyce 2001. Joyce nowadays prefers to speak of "nondoxastic acceptance" rather than make-believe. See Joyce, Chapter 13 of this volume.

believe the falsehoods.[11] I am using "pretence" here as a term of art to cover the various things which fictionalists and conservationists propose we do that are not abolition—the various ways they favor our *retaining* moral discourse in spite of its falsehood, whether that retention is understood as continued full-blooded belief or make-believe or nondoxastic acceptance or whatever. And I shall use "fictionalism" for views that favor such retentions in the face of suppose falsehood, including conservationists.

It's natural for an error theorist to be interested in the "What next?" question, the question what we should do next when we decide to believe the error theory. But I think this question is also of interest in deciding whether to believe the error theory in the first place, because I think reflection on it helps to make it clear why we should not.

It all starts with Mackie who, as is now notorious, wrote a book in two parts, the first of which is devoted to telling us that morality is bunk and the second of which is devoted to, um, moralizing. He explains in chapter 1, section eleven:

> The argument of the preceding sections is meant to apply quite generally to moral thought, but the terms in which it has been stated are largely those of the Kantian and post-Kantian tradition of English moral philosophy. To those who are more familiar with another tradition, which runs through Aristotle and Aquinas, it may well seem wide of the mark. For them, the fundamental notion is that of the good for man, or the general end or goal of human life, or perhaps of a set of basic goods or primary human purposes. Moral reasoning consists partly in achieving a more adequate understanding of this basic goal (or set of goals), partly in working out the best way of pursuing and realizing it.
> (1977: 46)

Mackie distinguishes between a descriptive and a prescriptive reading of this approach and goes on:

> I have no quarrel with this notion interpreted in the first way...Nor indeed have I any quarrel with the second, prescriptive interpretation, provided that it is recognized as subjectively prescriptive, that the speaker is putting forward his own demands or proposals, or those of some movement that he represents, though no doubt linking these demands or proposals with what he takes to be already in the first, descriptive, sense, fundamental human goals. In fact, I shall myself make use of the notion of the good for man, interpreted in both these ways, when I try in chapter 8 to sketch a positive moral system. (1977: 47)

---

[11] Defended by Olson 2014 and Isserow 2017.

In fact, the moralizing part of the book opens with chapter 5, section 1 of which is called "Consequences of moral scepticism." Morality, Mackie tells us here,

> is not to be discovered but to be made: we have to decide what moral views to adopt, what moral stands to take. (1977: 106)

But this is all rather queer. Having spent the first half of his book cheerfully refuting this morality thingummy that he thinks is full of errors, he proposes to rebuild the house he just demolished. The question that presses itself on us is "Then why demolish it in the first place?" And, indeed, very soon after Mackie's book, along comes Blackburn with the lovely challenge he raises in his classic essay "Errors and the phenomenology of value" (in Blackburn 1993). Blackburn, like me, finds the whole proceeding odd for reasons that I'll now recapitulate.

We all believe in this morality thing and everyone is happy. But then we decide, *No that morality thing was all wrong*. So we bin it. But now we think: *Hang on, what shall I do now? I want to go on living in society with other human beings and I want there to be some rules that say people are not allowed to kill me or beat me up or steal my lunch and we should keep our promises and not tell lies and so on*. And then, hey, it turns out that the other people are thinking this too. So we have a meeting and we discuss what rules to have and agree on some rules to begin with and we keep on meeting on the first Thursday of every month to try to refine and sometimes perhaps revise what we agreed so far. And of course what is more natural than that our language should come to have certain predicates in it to denote properties like that of *being required by the rules*, or even that of *what the rules would require were they subject to what we might all agree was a process of improvement*? And we make our rules and they bed in and become accepted, and they come to be central to our lives and the ways in which we came to understand and value what we are. Perhaps after some hundreds of years these new rules are deeply embedded in our shared lives, woven into our literature, our poems and our songs, our rituals and manners, the very conceptual water in which we swim. Almost as if…

But no! Please let us call this not "moralizing" but rather "schmoralizing," because we are now being ever so careful not to build in any of those pesky Ropey Metaphysical Presuppositions. So the result will look a bit different. Only, well, look, but it doesn't. When we sit down and try to imagine what schmoralizing might look like it's hard to resist the thought that it will end up looking *awfully* like moralizing. And indeed when we observe Mackie himself schmoralizing (as he must take it to be), it *does* look awfully like moralizing, at least as practiced by very clever and bookish academics of the late-twentieth century. We repudiate the Dao and make morality anew, but what we end up doing is remaking what we had before.[12]

---

[12] Cf. Walzer 1993: 20.

That's what I believe thinking about the "What next?" question teaches us: that the natural and right place to go next after coming to believe the error theory is backwards—back to the state you were in when you didn't believe it. What would it be like, the thing we might imagine ourselves constructing to replace a discredited morality, free of the ropey errors that effected the discrediting? If, as is all too credible, we think it would look exactly like morality, then the original diagnosis of error begins to look decidedly premature.

Jonas Olson addresses this concern and comes to Mackie's defense.[13]

> To some readers it may seem a puzzling fact that Mackie engaged seriously in these kinds of first-order normative debate. If moral error theory is true, then any conclusions reached in normative and applied ethics are false. It may seem obvious, then, that moral error theory discredits these disciplines completely. But there is no deep puzzle here. We have seen that philosophers from Protagoras through Hobbes and Hume to Warnock have taught us that human beings need morality to coexist peacefully, to prevent conflicts, to regulate and coordinate behaviour, and to counteract limited sympathies. Since most social life presupposes something like a system of morality and since something like a moral system will or is likely to occur, intentionally or not, wherever there is social interaction, we need, according to Mackie, "to find some set of principles which [are] themselves fairly acceptable to us and with which, along with their practical consequences and applications, our 'intuitive' (but really subjective) detailed moral judgements are in 'reflective equilibrium'". To this end, we need to engage in normative theorizing. Typical adequacy constraints on normative theories are intuitive plausibility and acceptability, comprehensiveness, systematicity, simplicity, and applicability. Moral error theorists can without tongues-in-cheeks engage in the pursuit of theories that meet these criteria. The one criterion that cannot be met is of course that of truth.   (Olson 2014: 197)

This defense of Mackie is pretty odd. We need moral rules to live by, Olson seems to be saying, so it makes sense to look for and agree on rules that we can live by well. This is something we can do without falling into any errors. This business of looking for rules can be done well or badly. It has adequacy criteria, as Olson says, that candidate codes of rules will meet to a greater or lesser degree. So theorizing about what these rules should be is subject to a regulative ideal constituted by those criteria. And if we can have rules and a regulative idea for choosing rules without falling into any errors, then we can certainly introduce a *property*: we can say some rules, or systems of rules, have the property of being robust under

---

[13] Olson's own case for error theory in his 2014 book is based on a different supposed RMP, what he calls *irreducibly normative favoring relations*. I don't discuss that here. A telling critical discussion with which I am in much agreement is Toppinen 2016.

critical theoretical scrutiny in the light of that regulative ideal. And if there is such a property for rules to have, we can also have (at this point, semantic ascent comes pretty cheap) *truths* about what does and does not have that property and to what degree. Mackie, like other error theorists, thinks morality is suspect because it has the Ropey Metaphysical Presupposition of "objective prescriptivity" that is supposed to underwrite the authority of morality. He most certainly does not think that it is *truth*.

There are Heavy Duty Realists who argue that without the RMP, whatever they take it to be, we really are in deep trouble and nothing makes sense. Notably, David Enoch argues that if Heavy Duty Realism were false, deliberation would not be possible at all—never mind co-deliberation. Intelligent practical thought would simply cease to be possible. We could only ever pick, quite arbitrarily, and never choose. Enoch makes an *indispensability argument* to this effect.[14] In this context, Mackie's project of quietly schmoralizing morality back into business so it can shape our lives in the ways we think so important acquires a great significance. If it succeeds it amounts to a *dispensability argument*. Sure we can make sense of this stuff without Ropey Presuppositions—look, we just did! But then it becomes puzzling why we should think there *ever was* an RMP and why, having successfully constructed an understanding of morality that doesn't make the Presupposition, anyone would want to insist that we continue to make-believe that any such Presupposition is true, never mind actually believe it, as Olson, a conservationist, advocates.

But where would the *authority* of morality come from if we stopped propping up our moral beliefs with RMPs, even supposing we ever did? Why would we think morality thus unpropped-up *important*? Well, that is not so hard to answer. In rejecting abolitionism, Olson approvingly quotes Nolan, Restall, and West:

> [M]oral discourse is extraordinary useful. Morality plays an important social role in coordinating attitudes and regulating interpersonal relations.[15]

Apart from the abolitionists—Hinckfuss, Garner, Marks, et al.—everyone in this literature agrees. Morality is really important. It is "precious and consequential." We would be in deep, deep trouble without it. (We say this in different ways. The fictionalist tries to confine the point to something about how very *useful* morality is. I am happy to say more: it would be a *moral* disaster if morality were to be lost) In any event, it is a point that gives us authority in abundance. And now that we have reconstructed the ethical in the way Mackie takes himself to be doing, and it all seems to be going so well, it gets less and less plausible that the supposed RMP is anything like as central—as "conceptually non-negotiable"—as we were

---

[14] Enoch 2011. I discuss Enoch's argument in my 2014.
[15] 2005: 307. Quoted in Olson 2014: 180.

first told. It starts to look like, at best, a fairly inessential add-on, something that can be sloughed off at little cost.

A few pages after the long passage quoted above, Olson's book ends with this peroration:

> To conclude, moral error theory does not discredit normative ethics. The human predicament is such that we need to "find principles of equity and ways of making and keeping agreements without which we cannot hold together." Our means of achieving this is to engage in first-order normative theorizing. This is not to discredit normative ethics, but to award it the highest importance.
> (Olson 2014: 197)

If we take this seriously, then nothing has been said to discredit normative ethics. But then moral error theory itself is beginning to look decidedly queer. If it is really, really important—not important only given a Ropey Metaphysical Presupposition, certainly not let's-pretend-important, but *for real* important—that we accept and respect some body of moral rules to regulate our lives together and so we do just that for just that reason, it's pretty hard to see where the mistake is supposed to be or why we should think we have fallen into error for having done so.

5. What Next? Joyce

The "What next?" question is brought very explicitly into focus by Joyce: "If there's nothing that we ought to do then what ought we to do?" (2001: 175). He quickly recognizes that this had better not be seen as itself a moral question.

> It might be thought that the question "If a moral error theory is the case, what should we do?" is self-undermining. And so it would be, if it were asking what we *morally* ought to do, but that is not what is being asked. It is just a straightforward, common-or-garden, *practical* "ought." In other words, the answer that the question invites will be a hypothetical imperative, and the arguments for a moral error theory have not threatened hypothetical imperatives. I do not want this issue to depend on any particular view of how we make such practical decisions. Let us just say that when morality is removed from the picture, what is practically called for is a matter of a cost-benefit analysis, where the costs and benefits can be understood liberally as preference satisfactions. By asking what *we* ought to do I am asking how a *group* of persons, who share a variety of broad interests, projects, ends—and who have come to the realization that morality is a bankrupt theory—might best carry on. (2001: 177; see also Joyce 2019)

Joyce then wants to think of the selection between the various items on the error theorist's supposed menu—abolitionism, fictionalism, conservationism—as guided by this supposedly morally neutral process of "cost-benefit analysis." We find the same thought in Nolan, Restall, and West:

> The fictionalist's answer, in brief, is that realist moral discourse should be retained, even though it is strictly speaking false, because it is useful. (The "should" here is pragmatic, not moral). (2005: 310)

This idea resurfaces in a different context later. We have to do more than decide which item on the "What next?" menu to choose. If we decide to choose one of the two options, fictionalism and conservationism, that invite us to go in for pretending, however thoroughgoing, we then have to make a *further* decision. We have to decide *which* set of falsehoods, of all the many moral codes we can dream up, we are going to pretend to believe. Again we are told to resort to non-moral, purely pragmatic selection: "the question of which fiction to be used is best settled by determining which fiction would be most useful to use" (Nolan et al. 2005: 327).

There is a problem with all this and it is a very big problem indeed. It's a problem we effectively already registered in noting Scanlon's response to Williams. It is just a fantasy that there is this thing we can do here—"cost-benefit analysis"—that is *morally neutral*. Joyce in *The Myth of Morality* takes this as something that we are imagining a group of people doing.[16] And these people are practicing Humean instrumental reasoning—what Joyce thinks is left standing when we have divested ourselves of believing in morality, safely insulated from the corrosive holism whereby error infects everything else. But to extend Humean instrumentalism in this way from person to group we need to come up with some kind of social welfare function, something that takes us from the preference profiles of individual people to a preference profile for the group as a whole. And how to do this is a massively and inescapably *moral* question. Whose welfare counts and how much? Everyone's? Equally? Really? Shall we give less weight to the preferences of poor people? Surely that would be really unfair. Shall we count women equally to men? Well yes, of course, unless we are sexist bigots. But using language like "unfair" and "sexist bigot" we are already deep inside the Dao; we have to already be under sail in the sea of moral language to speak this way. And who even is "everyone"? The group making the decision? But who are they? The competent adult members of the community that will have to live with it? All and only they count? What about their children who are not yet competent? Their children who are unborn? Adults who are not competent? What about people in other communities?

---

[16] 2001: 177. The emphasis on the "What next?" question as a question for a group is continued in Joyce 2005 and 2019. I think it a well-judged emphasis. We could ask the question from an individual standpoint but I don't think that will help much. Very briefly, we might hope to get satisfactory answers to it if we again take it to be an already inescapably moral question. But if we insist on the fantasy that there is available to us some pure, pragmatic understanding of practical reason purged of all moral direction that we can bring to bear here, it is a safe bet we are going to bump into some nasty free-rider problems.

What about animals? When we figure out who counts, what then? Are we to just aggregate and maximize? That's called *utilitarianism*. It's a *moral theory*. It's not morally neutral and is as controversial as hell.[17] As soon as we try to put this into action we are up to our necks in moral controversy. The "What next?" question is a moral question. Inescapably. That doesn't yet mean that error theory is false. It does mean you can forget about domesticating it. Without the Dao, we have, to echo Edmund Burke, no compass to govern us ([1790] 2004: 172–3) and we are quite lost.[18]

According to a certain kind of moral fictionalist, then, we can appeal to a cost-benefit analysis criterion for deciding whether we should make-believe any fiction or just jettison morality completely, which fiction we should choose to make-believe, and how thoroughly we should make-believe it. This is our criterion, we may say, of *pretenceworthiness*, and we are after the most pretenceworthy fiction to make-believe. There is a fatal dilemma here. We had better not be fictionalists or any kind of error theorists about *pretenceworthiness* itself. *It* has to be kosher. Some statements about what is pretenceworthy had better be true. Really true. Not pretend true. If not, then everything really is garbage all the way down; the Dao, all of it, is for the shredder, and domesticated skepticism is for the birds.

Pretenceworthiness, whatever it is, had better not be queer. Suppose we understand it in utilitarian terms: we should pick the moral code F to be our fiction, our make-believing of whose truth will generate most average (let us say) utility for members of the moral community doing the choosing. But hang on, this story is starting to look *really* familiar. It looks awfully like a familiar normative ethical position called *rule utilitarianism*.

> RU: We should adopt and follow the moral code our adopting and following of which will most effectively maximize average utility.

The "should" here is just the should of pretenceworthiness and, as we just noted, there had better be nothing queer or metaphysically ropey. So what started out meaning to be a bold new metaethical view just ends up being a very roundabout way of arriving at the idea that very familiar normative ethical theory is, simply, true.

---

[17] According to me it is also false, but that is another argument for another day.
[18] This pragmatic way of understanding the "What next?" question effectively seeks to accord a foundational role to personal preferences with morally substantive value judgments to be determined by and responsible to the former. Susan Hurley's book *Natural Reasons* is a sustained and powerful attack on just this way of understanding the normative world, which she characterizes as "the subjectivist view that all substantive evaluative questions may be reduced to formal problems about the relations among preferences, that solutions to the latter, as a conceptual matter, determine answers to the former" (1989: 106), making a strong case for its philosophical incoherence. Even before we start trying to figure out what our metric of social welfare is to be, preferences, she argues, are value-laden from the outset.

Well, maybe not quite. The thought may instead be:

FRU: We should adopt and follow the moral code our adopting and following of which will most effectively maximize average utility. We should *also* pretend we believe that the code in question derives its authority from Ropey Metaphysical Presuppositions which we will pretend to believe.

But it would be very queer to claim that FRU is a better plan than RU. Again we might think to prop up the authority of the rules. But that won't work, as we saw. If we think that maximizing average utility is *important* (*really* important), then we have authority aplenty already. If it is not, what are we even doing? If pretence-worthiness is a real thing with real normative clout, all we need is RU, in which case we don't need to pretend anything. We can be an open-eyed moral community whether or not RU is the best code for us to live by. So if our reasons to pretend are themselves more pretend reasons, then we have no reasons to pretend and the fictionalist project fails. But if our reasons to pretend are real reasons, then there is no need to pretend and the error theory itself is convicted of error.[19]

We cherish and respect the Dao, recognizing as we do that it is precious and consequential. To do this we don't need to pretend anything. Does the fictionalist think it in some way important not only that we cherish and respect the Dao but that we think our doing this requires validation for some Ropey Presupposition? That seems a queer thing for anyone to think. Ropey Presuppositions of the kind I here question are neither precious nor consequential. Whoever would want to pretend to believe them?[20]

References

Blackburn, S. 1984. *Spreading the Word: Groundings in the Philosophy of Language*. Oxford University Press.

Blackburn, S. 1993. *Essays in Quasi-Realism*. Oxford University Press.

---

[19] This strategy is followed very explicitly by Jaquet 2021. Jaquet offers a contractualist rationale for adopting a utilitarian criterion for selecting the moral fiction we have most reason to make-believe. But this is baffling. If this rationale works, we have good reasons, reasons for real, to adopt and follow the prescriptions of such a moral code. And if we have such reasons, we don't need to make-believe anything.

[20] I was pleased and honored to be invited to take part in the wonderful conference (during the Time of Coronavirus the word should be understood loosely) in Wellington from which this volume has emerged. I would like to thank Richard and Stuart for inviting my contribution and their detailed written comments. I would also like to thank all the other participants for the great discussion we enjoyed, not least Richard, Jess Isserow, and Jonas Olson for the good-natured and collegial spirit in which they engaged with my criticisms of their work. I also had an opportunity to present this material (alas, again online) to the Philosophy Department of Shandong University. I am grateful to the audience there for the great discussion we had and especially to Wen-fang Wang who organized my talk and to Matt Lutz for a lively and helpful response. Felicity Fu read a near final draft and said cool things. Work on this chapter was funded by the Swedish Research Council (Project Id: 2019-02828).

Burke, E. [1790] 2004. *Reflections on the Revolution in France*. Penguin.

Enoch, D. 2011. *Taking Morality Seriously: A Defence of Robust Realism*. Oxford University Press.

Garner, R. 1994. *Beyond Morality*. Temple University Press.

Gibbard, A. 1990. *Wise Choices, Apt Feelings: A Theory of Normative Judgement*. Oxford University Press.

Hinckfuss, I. 1987. "The moral society: Its structure and effects." *Discussion Papers in Environmental Philosophy* 16. Canberra: Philosophy Program [RSSS], Australian National University.

Hurley, S. 1989. *Natural Reasons: Personality and Polity*. Oxford University Press.

Isserow, J. 2017. *What to Do When the World Doesn't Play Along: Life after Moral Error Theory*. PhD Dissertation, Australian National University.

Jaquet, F. 2021. "Utilitarianism for the error theorist." *Journal of Ethics* 25: 39–55.

Joyce, R. 2001. *The Myth of Morality*. Cambridge University Press.

Joyce, R. 2005. "Moral fictionalism." In M. Kalderon (ed.), *Fictionalism in Metaphysics*. Oxford University Press. 287–313.

Joyce, R. 2019. "Moral fictionalism: How to have your cake and eat it too." In R. Garner & R. Joyce (eds.), *The End of Morality: Taking Moral Abolitionism Seriously*. Routledge. 150–65.

Lenman, J. 1999. "Michael Smith and the Daleks." *Utilitas* 11: 164–77.

Lenman, J. 2013. "Ethics without errors." *Ratio* 26: 391–409.

Lenman, J. 2014. "Deliberation, schmeliberation: Enoch's indispensability argument." *Philosophical Studies* 168: 835–42.

Lenman, J. Forthcoming. *The Possibility of Moral Community*. Oxford University Press.

Lewis, C. S. 1943. *The Abolition of Man*. Oxford University Press.

Lutz, M. 2014. "The 'now what' problem for error theory." *Philosophical Studies* 171: 351–71.

Mackie, J. L. 1977. *Ethics: Inventing Rights and Wrong*. Penguin.

Marks, J. 2013. *Ethics without Morality: In Defense of Amorality*. Routledge.

Nolan, D., Restall, G., & West, C. 2005. "Moral fictionalism versus the rest." *Australasian Journal of Philosophy* 83: 307–30.

Olson, J. 2014. *Moral Error Theory: History, Critique, Defence*. Oxford University Press.

Scanlon, T. M. 1998. *What We Owe to Each Other*. Harvard University Press.

Stevenson, C. L. 1944. *Ethics and Language*. Yale University Press.

Strawson, P. 1974. *Freedom and Resentment and Other Essays*. Methuen.

Street, S. 2009. "In defense of future Tuesday indifference: Ideally coherent eccentrics and the contingency of what matters." *Philosophical Issues* 19: 273–98.

Streumer, B. 2017. *Unbelievable Errors*. Oxford University Press.

Toppinen, T. 2016. "Is irreducible normativity impossibly queer?" *Journal of Moral Philosophy* 13: 437–60.

Walzer, M. 1993. *Interpretation and Social Criticism*. Harvard University Press.

Williams, B. 1981. *Moral Luck*. Cambridge University Press.

Williams, B. 1985. *Ethics and the Limits of Philosophy*. Fontana/Collins.

2
Should Moral Error Theorists Make Do with Make-Believe?

Jessica Isserow

1. Introduction

In his *On the Plurality of Worlds*, David Lewis recommends that we adopt a "simple maxim of honesty" when constructing our philosophical theories: "never put forward a...theory that you yourself cannot believe in your least philosophical and most commonsensical moments" (1986: 135). It is safe to say that not everyone has taken Lewis's suggestion to heart. Philosophers have told us that, contrary to what we believe, there are no beliefs (Churchland 1981)—nor any philosophers for that matter (Unger 1979). They have also denied the existence of colors (Boghossian & Velleman 1989), numbers (Field 1980), sexual perversion (Priest 1997), emotions (Griffiths 1997), and moral facts (Mackie 1977; Joyce 2001; Olson 2014).[1]

Assuming, as these philosophers do, that the sentences that figure in our talk of numbers, colors, and the like are usually used assertorically—to purport to state truths—this means that we ought to be *error theorists* about these discourses. Roughly, to be an error theorist about a discourse is to hold that certain sentences of that discourse, which seem to be clearly aiming at truth, do not (or, perhaps, *cannot*) achieve it; that is, the world is just not the right way for basic assertions made within that discourse to come out true. The error theorist about color discourse, for example, takes ordinary utterances like "roses are red" and "the sky is blue" to be stating purported truths—and she takes us to (usually) be giving expression to beliefs when we utter such declarative sentences. But she also holds that such sentences and beliefs are not true because, strictly speaking, there are no colors.

Just as error theorists about color deny that anything is really red or blue, moral error theorists deny that anything is really morally right or wrong (Mackie 1977; Joyce 2001; Olson 2014). According to them, moral discourse is guilty of a systematic error, and so no moral claims are true. For the purposes of this chapter,

---

[1] To be sure, some philosophers have reported to me that they believe moral error theory in their least philosophical and most commonsensical moments as well. But I expect not all will.

Jessica Isserow, *Should Moral Error Theorists Make Do with Make-Believe?* In: *Moral Fictionalism and Religious Fictionalism*. Edited by: Richard Joyce and Stuart Brock, Oxford University Press. © Jessica Isserow 2023.
DOI: 10.1093/oso/9780198881865.003.0003

moral error theory is assumed rather than defended. My interest lies with what *follows* our belief in moral error theory. Assuming that moral error theory is true—and moreover, that we believe it to be true—what ought we to do with our error-ridden moral discourse? I will refer to this as the "What Next? Question" (WNQ).

Moral error theorists are, as it turns out, spoiled for choice here. One response to the WNQ is *abolitionism*, which advises us to rid ourselves of moral discourse entirely (Hinckfuss 1987; Garner 1994, 2007; Burgess 2007; Marks 2013; Ingram 2015). Another is *conservationism*, which recommends that we hold onto moral discourse as it is; that we continue to believe and assert moral propositions that we know to be false (Olson 2014). It has even been suggested that a Platonic noble lie may make for a fitting response to our unsettling metaethical discovery; perhaps the truth of moral error theory ought to remain safeguarded by some secret guild of philosophers (Cuneo & Christy 2011).

My focus in this chapter lies not with any of these answers to the WNQ, but with another: *moral fictionalism*. As its name suggests, the essence of this solution is that moral error theorists ought to preserve moral discourse in the spirit of a useful fiction. My ambition will be to develop a challenge for a certain kind of moral fictionalist. Specifically, the fictionalist who interests me recommends that we preserve moral discourse in the spirit of a useful fiction by adopting attitudes of *make-believe* (rather than belief) towards moral propositions. When I speak of "fictionalism" or "moral fictionalism" in what follows, then, this should be taken to refer specifically to moral fictionalism of the make-believe variety, unless otherwise indicated.

Moral fictionalism is premised upon two key assumptions, and comes attached with two key promises. The first assumption is that moral discourse offers us a range of desirable practical goods. The second is that preserving these goods by participating in moral discourse as we have before—viz., by believing (what we now know to be false) moral propositions—is simply not an epistemically respectable option. Corresponding to these two assumptions are two important promises on behalf of the fictionalist. First, there is the practical promise that, qua fictionalists, we can hope to recoup (at least some of) our losses; we are told that by converting to fictionalism, we will preserve (at least some of) the benefits associated with ordinary moral discourse. Second, there is the epistemic promise that we can achieve this result without incurring the costs associated with preserving our erroneous moral beliefs.

The critical component of my discussion takes off from an important tension that Jonas Olson (2014) identifies in the dual promise that the fictionalist makes us: any earnest efforts on behalf of fictionalists to keep the practical promise will, he maintains, compromise their ability to keep the epistemic promise, and vice versa. Contra Olson, I will argue that the epistemic promise is not in jeopardy. However, I will also argue that a proper appreciation of *why* fictionalists can safely make good on their epistemic promise should also lead us to doubt whether they really can make good on their practical one. Make-believe is sufficiently distinct from belief to immunize the fictionalist from any illicit moral believing—but it is also arguably too distinct to secure the benefits of moral believing. I maintain that such fictionalist attitudes are neither a stable enough nor a strong enough basis for securing the desirable practical goods associated with our error-ridden moral discourse.

An important caveat is needed before getting down to business. Clearly, the question as to whether moral fictionalism (of any sort) is the right answer to the WNQ is going to depend upon how it fares in relative rather than absolute terms. Suppose I'm right in thinking that moral fictionalism spells a rather bleak future for the moral error theorist. It may still be that this future is *less* bleak than one which involves (say) adopting the abolitionist or conservationist solutions instead.[2] With this having been noted, a restricted critical focus upon the fictionalist option remains useful, for the bleaker the anticipated fictionalist future starts to look, the less well fictionalism is ultimately likely to fare in this comparative exercise.

2. Moral Fictionalism

I begin with some brief words about fictionalism more generally (§2.1), before motivating moral fictionalism (§2.2) and identifying the variety that will occupy my attention (§2.3).

2.1 Fictionalism

A fictionalist about some discourse *D* takes the sentences of *D* at face value; she holds that the relevant language has a representational semantics, and is in the market for truth and falsity. (See Daly 2008: 425–6; Friend 2008: 14; Kroon 2011: 791.) However, the fictionalist also maintains that all of these sentences are strictly-speaking false.[3] A fictionalist about *D*, then, does not *believe* any of the propositions expressed by the sentences of *D*. Typically, she adopts a wholly different attitude towards them: an attitude that is not likewise ontologically

---

[2] It is also possible (though not, I think, a foregone conclusion) that other varieties of moral fictionalism—such as those canvassed below—are better-placed than the make-believe variety to handle some of the problems that I point towards. For optimism on this score, see Jaquet, Chapter 4, and Joyce, Chapter 13 of this volume; for pessimism, see Lenman, Chapter 1, and Moberger & Olson, Chapter 3 of this volume.

[3] One complication that I skirt over here is that we should really restrict this claim to *a particular subset of* the sentences of *D*. Presumably, the fictionalist about Luke Skywalker will still want to say that the sentence "There was never really a famous Jedi named Luke Skywalker who was raised on Tatooine" is true. See Brock 2002 for discussion.

committing.[4] (Alternatively, she may adopt an attitude of belief towards the sentences of D, suitably modified—I return to this option shortly.)

Sometimes fictionalism is intended as a descriptive claim—as an account of how a discourse is in fact used. Other times fictionalism is a call for change; it is recommended that we modify our use of some discourse by using it in a fictive spirit. The former has been dubbed *hermeneutic fictionalism*, the latter, *revolutionary fictionalism*.[5]

My focus in this chapter will be fictionalism of the revolutionary variety. What makes revolutionary fictionalism *revolutionary* is that it recommends a radical change in the way that a discourse is used. Typically, its proponents recommend that we cease believing the propositions expressed by the sentences of D (on account of their falsity), and replace these beliefs with attitudes of some other kind (on account of their anticipated usefulness).

2.2 Moral Fictionalism as an Answer to the WNQ

As was noted earlier, the motivations underlying revolutionary moral fictionalism are two-fold. The first is epistemic: moral fictionalism is thought to be attractive in virtue of ridding us of our false moral beliefs. The second motivation is practical: moral fictionalism is expected to secure many of the desirable practical goods that we associate with moral discourse.

Among these practical goods is one identified by Richard Joyce, a prominent defender of revolutionary moral fictionalism: that of "combatting weakness of will" (228).[6] Joyce regards moral commitments as especially effective mechanisms of self-control (181). Even if a course of action is in our practical interests, and even if we judge it to be so, that is no guarantee that we will pursue it; for we are frequently weak-willed, and fail to act in accordance with our considered judgments (211). We might, for instance, succumb to the temptation to go back on our word, or to betray an unsuspecting friend.

These lapses may sometimes go unnoticed or unpunished, and so it may occasionally be in our immediate interests to be uncooperative. Yet being uncooperative is likely to be contrary to our *long-term* interests; one seldom does well by coming to earn a reputation as untrustworthy.[7] Generally speaking, it is plausibly

---

[4] Fictionalists might also enlist (or recommend enlisting) different kinds of *speech-acts* as far as D's propositions are concerned; for instance, they may recommend pretending-to-assert these propositions (though how one should—and, indeed, whether one even can—take on this advice is complicated; see Joyce, Introduction and Chapter 13 of this volume). I focus on fictionalist attitudes here rather than fictionalist speech-acts.
[5] The "hermeneutic/revolutionary" terminology originates (to my knowledge) with Burgess (1983).
[6] All unattributed citations henceforth are to Joyce 2001.
[7] Joyce acknowledges that it might be in an agent's short-term interests to (e.g.) break a promise when there is no possibility of being caught or developing a bad reputation. But given the very real

in our long-term interests to cooperate with others, and moral commitment is helpful in that regard (210). An agent who takes promise-keeping to be *morally required* of her is likely to be someone with a stronger resolve to keep her promises. Thus, morality is useful in offering us a kind of safeguard against weakness of will; when we enlist moral concepts in our deliberations, we are more likely to act in accordance with our (long-term) practical interests.

The purported benefits of moral discourse need not stop there, of course. Joyce also suggests that shared moral values may help to build social cohesion (228), and that moral judgments may function as "conversation-stoppers" of a useful sort (see Chapter 13 of this volume). Other fictionalists have drawn attention to the valuable role that moral discourse plays in directing our social lives, helping us to coordinate our attitudes and regulate interpersonal conflict (Nolan et al. 2005: 314).

All in all, then, there is good reason to take seriously the fictionalist's suggestion that moral discourse is worth preserving in some form, on account of its practical benefits. It is her contention that we can continue to enjoy such benefits—without believing moral propositions—by preserving moral discourse as a useful fiction.

2.3 Varieties of Moral Fictionalism

Suppose that the moral error theorist is seeking to put some variety of revolutionary moral fictionalism to work. There are several options available to her.

The first is what is sometimes called "Prefix Fictionalism." On this way of proceeding, the revolutionary moral fictionalist who claims to believe "It is wrong to break one's promises" does indeed believe something. However, what she believes is best understood by way of invoking some sort of (implicit or explicit) prefix (Eklund 2019). The Prefix Fictionalist might, for instance, want to say that what she really believes is "According to the moral fiction, it is wrong to break one's promises."[8]

The second option is what might be called "Distraction Fictionalism." This proposal takes off from the well-known idea that having our aims at the forefront of our minds can often be counterproductive. The socially awkward person only amplifies her awkwardness by questioning her every interaction at a dinner party. And the consequentialist who grows preoccupied with promoting the good may thereby miss her target (Railton 1984: 154). Generally speaking, we may do *worse*

---

danger of miscalculating the risks and the high costs of error, he argues that it is likely to be in an individual's long-term interests to adopt a policy of keeping her promises—and of being cooperative more generally. Though doing so may not benefit her on each and every occasion, the policy is likely to benefit her in the long run (212–13).

[8] Prefix fictionalism is a popular approach to discourse about paradigmatically fictional characters like Sherlock Holmes (see Lewis 1978; Brock 2002). It has also been developed for modal language (Rosen 1990; Brogaard 2006).

at achieving a particular goal if we are always explicitly aiming at it. Importantly, this need not entail that the social amateur should cease *believing* that she ought to work on her people-skills, nor that the consequentialist ought to back-track on her consequentialism. A more plausible resolution would be for these individuals not to *attend* to these beliefs quite so often. The Distraction Fictionalist offers parallel advice (Joyce, Chapter 13, and Jaquet, Chapter 4 of this volume; Joyce forthcoming): the fictionalist's belief that moral error theory is true should be "on the back burner most of the time." For the majority of her day-to-day life, the fictionalist's "thoughts, speech, and actions" should be guided by moral considerations in much the same way as a moral believer's would be.

The third item on our fictionalist menu is "Metaphor Fictionalism," which models our use of a fiction on the familiar practice of enlisting metaphors (see Joyce 2019, 2020). Joyce (2020: 109) appeals to the example of using the metaphorical description "She was a dragon" in order to convey something true: viz., that a particular person was bad-tempered. We might, so the thought goes, similarly convey something true—for instance, that we have good, desire-based reasons not to break our promises—by evoking moral language; by describing promise-breaking as "morally wrong," say. Why not simply appeal to the desire-based reasons themselves? One rationale for invoking metaphorical descriptions is that they typically engage our emotional and motivational energies in ways that literal descriptions do not. Couching our desire-based reasons in metaphorical (moral) terms can therefore be expected to generate more practical uptake (see Joyce 2020: 118–19).

Finally, there is the fictionalist option that will occupy my attention for the remainder of this chapter, which I suspect is the most well-known. This is "Make-Believe Fictionalism," which recommends that we adopt attitudes of make-believe towards moral propositions.[9] This proposal has been developed in detail by Joyce (2001, 2005), who takes make-believe to have a number of important properties that distinguish it from other sorts of attitudes. For one thing, make-believe involves *thoughts* unaccompanied by belief: when an agent make-believes that *p*, she is thinking the proposition *p* without believing it (197). Make-believing that *p* is also said to involve a disposition to withhold assent from *p* in "critical contexts": contexts wherein we "investigate and challenge the presuppositions of" ordinary thought (192). A moral fictionalist, for example, might still be disposed to attend to and express her belief that nothing is really morally right or wrong when she finds herself in a philosophy classroom.[10]

---

[9] It is not entirely clear whether "Metaphor Fictionalism" and "Make-Believe Fictionalism" are (i) best viewed as meaningfully distinct proposals (albeit ones that may overlap in certain ways), or if (ii) the former is better seen as a development of the latter. (See Joyce 2020: 110–12 for discussion.) I myself lean towards (i), and so I put the metaphor-proposal to the side in what follows.

[10] Cf. Cuneo & Christy (2011: 87–8), who characterize a critical context as one where there is a strong presumption of truth-telling. See also Jaquet, Chapter 4 of this volume.

On the matter of *what* we are to make-believe, Joyce suggests that a moral fiction "need consist primarily of a few general existential claims"—for instance, "there are obligations and prohibitions," and "people have character traits" (195). He adds some platitudinous claims (e.g., "Torturing babies to pass the time is always wrong") to partially constrain what these obligations and character traits could be. Thus, Joyce's moral fiction is effectively "a conceptual framework"—one that leaves many first-order moral questions open. Two moral fictionalists could not come to agree upon "whether a second-trimester abortion is permissible...simply by consulting the 'story of morality,' in the way that two Holmes fans may consult the canonical texts in order to settle a dispute about Watson's war wound" (195).

3. The Case against Moral Fictionalism

I begin my critical examination of moral fictionalism with Olson's (2014) critique of the proposal, which will serve as a useful launch-pad into the discussion. The moral fictionalist, recall, promises us the best of both worlds: it is her contention that we can continue to enjoy the advantages of engaging in moral discourse without holding onto our erroneous moral beliefs. Olson worries that there is a tension in this promise:

> One recommendation is to practice self-surveillance to make sure moral belief is avoided. This seems to involve occasionally attending to the belief that morality is fiction. A second recommendation is to suppress or silence belief to the effect that morality is fiction. This leads to instability in that while ways of thought and behaviour likely to prompt moral belief are recommended, moral belief is to be avoided. (2014: 190)

The moral fictionalist, then, seems to face the following dilemma. If she wants to make good on her epistemic promise, then she must take care to avoid becoming too immersed in her moral pretense. Otherwise, she risks a slip into moral belief (horn one). To avoid this slip, she must exercise epistemic caution, regularly attending to her belief that morality is merely a fiction. Such caution is, however, in tension with her practical promise; reminding herself that morality is a fiction is likely to prevent her from taking the pretense suitably seriously (horn two).

I think that the fictionalist can avoid impaling herself on Olson's first horn; she is not plausibly guilty of any moral believing. In what follows, I will argue for this claim on the fictionalist's behalf by drawing attention to important behavioral and psychological differences between attitudes of belief and make-believe (§3.1). However, I also think that avoiding Olson's first horn makes the second horn considerably *worse* for the fictionalist. Once we appreciate these important differences between belief and make-believe, we see why it is that the fictionalist cannot plausibly make good on her practical promise. Certain characteristic features of make-believe suggest that it would make for a rather poor substitute for moral belief (§3.2). None of the considerations that I raise should suggest to us that fictionalist attitudes would be *utterly useless*. But they should lead us to doubt the extent to which such attitudes are likely to be as useful as full-blooded moral beliefs—and this is, I think, a real worry for moral fictionalism inasmuch as it is proposed as a solution to the WNQ (§3.3).

3.1 The Slip into Belief

It is Olson's contention that an immersed moral fictionalist is apt to slip back into moral belief, reneging on her epistemic promise. Yet not much is said to motivate this claim. In its defense, Olson simply points out that moral make-believers would adopt incredibly similar behavioral and psychological dispositions to moral believers (with respect to moral propositions):

> [S]omeone who takes up a fictionalist stance to morality adopts certain behavioural dispositions and backs them up by moralizing her thoughts, i.e. by thinking of certain actions as wrong, unfair, or undeserved, etc.... But given successful adoption of the relevant behavioural dispositions, it seems difficult in many cases to avoid *believing* the relevant moral propositions, as opposed to merely *accepting* them or *thinking* about them.   (2014: 189, emphasis in original)
>
> [A]cquiring physical and psychological dispositions to behave in accordance with the fictional moral norms makes it all the more likely that one slips from moralized thought into moral belief.[11]   (2014: 189)

This at least gives us something to work with. In what follows, I build a case for Olson's first horn on his behalf, suggesting two ways in which it might be argued that an immersed moral fictionalist risks a slip into moral belief. Neither, I will argue, is promising.

First, the idea that make-believe is likely to lead to genuine belief might be advanced as an *empirical claim*. Perhaps it is simply a well-documented psychological fact about human beings that when immersed in a pretense, they usually find it difficult to avoid believing what they initially set out to merely pretend. Unfortunately, Olson doesn't provide us with any evidence to support this claim. And there is evidence that would seem to speak against it.

---

[11] Richard Garner briefly voices a similar suspicion when he suggests that if the moral fictionalist "begins to have moral feelings, moral outrage, moral guilt, and moral arguments, then we have every reason to say that he has reverted to his former moral beliefs, and to the error he once identified and abandoned" (2007: 509).

Experimental studies suggest that pretense-subserving representations are typically "quarantined" from representations of reality in games of make-believe (Leslie 1987). A child may pretend that a banana is a telephone, but she never loses sight of the fact that it is a banana. The events that occur within a pretense are taken to have effects only within that circumscribed domain: when the child pretends to talk to her father on the banana/telephone, she does not afterwards believe that she ever really had that conversation (Nichols & Stich 2000: 120). These events are not treated as relevant to guiding action in the outside world; if someone breaks a leg, no one uses a banana to call an ambulance.

Acts of pretense might therefore be said involve a kind of dual-representation; the child simultaneously represents the banana as a banana and as a telephone. What is important is that she does not surrender the capacity to distinguish what is real from what is imagined.[12] Indeed, this distinguishing capacity is so commonplace that some have taken its systematic absence to be a sign of pathology; it has been suggested that some mental disorders might profitably be explained in terms of a failure to quarantine what is real from what is imagined (Currie 2000). Absent any argument to the effect that immersed make-believe merits such a worrying prognosis, it seems uncharitable to deny the fictionalist a distinguishing capacity that is reliably present in young children.

Yet Olson might object[13] that the child's experience here is not appropriately analogous to that of our moral fictionalist. The moral fictionalist begins her epistemic journey believing that there are moral facts, prior to coming to believe that there aren't any. The expectation is then upon her to persist with moral make-believe indefinitely, taking care to avoid a relapse into moral belief. The child, by contrast, sets out by believing that bananas are not telephones, and only temporarily make-believes that they are. The epistemic challenge that she faces, then, hardly seems comparable to that of the moral fictionalist, whose moral beliefs have long influenced her actions, life plans, and deliberations. The substance of the child's make-believe—that bananas are telephones—is far from having ever occupied a parallel role in her cognitive economy.

More generally, Olson need not deny that there are propositions that we no longer believe but have come to take fictionalist attitudes towards, such that that we do not risk slipping back into believing them. His empirical conjecture, properly construed, is that it is difficult to adopt these fictionalist attitudes towards *certain kinds of* propositions without (at least occasionally) slipping back into believing those propositions. The person who comes to believe that the moral error theory is true may be thought to more closely resemble a former theist who

---

[12] This is not to deny that quarantining *can* sometimes fail; see Tamar Gendler's (2003) discussion of "contagion."

[13] Or, indeed, has objected; I am indebted to Jonas Olson for immensely helpful discussion on these points.

has been intellectually persuaded that God does not exist. Such a person might find herself deeply disturbed by the prospect of inhabiting a Godless world. And she may well find herself slipping back into believing that God exists on occasions when she is not attending closely to the evidence and arguments for atheism—especially if she chooses to immerse herself in any sort of religious pretense.

The latter case study may indeed make for a fairer point of comparison. Still, it's unclear to me how much help it will ultimately be to Olson, for there is evidence that the epistemic transition from theism to atheism is sustainable even following a return to religious practice. While many erstwhile theists undergo profound changes in how they navigate their way around the world (they no longer engage in prayer or attend church, for example (see Smith 2011)), many others return to religious institutions upon having children. Some choose to do so for moral-educational purposes, others because they want to foster a sense of communal belonging, or to expose their children to alternatives to atheistic worldviews (Ecklund & Lee 2011). However—and importantly for our purposes—such returns to religious practice are not marked by any return to theistic *belief* (Ecklund & Lee 2011: 736–9).[14] Isabella Kasselstrand's (2015) study of the phenomenon of "belonging without believing" across Swedish communities is also of relevance here; as she observes, participation in religious practices can remain high even among those who do not believe in God.[15]

While all such forms of religiously-engaged atheism admittedly fall short of a more thoroughgoing religious fictionalism, they do—together with the evidence concerning our capacity for quarantining—provide reason to be optimistic about the religious fictionalist's prospects—and indeed, those of her moral counterpart. At the very least, the available empirical evidence bearing upon this issue doesn't yield any obvious reason to worry that either species of fictionalist is at significant risk of reverting to her former beliefs.[16]

As an empirical claim, then, the idea that make-believe is likely to lead to belief seems unsubstantiated—or at least, under-substantiated. However, there is another kind of argument that could be developed on Olson's behalf. Perhaps we have simply been operating upon a faulty understanding of belief. Given certain assumptions about the conditions under which an agent believes that *p*, perhaps

---

[14] My diagnosis here rests upon the relevant experimental subjects' self-reports. This should not be taken for an outright dismissal of the possibility that people may sometimes be properly classified as believing that *p* even when they sincerely report that they do not believe that *p*. The conceptual interpretation of Olson's argument that I visit shortly allows for this possibility.

[15] Not all of these disbelievers in Kasselstrand's study may have once been believers. But such cases do further testify to the possibility of engaging in religious practices while rejecting the beliefs traditionally associated with it. It is, of course, also possible to believe in God while participating relatively little in religious institutions; a phenomenon richly explored in Davie's work on "believing without belonging" (1994).

[16] I thank Edward Elliott for helpful discussions about these issues.

immersed make-believe would—as a *conceptual* matter—properly be classified as genuine belief after all.

Developing this style of argument requires that we adopt a particular understanding of belief. Given Olson's remarks concerning the behavioral and psychological dispositions of moral make-believers, a natural route (at least for the sake of exploring this option) would be to appeal to a *dispositionalist* account of belief, which I shall understand as follows:

Dispositionalism:

Beliefs are to be characterized in terms of an agent's dispositions.

The common thread that runs through different varieties of dispositionalism is the idea that beliefs can be characterized in terms of their functional roles. The relevant roles here, being dispositions, are "forward-looking" in that they tell us what kinds of states a belief that p typically brings about (Stalnaker 1984). One who believes that p will, for instance, typically be disposed to assent to q if shown that p implies q, to express surprise upon hearing that not p, and so on. An agent who has these and other relevant psychological and behavioral dispositions can be said to believe that p. (These claims plausibly come attached with tacit "if" clauses; an agent who believes that p will typically be disposed to assert that p *if* she has not decided to deceive others about her beliefs, *if* she has not lost her voice, and so on. (See Schwitzgebel 2002: 253.) But the basic idea should suffice for my purposes.)

Here, then, is how we might go about arguing for the conceptual claim that immersed make-believe is properly classified as belief. We might begin with the idea that moral believers have particular dispositions in virtue of which they can be said to believe some moral proposition p. We might then point out that moral *make-believers* do not seem meaningfully different from moral believers with respect to these dispositions. Indeed, it would seem to be more or less business as usual for the convert to fictionalism; she is so immersed in her moral pretense that she scarcely pays any attention at all to the fact that it is but a mere fiction. Her moral thoughts come to be "well-rooted habits of thinking" (Joyce 2001: 218–19). She continues to enter into moral disputes, and to speak of "goodness and badness, rightness and wrongness, duties, justice, and obligations" (Nolan et al. 2005: 311–12).

All in all, the psychological and behavioral dispositions of make-believers seem *very similar* to those of moral believers. This is an alternative way to make sense of Olson's claim that an immersed fictionalist is a run-of-the-mill believer. An act of make-believe walks like a belief, talks like a belief, and sounds like a belief. So the onus is on the fictionalist to tell us why it *isn't* a belief. In the words of Douglas Adams (2014: 227), "If it looks like a duck, and quacks like a duck, we have at least to consider the possibility that we have a small aquatic bird of the family anatidae on our hands."

This problem is not new. Distinguishing fictionalist attitudes from beliefs has long been a challenge for fictionalist proposals. Many suspect that the distinction here is bogus; that it is a "distinction without a difference" (Horwich 1991: 3; see also O'Leary-Hawthorne 1994; Rosen & Burgess 2004). Since the psychological and behavioral profile of (certain) fictionalists attitudes seems indistinguishable from that of belief, it is tempting to think that there is not much if any daylight between them. It is my contention that this burden can be discharged as far as make-believe is concerned. I shall now argue that the moral fictionalist can address this challenge by pointing towards important differences between believers and make-believers.[17]

One possible difference between the dispositions of a believer and those of a make-believer was considered earlier (§2.2). Our moral fictionalist, recall, distinguishes the moral fictionalist from a moral believer by appealing to the former's disposition to *withhold assent from* positive, first-order moral claims in critical contexts. This suggests the following difference between belief and make-believe:

BEL_1

One who believes that p will typically be disposed to assent to p in critical and non-critical contexts.

$M\text{-}BEL_1$

One who make-believes that p will typically be disposed to assent to p in non-critical contexts and to withhold assent from or deny p in critical contexts.

This distinction has some initial appeal. However, I worry that BEL_1 is false. As Joyce characterizes a critical context, it is one in which an agent "investigates and challenges the presuppositions of ordinary thinking"—the philosophy classroom being a prime example (190–4). But it is far from obvious that we are disposed to assent even to very firmly held beliefs in critical contexts, so understood. Plausibly, the average student believes that she knows she has hands, that there are numbers, and that the sun will rise tomorrow. But she may not be so willing to assent to such claims in the philosophy classroom.

But no matter. There are other important differences between believers and make-believers. To begin with, make-believe can typically be resisted or acquired at will. Indeed, I would go so far as to say that it is *constitutive* of make-believe that it be tied to our will. We *choose* to participate in games of make-believe—we *elect* to imagine, we *decide* to pretend. It seems close to being analytic that an individual could not pretend to do something that she did not set out to pretend.

---

[17] Since I am responding here on behalf of moral fictionalists who recommend the attitude of make-believe, what I have to say may not double as a defense of the fictionalists targeted by Horwich (1991) and others, who often recommend attitudes of *acceptance*. Perhaps the slip-into-belief worry is harder to avoid in such cases.

Not only is make-believe the sort of attitude that we can choose to dispense with—it is also especially liable to being dispensed with when the practical stakes are high. Oddie and Demetriou offer a nice illustrative example:

> Suppose it is true in [a] play that two people are chatting comfortably on a couch in their home, and that their home is not on fire... we make-believe that that is true. Now, if smoke starts seeping onto the stage from backstage but it is clearly true, in the play, that there is no smoke in the room, we tend in such circumstances to abandon the make-belief (that there is no smoke in the room) and go with the belief (that there is smoke), and it is entirely reasonable to do so.
>
> (2007: 487)

Following Oddie and Demetriou, make-believe is a "highly overridable" attitude (2007: 487). When the practical stakes go up, we typically can and do dispense with it—and rightly so if it ceases to be useful to us.

In this respect, make-believe is markedly different from belief. Indeed, some claim that an attitude so intimately tied to one's will could not possibly be a belief (e.g., Railton 2014). But a weaker claim will serve the distinction that I am seeking to establish here. Whatever one has to say about the control that we may or may not be able to exert over our beliefs, it certainly doesn't seem *constitutive* of belief that it be tied to our will. There are attitudes that urge themselves upon us that are properly called beliefs. The clearest cases are perhaps the beliefs that we form on the basis of perception; our coming to believe that there is a house in front of us after having perceived a house, say. It's hard to make the case that one has any real say on the matter here.[18]

What I am proposing, then, is that we have comparatively little *control* over our beliefs. Make-believe is easily overridden—and rightly so when the pretense ceases to be useful to us. But we neither do nor can typically dispense with a belief that p after having come to appreciate that such a belief is contrary to our practical interests. This suggests the following difference between belief and make-believe:

BEL$_2$

One who believes that p will typically be disposed to persist with that belief even when the stakes are suitably high so as to render that belief contrary to her practical interests.

---

[18] I do not claim that we *always* acquire perceptual beliefs simply in virtue of seeing the world. (We might have independent evidence that what we are seeing is an illusion.) I claim only that when one sees that the world is thus-and-so, one also typically believes that the world is thus-and-so. (For discussion of belief being the "default state," see Egan 2008: 55–8).

M-BEL$_2$

One who make-believes that *p* will not typically be disposed to persist with that make-believe when the stakes are suitably high so as to render that make-believe contrary to her practical interests.

BEL$_2$ dovetails nicely with the well-worn idea that beliefs aim at truth (Williams 1973; Velleman 2000; Wedgwood 2002; Boghossian 2003; Shah 2003).[19] To maintain that we are typically capable of believing whatever we like at will would be to suggest that we can typically believe propositions without *any regard whatever* as to whether they are true (Williams 1973; Velleman 2000). Yet that seems to run contrary to the popular idea that part of what it is to believe that *p* is to hold that belief accountable to truth. Perhaps this is why it strikes many as odd to think we can choose beliefs at our fancy.

Yet another difference between belief and make-believe concerns the distinctive ways in which these attitudes integrate with the rest of our psychology and our behavior. I will here focus upon the different ways in which belief, as opposed to make-believe, elicits particular emotional responses. As Nichols (2006: 464) observes, our affective responses to fictions can differ strikingly from our responses to belief:

> At the end of Dr. Strangelove, we imagine that all human life is about to be destroyed, and we find this amusing in the context of the film. Presumably this is not how we would react if we had the real belief that all human life is about to be destroyed. Perhaps if we really believed that all human life was about to be destroyed, we could find some humor in the situation, but surely this would not be the predominant emotional response.

One shouldn't oversell the point here. Our affective responses to fictions don't always differ *strikingly* from our responses to belief. (Few feel warm and fuzzy inside when watching man-eating spiders on their television.) Nonetheless, these affective responses can be expected to differ in a number of important respects. As someone who grew up in Australia, I can testify that one who believes that there is a poisonous spider lurking beneath their bed is apt to feel a very real kind of fear—a fear that someone who make-believes that a rock is a spider is unlikely to experience.

---

[19] I acknowledge that claims regarding the truth-directedness of belief are open to a number of different interpretations. Such claims may be claims regarding what is *conceptually* constitutive of belief (as in Boghossian 2003) or what is constitutive of the *essence* of belief (as in Velleman 2000; Wedgwood 2002), or something else still. I leave this matter open here, since my basic point does not rest upon any particular precisification.

This is not to deny that our engagement with fictions can prompt emotional response. Nor is it to deny that these responses can prompt *similar* kinds of behavior. As Nichols and Stich note when reporting the results of a study:

> ...in our burglar in the basement scenario, one subject picked up the phone that was available and dialed 9-1-1. However, she took precautions to ensure that the call did not really go through. She didn't want her behavior to be that similar... she wanted to be sure that the police didn't really come. (2000: 129)

The important point to appreciate is that whatever affective responses make-believe is capable of eliciting, these can be expected to integrate with the rest of our psychology and our behavior in importantly different ways than the affective responses triggered by belief. Someone who believes that Freddie Kruger exists is likely to fear encountering him in her dreams, and to take steps to ensure her safety. (She might sleep less often or bring a crucifix to bed.) One who merely make-believes that Freddie Kruger exists while watching *A Nightmare on Elm Street* is unlikely to take such steps to avoid him (though she may have more trouble than usual falling asleep).

This suggests another important difference between attitudes of belief and make-believe, which concerns their integration with emotions and behavior:

BEL_3
One who believes that *p* will typically be disposed to experience the emotions stereotypically associated with believing that *p*, and to engage in the behavior stereotypically associated with believing that *p*.

$M\text{-}BEL_3$
One who make-believes that *p* will not typically be disposed to experience the emotions stereotypically associated with believing that *p*, or to engage in the behavior stereotypically associated with believing that *p*.

Three quick caveats here. First, although talk of stereotypical emotions and behavior seems sensible enough, we may well want to relativize stereotypical responses to a particular individual. Second, and as I have suggested, it is consistent with $M\text{-}BEL_3$ that make-believe can prompt *somewhat similar* emotions and behavior to belief. Finally, although I have used fear as a demonstrative example, it is not implausible that the same holds true for other kinds of affective response. One who loves their neighbor will be motivated to seek him out and win his affections, but someone who feels for Emily Brontë's Heathcliff will make no attempts to get in touch. One who loses a pet will mourn and grieve, but no one holds a funeral for Lassie.

Let's take stock. We began with Olson's suspicion that an immersed moral make-believer is at risk of relapsing into moral belief. I made two attempts to put some flesh on the bones of this suspicion. The first attempt was to construe the claim as an empirical one—an unpromising move, I argued. The second was to understand Olson's suspicion as stemming from particular conceptual presuppositions regarding the conditions under which an agent believes that p. In order to address the latter concern, the moral fictionalist needed to make the case for a meaningful distinction between make-believers and believers. I have argued that she is up to the task; attitudes of make-believe are importantly different from beliefs. So the fictionalist evades Olson's first horn—she is no moral believer. However, and as I will now argue, these insights only serve to sharpen the second horn. Make-believe may very well be *too* different from belief to sustain a practically useful moral discourse.

Before diving into things, though, I want to briefly comment upon the implications of these arguments for the wider intra-moral-fictionalism debate. As should now be clear, it is in virtue of make-believe reflecting a *distinct* attitude from belief that the fictionalist evades Olson's first horn. But while this particular escape-route is available to the Make-Believe Fictionalist, I am skeptical that it would likewise be available to the Distraction Fictionalist. For all that I've said, Olson may be right to worry that *this* fictionalist risks reverting to moral belief insofar as she insists upon distracting herself from the metaethical truth. Given this, it may ultimately be possible to re-work my arguments here into a dilemma for moral fictionalism, whereby Distraction Fictionalism faces Olson's epistemic horn, and Make-Believe Fictionalism his practical one. (A full implementation of this strategy would need to incorporate Prefix Fictionalism and Metaphor Fictionalism as well.) Although I do not develop that dilemma here, it is worth keeping in mind for those interested in the potentially wider reach of my arguments.

3.2 The Practical Shortcomings of Moral Make-Believe

My challenge for the fictionalist in what follows is similar to Olson's in spirit, but differs in its letter. Olson, recall, thinks that a moral make-believer must constantly remind herself that morality is a fiction in order to avoid becoming a moral believer. According to him, however, this act of constantly reminding herself that morality is merely a fiction will undo the practical benefits that the moral pretense promises to supply. I have rejected Olson's claim that the fictionalist must regularly attend to her belief that morality is a fiction in order to avoid a slip into belief—and accordingly, there is no threat of these reminders undermining the practical pay-offs of the pretense.

However, there is a more fundamental worry in the vicinity. Even if make-believe is not liable to slip into belief, the important differences between these attitudes suggest that moral discourse would be far less *useful* if it were preserved as a fiction. The problem isn't merely that make-believe wouldn't play the *same* role as beliefs—that is to be expected. The criticism that I will now proceed to develop is that moral make-believe is unfit to play even a *suitably similar* role.

By way of contrast, it will be helpful to begin by reflecting upon the nature of moral beliefs. Consider someone in dire financial straits who is tempted to siphon some funds from a naïve and trusting friend. She believes that doing so would be morally wrong, and so, she is ultimately motivated to refrain. Joyce, recall, identifies precisely this feature of moral beliefs as a key element in accounting for their usefulness; they prompt us to behave in ways that accord with our long-term interests (181). True, a cash injection might further an agent's immediate interests. But stealing from her friends is also likely to be contrary to her long-term interests, insofar as friendship and a trustworthy reputation are the sorts of things that benefit her in the long run.

Now, moral beliefs are beliefs, and so they plausibly have the following feature which, I have argued, is characteristic of belief: they persist even when the stakes are sufficiently high to render them contrary to our practical interests. And this is, in large part, what accounts for their usefulness. Just imagine what would follow if we could simply make our moral beliefs *disappear* whenever we judged doing so to be convenient. Suppose that we were accustomed to cease believing in the cruelty of the animal fur industry whenever we eyed an attractive pair of leather boots, or to cease believing that stealing from a friend was morally wrong whenever our pockets began to feel light.[20] It is doubtful that moral beliefs would play the same role if they were apt to disappear when they were most needed to stave off temptation.

Yet acts of *make-believe* have precisely this feature; they are highly overridable, and they typically *are* overridden when the practical stakes are high (Oddie & Demetriou 2007: 487). And the practical stakes can be incredibly high in moral decision-making. As Lillehammer points out, morality "frequently prescribes costly sacrifices, such as the abandonment of basic personal projects" (2004: 103; see also Cuneo & Christy 2011: 99). Whatever long-term gains the fiction affords us, then, it is doubtful that these will be sufficient to motivate persisting with the pretense when our important personal interests are at stake. The situations in which we would most want moral make-believe to work for us are precisely those situations in which it is most likely to let us down.[21]

A related concern pertains to the ways in which moral beliefs integrate with our psychology and behavior. Most of us are emotionally invested in moral issues. We grow angry when we believe that others have done wrong, and feel guilty upon coming to believe that we ourselves have engaged in wrongdoing. These affective

---

[20] Of course, people do sometimes act contrary to their moral beliefs, and they often have creative ways of justifying these transgressions to themselves. But moral beliefs don't typically *disappear* whenever convenient. In this respect, they seem to me to be more reliable than acts of make-believe.

[21] Interestingly, Joyce (forthcoming) sees a feature here where I see a bug. He argues that some flexibility in our commitments may (generally) be beneficial—and that we may have reasons to favor a fictionalized morality over a believed one as a result. While I don't dispute the general point, I am skeptical of its degree of applicability to the case at hand.

experiences also typically motivate distinct sorts of behavior. Moral transgressions are usually met with punishment (Boyd et al. 2003); guilt usually prompts us to make amends (Wicker et al. 1983; Ferguson et al. 1991; Tangney et al. 2013). All in all, our moral beliefs tend to *integrate* with our behavior (and the rest of our psychology) in fairly distinctive ways.

An important question for the moral fictionalist is whether moral make-believe is likely to integrate with our behavior and our psychology in a suitably similar way; is make-believe capable of eliciting these powerful emotions and the behaviors that they usually motivate? This is far from obvious. If a spider the size of Tolkien's Shelob appeared at my window (and if I believed it were there), I would experience a very real kind of fear—something I plausibly don't experience when I watch Shelob pursuing Frodo Baggins. In the former case, I would be motivated to barricade the windows and seek out help. When watching Frodo flee, I merely avert my eyes in horror.

Yet moral fictionalists are confident that moral make-believe *would* be capable of eliciting affective responses that are sufficiently similar to those prompted by moral beliefs. Joyce proposes that fictive thoughts

> …can engage our emotions. If one sits vividly thinking about one's house burning down and all one's worldly belongings with it—not believing it, nor even believing it particularly likely—that may be sufficient to prompt anxiety or fear. This, I take it, is what happens when we engage emotionally with fiction—when we feel fear at horror movies or sadness at novels. (197; see also Joyce 2006: 99)

As I understand Joyce, the basic idea here is that a lack of belief doesn't necessarily imply a lack of emotion. We very often *do* seem to be emotionally responsive to fiction. So perhaps beliefs have limited penetration into emotion; even when we don't believe that the objects of our fear are instantiated, we are still apt to feel (at least something meaningfully like) fear. And perhaps this lesson applies to moral fictions: they may engage us emotionally, even if we no longer believe that there is really any such thing as moral wrongness.

Yet the analogy with paradigmatic fictions will only get the moral fictionalist so far. In order for the moral fictionalist to establish that a moral fiction is likely to engage us emotionally, it won't suffice to point out that fictions are generally capable of prompting emotion. She must make the case that *a moral fiction* will be so capable. This isn't straightforward—especially once we reflect upon why it is that fictions often elicit affective responses. There is strong empirical evidence that our emotional engagement with fictions is often the result of our having identified with *the characters* that are portrayed. People usually adopt the standpoint of the protagonist (Rinck & Bower 1995), and process the emotional implications of the fiction's events from their perspective (Gernsbacher et al. 1992). For this reason, empathetic perspective-taking is increasingly thought to be "a standard part of...engagement with fictional narratives" (Coplan 2004: 143; see also Harris 2000: 70–8; Bourg 1996: 246–57; Rall & Harris 2000: 206–7). It is plausibly because of this identification with fictional characters that we often feel on behalf of them; we share in Captain Kirk's sadness when Spock sacrifices himself for the needs of the many. (And we share in his apathy when those unfortunate enough to be wearing red shirts suffer an untimely demise.)

Yet in what way are such cases analogous to the case of a moral fiction? They seem to me to be rather disanalogous. The features in virtue of which we are emotionally "taken in" by fictions would seem to be altogether absent in *moral* fictions. There are no protagonists to be found in this moral story. There may be a few abstract entities floating around, to be sure (rights, obligations, and what-have-you). But these presumably aren't the sorts of characters with whom we are likely to engage.

I am not arguing here that a moral fiction could not engage us emotionally. What I am rather arguing is that pointing towards our engagement with paradigmatic fictions does not seem to provide us with strong evidence that it could. The issue is that the fictionalist is using our emotional engagement with paradigmatic fictions as evidence for her claim that a moral fiction can be expected to engage us emotionally. Yet the features that explain our emotional engagement with paradigmatic fictions would seem to be wholly absent in the case of moral fictions.

For those unconvinced, let me simply grant for the sake of argument that the moral fiction itself would engage us emotionally in the manner that more familiar fictions can and do. A further problem for the moral fictionalist remains. It is not merely that moral beliefs prompt emotions; these emotions also tend to motivate distinct kinds of behavior—punishment, reparations, and the like. Even if we conceded that a moral fiction could elicit *bona fide* emotions, then, we are still left with the following question: are these emotions likely to motivate useful sorts of behavior?

It is not unlikely that the emotions prompted by make-believe can motivate *somewhat similar* sorts of behavior as those prompted by belief—especially within the confines of the pretense. One plausible understanding of participation in make-believe takes it to be driven by a desire to behave in a *similar* way to how one would behave were the pretense a reality (Nichols & Stich 2000: 128). But there are important limits, especially when behaving in *too similar* a way would carry real life costs. Someone pretending that there is a burglar in her house is careful not to actually call 9-1-1.

This suggests a worry for the moral fictionalist. Even if moral make-believe prompted the relevant emotional responses, it remains debatable whether these would motivate the relevant cooperative behaviors. Agents who participate in moral make-believe may very well desire to behave in a somewhat similar manner to how they would were the moral fiction reality. Yet they are likely to stop short of behaving in the same manner when that behavior is sufficiently costly—as punishment and making amends can often be.

3.3 How Worried Should Moral Fictionalists Be?

Even with these criticisms having been granted, there are several ways that moral fictionalists might try to soften the blow to their proposal. One strategy would be to temper the strength of their advice. As I have construed fictionalism as a response to the WNQ, it presents us with an answer to the question as to what we *all-things-considered ought to do*, given our belief in the moral error theory. But perhaps some among the fictionalist's ranks are lacking in any such vaulting ambition; they may want to insist that they are merely pointing towards some good-making features of going fictionalist. (See Jay 2014: 211 and Deng 2015: 198 for discussion.) Call this strategy "the evaluative-retreat." Relatedly, some fictionalists may qualify that they merely view these good-making features as *sufficient* reason to convert to the fictionalist camp, and only take their arguments to favor the rational *permissibility* of the fictionalist option. Call this strategy the "permissibility-gambit."

Suppose a fictionalist were to avail herself of either strategy. Would this leave my arguments moot? Not necessarily. For one thing, the problems that I have raised cast doubt upon just how good the relevant good-making features associated with the fictionalist option are. Admittedly, this observation doesn't undercut the evaluative-retreat completely, but it certainly seems to me to take the wind out of its sails. Moreover, and insofar as we *are* left questioning just how good these good-making features are, the "permissibility-gambit" may be in trouble as well. In order for the fictionalist option to be rationally permissible, we must have at least as much reason to adopt it as we do to adopt other solutions. And the more we come to doubt that fictionalism's good-making features really are quite so good, the more likely it becomes that we may ultimately have stronger reasons to seek out conservationist or abolitionist options instead—in which case, fictionalism will not turn out to be rationally permissible after all.

4. Conclusion

I have argued that the moral fictionalist can make good on her epistemic promise: moral error theorists cum fictionalists can reasonably hope to avoid any slip into moral belief. However, the moral fictionalist is likely to have trouble keeping up the practical end of the bargain. The attitudes of make-believe that she recommends seem neither a stable enough nor a strong enough basis for securing the practical benefits that she promises us.

It would be premature to conclude that moral fictionalism is the wrong answer to the WNQ. I have shown that one much-discussed variety of moral fictionalism— one that enlists attitudes of make-believe—has important shortcomings. But it remains to be seen whether other more recent implementations of the moral fictionalist project (of the sort visited in §2.2) are likewise limited. It is possible that these varieties do not fall prey to the same pitfalls (though, as I've noted, some varieties may well fall prey to the epistemic horn of Olson's dilemma). It also remains to be seen whether conservationism or abolitionism fare any better, and so it still remains an open question whether a fictional moral discourse is ultimately the best that moral error theorists can do. Determining whether this is so will require a serious consideration of their other options.[22]

References

Adams, D. 2014. *Dirk Gently's Holistic Detective Agency*. Simon and Schuster.

Boghossian, P. 2003. "The normativity of content." *Philosophical Issues* 13: 31–45.

Boghossian, P. & Velleman, D. 1989. "Colour as a secondary quality." *Mind* 98: 81–103.

Bourg, T. 1996. "The role of emotion, empathy, and text structure in children's and adults' narrative text comprehension." In R. Kreuz & M. MacNealy (eds.), *Empirical Approaches to Literature and Aesthetics*. Ablex. 241–60.

Boyd, R., Gintis, H., Bowles, S., & Richerson, P. 2003. "The evolution of altruistic punishment." *Proceedings of the National Academy of Sciences* 100: 3531–5.

Brock, S. 2002. "Fictionalism about fictional characters." *Noûs* 36: 1–21.

Brogaard, B. 2006. "Two modal -isms: Fictionalism and ersatzism." *Philosophical Perspectives* 20: 77–94.

Burgess, J. 1983. "Why I am not a nominalist." *Notre Dame Journal of Formal Logic* 24: 93–105.

Burgess, J. 2007. "Against ethics." *Ethical Theory and Moral Practice* 10: 427–39.

Churchland, P. 1981. "Eliminative materialism and the propositional attitudes." *Journal of Philosophy* 78: 67–90.

Coplan, A. 2004. "Empathic engagement with narrative fictions." *Journal of Aesthetics and Art Criticism* 62: 141–52.

Cuneo, T. & Christy, S. 2011. "The myth of moral fictionalism." In M. Brady (ed.), *New Waves in Metaethics*. Palgrave MacMillan. 85–102.

Currie, G. 2000. "Imagination, delusion, and hallucinations." *Mind & Language* 15: 168–83.

Daly, C. 2008. "Fictionalism and the attitudes." *Philosophical Studies* 139: 423–40.

Davie, G. 1994. *Religion in Britain since 1945: Believing without Belonging*. Blackwell.

Deng, N. 2015. "Religion for naturalists." *International Journal for Philosophy of Religion* 78: 195–214.

---

[22] I thank Edward Elliott, Ben Fraser, Daniel Nolan, and Rach Rowland for constructive feedback on earlier drafts of this work. I am also grateful to audiences who provided feedback at the Australian National University, the University of Luxembourg, and Victoria University of Wellington.

Ecklund, E. & Lee, K. 2011. "Atheists and agnostics negotiate religion and family." *Journal for the Scientific Study of Religion* 50: 728–43.

Egan, A. 2008. "Seeing and believing: Perception, belief formation and the divided mind." *Philosophical Studies* 140: 47–63.

Eklund, M. 2019. "Fictionalism." In E. Zalta (ed.), *The Stanford Encyclopedia of Philosophy*. <https://plato.stanford.edu/entries/fictionalism/>.

Ferguson, T., Stegge, H., & Damhuis, I. 1991. "Children's understanding of guilt and shame." *Child Development* 62: 827–39.

Field, H. 1980. *Science without Numbers*. Princeton University Press.

Friend, S. 2008. "Hermeneutic moral fictionalism as an anti-realist strategy." *Philosophical Books*, 49: 14–22.

Garner, R. 1994. *Beyond Morality*. Temple University Press.

Garner, R. 2007. "Abolishing morality." *Ethical Theory and Moral Practice* 10: 499–513.

Gendler, T. 2003 "On the relation between pretense and belief." In D. Lopes & M. Kiernan (eds.), *Imagination, Philosophy and the Arts*. Routledge. 125–41.

Gernsbacher, M., Goldsmith, H., & Robertson, R. 1992. "Do readers mentally represent characters' emotional states?" *Cognition and Emotion* 6: 89–111.

Griffiths, P. 1997. *What Emotions Really Are*. University of Chicago Press.

Harris, P. 2000. *The Work of the Imagination*. Blackwell.

Hinckfuss, I. 1987. "The moral society: Its structure and effects." *Discussion Papers in Environmental Philosophy* 16. Canberra: Philosophy Program [RSSS], Australian National University.

Horwich, P. 1991. "On the nature and norms of theoretical commitment." *Philosophy of Science* 58: 1–14.

Ingram, S. 2015. "After moral error theory, after moral realism." *Southern Journal of Philosophy* 53: 227–48.

Jay, C. 2014. "The Kantian Moral Hazard Argument for religious fictionalism." *International Journal for Philosophy of Religion* 75: 207–32.

Joyce, R. 2001. *The Myth of Morality*. Cambridge University Press.

Joyce, R. 2005. "Moral fictionalism." In M. Kalderon (ed.), *Fictionalism in Metaphysics*. Oxford University Press. 287–313.

Joyce, R. 2006. *The Evolution of Morality*. MIT Press.

Joyce, R. 2019. "Moral fictionalism: How to have your cake and eat it too." In R. Garner & R. Joyce (eds.), *The End of Morality: Taking Moral Abolitionism Seriously*. Routledge. 150–65.

Joyce, R. 2020. "Fictionalism: Morality and metaphor." In B. Armour-Garb & F. Kroon (eds.), *Fictionalism in Philosophy*. Oxford University Press. 103–21.

Joyce, R. Forthcoming. *Morality: From Error to Fiction*. Oxford University Press.

Kasselstrand, I. 2015. "Nonbelievers in the church: A study of cultural religion in Sweden." *Sociology of Religion* 76: 275–94.

Kroon F. 2011. "Fictionalism in metaphysics." *Philosophy Compass* 6: 786–803.

Leslie, A. 1987. "Pretense and representation: The origins of 'theory of mind.'" *Psychological Review* 94: 412–26.

Lewis, D. 1978. "Truth in fiction." *American Philosophical Quarterly* 15: 37–46.

Lewis, D. 1986. *On the Plurality of Worlds*. Blackwell.

Lillehammer, H. 2004. "Moral error theory." *Proceedings of the Aristotelian Society* 104: 93–109.

Mackie, J. L. 1977. *Ethics: Inventing Right and Wrong*. Penguin.

Marks, J. 2013. *Ethics without Morals: In Defence of Amorality*. Routledge.

Nichols, S. 2006. "Just the imagination: Why imagining doesn't behave like believing." *Mind & Language* 21: 459–74.

Nichols, S. & Stich, S. 2000. "A cognitive theory of pretense." *Cognition* 74: 115–47.

Nolan, D., Restall, G., & West, C. 2005. "Moral fictionalism versus the rest." *Australasian Journal of Philosophy* 83: 307–30.

Oddie, G. & Demetriou, D. 2007. "The fictionalist's attitude problem." *Ethical Theory and Moral Practice* 10: 485–98.

O'Leary-Hawthorne, J. 1994. "What does van Fraassen's critique of scientific realism show?" *Monist* 77: 128–45.

Olson, J. 2014. *Moral Error Theory: History, Critique, Defence*. Oxford University Press.

Priest, G. 1997. "Sexual perversion." *Australasian Journal of Philosophy* 75: 360–72.

Railton, P. 1984. "Alienation, consequentialism, and the demands of morality." *Philosophy & Public Affairs* 13: 134–71.

Railton, P. 2014. "Reliance, trust, and belief." *Inquiry* 57: 122–50.

Rall, J. & Harris, P. 2000. "In Cinderella's slippers? Story comprehension from the protagonist's point of view." *Developmental Psychology* 36: 202–8.

Rinck, M. & Bower, G. 1995. "Anaphora resolution and the focus of attention in situation models." *Journal of Memory and Language* 34: 110–31.

Rosen, G. 1990. "Modal fictionalism." *Mind* 99: 327–54.

Rosen, G. & Burgess, J. 2004. "Nominalism reconsidered." In S. Shapiro (ed.), *The Oxford Handbook of Philosophy of Mathematics and Logic*. Oxford University Press. 515–35.

Schwitzgebel, E. 2002. "A phenomenal, dispositional account of belief." *Noûs* 36: 249–75.

Shah, N. 2003. "How truth governs belief." *Philosophical Review* 112: 447–82.

Smith, J. 2011. "Becoming an atheist in America: Constructing identity and meaning from the rejection of theism." *Sociology of Religion* 72: 215–37.

Stalnaker, R. 1984. *Inquiry*. MIT Press.

Tangney, J., Stuewig, J., Malouf, E., & Youman, K. 2013. "Communicative functions of shame and guilt." In K. Sterelny, R. Joyce, B. Calcott, & B. Fraser (eds.), *Cooperation and its Evolution*. MIT Press. 485–502.

Unger, P. 1979. "Why there are no people." *Midwest Studies in Philosophy* 4: 177–222.

Velleman, D. 2000. "On the aim of belief." In his *The Possibility of Practical Reason*. Oxford University Press. 244–81.

Wedgwood, R. 2002. "The aim of belief." *Philosophical Perspectives* 16: 267–97.

Wicker, F., Payne, G., & Morgan, R. 1983. "Measurement of social-evaluative anxiety." *Journal of Consulting and Clinical Psychology* 33: 448–57.

Williams, B. 1973. "Deciding to believe." In his *Problems of the Self*. Cambridge University Press. 136–51.

3
Moral Fictionalism
How and Why?

Victor Moberger and Jonas Olson

1. Introduction: Moral Error Theory and the "What Now?" Question

According to moral error theorists, our actual moral thought and discourse are ridden with error. Moral beliefs and assertions are systematically mistaken in much the same way as religious beliefs and assertions are, according to atheists. Moral beliefs purport to attribute moral properties and moral assertions purport to state moral facts. But since there are no moral facts or instantiated moral properties, there are no moral truths. Hence, our moral beliefs and assertions are systematically false, or at least untrue.

If we become convinced that the moral error theory is true, then what is to be done with our moral thought and discourse? This is the "what now?" question for moral error theorists. A natural response is that morality is to be abolished, just like we have abolished thought and discourse about witches and phlogiston. Error theorists have by and large been reluctant to make this suggestion, however, the reason being morality's apparent practical benefits. As J. L. Mackie put it:

> We need morality to regulate interpersonal relations, to control some of the ways in which people behave towards one another, often in opposition to contrary inclinations. (1977: 43)

Due to considerations of this kind, most error theorists have agreed with Mackie that moral thought and discourse, in some form or another, are to be retained. *Conservationists* (Olson 2014; Eriksson & Olson 2019) respond to the "what now?" question by suggesting that we go on as before, making (false) moral assertions and (at least aspiring to) forming (false) moral beliefs. To abide by this suggestion will thus involve compartmentalization between one's metaethical thought and talk on the one hand, and one's first order moral thought and talk on the other. *Fictionalists* (Joyce 2001, 2019, 2020; Nolan et al. 2005) instead suggest that we stop believing and asserting moral propositions, and instead accept them "nondoxastically" and express them without assertoric force. According to fictionalists, this would afford us the practical benefits of morality without requiring us to continue believing and asserting falsehoods. It thus appears that fictionalism can deliver the goods, but without the conservationist price tag of irrationality and falsity.[1]

Fictionalism faces two serious challenges, however. We call them the *how-challenge* and the *why-challenge*. The how-challenge consists in explaining how the fictionalist reform proposal can indeed preserve the practical benefits of morality. After all, those practical benefits are largely due to the supposed *motivational efficacy* of moral thought and discourse, and one might suspect that this efficacy is due precisely to the efficacy of moral *belief* and *assertion*.[2] Thus, it isn't obvious that fictionalism's recommendation that we abandon moral belief and assertion can be reconciled with its rationale of preserving the motivational impact of morality. To put it somewhat rhetorically, how can we get the practical benefits of morality if we don't take it seriously enough to believe in it?

The why-challenge consists in explaining why replacing moral belief and assertion is sufficiently important to begin with. Why not just stick with what we know works? There is a lot at stake, after all, and it is not clear that the benefits of avoiding what appear to be highly local forms of irrationality and falsity are significant enough to outweigh the hazards of tampering with our tried and tested morality device.

If these two challenges cannot be met, then conservationism has the upper hand. In this chapter we argue that fictionalists have yet to provide persuasive answers to the two challenges. We will focus on a particular version of moral fictionalism, recently developed by Richard Joyce (2019, 2020), but we will also tie the discussion to moral fictionalism in general. In §3, we discuss the how-challenge, and in §4, we turn to the why-challenge. In §5, we reflect briefly on an important background issue of the debate between fictionalism and conservationism—namely, the nature of belief—and consider its implications for the two rival positions. We end in §6 with a brief summary of the main points. First of all, however, we want to make two preliminary observations.

2. The "What Now?" Question: Two Observations

The "what now?" question is typically framed as the question of what to do with moral thought and discourse if we become *convinced* or *intellectually persuaded*

---

[1] In this chapter, we are exclusively concerned with *revolutionary* moral fictionalism, which is a reform proposal that one may adopt in light of the discovery or belief that moral thought and discourse involve profound and systematic error, as described in the main text. It is commonplace to distinguish revolutionary moral fictionalism from *hermeneutic* moral fictionalism (Kalderon 2005). The latter is the view that ordinary moral thought and discourse are already fictional and involve no profound or systematic error. Hermeneutic moral fictionalism thus stands in opposition to moral error theory.

[2] Note that moral thought and talk having the requisite motivational impact does not presuppose motivational *internalism* (i.e., the view that there is a *necessary* connection between making a moral judgment and being (to some degree) motivated to act accordingly). For discussion, see Olson 2010: 95–6.

that moral error theory is true. But philosophical arguments are seldom conclusive, fully convincing, or intellectually persuasive. Arguments for moral error theory are no exceptions to this rule. One might thus believe in a philosophical view, such as moral error theory, to a high degree—or believe that some view, like moral error theory, is likely to be true—without being fully convinced or intellectually persuaded that it is true.

Believing to a high degree that moral error theory is true, or believing that moral error theory is likely to be true, is compatible with having some positive credence that some other, incompatible, metaethical theory is true. So the "what now?" question is perhaps more adequately framed as the question of what to do with moral thought and discourse if we come to believe to a high degree that moral error theory is true, or if we come to believe that moral error theory is likely to be true. This complication is relevant to some arguments made in the "what now?" debate, as we will briefly indicate in §3.3 below. For most of the chapter, however, we follow common practice and simply assume that the "what now?" question concerns what to do with moral thought and discourse if we become convinced or intellectually persuaded that moral error theory is true.

Our second observation is that there is a parallel "what now?" question about what to do with *religious* thought and discourse if we become convinced that religious beliefs and assertions are systematically erroneous, as atheists maintain.[3] Atheists' response does not have to be abolitionism. If religious thought and discourse have practical benefits akin to those of moral thought and discourse, there are parallel options available to atheists, including fictionalism and conservationism about religious thought and discourse. Our focus in this chapter is on the "what now?" question for moral error theory, and in particular on moral fictionalism, but we believe that many moves made in this debate can also be made, *mutatis mutandis*, in the debate about religious fictionalism and other available responses to the "what now?" question for atheism. This is also briefly indicated in §3.3 and §4.2 below.

3. Moral Fictionalism: How?

In order to arrive at an answer to the how-challenge, moral fictionalists need to clarify the kind of nonassertoric speech act that is to replace moral assertion and the kind of nondoxastic acceptance that is to replace moral belief. In this chapter, we focus mainly on two of Joyce's proposals: the first attempts an analogy with story-telling and engagement with fictitious narratives; the second with the use of metaphors. Both accounts face similar problems, as we shall see.

---

[3] There is also a "what now?" question about religious thought and discourse for agnostics, who maintain that there is sufficient evidence for neither theism nor atheism.

Before we come to that, let us comment briefly on a different proposal, according to which a useful analogy can be made between moral fictionalism's nondoxastic attitude of acceptance and the kind of attitude consequentialists take towards "secondary principles." Examples of secondary principles that many consequentialists endorse are "killing is wrong," "breaking promises is wrong," etc.[4] We find this attempted analogy unhelpful. The reason is that consequentialists typically *believe* that killing, breaking promises, etc., is suboptimal in the vast majority of cases and, therefore, morally wrong in the vast majority of cases. For related reasons, many consequentialists hold that it tends to have good consequences to believe that killing, breaking promises, etc., is wrong. The bottom line is that the kind of attitude consequentialists ordinarily take, and recommend, to secondary principles is straightforward belief, rather than some kind of nondoxastic acceptance.[5]

3.1 Narrationist Fictionalism

In his highly influential discussion of moral fictionalism in *The Myth of Morality* (2001), Joyce suggested that the appropriate replacement for assertion of moral propositions is *pretense-assertion*. This is the type of speech act that we perform when *telling* a fictional story (as opposed to describing it from the outside). For example, while telling the story of *The Lord of the Rings*, we might utter the sentence "Sauron forged a Ring of Power," thereby pretending to assert the proposition that Sauron forged a Ring of Power. And the appropriate replacement for belief in moral propositions is *make-believe*. This is the kind of attitude that we take up when *engaging in* a fictional story (as opposed to thinking about it from the outside). For example, while reading *The Lord of the Rings*, we might entertain or make-believe the proposition that Sauron forged a Ring of Power. Thus, moral belief and assertion are to be replaced by moral make-believe and pretense-assertion. Just as we can pretend that we live in a world containing witches or phlogiston, we can pretend that we live in a world containing moral facts or instantiated moral properties. We are to engage in and tell a fictional moral realist story about our world, as it were. Let us call this view *narrationist* fictionalism.

---

[4] See Jaquet, Chapter 4 of this volume.
[5] See, for example, Mill 1863; Hare 1981. Both Mill and Hare are well-known for propounding *levels* of moral thinking; in Hare's terms an "intuitive" and a "critical" level. We take it that both Mill and Hare held that in unexceptional circumstances we should *believe* the intuitive moral principles that are justifiable on a consequentialist foundation at the critical level, or at least that we should take the same kind of attitude to justifiable secondary principles in unexceptional circumstances that we take to the utilitarian principle at the critical level. (We make the latter reservation because of Hare's prescriptivism; it is not clear whether Hare held that belief is a kind of attitude that we can take to any kind of moral principle.)

3.2 Metaphorist Fictionalism

In recent work (2019, 2020), Joyce has developed a different account of the fictionalist reform proposal. The idea is that the kind of nonassertoric declarative speech that is to replace moral assertion can be understood along the lines of the kind of speech act that we perform when using *metaphor*.[6] One of Joyce's examples (2019: 155) is that of describing someone as a "spineless snake" in order to convey metaphorically the information that the person is dishonest and cowardly. That information could be conveyed straightforwardly by simply describing the person as dishonest and cowardly, but by using the metaphor of a spineless snake the information is conveyed "more evocatively and dramatically," as Joyce puts it. The speaker does not assert that the person is literally a spineless snake (i.e., an invertebrate reptile). Rather, the speaker pretense-asserts that false proposition in order to draw attention to the truth of *another* proposition, but in a way that serves to enhance the emotional impact of that other piece of information.[7]

Let us introduce some terminology. In the case of the metaphorical sentence "Jake is a spineless snake," let us say that the proposition that Jake is a spineless snake is the *literal* content, and that the proposition that Jake is dishonest and cowardly is the *conveyed* content. Metaphorical sentences like "Jake is a spineless snake" thus pretense-assert the literal content, while (evocatively) drawing attention to the conveyed content.

According to metaphorist fictionalism, this account serves as a model for a reformed use of moral language. For example, instead of "spineless snake," the expression "immoral spineless snake," or just "immoral," could be used to similar effect. Here is Joyce:

> The [metaphorist] fictionalist pictures a world where what goes for "spineless snake" goes for "immoral." In this world, if you ask me whether I really believe in immorality—where immorality involves (let's suppose) things that mustn't be done regardless of one's goals (i.e., non-Humean norms)—then at some point I'll back off: "No, of course I don't really think *that*, but you're missing the point!" There are facts about Jake that I will want to convey—this time concerning his frustrating of the group's Humean goals—and by saying something that is

---

[6] Joyce has explained to us that he nowadays advocates neither narrationist fictionalism nor metaphorist fictionalism. Nevertheless, we find the two accounts interesting enough to merit discussion of how they meet the how- and why-challenges. See Chapter 13 of this volume for Joyce's current views on how to understand the kind of nondoxastic acceptance and nonassertoric declarative speech act that moral fictionalism propounds. We comment briefly on them in §4.4 and §5 below.

[7] Joyce (2020: 112) notes that it is controversial whether metaphor does indeed involve pretense, and he goes on to provide some defense of the view that it does. If it does not, then it is not clear that metaphorist fictionalism is consistent with the kind of "force" fictionalism that Joyce endorses elsewhere (Joyce 2001: 199–200).

literally false I draw attention to those facts more evocatively and dramatically, which might serve my goals (or the group's goals) better than straight talk.

(Joyce 2019: 155)

According to metaphorist fictionalism, then, while we currently use sentences like "Jake is immoral" to assert their literal content—that is, (false) moral propositions—we are to start using moral sentences metaphorically instead, thus merely pretense-asserting those propositions while (evocatively) drawing attention to something else. But what, exactly?

In the passage just quoted, Joyce mentions "Humean goals." He thinks of Humean goals as set by individuals' desires (which need not be selfish) and of a group's Humean goals as "some kind of function of individuals' desires" (2019: 151; 2020: §5). A community of moral error theorists will recognize that they have certain Humean goals, deriving from their individual goals, and they will be interested in furthering those goals. For example, they will all want the members of their community to be robustly disposed not to harm, kill, steal, break promises, etc. Thus, there will be true propositions about certain shared purposes of the group, deriving from the purposes of its individual members, and those are the propositions that moral pretense-assertions are to draw attention to. In other words, the appropriate conveyed content of moral utterances concerns such Humean goals, for example that they are frustrated, as in the case of the allegedly immoral Jake. Following Joyce, we will refer to the propositions in question as propositions about *Humean reasons* (Joyce 2020: §5).

Although of central importance, Humean reasons might in various circumstances fail to motivate, due to distorting psychological factors like temptation, obsession, short-sightedness, weakness of will, and self-deception. The point of retaining moral language in metaphorical form is to provide an evocative, mystical overlay which helps bolster the motivational impact of Humean reasons.

To sum up: Moral language is to be used to pretense-assert (false) moral propositions (the literal content), in order to convey important information about Humean reasons (the conveyed content). The idea is that this metaphorical use of moral language will have additional motivational impact in comparison with straightforward and mundane assertions about Humean reasons.

Joyce (2019: §3) goes on to argue that this metaphorist version of fictionalism can successfully deal with the how-challenge. To repeat, the how-challenge is to explain how the recommendation that we abandon moral belief and assertion can be reconciled with the rationale of preserving the motivational impact of moralizing. To get a firmer grip on the challenge, let us begin by explaining how it applies to Joyce's previous (2001) narrationist version of fictionalism, according to which moral thought and talk are to be reformed into something like engaging in and telling a fictional moral realist story about our world. We then proceed to the metaphorist solution.

3.3 Narrationist Fictionalism and the How-Challenge

The worry about narrationist fictionalism is that it does not take the moral realist story *seriously* enough for us to be sufficiently motivated by it. To illustrate, suppose you are in a position to steal a philanthropist's entire fortune without any risk whatsoever of getting caught. You start to visualize the private jet, the yacht, and the Lamborghini. Something gives you pause, however: "It would be *wrong* to steal the fortune," you think to yourself, "especially since it is continuously being used for humanitarian purposes." Another thought might instantly appear: "But wait, morality is just a story! It isn't *really* wrong to steal the money. So why not?" Similarly, if you seek the counsel of a friend who moralizes against the prospective theft, your friend's speech might not be very effective as a conversation-stopper, since you might reply: "But that's just a story, and you know it!"

Thus, in order for moral thought and talk to be motivationally efficacious, morality's status as a mere story has to be suppressed. An analogous issue arises for conservationism with respect to morality's status as falsehood, of course. But there is a crucial difference. While the conservationist can recommend *deep* suppression of metaethical thought in everyday life, the fictionalist has to recommend that we keep on our metaethical toes, lest we slip into moral belief and assertion. But how can we manage to combine such *vigilance* with the requisite *suppression* of morality's status as a mere story (cf. Olson 2014: §9.2; Eriksson & Olson 2019: §6)? There are three distinct worries here.

First, one might wonder whether the fictionalist recommendation is even coherent. Insofar as we manage to suppress the motivation-depleting thought "It's just a story," then haven't we in effect slipped into moral belief? If so, the fictionalist recommendation that we suppress morality's mere-story status while simultaneously staying away from moral belief is incoherent. (This raises questions about the nature of belief, which we will return to briefly in §5 below.)

Second, one might wonder whether the kind of metaethically monitored self-control that the fictionalist is recommending, even if coherent, is at all feasible. In order to suppress the mere-story thought, it seems that we would at the very least have to come rather *close* to full-blown moral belief and assertion. How would we know whether we have succeeded in avoiding the real thing? Even if there is a conceptual or metaphysical distinction to be drawn here, it is not clear how we might be able to tell the difference, at least from the "inside." Thus, the fictionalist recommendation may be one that we are not able to follow consciously and wittingly.

Third, even if the fictionalist recommendation is both coherent and feasible, the requisite cognitive self-surveillance would seem to be a very difficult and burdensome thing to pull off in everyday life. At the very least, then, the fictionalist recommendation looks psychologically austere and therefore rather unattractive next to the conservationist one.

Note that this last claim does not rely on the premise that there is always a danger of slipping into genuine belief when engaging in make-believe. For example, it is normally not difficult to engage in make-believe concerning Santa Claus, without coming to believe that there is a bearded man at the North Pole who brings gifts every December. Similarly, we seem able to talk and think about sunsets and sunrises without risk of slipping into belief in the Ptolemaic view of the universe. Instead, our claim about psychological austerity relies on the restricted empirical conjecture that it is difficult for someone who has come to believe that moral error theory is (likely to be) true to take the kind of nondoxastic attitude that fictionalism recommends towards moral propositions, without (at least occasionally) slipping back into believing these propositions. This is especially so since philosophical arguments, including arguments for moral error theory, are often less than conclusive or not fully intellectually persuasive, as we pointed out in §2 above.

There are several reasons why the difficulty of avoiding genuine belief arises with respect to moral propositions, but not with respect to the propositions that Santa Claus exists and that the sun sets and rises. First, we have not believed as adults that Santa Claus exists or that the sun literally sets and rises, but we have had many moral beliefs as adults. Second, the belief that Santa Claus exists and that the sun literally sets and rises have not influenced our actions, life plans, and practical deliberation in anything like the way our moral beliefs have (as adults). Third, we have not debated with our peers whether the sun literally sets and rises, and whether Santa Claus exists, with anything like the seriousness with which we have debated moral issues.

A person who comes to believe that moral error theory is true is in a situation that resembles that of a person who used to be a theist but who has come to believe that God does not exist. The latter kind of person is likely to find the belief that God does not exist emotionally disturbing. Partly for this reason, and partly for reasons having to do with more general existential angst, peer pressure, and the like, she might slip back into believing that God exists, at least on occasions when she does not attend to the (presumably non-conclusive) evidence and arguments to the effect that God does not exist. In a similar way, a person who has come to believe that there are no moral truths does not thereby cease to be emotionally engaged by what she formerly judged to be instances of injustice and rights violations. There is thus a similar risk that such a person slips back into holding occurrent beliefs in moral propositions, at least on occasions when she does not attend to the (again presumably non-conclusive) evidence and arguments to the effect that there are no moral truths.

But what would be so terrible about occasionally slipping into moral belief, one might ask.[8] "Nothing," is the short answer. The point is that *according to moral*

---

[8] Joyce posed this question, in correspondence.

fictionalism, moral belief is to be avoided. In order to abide by this advice, we would have to engage in cognitive self-surveillance. Conservationism, by contrast, sees no similar need for cognitive self-surveillance since it does not view moral belief as something to be avoided. This is a crucial difference between fictionalism and conservationism. We will return to this point presently.

3.4 Metaphorist Fictionalism and the How-Challenge

Joyce (2019: §3) argues that these worries about coherence, feasibility, and psychological austerity all dissipate if we understand the fictionalist reform proposal in metaphorist terms. The basic point is that, in the case of metaphor, the motivational efficacy of the evocatively overlaid literal content does not require *suppression* of one's insight about its falsity. Thus, Joyce points out that when we think and say that Jake is a spineless snake, we come "nowhere near" believing and asserting the literal content (i.e., that Jake is an invertebrate reptile) (Joyce 2019: 159). Here the distinctions between make-believe and belief, and between pretense-assertion and assertion, seem conceptually, metaphysically, and epistemically straightforward, and no effort is required to avoid believing and asserting the literal content. And yet, according to Joyce, the evocative overlay has emotional impact despite our effortless recognition of its literal falsity:

> On the assumption that no moral claims are true, we can picture a world where in certain contexts their utterance might nevertheless usefully convey information about real truths of great importance (concerning Humean values). And, indeed, uttering these false sentences may well convey those truths more effectively than trying to do so using straight-talk. Yet there need be no risk of sliding into really *believing* any moral claims—any more than one who declares "I love you with all my heart" risks sliding into believing an Aristotelian view of the physiology of emotions. (Joyce 2019: 158)

Thus, if we use "immoral" instead of "spineless snake" as a metaphor for (our Humean reasons relating to) Jake's dishonesty and cowardice, there will be no need to suppress our recognition of the falsity of the overlaid literal content (i.e., that Jake literally has a moral property—that of being immoral)[9] in order to get the requisite motivational impact. And since the recognition of the literal content's falsity need not be suppressed, there is no need for cognitive self-surveillance in order to avoid slipping into moral belief and assertion.

---

[9] While dishonesty and cowardice are often thought to be relevant to moral judgments, we assume here that they are not themselves moral properties.

As elegant and clever as this is, in what follows we argue that metaphorist fictionalism does not, in the end, successfully answer the how-challenge.

3.5 Why the Metaphorist Solution Fails

We see three distinct problems for metaphorist fictionalism with respect to the how-challenge. We call them *the mismatch problem, the inertness problem*, and *the (new) self-surveillance problem*. We begin with the mismatch problem.

3.5.1 The Mismatch Problem

A first problem for metaphorist fictionalism is that metaphors require a certain degree of (perceived) *correspondence* between the literal and the conveyed content, whereas, on Joyce's proposal, the literal and the conveyed content of moral thought and talk will be significantly mismatched.

Consider the romantically metaphorical sentence "Juliet is the sun." Its literal content is the proposition that Juliet is the star at the center of our solar system. The conveyed content is not entirely perspicuous, but it would seem to be something like one or more of the following propositions (some of which are themselves metaphorical):

Juliet is (perceived as)
...radiant.
...warm.
...centrally placed.
...a source of life.
...unique.
...irreplaceable.

These are all properties of the star at the center of our solar system. And assuming that Romeo is sincere when thinking or uttering the sentence, he can be expected to perceive Juliet along analogous lines, as warm and radiant, centrally placed in his life, and so on. In this case, then, there is significant correspondence between the literal and the conveyed content, and that is why the metaphor works. Romeo could not have used the sentence "Juliet is the moon," for example, to metaphorically convey the same content, since the correspondence between literal and conveyed content would be lost.

Consider also the sentence "Jake is a spineless snake." Again, there is significant correspondence between the literal and the conveyed content. Spineless creatures do not stand up straight and are easily bent. Analogously, cowardly people do not stand up to, and are easily bent by, the will of others. And just like snakes, dishonest people attack in sneaky ways, often from behind, and they maneuver in an undignified, often groveling sort of way. This is why the sentence can be used to metaphorically convey Jake's cowardice and dishonesty. One could not use the sentence "Jake is an upright elephant," for example, to convey that same content.

This correspondence requirement spells trouble for metaphorist fictionalism. To see why, note that among proponents of moral error theory, Joyce included, there seems to be a consensus that the motivational impact of morality stems from the belief that moral requirements are imbued with an especially robust kind of normativity. Mackie called it "authoritative prescriptivity" (1977), and Joyce has used the terms "must-be-doneness" (2001) and "practical oomph" (2006). Although there are several different explications of this notion in the literature, reasons imbued with must-be-doneness are standardly taken to be *objectively* or *desire-independently* prescriptive, whereas Humean reasons are transparently *subjective*, ultimately deriving their prescriptivity from desires or desire-like states. And it is not clear how propositions about transparently objective or desire-independent prescriptivity can be used to metaphorically convey propositions about transparently subjective or desire-dependent prescriptivity.

To illustrate, suppose someone who knows you very well tells you that it would be morally wrong for you to steal the philanthropist's fortune. You reply that you don't really care about strangers. Your friend replies that you have misunderstood; the point was merely that you have Humean reasons not to steal the money, since having a yacht, a Lamborghini etc. will in fact lead to your imminent, cocaine-fueled demise; or that you have Humean reasons not to steal the money, since you yourself want to live in a society where people don't steal, and the theft would contribute (if only marginally) to frustrating this desire of yours. Clearly, the expression "morally wrong" would be misleading here, and it seems that the reason is precisely that moral wrongness, unlike Humean reasons, is supposed to be desire-independently prescriptive.

What this mismatch shows is that moral propositions can be used as metaphors for propositions about Humean reasons only if very odd linguistic conventions are put in place. It would be like a community coming to an agreement that, without changing the meanings of the terms, the expression "upright elephant" is to be used as a metaphor for dishonesty and cowardice, or that "is the moon" is to be used as a romantic metaphor. Assuming that this is even feasible, it would presumably have a rather unnatural and awkward feel to it. How could the mystical, evocative flavor of moral thought and talk be retained under such circumstances? And how could the motivational force of moral thought and discourse be preserved? This brings us to the second problem for metaphorist fictionalism.

3.5.2 The Inertness Problem

Some of the metaphors on which Joyce models his reform proposal seem to derive most, if not all, of their emotional/motivational impact from the *conveyed* content, with the evocatively overlaid literal content playing only a minor, if any, role. In the case of Jake the spineless snake, the motivational impact of the metaphorical thought or utterance would appear to be roughly the same as that of the straightforward thought or utterance that Jake is dishonest and cowardly. Suppose you are thinking of getting involved with Jake somehow, perhaps starting a business with him, lending him some money, hiring him to fix your car, voting for him in an election, or publicly praising him for his honesty and courage. Would it make any difference to your decision-making whether you were informed about his dishonesty and cowardice in metaphorical terms or not, or whether you represented that information in metaphorical terms or not? It is difficult to think of a situation where hearing or thinking that Jake is a spineless snake makes one more motivated not to get involved with Jake than one already is upon hearing or thinking that he is dishonest and a coward. Another of Joyce's examples is the sentence "My high school math teacher was a dragon," used to convey the information that the teacher was bad-tempered (2020: §3). Again, it is difficult to think of a situation where the literal content adds much to the motivational impact of the conveyed content. Thus, in both these cases the overlaid literal content seems to be more or less inert in terms of making a difference to motivational impact.

Joyce also points to *romantic* metaphors, however, such as "Juliet is the sun" and "I love you with all my heart" (2019: §3; 2020: §3). Admittedly, this kind of speech and thought can have significant emotional impact in comparison with straight talk and thought. Another of his examples is of someone being accused of having been "a pig at dinner" (2019: 157). Such *dehumanizing* metaphors also seem capable of influencing our emotions in ways that outstrip the conveyed content. Although Joyce's example concerning table manners is relatively innocuous, history teaches us that dehumanizing metaphors can get quite ugly, and can motivate people in ugly ways. But perhaps they can also motivate us in beneficial ways.

Thus, while certain metaphors do seem to have significant emotional/motivational impact, others seem not to make much of a motivational difference, and so it cannot just be assumed that moral metaphors will even slightly enhance the motivational impact of Humean reasons. The question, then, is why we should think that moral metaphors will indeed have significant motivational impact.

To answer this question, we need a hypothesis concerning what it is about our actual moral thought and talk that accounts for their motivational impact. As we explained in the previous subsection, error theorists (Joyce included) largely agree that moral language is primarily and saliently used to assert propositions about *must-be-doneness*. There are various ways of explicating this notion, and its precise relation to motivation is contentious. But error theorists seem largely to agree that the motivational impact of belief in such normativity is crucial for understanding why moral thought and talk evolved in the first place. Indeed, this case has been forcefully made by Joyce himself (2006).

The belief in must-be-doneness is lost on metaphorist fictionalism. Recall Joyce's claim that when we use a metaphorical expression like "Jake is a spineless snake" we come "nowhere near" believing or asserting its literal content. We take Joyce's point to be that the same will hold for "moral metaphors" like "Stealing is wrong." That is, when we use that phrase metaphorically, we will come nowhere near believing or asserting that stealing has the authoritatively prescriptive property of being morally wrong.[10] This point is supposed to allay the worry that compliance with narrationist fictionalism, which requires that we act and speak as if we believe that stealing is wrong, involves a risk of slipping into genuine moral belief and assertion. But the move to metaphorist fictionalism is a two-edged sword: while it enables the fictionalist to avoid the worry about slipping into genuine moral belief, and hence avoid the aforementioned worries about incoherence, feasibility, and psychological austerity, it leaves it entirely unclear how moral judgments are supposed to motivate. For if we understand a metaphor like "Stealing is wrong," we understand that its literal content (i.e., that stealing has the moral property of *must-not-be-doneness*) is false and that the conveyed content is that we have Humean reasons not to steal. But the whole point of revolutionary fictionalism is to ensure that moral thought and talk continue to regulate our behavior and work as an antidote to weakness of will when other kinds of considerations, for example concerning Humean reasons, are motivationally insufficient to do so!

In other words, insofar as the metaphorical overlay fails to have motivational impact, or has only limited motivational impact, it will leave motivational work to be done by the conveyed content (i.e., propositions about Humean reasons). In the case of certain metaphors, the conveyed content can indeed do such work. For example, in the case of Jake the spineless snake, the conveyed content seems quite capable of motivating us on its own, and so inertness on the part of the metaphorical overlay will not matter much, if at all. But in the case of moral sentences on Joyce's proposal, the conveyed content will *itself* be motivationally inert, at least in many central cases.

To see this, let us again consider the scenario in which you are in a position to steal a philanthropist's entire fortune without risk of getting caught. Do you have Humean reasons not to proceed with the theft? Well, assuming that you desire the comforts that wealth brings, and assuming that you will not feel much guilt or shame as a consequence, then presumably you *don't* have such reasons; indeed, you appear to have Humean reasons in the opposite direction. How, then, is information about your Humean reasons supposed to have the requisite motivational impact? It would be like Romeo entertaining the thought that Juliet is the sun in order to motivate himself to stay with her, when he has in fact fallen out of love.[11]

---

[10] As we will see in §5 below, Joyce's present view is that we come *very near* believing that stealing is wrong when we accept nondoxastically the proposition that stealing is wrong.

[11] We assume that a chief rationale for retaining moral discourse in some form is the observation that Mackie expressed in the quote that appeared in the introduction of this chapter, *viz.* that "[w]e need morality to regulate interpersonal relations, to control some of the ways in which people behave

Perhaps this is too quick, however. As selfish as you may be, presumably you still want to live in a society where people don't steal, and if so, there is at least something to be said in Humean terms for you not to proceed with the theft. But suppose that consideration of this Humean reason is insufficient to motivate you to refrain. This is precisely the kind of case in which moral thought is supposed to kick in as an antidote to selfishness and short-sighted temptation. But how can it, if you know that the thought or claim that stealing is wrong is literally false and that its conveyed content is about Humean reasons that you recognize already, but which are, in the case at hand, insufficient to provide motivation? It would be like Romeo entertaining the thought that Juliet is the sun in order to motivate himself to stay with her, when he has in fact fallen more deeply in love with someone else.

The problem also has an interpersonal dimension. It is difficult to see how a metaphorical use of moral terms can be used in dialogues to put pressure on others or to function as conversation-stoppers (Joyce 2006: 165–8). Imagine that your interlocutor endeavors to put a halt on your thieving plans by insisting that stealing is wrong. How can such an insistence have the intended impact on your plans and course of action if both you and your interlocutor realize both that it is merely a metaphorical way of conveying information about your Humean reasons and that these reasons are either non-existent or at least insufficient to bring about motivation to act?

The upshot is that if the conveyed content is understood in terms of Humean reasons, it will typically fail to motivate in the crucial contexts, since it will be either transparently false or insufficiently forceful. Hence, on Joyce's proposal, it appears that the metaphorical overlay in the form of moral propositions will have to do most, if not all, of the motivational work single-handedly. But, as we have seen, it isn't clear that it can do any such work at all.

3.5.3 The (New) Self-Surveillance Problem

Yet another problem for metaphorist fictionalism is that metaphors, as Joyce (2020: §4) recognizes, tend to have a limited life-span, or at least tend to lose much of their vitality over time as they get increasingly entrenched in language. Joyce mentions the expression "the mouth of the river," which in current usage simply denotes the egress of a river, without much, if any, phenomenological association with the mouths of humans or animals. What has happened here is that the conveyed content has become the literal content, with at most vestiges of the original literal content remaining.

---

towards one another, often in opposition to contrary inclinations." We believe that it is a plausible assumption that a moral fiction that is efficient in these regards will consider stealing (*pro tanto*) wrong. We also believe that the prescriptions of such a moral fiction can conflict with a person's Humean reasons.

If this were to happen with moral vocabulary in Joyce's proposed scenario, then any emotional/motivational enhancement it once provided would be all but lost. Since this is a possible turn of events, the group that uses moral vocabulary metaphorically must continuously make efforts to ensure that it does not become a set of dead metaphors. This parallels the self-surveillance problem for narrationist fictionalism, where individuals need to exercise cognitive self-surveillance to make sure they don't end up believing moral propositions; the fictionalist group must exercise a kind of collective self-surveillance to ensure that their talk of moral wrongness (etc.) remains metaphorical.

This issue is related to the mismatch problem in that, in both cases, a kind of continuous, self-conscious engineering of moral thought and talk is needed in order to preserve its requisite functionality (assuming that this is even possible to begin with). At the very least, then, the fictionalist reform proposal appears less attractive than the conservationist one.

4. Moral Fictionalism: Why?

Even if the above issues are somehow dealt with, moral fictionalism (metaphorist as well as narrationist) will still face a troubling question: Why replace our battle-tested morality device in the first place? After all, fictionalism cannot *beat* conservationism with respect to the how-challenge; at most it can do equally well. And we know that the human psyche is potentially destructive beyond belief. Since there is thus no potential upside in terms of beneficial motivational enhancement—and a lot of potential downside—why take a chance on fictionalism?

Joyce (2001: §7.0; 2019: §2) suggests that the why-challenge can be at least partly answered by appealing to the benefits of avoiding *falsity* and *irrationality*. The conservationist proposal would have us embrace first order moral beliefs that we recognize to be false in metaethically alert contexts. Joyce points to three more specific problems attached to this kind of compartmentalization: (1) the instrumental disadvantage of having false beliefs; (2) the instrumental disadvantage of knowingly cultivating inconsistent beliefs; and, less explicitly, (3) the intrinsic repugnance of embracing such irrationality. We consider these in turn (cf. Olson 2014: §9.2). More recently, Joyce has argued that fictionalism allows for a greater degree of desirable flexibility than does conservationism. We consider this point in §4.4.

4.1 The Instrumental Disadvantage of False Beliefs

We agree with Joyce, of course, that having true beliefs is in general instrumentally beneficial, and that having false beliefs is in general instrumentally disadvantageous.

As Joyce puts it, "true beliefs are an extremely valuable commodity" (2001: 178). But we are dealing with a very special case here. As we mentioned earlier, error theorists (Joyce included) largely agree that false *moral* beliefs, with their salient commitment to must-be-doneness, are instrumentally beneficial overall (in Humean terms), and that this is precisely why they have been biologically and culturally selected for. Thus, a guiding assumption of this whole debate is that false moral beliefs are an exception to the rule.

This response is admittedly too easy, however, since false moral beliefs may be advantageous only in ways that fictionalism can also accommodate (assuming that the how-challenge can be answered), while being disadvantageous in certain other respects. Here Joyce points to their disruptive influence on our broader web of belief, in that they "will require all manner of compensating false beliefs to... fit with what else one knows" (Joyce 2001: 179). Thus, even if false moral beliefs are motivationally efficacious in beneficial ways, then as long as the fictionalist's ersatz is equally so, any negative impact of false moral beliefs on our broader web of belief will count in favor of fictionalism vis-à-vis conservationism.

However, it is not the case that false moral beliefs will require all manner of compensating false beliefs. Due to the autonomy of ethics, or the "is-ought gap," our moral beliefs will form a largely isolated tangle in our broader web of belief. There will be inferential connections between various moral propositions, of course, and some of these will hook up with various non-moral propositions as bridge premises. However, only rarely will belief in the false moral propositions in such inferential clusters require belief in false non-moral propositions for coherence. To think otherwise would be to presuppose some form of reductive naturalism, but reductive naturalism is presumably ruled out by the error theoretic starting points of the present debate.[12]

4.2 The Instrumental Disadvantage of Cultivating Inconsistency

Joyce (2001: 179) also suggests that the conservationist *policy* of compartmentalization is "likely to have negative repercussions." Quoting C. S. Peirce, he worries that such a policy will lead to "a rapid deterioration of intellectual vigor." Here the point is not that the false moral beliefs themselves will have negative consequences, but rather that the policy of endorsing and nurturing them while ultimately recognizing their falsity will open the door to epistemic chaos. Joyce writes:

---

[12] In correspondence, Joyce asked us to imagine a person who believes that ethics is not autonomous. In such a person's web of beliefs, false moral beliefs may require compensating false non-moral beliefs. We agree, but the culprit here is the person's (false) belief that the "is-ought gap" is bridgeable. This does not show that false moral beliefs per se require compensating false non-moral beliefs, regardless of background beliefs.

> [T]he conservationist's recommendation involves doxastic practices that are likely to lead to deleterious consequences. The conservationist is, after all, recommending that we knowingly cultivate inconsistent beliefs, which is, arguably, a recommendation of irrationality. (Joyce 2019: 154)

It is indeed a recommendation of irrationality, at least in some sense (see §4.3 below). But why think that "deleterious consequences" will likely follow?

To get a grip on this issue we need to consider what those consequences might be, more precisely. The worry appears to be that adopting the conservationist policy with respect to morality will likely lead us to adopt similar policies in other domains, where belief in the non-existent facts or properties is not beneficial but rather harmful. Which domains are those? Joyce doesn't really tell us, but two obvious candidates are the domains of *superstition* and *pseudoscience*. Superstitious and pseudoscientific beliefs can be very tempting, as they often provide easily accessible and comforting answers to important questions. And while they often appear mostly harmless and silly, they can sometimes be highly destructive. Phenomena such as witch trials, quack medicine, conspiracy theories, and religious or political cults come to mind. If conservationist compartmentalization with respect to morality will likely make us more self-indulgent with respect to our superstitious and pseudoscientific inclinations, by licensing their insulation from our rational selves, then this does present a problem for conservationism.

It's not clear, however, why we wouldn't be able to contain the irrationality in question. A salient feature of superstitious and pseudoscientific beliefs is that they are typically beliefs about *empirical* or *causal* matters, and so they typically come into conflict not only with our best science but also with everyday observation and common sense. Belief in flat-earthism or anti-vax, for example, will constantly run up against manifest contrary evidence, the suppression of which will require some sort of ridiculous conspiracy theory. Thus, insulating such beliefs from our rational selves will not be easy. By contrast, and as we noted earlier, the content of moral beliefs will only rarely have empirical or causal implications (at least given the error theoretic assumptions of the present debate). Thus, there will be virtually nothing tangible to wake us up from our self-imposed metaethical slumber.[13]

Indeed, a claim can be made that we already have sustainable conservationist or conservationist-like policies implemented in various other philosophical areas. For example, skeptical arguments concerning things like free will, personal identity, the moving now, other minds, and the external world present difficult and disturbing philosophical challenges, but most of us don't really take them

---

[13] This suggests that religious conservationism is less plausible than moral conservationism, since many religions do make (manifestly false) claims about the natural world, which will not be easy to contain. This, in turn, suggests that religious fictionalism is more plausible than moral fictionalism.

seriously in our daily lives. This type of compartmentalization is described by Hume in a familiar passage:

> I am confounded with all these questions, and begin to fancy myself in the most deplorable condition imaginable, environ'd with the deepest darkness, and utterly depriv'd of the use of every member and faculty.
>
> Most fortunately it happens, that since reason is incapable of dispelling these clouds, nature herself suffices to that purpose, and cures me of this philosophical melancholy and delirium, either by relaxing this bent of mind, or by some avocation, and lively impression of my senses, which obliterate all these chimeras. I dine, I play a game of back-gammon, I converse, and am merry with my friends; and when after three or four hour's amusement, I wou'd return to these speculations, they appear so cold, and strain'd, and ridiculous, that I cannot find in my heart to enter into them any farther. (Hume [1740] 1978: 269)

Thus, when engaged in everyday life it takes *effort* to feel the force of skeptical philosophical challenges or conclusions. But in the case of superstition and pseudoscience, the opposite is the case; everyday life will present constant reminders of falsity. This asymmetry should help prevent the irrationality of moral/metaethical compartmentalization from spreading to potentially more dangerous areas.

Note that we do not mean to take a stand on the vexed exegetical question whether Hume genuinely believed the conclusions of his skeptical arguments while pursuing his speculations in his study, and believed something inconsistent with these conclusions while relaxing and dining with his friends.[14] Our point is merely that this is a possible scenario, and were it also an actual one, the kind of inconsistency Hume would be committed to does not seem disadvantageous at all. Indeed, given the usefulness in daily life of reasoning concerning cause and effect—famously one of the targets of Hume's skepticism—it seems clearly instrumentally advantageous.

4.3 The Intrinsic Repugnance of Irrationality

Although it is less explicitly articulated than the previous two points, Joyce in addition seems to find the conservationist policy intrinsically repugnant, independently of any negative consequences. Having set forth the conservationist "recommendation of irrationality," he says that he "recoil[s] at such a violation of epistemic norms" (Joyce 2019: 154).

---

[14] As Joyce pointed out to us in correspondence, Hume's remarks might also be interpreted along fictionalist lines.

This seems like an overreaction, however. First, as we pointed out in the previous section, the kinds of violations of epistemic norms that the conservationist is recommending are not exactly unheard of. Indeed, keeping a firm distance in everyday life to what one is disposed to believe in philosophically alert modes is arguably a prerequisite for mental health, at least for many or most of us. Moreover, while the conservationist is indeed recommending a violation of *theoretical* rationality, ideally this violation is sanctioned by *practical* rationality. Given the conservationist's empirical assumptions concerning the utility of moral belief and assertion, going on with morality is not some arbitrary manifestation of epistemic negligence or arrogance, but rather the *wise* thing to do. With these mitigating factors in mind there is little reason to recoil.

4.4 Nondoxastic Acceptance, Belief, and Flexibility

We have already remarked that one useful feature of moral thought and discourse is their function as conversation-stoppers; the judgment that some course of action would be morally wrong can often serve to put an end to individual or collective deliberation about whether to take that course of action. As Joyce points out, this requires a degree of steadfastness and inflexibility in our moral thinking. As he also points out, however,

> we don't want to be so committed to moral values that we refuse to recognize any context wherein they can be critically examined.... [W]hat was once a useful conversation-stopper might become a destructive conversation-stopper.... [A] moral system that is *utterly* steadfast and inflexible—that will crash and burn rather than adapt—is very probably less beneficial overall than a moral system that is able, *in extremis*, to adjust and evolve.[15]

It is easy to agree with all of this, but it is difficult to see why any of it licenses the conclusion that "an attitude of nondoxastic acceptance toward morality may serve us better than sincere moral belief."[16] First, a conservationist policy does not preclude occasional assessment of moral beliefs in terms of how well they conduce to our practical ends. Compare how utilitarians occasionally step back from their sincere belief in secondary principles and assess those beliefs in terms of how well they promote the general happiness. Compare also how, in reflective moments, we can assess our sincere religious—or atheist—beliefs in terms of the extent to which they provide comfort or bring a sense of purpose to life. Second, flexibility in the content of a moral system seems clearly desirable. For example, a moral

---

[15] Joyce, Chapter 13 of this volume, §5 (italics preserved).
[16] Joyce, Chapter 13 of this volume, §5.

system that contains an absolute prohibition against lying is less flexible—in that respect, at least—than an alternative moral system that permits lying in special circumstances. But this kind of flexibility is a feature of the *content* of moral systems and does not speak in favor of any particular kind of attitude—such as belief or nondoxastic acceptance—that we may take toward moral systems. Third, one of us has argued elsewhere that conservationists should be wary about when and where to use the device of moral talk and employ moral claims as conversation-stoppers. This is yet another dimension in which conservationism allows for flexibility.[17]

5. A General Reflection: Fictionalism, Conservationism, and the Nature of Belief

Throughout this chapter, some readers might have had the nagging suspicion that looming in the background of the debate between fictionalism and conservationism is the question of the nature of belief. We think that this is correct but that the situation is more precarious for fictionalism than for conservationism. To begin to see this, consider how Joyce describes your situation if you manage to follow the advice of moral fictionalism "studiously":

> In everyday contexts, your attitude toward morality will have all the *phenomenology* of belief—all the *emotional, motivational*, and *practical advantages* of moral belief—without being moral belief.[18]

This attitude does not count as belief, however, since if you were asked about morality "in all seriousness," you would reject it as false.

This reintroduces worries about coherence, voiced in §3.3 above. Moral fictionalism is a coherent position only if belief is defined in a certain way. More specifically, Joyce's view seems to be that you believe that *p* only if you affirm *p* when asked about whether *p* "in all seriousness." But a view that defines belief rather as a state with a certain role in our psychology (e.g., in motivating intentional action) might imply that any state that has the phenomenology and the emotional, motivational, and practical implications of moral belief *is* a belief. Such accounts may allow that some of our *occurrent* beliefs conflict with some of our *dispositional* beliefs (e.g., what we would occurrently believe if we were asked about the matter "in all seriousness"). Moral fictionalism appears to rule out this possibility.

---

[17] See Eriksson & Olson 2019. In that paper it is argued that conservationism should be morphed into *negotiationism*.
[18] Joyce, Chapter 13 of this volume, §4 (italics added). See also Jaquet, Chapter 4 of this volume.

Conservationism is not in the same way held hostage to accounts of the nature of belief since it involves no recommendation against belief. It advises those who come to believe that moral error theory is true to—as far as possible—preserve ordinary (error-ridden) moral thought, including moral belief. The crucial difference between conservationism and fictionalism, remember, is that while the latter sees moral belief as something to be avoided, the former does not.[19] That is why the situation with respect to the issue of the nature of belief is less precarious for conservationism.

6. Conclusion

In this chapter we have clarified central challenges faced by moral fictionalism, and we have argued that metaphorist fictionalism fares no better with respect to these challenges than narrationist fictionalism. Just like its narrationist predecessor, metaphorist fictionalism fails to secure the motivational efficacy of moral thought and talk. We have also found faults with more recent attempts at answering the *how* and *why* challenges for moral fictionalism, leaving the conservationist recommendation a more attractive alternative. This conclusion could be overturned if the conservationist proposal were sufficiently problematic in other respects, but we have argued that it isn't.[20]

References

Eriksson, B. & Olson, J. 2019. "Moral practice after error theory: Negotiationism." In R. Garner and R. Joyce (eds), *The End of Morality: Taking Moral Abolitionism Seriously*. Routledge. 113–30.

Hare, R. M. 1981. *Moral Thinking: Its Levels, Method, and Point*. Clarendon Press.

Hume, D. [1740] 1978. *A Treatise of Human Nature* (2nd edition). Clarendon Press.

Joyce, R. 2001. *The Myth of Morality*. Cambridge University Press.

Joyce, R. 2006. *The Evolution of Morality*. MIT Press.

Joyce, R. 2019. "Moral fictionalism: How to have your cake and eat it too." In R. Garner & R. Joyce (eds.), *The End of Morality: Taking Moral Abolitionism Seriously*. Routledge. 150–65.

Joyce, R. 2020. "Fictionalism: Morality and metaphor." In B. Armour-Garb & F. Kroon (eds), *Fictionalism in Philosophy*. Oxford University Press. 103–21.

---

[19] See Olson 2014: 190.
[20] For helpful comments and suggestions, we are grateful to Natalja Deng, Jessica Isserow, Fred Kroon, and, especially, to the editors of this volume. Work on this chapter was funded by the Swedish Research Council (Project Id: 2019-02828).

Kalderon, M. 2005. *Moral Fictionalism*. Oxford University Press.

Mackie, J. L. 1977. *Ethics: Inventing Right and Wrong*. Penguin.

Mill, J. S. [1863] 1998. *Utilitarianism*. Oxford University Press.

Nolan, D., Restall, G., & West, C. 2005. "Moral fictionalism versus the rest." *Australasian Journal of Philosophy* 83: 307–30.

Olson, J. 2010. "The freshman objection to expressivism and what to make of it." *Ratio* 23: 87–101.

Olson, J. 2014. *Moral Error Theory: History, Critique, Defence*. Oxford University Press.

4
Moral Fictionalism and Misleading Analogies

François Jaquet

1. Introduction

Imagine. After taking a course in the metaphysics of ordinary material objects, you become convinced that there are no such things. Though there appear to be cows and horses, roads and cars, chairs, shelves, and books, this appearance is deceptive. There are in fact no such things; there exist only microscopic objects, simples arranged cow-wise, car-wise, or chair-wise. In light of this finding, you naturally conclude that everyone is in massive error. Whenever someone believes, say, that there is a horse on the road or a book on the shelf, they believe something false. And that, of course, includes you. So, what should you do? Should you get rid of all your judgments about macroscopic objects and think only in terms of atoms? That sounds like terrible advice—way too impractical to be worth acting upon. Much more plausibly, in your everyday life, you should keep thinking as if there is a horse on the road (when there are atoms arranged horse-wise on atoms arranged road-wise) and as if there is a book on the shelf (when there are simples arranged book-wise on simples arranged shelf-wise). In short, you should make a fiction of propositions about ordinary objects. This piece of advice is a form of fictionalism about material objects.

The present chapter is not concerned with material objects, but it is with fictionalism. More precisely, it provides a defense of revolutionary moral fictionalism. Proponents of this view accept a moral error theory: they believe that all moral propositions are false because they purport to represent moral facts and properties that actually do not exist. Yet, they maintain that we should make a fiction of some moral propositions, thinking and talking as if killing is wrong and people ought to keep their promises. I will proceed in seven steps. In section 2, I present the question that moral fictionalists purport to answer—the "now-what question." Section 3 contains a more detailed characterization of moral fictionalism. In section 4, I criticize some analogies that are commonly used to introduce the view. The next three sections defend fictionalism against a set of objections. The bulk of this defense is that all three objections rest on a misconception of the view which is due to the use of some of the misleading analogies previously discarded.

François Jaquet, *Moral Fictionalism and Misleading Analogies* In: *Moral Fictionalism and Religious Fictionalism*. Edited by: Richard Joyce and Stuart Brock, Oxford University Press. © François Jaquet 2023.
DOI: 10.1093/oso/9780198881865.003.0005

Once it is understood through better analogies, fictionalism escapes these objections. However, it becomes very similar to another answer to the now-what question, so much so that one might think it inherits this other view's main problem. In the final section, I argue that it doesn't.

2. Now What?

Moral error theorists face the now-what question: What should we do with our moral judgments if they are all false? Three components of this question call for clarification. In what sense *should* we do something with our moral judgments? Who are the *we* who should do something with their moral judgments? And what exactly are these *judgments* that we should do something with? Let me clarify each point in turn.

The idea that we *should* do something with our moral judgments if they are all false has an air of paradox. Assuming a moral error theory, one might reason, there is nothing we should do. On the one hand, the now-what question is premised on the assumption that all moral judgments are false. On the other hand, it makes no sense on this very assumption. How weird! Well, not really. The key to unlocking the paradox is to appreciate that the now-what question is not a moral question. Trivially, there is nothing that we *morally* ought to do with our moral judgments if there is nothing we morally ought to do at all. But there might still be something we ought to do with our moral judgments in a non-moral sense. So, what is this sense? The suggestion I will retain is that the *should* that is at stake is prudential.[1] The now-what question is really "What policy concerning our moral judgments would be in our best interests?"

What about the *we*? A first observation in this respect is that the now-what question concerns error theorists rather than success theorists. Assuming that all moral judgments are false, one may wonder what people who still mistakenly believe that some moral judgments are true should do with these judgments. This is not our concern. Instead, we will wonder what those people who have reached the conclusion that all moral judgments are false should do with their moral judgments. This point is worth stressing, for the discovery that all moral judgments are false might significantly affect the outcome of our cost–benefit analysis. For instance, it might be much more irrational to keep believing moral propositions for an error theorist than for a success theorist. A policy worth pursuing for a success theorist might therefore be bad advice for an error theorist (Joyce 2019: 152).

---

[1] Some authors rather understand it as a pragmatic *should*, where a subject pragmatically should do whatever best satisfies their desires (e.g., Joyce, Chapter 13 of this volume). While the distinction between prudential and pragmatic *should*s is essential in accounts of well-being other than the desire-fulfilment view, it will not be for my purposes here. Feel free to translate every occurrence of "prudential" into "pragmatic."

Richard Joyce (2001: 204; 2016: 228–9) draws a further distinction about the *we*, which concerns the context we occupy. One question is what a lone error theorist—an error theorist living among success theorists—should do with their moral judgments. Another is what a whole community of error theorists should do with its moral judgments. Whilst the first question is not uninteresting, the latter has more of an "existential" touch. It is more directly connected to the common worry that widespread acceptance of a moral error theory might result in a society of liars, thieves, and murderers. However, there is a worry that this collective question rests on a false assumption. As Joyce acknowledges (2019: 155), maybe only individuals have a good of their own, and thus maybe nothing is in the interests of a group. Should that be the case, there would be nothing a community of error theorists prudentially ought to do with its moral judgments. To sidestep this issue, I propose that we ask a slightly different question: What should individual error theorists do with their moral judgments within a community of error theorists? (Jaquet 2021: 40). This question is still importantly different from that concerning a lone error theorist. What's best for a lone error theorist might differ drastically from what's best for an error theorist surrounded by fellow skeptics. Should a group of error theorists decide together to adopt a moral fiction, they might be willing to negotiate the content of this fiction. By contrast, such negotiation would be impossible with people who believe that there are mind-independent moral truths. This openness to negotiation might deeply affect our error theorists' cost–benefit analysis.

The *we* raises yet another issue that deserves attention. Not all error theorists have the same interests. Prudential advice that is adequate for one need not therefore be for another: even within a community of error theorists, not everyone ought to act in the same way. This means that there will be no unique answer to the question, "What should individual error theorists do with their moral judgments?" What we must aim for, given this complication, is an answer that makes prudential sense for error theorists who share a set of core interests. Fortunately, if the current philosophical literature is any indication, error theorists seem to converge pretty much in their ends. All parties to the now-what debate appear to agree that it would be best to ease the resolution of our practical conflicts, to be able to cooperate more fruitfully, and to strengthen our will. All they disagree about is how to achieve these common ends.

A final clarification concerns the notion of *judgments* involved in the now-what question. In the metaethics literature, the word "judgment" is often used to refer to *speech* acts. In this sense, to judge that the book is on the shelf amounts to uttering the sentence "The book is on the shelf." Accordingly, many philosophers ask a now-what question about moral discourse: What should we do with moral words and sentences? If moral words fail to denote anything and all moral sentences are false as a result, should we keep or stop using them to communicate? Should we preserve or abolish moral utterances? But the word "judgment" sometimes also refers to *mental* acts. In this other sense, to judge that the book is on the shelf amounts to accepting the proposition *The book is on the shelf*. We can thus ask a now-what question about moral thought: What should we do with our moral beliefs? Should we keep them, get rid of them, or revise them in some way? Since I believe that fewer of the benefits of morality are at bottom attributable to moral discourse than to moral thought (Jaquet 2020: 248–9), I will focus on the latter kind of inquiry.

To recap, the question we will be dealing with is: "From a prudential standpoint, what should individual error theorists with standard interests do with their moral beliefs, within a community of like-minded error theorists?" According to the fictionalist answer that I will defend, they should replace their moral beliefs with fictional attitudes. Let us now spell out this view in more detail.

3. Fictionalism

According to the fictionalist, we should replace our moral beliefs with attitudes that, to some extent, resemble the attitudes we entertain towards pieces of fiction. We should think that killing is wrong very broadly in the way we think that the Joker is Batman's archenemy. Thinking that the Joker is Batman's archenemy commits us neither to the existence of Batman nor to the truth of the proposition *The Joker is Batman's archenemy*. Thinking in a similar manner that killing is wrong would commit us neither to the existence of wrongness nor to the truth of the proposition *Killing is wrong*. What would it amount to exactly?

Depending on context, pieces of fiction can generate two distinct types of attitudes (Joyce 2001: 199–200; Walton 1990: 393). Suppose I am trying to improve the Wikipedia page of the movie *Joker* and, after wondering how to start for a while, I think: Arthur Fleck lives with his mother. My thought, in this case, is not the belief that Arthur Fleck lives with his mother. But it is a belief nonetheless—the belief that *in the movie* Arthur Fleck lives with his mother. I have a genuine belief whose content contains the fictional operator "in the movie." Consider now what happened earlier on, when I was at the movies. As I was completely immersed in the fiction, I thought: Arthur Fleck lives with his mother. Again, my thought was not the belief that Arthur Fleck lives with his mother. But, in this instance, neither was it the belief that in the movie Arthur Fleck lives with his mother, for I did not adopt such an external perspective on the story. I was not thinking *about* the fiction but *within* the fiction. I did not have a belief whose content was fictional; what I had was a fictional attitude whose content was literally that Arthur Fleck lives with his mother. I *make*-believed that Arthur Fleck lives with his mother.

With this in mind, we can distinguish two forms of fictionalism (Eklund 2007: 8). Content fictionalism is the view that we should use a kind of external viewpoint, like the one that I adopt when, updating Wikipedia, I believe that *in the movie* Arthur Fleck lives with his mother. So instead of believing, for example, that killing is wrong (period), I should believe that killing is wrong in the moral fiction. Force fictionalism, by contrast, urges us to make-believe that killing is wrong, in a way more or less analogous to that in which, immersed in the movie, I make-believe that Arthur Fleck lives with his mother.[2] Moral thought revised as prescribed by force fictionalism is thus thought *in* a moral fiction as opposed to thought *about* a moral fiction. Let us set aside content fictionalism and focus on force fictionalism. This is the view I want to defend in this chapter.

What exactly is this attitude of make-believe that fictionalists advise us to adopt towards moral propositions? And how exactly does it differ from full-blown belief? This is where things get complicated, for many features of the attitudes that are typical of our engagement with fiction might in principle be used to characterize make-believe and to distinguish it from proper belief. That being said, moral fictionalists generally appeal to one feature in particular (Joyce 2001: 192–3). On this account of the difference between belief and make-believe,

(B)   S believes that φ if and only if S has accepted φ in her most critical contexts, and S is disposed to accept φ in her most critical contexts.

(MB)   S make-believes that φ if and only if S is disposed to accept φ in some contexts, and S is disposed to accept not-φ in her most critical contexts.[3]

What is it, then, that makes a context more or less critical than another? Ask and you shall receive:

(C)   For any pair of contexts C1 and C2, C1 is more critical than C2 if and only if an assumption that is made in C2 is questioned in C1, but not vice versa.

Call this dimension of the distinction "context dependence."

Typical cases of engagement with fiction seem to fall under this description of make-believe. Consider my attitude to the proposition *Arthur Fleck lives with his mother*. I am disposed to accept this proposition while watching the movie. But I am also disposed to reject it when I update the Wikipedia page. Importantly, the former context is less critical than the latter. While watching the movie, I assume the truth of everything I am seeing on the screen. As I am shown an Arthur Fleck, for example, I assume his existence. Later, when I am in front of my computer,

---

[2] Please do not read the word "make-believe" too literally. As we shall see, the attitudes recommended by moral fictionalism differ from typical engagement with fiction in several respects. This has led some proponents of the view to switch terminology. For instance, Joyce (Chapter 13 of this volume) now speaks of "nondoxastic acceptance" instead of "make-believe."

[3] Joyce adds a third condition: S has dissented from φ in her most critical contexts. In my opinion, this condition is too demanding on make-believe. The first time I watched *Joker*, I had never rejected the proposition *Arthur Fleck lives with his mother*.

I have switched to an altogether different context. I no longer assume that Arthur Fleck exists. Being aware that *Joker* is a piece of fiction rather than a documentary, I question everything the movie depicts. Insofar as I am disposed to accept the proposition *Arthur Fleck lives with his mother* in some context and to reject it in a more critical context, I make-believe that Arthur Fleck lives with his mother.

Moral fictionalism, as I will use the label hereafter, is thus the view that we should both accept some moral propositions in certain contexts and reject these propositions in more critical contexts. Now, in the relevant sense, the context of a metaethical discussion is more critical than that of moral deliberation. In discussing the ethics of abortion or the death penalty, we assume that there is a truth to the matter. But we question this assumption when we do metaethics—one of the central questions in such contexts is whether there are moral truths at all. Conversely, we make no assumption while discussing metaethics that we would question when we deliberate. (Of course, metaethical contexts involve assumptions too—for instance, the assumption that there is a true answer to the question "Are there moral truths?" But this is not the kind of assumption we question when in deliberative contexts.) Concretely, moral fictionalists advise us to be disposed both to accept moral propositions when we deliberate about what to do and to reject these propositions when we do metaethics. And when they say we should get rid of our moral beliefs, what they mean is that we should not be disposed to assent to moral propositions when we do metaethics.

It is not the purpose of this chapter to provide a compelling argument for fictionalism; my more modest ambition is to counter some common objections. Let me nonetheless say a few words to motivate the view. Moral fictionalism is basically grounded in a series of observations. Imbued with error as it may be, the whole moral practice is far from useless. For instance, having moral beliefs arguably helps us resolve our practical conflicts (Nolan et al. 2005: 307). Provided that our respective moral principles overlap to some extent, we have an easier time agreeing on what to do. In addition, our moral beliefs help us overcome weakness of will (Joyce 2001: 184; Olson 2014: 195). We are all sometimes tempted to act on the basis of selfish calculations, but this is often against our long-term interest. Most of the time, we end up better off if we refrain from harming people (even if feeling a temptation to do so). It is thus in our best interest to cultivate a strong disposition not to harm others. And it is quite plausible that moral beliefs can help with this—that they bolster self-control by blocking such hazardous calculations. These considerations provide us with prudential reasons to keep believing in moral propositions.

On the other side, we also have prudential reasons *not* to believe in moral propositions. If it is possible at all, believing propositions that one knows to be false appears to be plainly irrational (Joyce 2001: 178). Remember: the belief that φ involves a disposition to accept φ in one's most critical context. An error theorist who would believe moral propositions would therefore be disposed to accept them in the metaethics classroom. It is unclear how she could even do that qua error theorist. Assuming she could, one thing at least is clear: she would qualify as irrational if she did. Indulging in such irrationality might open the door to many false beliefs and provoke the deterioration of her critical thinking. All this is in turn likely to lead to the frustration of her interests. (See Moberger & Olson, Chapter 3 of this volume, for advocacy of this conservationist option.)

In view of these conflicting prudential reasons, it would be ideal to have at our disposal an attitude that would at the same time meet the functions of moral beliefs (helping us combat *akrasia* and resolve our conflicts) and avoid the issues raised by moral beliefs (irrationality and the deterioration of critical thinking). This is where moral make-believe steps in, for the hope is that it can do reasonably well on both counts.

4. Misleading Analogies and the Nature of Moral Make-Believe

Not everyone is convinced by the fictionalist's preferred way of distinguishing belief from make-believe. Jessica Isserow makes the following objection:

> As Joyce characterizes a critical context, it is one in which an agent "investigates and challenges the presuppositions of ordinary thinking"—the philosophy classroom being a prime example. But it is far from obvious that we are disposed to assent even to very firmly held beliefs in critical contexts, so understood. Plausibly, the average student believes that she knows she has hands, that there are numbers, and that the sun will rise tomorrow. But she may not be so willing to assent to such claims in the philosophy classroom. (Isserow, Chapter 2 of this volume)

There may well be something to this objection. For my part, I am unsure that the student who genuinely suspends her judgment about the existence of numbers or the external world can truly be said to have beliefs in these domains. But I would not want to bite the bullet and say that she does not. The safe route for the fictionalist, I suspect, is to retreat to a weaker account of belief that would still make belief mutually exclusive with make-believe as characterized above. Here is such an account:

(B*) S believes that φ if and only if S accepts φ in some contexts, and S is not disposed to reject φ in her most critical contexts.

Our average student might believe that she knows she has hands, that there are numbers, and that the sun will rise tomorrow, and yet not be disposed to accept these claims in the philosophy classroom. That much I will concede, if only for the sake of argument. However, assuming that she is disposed to deny that she knows she has hands, that there are numbers, and that the sun will rise tomorrow in the philosophy classroom, I have a firm intuition that she does not really believe these propositions. A plausible interpretation, I submit, is that she make-believes them. If this is on the right track, then belief and make-believe can indeed be distinguished in terms of context dependence.

Be that as it may, Isserow further points out two other dimensions along which belief typically differs from engagement with fiction. First, whereas our beliefs tend to persist even when having them runs contrary to our interests, our attitudes to fiction usually evaporate in such circumstances (Isserow, Chapter 2 of this volume). I would easily abandon my make-believe that Arthur Fleck lives with his mother should that be in my best interests—I'll be happy to make-believe that he lives with Catwoman if you offer me a thousand dollars on this condition. Call this dimension of the distinction "stake sensitivity." Second, whereas our beliefs typically dispose us to act in specific ways, our attitudes to fiction translate much less directly into action (Isserow, Chapter 2 of this volume). My make-believe that Arthur Fleck is a killer does not dispose me to act as the equivalent belief would—it doesn't even cross my mind to call the police and report him. Call this dimension of the distinction "action tendency."

All in all, attitudes that are typical of our engagement with pieces of fiction fall on the "make-believe" side of the divide along at least three dimensions: context dependence, stake sensitivity, and action tendency. It is worth noting, however, that the dimension of context dependence is relatively independent of the other two. Even though it is atypical of fictional engagement, a person could be disposed to accept a proposition only in everyday contexts, stick to that state of acceptance when the stakes are high, and act on it as though it were a belief. Should you come to the conclusion that there are no macroscopic objects, for example, you would presumably keep accepting the proposition *Throwing oneself under a car is dangerous* even if offered a large amount of money to stop. Furthermore, the fictionalist is committed only to the view that we should adopt attitudes that are *to some extent* similar to the attitudes that are typical of engagement with fiction. They need not claim that we should adopt attitudes that resemble them in all respects. The suggestion, then, is that an attitude that qualifies as make-believe in terms of context dependence is close enough.

While moral make-believe should be like our attitude to pieces of fiction in this respect, maybe it should be unlike this attitude in other respects. Maybe it should be like other types of make-believe. Besides engagement with fictions, moral fictionalists tend to appeal to all sorts of analogies to introduce their view. Moral make-believe would be analogous to storytelling (Joyce 2001: 200; Nolan et al. 2005: 308–9), acting (Joyce 2007: 70; 2016: 225), and games of make-believe (Joyce 2001: 197; 2019: 154). Just like engagement with fictions, all three activities are proper instances of make-believe. When a parent tells a story, an actor plays a role, or a child pretends to be a pirate, they accept some propositions that they are nonetheless disposed to reject as soon as they step out of their fictional engagement. Inasmuch as the purpose is to illustrate our account of make-believe, then, these examples perfectly fit the bill. However, just like engagement with fiction, they are not the kind of make-believe we should adopt towards moral propositions. These analogies are misleading.[4]

Better analogies are available. For instance, skeptics about colors, numbers, or the external world generally practice make-believe (Joyce 2001: 191, 220). In everyday contexts, they accept that grass is green, that $\sqrt{9} = 3$, and that there are other people. Only, they reject these propositions in more philosophical moments. Another example concerns the "paradox of hedonism" (Joyce, Chapter 13 of this volume). Hedonists believe that one and only one thing is intrinsically valuable: happiness. However, it is a well-known fact of human psychology that those who seek only happiness get very little of it. One will find happiness only by treating other things as if they were valuable in themselves. A consistent hedonist would therefore make-believe that friendship, knowledge, and freedom are intrinsically good; they would accept this proposition in everyday contexts so as to increase their own happiness and yet be disposed to reject it in a more critical context, such as a seminar on well-being. Consequentialism provides a final example (Olson 2014: 192; Jaquet & Naar 2016: 204; Jaquet 2021: 42–3). Just like with our own happiness, we will fail to produce the best consequences if we seek nothing else, for we are not so good at anticipating the effects of our acts. This is why consequentialists rarely follow the general principle that one should always produce the best consequence in their deliberations. Instead, in everyday circumstances, they accept a set of more specific rules—such as "Killing is always wrong" and "One always ought to keep one's promises"—whose general acceptance would bring the best outcomes. Still, they remain disposed to reject these specific rules in a more critical context: the ethics classroom. In a nutshell, they make-believe these rules.

Why are these better analogies? Because they make it plain that the principal objections levelled against moral fictionalism fail. Indeed, it will be my contention that these objections rest on the misrepresentation that fictionalism recommends that we adopt towards moral propositions the kind of attitudes that are typical of engagement with fictions, storytelling, or games of make-believe. As we shall see, there is not much left of these criticisms once this misrepresentation is fixed.

---

[4] Another analogy that is sometimes used is that of metaphors (Joyce 2017: 83; 2019: 155). But metaphors do not fall under our description of make-believe. When I think "Jake is a spineless snake," it is not the case that I accept the proposition *Jake is a spineless snake* in one context but remain disposed to reject it in a more critical context. Rather, I accept the proposition *Jake is a dishonest coward*, and I am disposed to do so even in more critical contexts. There is nothing I make-believe. All I do is believe that Jake is a dishonest coward.

5. The Inference Problem

A satisfactory answer to the now-what question would allow for moral reasoning; it would not face the Frege-Geach problem fatal to metaethical expressivism (Olson 2011; Husi 2014: 92; Svoboda 2017: 55). Consider this *modus ponens*:

> Killing animals is wrong.
> If killing animals is wrong, then so is buying meat.
> Therefore, buying meat is wrong.

If the meaning of moral sentences consists only of the expression of conative attitudes, then the phrase "Killing animals is wrong" means one thing in the first premise (where it expresses disapproval of killing animals) and another in the second (where it expresses no such thing). The argument commits a fallacy of equivocation and is therefore invalid. But, as anyone can see, this argument is *not* invalid—it is perfectly kosher from the logical point of view. So, expressivism must be false: the meaning of moral sentences does not consist only of the expression of conative states. A related worry is that expressivism does not allow for moral *reasoning*. If our toy argument were invalid, then one could without inconsistency accept both its premises and yet reject its conclusion. In sum, on the expressivist picture, moral inferences are always optional, never mandatory. We can call this the "inference problem."

The point is slightly different in the present context. Answers to the now-what question purport not to describe the current moral practice but to prescribe a policy for moral error theorists. Moral fictionalists, for instance, hold that moral error theorists should make-believe moral propositions, not that people currently make-believe moral propositions. As a result, they need not accommodate the validity of arguments in the current moral practice. It would, however, still be problematic should apparently valid arguments turn out to be invalid in the revised moral practice. For the revised practice had better allow us to distinguish between reasonable and unreasonable deductive inferences: if it is to guide our actions effectively, it must make room for moral deliberation and thus moral reasoning.

Does moral fictionalism face the inference problem? Well, it's complicated. Why is it that expressivism cannot accommodate the validity of our moral *modus ponens*? Because it entails that the meaning of the phrase "killing animals is wrong" shifts between the first premise and the second. But moral fictionalism entails no such thing, even if we focus now on the revised moral practice. In the practice revised along fictionalist lines, the phrase "killing animals is wrong" would mean the same in both premises—just like in the current moral practice, its meaning would consist in the proposition *Killing animals is wrong*. Accordingly, the argument would not commit a fallacy of equivocation. It would be as valid in the revised moral practice as it is in the current one (Joyce 2016: 225). To that extent, moral fictionalism does not face the inference problem; it can account for *semantic entailment*.

A problem remains, though. In the current practice, not only is our *modus ponens* valid—not only does the truth of the premises guarantee that of the conclusion—in addition, someone who accepts the premises is committed to accepting the conclusion. And that is because it is a property of belief that, if you believe proposition φ, and φ entails proposition ψ, then you are committed to believing ψ as well (Oddie & Demetriou 2007: 492). But, crucially, this might be a property of belief that is not instantiated by make-believe. So, is it the case that make-believing a certain proposition commits us to make-believing the propositions it entails? Jonas Olson and James Lenman think not (see also Dain 2012: 204):

> [P]retending to believe the premises of a logically valid argument does not commit one to pretend[ing] to believe the conclusion. Acts of pretence and pretence attitudes, I submit, are not subject to norms of consistency. The explanation of this is that unlike assertion and belief, acts of pretence and pretence attitudes do not aim at correct representation of the world; their function is not to fit the world. In this respect, they are more akin to desires and expressions thereof, than to belief and assertion. (Olson 2011: 191)

> That it is true in the fiction that p and that it is true in the fiction that if p then q do not entail that it is true in the fiction that q. If I believe that p and believe that if p then q, logic requires me to believe that q. But if I pretend that p and pretend that if p then q, logic doesn't require me to do anything. Given that fictions are not in the market for truth, why should only consistent fictions be eligible?
> (Lenman 2013: 406)

The objection, then, is that moral fictionalism can accommodate semantic entailment but not deductive inference. Insofar as semantic entailment is of little use in practical deliberation without deductive inference, fictionalism does not satisfy our desideratum and it faces the inference problem.

All this sounds plausible as long as we focus on storytelling, engagement with fictions, and games of make-believe. Novels, movies, and children's play are often consistent, but they need not be. Some indeed maintain that we are able to make-believe inconsistent fictions. To mention just two: Tamar Szabó Gendler (2000) tells a story in which seven and five do not make twelve, and Graham Priest (1997) writes about an empty box that contains an object. In engaging with Gendler's fiction, we are supposed to make-believe that there are five and seven righteous souls and yet not make-believe that there are twelve righteous souls, even though the first proposition clearly entails the second. Likewise, while imagining Priest's story, we are meant to make-believe that the box is empty and yet not make-believe that it contains no object, even though the first proposition obviously entails the second. As far as engagement with fiction is concerned, maybe make-believing a proposition does not always commit us to make-believing the propositions it entails.

Consider now the analogy with consequentialism. As we saw, consequentialists advise us to make-believe a moral fiction consisting of a set of simple moral rules. While we should reject these rules in the ethics classroom, we should nonetheless accept them in the less critical contexts of practical deliberation. Yet, in the latter contexts, a consequentialist who accepts the propositions *Killing animals is always wrong* and *If killing animals is always wrong, then eating meat is wrong* appears to be committed to also accepting the proposition *Eating meat is wrong*. A consequentialist who would accept the first two propositions and yet reject the third would strike us as unreasonable. So, how come consequentialists must accept the logical consequences of the propositions they accept but we need not do so when we engage with Gendler's and Priest's stories? The answer is quite obvious: the consequentialist's fiction is designed to be consistent; Gendler's and Priest's aren't. Whenever we make-believe in a consistent fiction, accepting a proposition commits us to accepting its logical consequences.

Getting back to moral fictionalism, the question we need to ask is really "Should we make-believe a consistent moral fiction?" And the answer is that we very probably should. The consequentialist fiction needs to be consistent, for it would fail to meet its purpose if it were not—accepting an inconsistent set of principles is likely to have undesirable effects. Of a pair of inconsistent principles, this would always leave us with the option to pick that which aligns best with our personal interests, whatever the overall consequences. In the same way, the error theorist's moral fiction must be consistent if it is to meet the desideratum that it allow for moral reasoning. A fiction in which it could be true that killing animals is wrong, that if killing animals is wrong then eating meat is wrong, and yet that eating meat is not wrong, would leave this desideratum unsatisfied. In the end, the claim that a good answer to the now-what question would allow for moral reasoning cannot be mobilized against moral fictionalism. It implies only that moral make-believers should accept a consistent moral fiction.

6. The Disagreement Problem

Besides moral reasoning, a suitable answer to the now what question would allow for the existence of moral disagreement; it would not face the disagreement problem that is fatal to speaker subjectivism (Olson 2011: 186; Svoboda 2017: 60). Suppose I judge that killing animals is wrong while you judge that it is right. It is manifest that we disagree. But speaker subjectivism entails that we do not. On this view, my moral judgment amounts to the belief that I disapprove of killing animals, whereas your moral judgment amounts to the belief that you approve of killing animals. Our judgments are mutually consistent—they are both true provided that I do disapprove of killing animals and you do approve of it. So, speaker subjectivism cannot accommodate the existence of moral disagreement. This is the "disagreement problem."

As was the case with the inference problem, the issue is slightly different in the present context. Since answers to the now-what question are not in the business of describing the current moral practice, they need not accommodate the existence of moral disagreement in that practice. Still, it would be problematic should apparent moral disagreement turn out to be merely apparent in the revised moral practice. If it is to help us address and resolve our practical conflicts effectively, the revised moral practice had better allow us to articulate them in the first place. In the revised practice, you and I should have a genuine disagreement when I judge that killing animals is wrong and you judge that it is right. If we are thinking and talking past each other, as we are according to speaker subjectivism, we will be unable to address the issue that needs addressing.

Does moral fictionalism face the disagreement problem? Some philosophers think so. Olson imagines a dispute between a consequentialist named Con and a deontologist named Don, and makes the following observation:

> One leading thought in moral fictionalism is that to make moral judgements is to tell stories. In debating whether diverting the trolley is morally required or morally impermissible, Con and Don are thus engaging in story telling. But…they are telling different stories. Con tells a consequentialist story while Don tells a deontological story. But how does telling different stories amount to disagreement? We would not normally say that two storytellers who tell different stories are thereby disagreeing with one another.
> (Olson 2011: 187; see also Svoboda 2017: 61)

This objection explicitly rests on an analogy between moral make-believe and storytelling. If moral make-believe were a kind of storytelling, then there could be no moral disagreement in the fictional moral practice, for people who tell different stories do not disagree. But what if it were a different kind of make-believe?

Since the analogy with storytelling is misleading, consider a better one again, and imagine a dispute between two consequentialists. Connie judges that eating meat is wrong (except in life and death situations); Connor judges that it is permissible. Intuitively, they have a disagreement. Yet, their respective judgments are instances of make-believe rather than belief. When in everyday contexts, Connie accepts that eating meat is wrong and Connor accepts that eating meat is permissible; yet they are disposed to reject these rules when in the ethics classroom, where they accept only the general consequentialist principle. In contrast with storytellers, consequentialists do disagree when they make-believe mutually inconsistent propositions. Why is that? I believe the reason is that storytellers who make-believe mutually inconsistent propositions *ipso facto* engage with different fictions, whereas this need not be the case with consequentialists. Even though they disagree about the ethics of eating meat, Connie and Connor are both (supposedly) immersed in the moral fiction whose acceptance would produce the best consequences. Suppose killing animals is wrong in that fiction. Then, presumably Connie thinks that this implies that eating meat is wrong, whereas Connor doesn't. All the same, they make-believe the same moral fiction. This is enough for them to have a genuine disagreement.

If all this is correct and consequentialists can disagree within their moral fiction, then the same must be true *mutatis mutandis* of moral error theorists. Moral fictionalism allows for moral disagreement provided that we would all engage with the same moral fiction. In the end, the disagreement problem turns out to be not much of a problem. What we have instead is a reason for moral fictionalists to recommend the adoption of a unique moral fiction for all standard error theorists (Jaquet 2021: 46–7).

7. The Motivation Problem

In addition to moral reasoning and moral disagreement, there is a third feature of the current moral practice that seems worth preserving: moral motivation (Lutz 2014: 358; Svoboda 2017: 67). Even assuming the falsity of motivation internalism—even assuming, that is, that we are not necessarily motivated by our moral judgments—it remains true that, most of the time, most of us feel the pull to act in conformity with our beliefs about right and wrong. A satisfactory answer to the now-what question would retain this feature of moral judgments. Indeed, the kind of practical commitment involved in these attitudes brings us precious support in our fight against weakness of will. A revised practice made of motivationally inert attitudes would be powerless in front of *akrasia* and would therefore fail to fulfil one of its main functions. As it happens, some philosophers maintain that this is the case with the fictionalist moral practice. In their view, moral make-believe would simply lack the motivational force typical of moral belief. Call this the "motivation problem."

This is a front on which all competing teams unite against fictionalists. Here are a couple representative quotes (see also Garner 2007: 511; Cuneo & Christy 2011: 99; Hussain 2010: 341; Lutz 2014: 361; Olson 2014: 187; Isserow, Chapter 2; Moberger & Olson, Chapter 3).

> Although engaging with fictions can undoubtedly provoke emotional sensations, it is questionable whether those sensations engage our motivations like

real emotions. While we feel something like fear while watching a scary movie, this sensation clearly lacks the motivational profile of real fear.
(Köhler & Ridge 2013: 442)

Make-belief sounds a bit feeble for the kind of attitude which morality, on the surface, demands. Make-belief is, after all, a highly overridable attitude. Whenever we make-believe something we are primed to abandon the attitude if reality intrudes in a rude or demanding way, and it is entirely appropriate to be so primed. Suppose make-belief is the appropriate attitude of an audience to the propositions explicitly or implicitly true in a work of fiction—like a play one is attending. Suppose it is true in the play that two people are chatting comfortably on a couch in their home, and that their home is not on fire. As we get into the play, we make-believe that that is true. Now, if smoke starts seeping onto the stage from backstage but it is clearly true, in the play, that there is no smoke in the room, we tend in such circumstances to abandon the make-belief (that there is no smoke in the room) and go with the belief (that there is smoke), and it is entirely reasonable to do so. When push comes to practical shove, make-belief will rightly give way to genuine belief. (Oddie & Demetriou 2007: 487)

Long story short: moral belief may well have the binding force required to bolster self-control against the temptations of short-term profit, but this force would be lost in the transition to moral make-believe.

Just like with the previous two problems, I think it is no accident that, in both quotes, the criticism is phrased in the way it is, one that appeals to a comparison with attitudes typical of fictional engagement. The make-believe we engage in as a response to a movie or a play does not move us as the equivalent beliefs would, and it tends to fade when its presence runs against our interests—these are the dimensions of action tendency and stake sensitivity that we met in section 4. Be that as it may, the objection is much less convincing as soon as it is considered through the lens of more felicitous analogies. I will stick to the example of consequentialism. In terms of motivational pull too, the consequentialist's make-believe is much more akin to proper belief than it is to engagement with a movie or a play. Provided that consequentialists have selected a certain principle in the critical context of their philosophical reflections, they will feel just as motivated to act in accordance with it in the circumstances of everyday deliberation as if they believed it. In this less critical context, they will accept that killing is wrong and that one should keep one's promises, and these states of acceptance will motivate them not to kill and to keep their promises.

This should come as no surprise, upon reflection. For moral belief and make-believe differ only as to what they dispose us to do in our most critical contexts—respectively, accepting and rejecting their content. In the ethics classroom, a true believer will hold fast to the rule that killing is always wrong, whereas a consequentialist will reject it in favor of the more general principle that one should do whatever produces the best outcome. As far as less critical contexts are concerned, moral belief and make-believe dispose us to the exact same attitude towards their content: acceptance. When they deliberate about what to do, the true believer and the consequentialist will therefore be indistinguishable; they will accept the rule that killing is always wrong in the exact same manner. Accordingly, the consequentialist's habit of make-believe will have just as much motivational force as an equivalent belief. But, then, the same should be true of error theorists who would follow the fictionalist's advice to make-believe moral propositions. In everyday contexts, they will accept moral propositions in the same way that consequentialists make-believe simple moral principles, and they will be just as motivated by their make-believe. Crucially, these are the contexts in which we need the motivational pull afforded by moral attitudes. It is in the everyday circumstances of practical deliberation that we need the support of moral make-believe to neutralize the threat of temptation. All this indicates that the motivational pull of moral belief would not be lost in the transition to moral make-believe.

Moral make-believe would motivate us no less than moral belief as long as we occupy a non-critical context. That is already something. But wouldn't we run the risk of slipping into a critical context whenever the stakes are high? Victor Moberger and Jonas Olson raise this issue with a thought experiment:

> Suppose you are in a position to steal a philanthropist's entire fortune without any risk whatsoever of getting caught. You start to visualize the private jet, the yacht, and the Lamborghini. Something gives you pause, however: "It would be *wrong* to steal the fortune," you think to yourself, "especially since it is continuously being used for humanitarian purposes." Another thought might instantly appear: "But wait, morality is just a story! It isn't *really* wrong to steal the money. So why not?"...Thus, in order for moral thought and talk to be motivationally efficacious, morality's status as a mere story has to be suppressed.
>
> (Moberger & Olson, Chapter 3 of this volume)

High stakes tend to lure us into critical contexts, ones in which we question the assumption that there are moral truths and naturally remember our commitment to the moral error theory. When that happens, we stop accepting moral propositions and lose the motivational support that comes with them.

Once again, it seems to me that the reliance on the lexicon of narration is not innocent. Surely, if you think of the moral fiction as "just a story," you will emerge from your fictional engagement whenever your interests are at stake. The objection loses much of its plausibility, however, if we consider instead the case of consequentialists. Insofar as they manage to cultivate a strong disposition to accept the moral rules whose acceptance produces good consequences, consequentialists will not easily slip into the more critical contexts in which they question the truth of these rules and think only in terms of best outcomes. Not that they won't ever appeal to consequences in their deliberation—they will if encountering very solid evidence that sticking to the fiction on this occasion would have suboptimal effects. Such cases will no doubt occur from time to time, but they will constitute the exception rather than the rule. Their existence lends little support to the claim that consequentialists are never motivated by their fictional engagement.

To drive the point home: assuming that the error theorist's moral make-believe would be psychologically similar to the consequentialist's, it should be no more prone to evaporate when morality becomes demanding. With some rare exceptions, error theorists would keep accepting moral propositions in those circumstances. And their moral make-believe would motivate them, to some extent at least.

8. The Irrationality Problem

Fictionalism escapes all the above objections because moral make-believe resembles belief much more than the usual analogies with storytelling, immersion in fiction, and games of make-believe suggest. Considering the strong resemblance moral make-believe bears to moral belief, one might even think that fictionalism is ultimately identical to conservationism, the view that we should go on believing moral propositions (Jaquet & Naar 2016). As a matter of fact, both views recommend that we keep accepting moral propositions in everyday circumstances but reject them in the more critical contexts where we question the existence of moral truths. The fictionalist calls this double disposition "make-believe," whereas the conservationist thinks of it as "belief." More than this: conservationists sometimes appeal to the very same analogies that I have mobilized in support of fictionalism. Olson, for example, argues that we should accept moral propositions just as the consequentialist accepts the moral principles whose acceptance has the best effects. Only, he describes the consequentialist's attitude towards these principles as belief rather than make-believe (Olson 2014: 192). In substance, fictionalists and conservationists put forward the same recommendation.

In and of itself, this is not a problem for moral fictionalism. Looking on the bright side, it might even mean good news—after all, if we take conservationists into account, fictionalism turns out to have more supporters (including in this volume). This comes with a worry, though. If fictionalism can avoid the problems that it was thought to face because it is indistinguishable from conservationism, then chances are that it will now face the problems associated with conservationism. Just when we thought we had made progress...

The main obstacle to conservationism is that it seems irrational to hold beliefs that one believes to be false (Husi 2014: 88; Lutz 2014: 355; Svoboda 2017: 57). Part of the problem pertains to epistemology: it seems like an obvious epistemic truth that we should not believe propositions against which we have strong overall evidence, and moral error theorists believe that they have strong overall evidence against moral propositions. But the problem is also partly prudential. Believing moral propositions against which we have strong evidence—so strong indeed that we believe that these propositions are false—could lead us to slip onto a slope; it could lead us to relax our evidential standards for belief too much. Over time, we would be likely to adopt all sorts of irrational beliefs, including ones that would prove detrimental to our welfare (Joyce 2001: 178–9). Let us call this the "irrationality problem."

Does fictionalism face the irrationality problem? I think not. And I think the reason that it doesn't indicates that the attitudes that fictionalists and conservationists advise us to adopt towards moral propositions are best characterized as make-believe. To begin with, notice that it is not irrational to be disposed to accept some propositions in certain contexts and yet reject them in more critical contexts. This is quite clear if we consider cases of make-believe that are most distant from typical beliefs—cases involving storytelling, engagement with fiction, and games of make-believe. There is nothing irrational about accepting, for the duration of the movie, that Arthur Fleck lives with his mother, while remaining disposed to reject this proposition outside the context of fictional engagement. But the same observation applies to more controversial cases of make-believe, those that resemble belief to a much greater extent—of course, I am thinking here of the more adequate analogies I have relied on throughout this chapter. Consequentialists, for instance, do not indulge in irrationality when they accept simple and workable principles in everyday life that they are nonetheless disposed to reject in the ethics classroom.

This observation is good news for fictionalists on two counts. First, it establishes quite directly that they escape the irrationality problem—if it is rational for consequentialists to accept moral rules that they reject in critical contexts, why would it be irrational for moral error theorists to accept moral propositions that they reject in critical contexts? Second, it means that fictionalists are correct when they label the attitude they recommend "make-believe" rather than "belief." The reason is straightforward: it is always epistemically irrational to believe both a proposition and its negation. Accordingly, if being disposed to accept a proposition in non-critical contexts and its negation in more critical contexts amounted to believing both the proposition and its negation, then it would always be irrational to be so disposed. But we have just seen that it is sometimes rational to have that double disposition. It follows that being disposed to accept a proposition in non-critical contexts and its negation in more critical contexts does not amount to believing both the proposition and its negation. It amounts to make-believing the proposition.

Wait a minute. Perhaps fictionalists cannot escape the irrationality problem so easily. Even if the attitudes they recommend are not irrational because they are not beliefs, maybe they could, one thing leading to another, result in irrational attitudes. This would be the case if moral make-believers constantly risked slipping into full-blown moral belief, a hypothesis that has been defended most forcefully by Olson (Olson 2011; Olson 2014: 189; Eriksson & Olson 2019: 120; Moberger & Olson, Chapter 3 of this volume):

> Imagine that a moral fictionalist has been trusted with some private information by a friend. Imagine also that the fictionalist realizes that were she to break the promise not to reveal this information to third parties, she can make personal gains. Still, she might not be at all inclined to break the promise. Given her moral precommitment and her concern for her friend it does not seem unrealistic that this is partly because she has slipped into believing that breaking the promise would be wrong. But by the lights of moral fictionalism, this would amount to a failure on her part, for moral beliefs are to be avoided.
> (Olson 2014: 189)

The same rejoinder that we mobilized against other objections applies here too. Olson would be right if make-believe were to be understood in the strict sense that applies to common engagement with fiction. As we have seen in the previous section, such engagement does not have the motivational pull that is typical of moral beliefs. If our fictionalist's attitude to the proposition *One ought to keep one's promises* motivates her to keep her promise, then it is no longer make-believe in this restricted sense. For all that, it need not have slipped into something else. Maybe it was, all along, an instance of make-believe in the broader sense in which fictionalists use the term. Olson's objection is indeed much less powerful as soon as we consider fictionalism in the light of better analogies. Consequentialists are motivated to keep their promises by their acceptance of the principle that one always ought to keep one's promises, yet they remain disposed to reject this principle in their more critical contexts. They never slip into full-blown belief in this principle. By the same token, it is unclear why moral make-believers would risk slipping into moral belief just because they accept moral propositions most of the time.

9. Conclusion

Once misleading analogies for moral make-believe are discarded and moral fictionalism is understood correctly, it appears clear that it has the resources needed to solve the inference problem, the disagreement problem, and the motivation problem. Furthermore, fictionalism does not face the irrationality problem that afflicts conservationism, for the attitudes it recommends are best described as make-believe, and it is a distinctive feature of this kind of attitude that there is nothing irrational about make-believing a proposition one believes to be false. Pending a better objection, fictionalism looks like a fine answer to the now-what question.[5]

---

[5] I would like to thank Richard Joyce and Stuart Brock for inviting me to be part of this volume and for their very helpful feedback on several drafts of this chapter.

References

Cuneo, T. & Christy, S. 2011. "The myth of moral fictionalism." In M. Brady (ed.), *New Waves in Metaethics*. Palgrave Macmillan. 85–102.

Dain, E. 2012. "Projection and pretence in ethics." *Philosophical Papers* 41: 181–208.

Eklund, M. 2007. "Fictionalism." In E. Zalta (ed.), *Stanford Encyclopedia of Philosophy*. <https://plato.stanford.edu/entries/fictionalism/>.

Eriksson, B. & Olson, J. 2019. "Moral practice after error theory: Negotiationism." In R. Garner & R. Joyce (eds.), *The End of Morality: Taking Moral Abolitionism Seriously*. Routledge. 113–30.

Garner, R. 2007. "Abolishing morality." *Ethical Theory and Moral Practice* 10: 499–513.

Gendler, T. 2000. "The puzzle of imaginative resistance." *Journal of Philosophy* 97: 55–81.

Husi, S. 2014. "Against moral fictionalism." *Journal of Moral Philosophy* 11: 80–96.

Hussain, N. 2010. "Error theory and fictionalism." In J. Skorupski (ed.), *The Routledge Companion to Ethics*. Routledge. 335–45.

Jaquet, F. 2020. "Sorting out solutions to the now-what problem." *Journal of Ethics & Social Philosophy* 17: 239–58.

Jaquet, F. 2021. "Utilitarianism for the error theorist." *Journal of Ethics* 25: 39–55.

Jaquet, F. & Naar, H. 2016. "Moral beliefs for the error theorist?" *Ethical Theory and Moral Practice* 19: 193–207.

Joyce, R. 2001. *The Myth of Morality*. Cambridge University Press.

Joyce, R. 2007. "Morality, schmorality." In P. Bloomfield (ed.), *Morality and Self-Interest*. Oxford University Press. 51–75.

Joyce, R. 2016. "Moral fictionalism." In his *Essays in Moral Skepticism*. Oxford University Press. 219–39.

Joyce, R. 2017. "Fictionalism in metaethics." In T. McPherson & D. Plunkett (eds.), *Routledge Handbook of Metaethics*. Routledge. 72–86.

Joyce, R. 2019. "Moral fictionalism: How to have your cake and eat it too." In R. Garner & R. Joyce (eds.), *The End of Morality: Taking Moral Abolitionism Seriously*. Routledge. 150–65.

Köhler, S. & Ridge, M. 2013. "Revolutionary expressivism." *Ratio* 26: 428–49.

Lenman, J. 2013. "Ethics without errors." *Ratio* 26: 391–409.

Lutz, M. 2014. "The 'now what' problem for error theory." *Philosophical Studies* 171: 351–71.

Nolan, D., Restall, G., & West, C. 2005. "Moral fictionalism versus the rest." *Australasian Journal of Philosophy* 83: 307–30.

Oddie, G. & Demetriou, D. 2007. "The fictionalist's attitude problem." *Ethical Theory and Moral Practice* 10: 485–98.

Olson, J. 2011. "Getting real about moral fictionalism." In R. Shafer-Landau (ed.), *Oxford Studies in Metaethics*, Vol. 6. Oxford University Press. 181–204.

Olson, J. 2014. *Moral Error Theory: History, Critique, Defence*. Oxford University Press.

Priest, G. 1997. "Sylvan's box: A short story and ten morals." *Notre Dame Journal of Formal Logic* 38: 573–82.

Svoboda, T. 2017. "Why moral error theorists should become revisionary moral expressivists." *Journal of Moral Philosophy* 14: 48–72.

Walton, K. L. 1990. *Mimesis as Make-Believe: On the Foundations of the Representational Arts*. Harvard University Press.

5
Religious Fictionalism

Graham Oppy

1. Religious Error Theory

One straightforward error-theoretic treatment says that key terms and primitive predicates of religious language are empty. Atheists who adopts this approach will claim that "God" has no referent and "…is omnipotent" has null extension. While there are other theoretical options, Quineans of this persuasion will claim that atomic sentences framed using these key terms and predicates—for example, "God is omnipotent"—are false.

No one who wishes to give an error-theoretic account of religious language will believe atomic religious claims. Of course, such people might have various kinds of reasons for uttering the sentence "God is omnipotent." However, no knowledgeable, sympathetic interpreters will take these people to believe that God is omnipotent. Perhaps, for example, in context, what they are saying is that according to religious believers, God is omnipotent. Or perhaps, in context, they are pretending to be religious believers and so are merely pretending to believe that God is omnipotent.

A corresponding straightforward realist treatment says that key terms and primitive predicates of religious language are not empty. Theists who adopt this approach will claim that "God" has a referent, and "…is omnipotent" has a non-null extension. (Of course, theists vary over which primitive predicates of religious language apply to God. Not all theists agree that God is omnipotent. However, for the sake of having a simple example, it will do no harm here to pretend that theists are all committed to divine omnipotence.) People of this persuasion will claim that some atomic sentences framed using the key terms and predicates—for example, "God is omnipotent"—are true. At least in a significant range of contexts, when people of this persuasion utter the words "God is omnipotent," they are properly taken to believe that God is omnipotent.

Setting agnosticism aside, one might be tempted to think that there are no further options for the interpretation of atomic religious sentences. In other domains, there are noncognitivist positions: expressivism, emotivism, norm-expressivism, imperativism, prescriptivism, quasi-realism, and their ilk. However, nothing of this sort is at all plausible for the interpretation of atomic religious sentences. Braithwaite (1955) does claim that atomic religious sentences are declarations of commitment to a way of life. But, apart from the implausibility of the claim that "God is omnipotent" is a declaration of commitment to a way of life, the view seems to founder on the impossibility of assigning distinct declarations to all of the different atomic religious sentences. Since they obviously mean different things, it cannot be that "God is omnipotent" and "God is omniscient" make the same declaration of commitment to a religious way of life. But, if they make different declarations, that is presumably because they declare different commitments. And the same is true for all of the other independent atomic religious sentences. Moreover, even if there are enough different declarations of commitments to a religious way of life, it is hard to see how those different declarations are systematically linked to the atomic religious sentences that are properly said to express them.

Plausibly, agnostics will suspend judgment between realist and error-theoretic approaches to the key terms and primitive predicates of religious language. That is, agnostics will be undecided whether "God" has a referent that lies in the non-null extension of "…is omnipotent," etc. Moreover, while agnostics may have various kinds of reasons for uttering the words "God is omnipotent," no knowledgeable, sympathetic interpreters will take such people to believe that God is omnipotent. Like realists, agnostics might pretend or make-believe that they are theists; but, if they do so, these utterances of "God is omnipotent" are not expressions of their belief that God is omnipotent.

2. Fictionalism

In general, we can think of fictionalism as a response to error theory (or—though I shall largely stop mentioning this possibility from here on—suspension of judgment with respect to error theory). Granted that the atomic sentences of a discourse are all false, it might be tempting to suppose that we could have no further use for that discourse. But, of course, fictions provide a paradigm example of discourse in which there are empty terms: "Christian Moosbrugger," "Gloria Munde," "Slartibartfast," and so on. What matters, in this case, is that we find value in the production and consumption of fiction even though the atomic sentences of fictional discourse are straightforwardly false.

There are many domains about which we might be fictionalists. The obvious advantage of error theory about the atomic sentences in a domain of discourse is that we avoid theoretical commitment to referents for the terms in that discourse, or to extensions for the predicates of that discourse, or both. However, an obvious disadvantage of error theory about the atomic sentences in a domain of discourse is the loss of benefits that we obtain via the production and consumption of those atomic sentences. The promise of fictionalism about the atomic sentences of a domain of discourse is that we can be error theorists about those atomic sentences while continuing to enjoy benefits that we obtain from their production and consumption.

Consider numbers. If we think that there are no numbers, then—on a straightforward account—we shall suppose that it is false that $2+2=4$. But there are many situations in which we make use of arithmetic in the course of our lives—for example, when engaging in financial transactions. One strategy for reconciling error theory and continuing use in this case is to argue that number talk is in principle dispensable: there is no claim in purely non-number talk that can be arrived at through a detour via number talk that could not, at least in principle, be arrived at without the detour through number talk. If this is so, then it is fine for us to go on using number talk even if we think that there are no numbers. Adopting the number fiction simplifies our lives: in practice, we would be much worse off if we abandoned number talk. But—according to mathematical fictionalists—we can continue to use number talk in good conscience while supposing that there are no numbers. (See, for example, Field 1980; Leng 2010; Yablo 2005.)

Consider electrons. If we think that there are no electrons, then—on a straightforward account—much of our fundamental physics and chemistry is just false. But there are many situations in which scientists and engineers make use of electron talk in the course of their working lives. One strategy for reconciling error theory and continuing use in this case is to argue that electron talk has no more than instrumental justification: while it enables us to make accurate predictions about future observations, this is not a sufficient reason for being realists about electron talk. Or, at any rate, so scientific instrumentalists and constructive empiricists are wont to claim. On their view, it is fine for us to accept and positively evaluate electron talk, even though we do not believe that there are electrons. (See, for example, Vaihinger 1924; Van Fraassen 1980.)

It is tempting to generalize. If we want to support a move away from realism about some domain of atomic discourse for which error theory and fictionalism are the plausible alternatives—or even if we are merely undecided about whether we want to support a move away from realism about some domain of atomic discourse for which error theory and fictionalism are the plausible alternatives—then, if we are to defend fictionalism, we need to have a satisfying story to tell about (1) the value that is, or the values that are, obtained by turning to fictionalism and (2) how it is that fictionalism secures that value, or those values.

3. Religious Fictionalism

There has been a recent surge of interest in religious fictionalism. At least roughly, following Stuart Brock (2020), we might think about "standard" religious fictionalism in the following way. The doctrines of particular religions entail truth-apt claims about supernatural realms. Fictionalists about the doctrinal claims of a particular religion (1) do not believe those claims; but (2) accept those claims and evaluate them positively; and (3) participate fully in prescribed practices and rituals of the religion in question.

Brock claims that his account of religious fictionalism is an account in terms of religious faith: to accept and positively evaluate a religious claim that p just is to have faith that p. So, on Brock's account, fictionalists about the doctrinal claims of a particular religion (1) do not believe those claims, but (2) have propositional faith in those claims; and (3) participate fully in prescribed practices and rituals.

It is not clear that we should accept Brock's account of (religious) faith. Compare the account of Daniel Howard-Snyder (2019): roughly, S has faith that p iff (1) S does not disbelieve that p; (2) S has [positive, evidence-sensitive attitude] that p; (3) S has [positive conative-evaluative attitude] that p; (4) S lives in the light of (2) and (3); and (5) S's living in the light of (2) and (3) is resilient to challenges. Whether Brock's account of (religious) faith is thought to be sufficiently "thick" will plausibly depend upon exactly what it is taken to be sufficient for "acceptance and positive evaluation" of religious claims.

It is also not clear, on Brock's account, exactly what are the values to be obtained by turning to religious fictionalism; hence, it is further not clear how turning to religious fictionalism secures those values. One thought is that the most important values are just the values of participating fully in prescribed practices and rituals. Another thought is that the most important values are the values of possessing religious faith. And a third thought is that both of these kinds of values—the values of participating fully in prescribed practices and rituals, and the values afforded by possession of religious faith—are equally important values attained by those who turn to religious fictionalism.

The decision to be made here seems likely to have implications for the question whether there could be *original* religious fictionalism: could there be religions in which, across the entire history of the religion, every participant is a religious fictionalist? On the plausible assumption that there could not be religions whose entire content is just its practices and rituals, it seems that taking value for religious fictionalists to lie entirely in the values of participating fully in prescribed practices and rituals yields the conclusion that there could not be original religious fictionalism. If this is so, then it marks an interesting point of contrast with fictionalism about numbers or electrons. Taking the values of engaging in arithmetic and scientific practice to lie entirely in simplification of financial transactions and production of computationally tractable predictions of future observations is entirely consistent with original fictionalism about numbers and electrons.

Suppose, instead, that we take the values to be secured by religious fictionalism to be the values of possessing religious faith. On the plausible assumption that there could not be religions whose entire content is just the having of faith in that very religion, it seems that taking the value for religious fictionalists to lie entirely in the values of having religious faith yields the conclusion that there could not be original religious fictionalism.

Suppose, finally, that we take the values to be secured by religious fictionalism to be the twin values of possessing religious faith and participating fully in prescribed practices and rituals. On the plausible assumption that there could not be religions whose entire content is just a combination of practices, rituals, and the having of religious faith, it seems that taking the value for religious fictionalists to lie entirely in the values of having religious faith and participating fully in prescribed rituals and practices yields the conclusion that there could not be original religious fictionalism.

Since it is open to religious fictionalists to provide some other account of the value of religious fictionalism, the argument sketched here hardly establishes that there cannot be original religious fictionalism. However, this discussion does suggest that it is worth thinking about the contrast between *original* fictionalism and *parasitic* fictionalism. If something like the above line of thought could be carried through, then we would have reason to suppose that religious fictionalism requires, at least originally, a non-fictionalist host.

The distinction that I have drawn between original and parasitic fictionalism might be taken to suggest further distinctions. It is one question whether a species of fictionalism at least originally requires a non-fictionalist host; it is a quite different question whether a species of fictionalism requires a *current* non-fictionalist host. Even if there could not be a religion in which all of the participants throughout its entire history have been fictionalists, it might be that there are religions all of whose current participants are fictionalists.

In the literature, there is a familiar distinction between hermeneutic and revolutionary fictionalism (see the Introduction to this volume). Hermeneutic fictionalists undertake to provide an accurate *description* of what those currently engaged in a particular discourse are doing. Revolutionary fictionalists offer, to those who have come to doubt or deny the truth of the atomic statements of a particular discourse, a *prescription* for what they should now do. It seems that hermeneutic fictionalists could suppose that their description applies to everyone who has ever engaged in the discourse in question, but that they need not do so. If this is right, then hermeneutic fictionalism can crosscut the distinction between original and parasitic fictionalism. On the other hand, given that revolutionary fictionalists suppose that there was a time when many participants in a discourse were not fictionalists, it seems that revolutionary fictionalism can only be parasitic.

In order to think about whether religious fictionalism requires a *current* non-fictional host, we need to think about the goods that are taken to be attendant on participation in religion. And, in order to think about the goods that are taken to be attendant on participation in religion, we need to think a bit about the nature of religion.

4. Religion

The nature of religion is hotly contested. While, in ordinary discourse, we take it for granted that there are many different religions that have risen and fallen across the course of human history, there is significant skepticism, in some parts of the academy, about whether we should persist with talk about "religion" and "religions." I do not propose to examine this controversy here; instead, I shall simply offer an account of religion, and then consider what the consequences of this account might be for collective religious fictionalism. The account that I give is adapted from Scott Atran (2002). In his hands, it is a stipulative account. I hope that it can be something more than that.

At least roughly: *religions* are passionate communal displays of costly commitments to the satisfaction of non-natural causal beings—gods or ancestor spirits—and/or the overcoming of non-natural causal regulative structures—reincarnation and karmic reward—that result from evolutionary canalization and convergence of: (1) widespread belief in non-natural causal agents and/or non-natural causal regulative structures; (2) hard-to-fake public expressions of costly material commitments—offerings and/or sacrifices of goods, property, time, and/or life—to the satisfaction of those non-natural causal agents and/or the overcoming of, or escape from, those non-natural causal regulative structures; (3) mastering of people's existential anxieties—about death, deception, disease, catastrophe, pain, loneliness, injustice, want, loss, and so forth—by those costly commitments; and (4) ritualized, rhythmic, sensory coordination of all of the above in communion, congregation, intimate fellowship, and the like. Given what religions are, there are many importantly different dimensions to religion, including: (a) doctrines (theories, teachings, creeds); (b) behaviors and practices; (c) hierarchies; (d) institutions and organizations; (e) codes; (f) service; (g) leaders; (h) sacred objects and sites; and (i) oral and/or written records. Religious behaviors and practices take in, for example, art, dance, feasts, festivals, funerary rites, initiations, marriage ceremonies, meditation, music, prayer, rituals, sacrifices, sermons, trances, and veneration.

For our current purposes, the important features to pick out from this account are: (1) widespread belief in non-natural causal agents and/or non-natural causal regulative structures; (2) hard-to-fake public expressions of costly material commitments to the satisfaction of those non-natural causal agents and/or the overcoming of, or escape from, those non-natural causal regulative structures; and (3) mastering of people's existential anxieties by those costly commitments. In an important sense, the most fundamental part of the story is the mastering of existential anxieties: it is essential to the development and continuation of religions that they enable followers to deal with their emotionally eruptive existential anxieties about death, deception, etc. How religions enable people to do this is a complex tale, partly concerned with fostering certain kinds of beliefs, and partly concerned with markings of identity—including hard-to-fake public expressions of costly commitments—that facilitate in-group identification. In turn, the story about what facilitates the fostering of supernatural belief is another complex tale, the details of which are still much debated in current cognitive science of religion.

As I noted above, this account of religion is controversial. However, even if you are not inclined to accept it, you may be interested in the possible consequences of an account of religion of this kind for proposed kinds of religious fictionalism. (For a not altogether different account of religion, see Crane (2017): his "religious impulse" and "identification" map reasonably well onto "fostering belief" and "marking... that facilitates in-group identification.")

5. Original Religious Fictionalism

Suppose that it is true that it is essential to the development and continuation of religions that they enable adherents to deal with their emotionally eruptive existential anxieties about catastrophe, death, deception, disability, disease, injustice, loneliness, loss, pain, suffering, and want. It is, at the very least, intelligible how (1) belief in non-natural causal agents and/or non-natural causal regulative structures, in combination with (2) hard-to-fake public expressions of costly commitments to the satisfaction of those non-natural agents and/or the overcoming of, or escape from, those non-natural causal regulative structures, and (3) ritualized, rhythmic, sensory coordination of the above in communion, congregation, and fellowship, enables adherents to deal with the emotionally eruptive existential anxieties. However, it seems doubtful that it is so much as intelligible that mere make-believe that there are—or mere pretense that there are, or mere acting as if there are, or mere acceptance that there are—non-natural causal agents and/or non-natural causal regulative structures, even when combined with the other operative factors, could enable adherents to deal with the specified emotionally eruptive existential anxieties.

Consider death. It is easy to see how, for example, having the *belief* that we go to be with the gods or the ancestors when we die can enable us to deal with emotionally eruptive existential anxieties about death. If we believe that we will have good, unending lives after death then, very plausibly, we are better placed to manage anxieties about death than those who believe that death is total annihilation. However, if we are plagued by emotionally eruptive existential anxiety about death, it is hard to see how taking fictionalist approaches towards the claim that we will have good, unending lives after death will be of any assistance in managing that anxiety. Mere engagement in make-believe, or pretense, or acting-as-if seems hopeless: if we are genuinely anxious about death, then, for example, merely pretending that we are going to live forever is not up to the job of quieting that anxiety. Of course, engagement in make-believe, or pretense, or acting-as-if, offers *distraction* while we are engaged in the make-believe, or pretense, or acting-as-if. But, once we step back from the make-believe, or pretense, or acting-as-if, the temporary solace offered by distraction simply disappears. Moreover, it seems that the same is true for mere acceptance, given that acceptance is an attitude that falls short of belief: if we believe that there is no more than a 50/50 chance that we shall live forever, then, in contexts in which this belief is salient, it is hard to see how existential anxiety about death is going to be silenced or even diminished by our "accepting" that we shall live forever. (I assume here that acceptance has no effect on credence: fictionalist acceptance that you will live forever does not boost the credence that you give to the claim that you will live forever above 0.5.) If we merely accept—but do not believe—that we will live forever, then, in contexts in which we pay attention to what we do and do not believe, the anxiety will simply flood back in.

Suppose catastrophe strikes. It is not too hard to see how, for example, having the belief that we go to a much better, non-catastrophic, future with the gods or the ancestors when we die may help us to deal with the kind of suffering that typically follows in the wake of catastrophe. However, it is hard to see how taking a fictionalist stance towards the claim that we go to a much better, non-catastrophic, future with the gods or the ancestors when we die offers any similar assistance. Mere engagement in make-believe, or pretense, or acting-as-if seems hopeless: if we are suffering in the wake of catastrophe, then, for example, merely pretending that we have a future in heaven is not up to the job of even beginning to relieve our suffering (considerations about distraction aside). And, as in the case of death, the same seems true for mere acceptance, given that acceptance is an attitude that falls short of belief. Thinking that there is a no more than 50/50 chance that we have a future in heaven is no kind of rod on which to lean when we are victims of catastrophe.

Perhaps it might be objected that some emotionally eruptive existential anxieties can be managed by mere community membership. Consider loneliness. If I am an accepted and valued member of a community, then the odds are pretty good that I will not be the victim of corrosive loneliness. A religious fictionalist who is genuinely accepted into a religious community has a buffer against loneliness and, plausibly, some community resources for dealing with at least some kinds of deception, disability, disease, injustice, loss, pain, suffering, and want. However, it is not clear that this is any kind of recommendation for religious fictionalism. After all, a (non-fictionalist) religious non-believer who is genuinely accepted into a religious community has exactly the same buffer against deception, disability, disease, injustice, loss, pain, suffering, and want. Moreover, this is also true for a (non-fictionalist) religious non-believer who is genuinely accepted into a *non-religious* community. We should not think that the generic goods of community membership are the goods that motivate and justify religious fictionalism.

(There are interesting questions about genuine acceptance into religious communities. For example, should we suppose that religious communities are more likely to genuinely accept religious fictionalists than they are to accept (non-fictionalist) religious non-believers? If you are not a religious believer, and you are looking for genuine community acceptance in a religious community, should you prefer religious communities that are equally open to religious fictionalist and non-believers above those who give preferential treatment to religious fictionalists? Is there reason to suppose that religious non-believers are more likely than religious fictionalists to need to deceive religious believers about their cognitive attitudes in order to gain "acceptance" in religious communities? I do not propose to investigate these kinds of questions here.)

Once we distinguish between the kinds of goods that are unique to religion and the kinds of goods that are also on offer from other sources, it seems plausible to think that the goods that are unique to religion are no more available to religious fictionalists than they are to (non-fictionalist) religious non-believers. But, if this is right, then it seems unlikely that religions could be launched solely by religious fictionalists; *and* it seems implausible that religions could be sustained solely by religious fictionalists. Perhaps it might be said that, for example, scientology provides a contemporary counterexample. Nevertheless, even if it is accepted that scientology is a religion, it must be remembered that (a) according to scientology, we are immortal spiritual beings destined for heavenly union with God and (b) many scientologists *believe* these teachings of scientology. I think that there is no plausible historical example of a religion launched and sustained by religious fictionalists. Moreover, there are many historical examples of attempts to launch secular substitutes for religion that have floundered in short order: Chaumette's cult of reason, Comte's religion of humanity, Evans' Sunday Assembly, and so forth. While there are other reasons that these secular ventures have all had no more than a very fleeting presence, I think it is plausible that a significant common factor is their inability to deliver the belief-based benefits that are unique to religion.

6. Parasitic Religious Fictionalism

There is an extensive literature on parasitic religious fictionalism. *Pro*: Brock 2020; Deng 2015, 2019, 2020; Eshleman 2005, 2010, 2016; Hesse 2020; Jay 2014, 2016; Kitcher 2016; Klassen 2012; Le Poidevin 1996, 2016, 2019; Lipton 2007; Robson 2015; Sauchelli 2018; Stone 2012; van Leeuwen 2014; and Wettstein 2012. *Contra*: Blackburn 2007; Cordry 2010; Dennett 2016; Đurković 2016; Ekstrom 2015; Gäb 2020; Malcolm 2018; Malcolm & Scott 2017; Palmqvist 2019; Park 2021; Pouivet 2011; Scott 2020; and Scott & Malcolm 2018. (No doubt I have missed some pieces.)

In the literature on parasitic religious fictionalism, there is a division between (a) approaches that take religious fictionalism to involve engaging in make-believe, or pretense, or acting as-if in carefully chosen contexts (Deng, Sauchelli), (b) approaches that take religious fictionalism to involve engaging in make-believe, or pretense, or acting as-if in all contexts (Đurković), and (c) approaches that take religious fictionalism to involve nondoxastic acceptance of religious claims in all but "critical" contexts (everyone else).

On the approach that takes religious fictionalism to involve engaging in make-believe, or pretense, or acting as-if in carefully chosen contexts, it is assumed that religious fictionalists have local, context-specific reasons for engaging in the relevant forms of make-believe, or pretense, or acting as-if. Andrea Sauchelli suggests, roughly, that those reasons might concern one's desire to understand, or to engage with, religious art. Natalja Deng canvasses a wider range of reasons: wanting to walk in the world of the religious story one treasures, or wishing to exercise certain capacities, or wanting to have certain kinds of inspiration, or wishing to give expression to certain kinds of heartfelt wishes for oneself and others, and so forth. While, as Deng notes, one might raise objections to this kind of "dipping in" because of reservations that one has about what is being dipped into, it seems that there are no serious barriers to understanding the possible attractions of this kind of dipping in. However, as Deng also notes, it is not clear that what is here under consideration is properly called "religious fictionalism." It feels a bit of a stretch to say that someone who dips into a Sherlock Holmes story in this way—for example, by tracing the London route that Holmes followed when engaged in the adventure of the speckled band—in order to walk in the world of a story they treasure is a "Sherlock Holmes fictionalist." Moreover, even if we suppose that we do count this as parasitic religious fictionalism, it is not clear that there are, or will be, religions in which there are many participants who are parasitic religious fictionalists of this kind.

On the approach that takes religious fictionalism to involve engaging in make-believe, or pretense, or acting as-if in *all* contexts, it is assumed that religious fictionalists are obsessive method actors: they remain at all times in character while never entirely forgetting that they are merely in character. As Nikola Đurković points out, it is not plausible that human beings can meet the psychological demands: method actors who remain in character for more than a couple of months tend to become highly mentally unstable. If it were conceivable that individual human beings could meet the psychological demands, then perhaps it would also be conceivable that collections of human beings could meet the psychological demands: but it is not at all clear that collections of human beings could have plausible motives for being "religious" method actors. After all, method acting is a means to a very particular end—namely, producing better performances on stage and screen. It is not at all plausible that method acting is the kind of thing that might be pursued in a whole-of-life context.

On the approach that takes religious fictionalism to involve nondoxastic acceptance of religious claims in all but "critical" contexts, it is assumed that we can make sense of "nondoxastic acceptance" and "critical context." In order to distinguish our religious fictionalist from a religious adherent who is subject to periods of doubt, we need to suppose that the "critical contexts" are normative for the religious fictionalist: they inform us about what the religious fictionalist really believes. There are two options: either the religious fictionalist really believes that there is no afterlife, or the religious fictionalist really suspends judgment on the question whether there is an afterlife. If the religious fictionalist really believes that there is no afterlife, then there is no plausible defense against emotionally eruptive existential anxiety about death in the fictionalist's nondoxastic acceptance of the claim that there is an afterlife. On the other hand, if the religious fictionalist merely suspends judgment on the question whether there is an afterlife, then matters are less straightforward. As I argued earlier, it will not be enough, to silence or even significantly rein in existential anxiety about death, for the religious fictionalist merely to hope that there is an afterlife. Perhaps it might be suggested that the religious fictionalist could have faith that there is an afterlife. But how could that be? Recall Howard-Snyder's account. In order to have faith that there is an afterlife, a religious fictionalist would need to: (1) not disbelieve that there is an afterlife; (2) have some positive, evidence-sensitive attitude that there is an afterlife; (3) have some positive conative attitude that there is an afterlife; (4) live in light of these attitudes; and (5) resiliently live in the light of these positive attitudes. But what, exactly, could the positive, evidence-based attitude that there is an afterlife be, other than some kind of weak belief that there is an afterlife? If our putative religious fictionalist *leans towards* the claim that there is an afterlife, then our putative religious fictionalist simply does not suspend judgment on the question of whether there is an afterlife. But, if this is right, then—if the religious fictionalist really does suspend judgment on the question of whether there is an afterlife—then there is no defense against emotionally eruptive existential anxiety about death in the fictionalist's nondoxastic acceptance of the claim that there is an afterlife.

While the argument here has gone rather quickly, it seems to me to be not implausible to suggest that, on a reasonably strict interpretation of what counts as fictionalism, the only potentially satisfying account of parasitic religious fictionalism is the "dipping in" account. It seems clear enough that there can be religious make-believe, or religious pretense, or religious acting as-if in carefully chosen contexts. But it is not plausible that "dipping in" can deliver the benefits whose delivery is fundamental to the existence of religion. And there is no alternative kind of "religious fictionalism" that plausibly offers the kinds of benefits that are uniquely conferred by full participation in religion.

7. Some Objections Considered

There are many objections that can be raised against what I have said to this point. I will try to address some of these objections here. Of course, there may be other—perhaps better—objections that I do not consider because I have not yet encountered them.

1. Even if you allow that there is no alternative that plausibly offers the kinds of benefits that are uniquely conferred by full participation in religion, you might claim that there is a long list of reasons that some might give to justify their fictionalist participation in a particular religion. You might think that fictionalist participation in religion can contribute towards a sense of self-worth and a sense of hope and optimism in decision and action. You might think that there are benefits to be gained from participating in a community that has at least one eye focused on goods that go beyond the goods of that particular community. You might think that there are benefits to be gained from engaging in prayer and meditation. You might think that there are benefits to be gained from participating in a community that has a sense of shared moral purpose, and, in particular, a commitment to justice and equality. You might think that there are benefits to be gained from participating in a community in which there is commitment to cultivation of particular virtues, such as humility, compassion, and concern for the least well-off. You might think that there are benefits to be gained from participating in a community in which there is commitment to the development of spirituality through engagement in the arts. And so on.

I think that the obvious question to ask in response to this kind of objection is: why suppose that being a *fictionalist* atheist or agnostic about the religion offers you advantages that you cannot have just by being a non-fictionalist atheist or agnostic about the religion? I do not see any benefits here that you could not obtain by being a non-fictionalist atheistic or agnostic member of the religious community. There is no reason that a non-fictionalist atheist or agnostic cannot make common cause with those who are committed to justice, equality, and the improvement of the lot of the worst off beyond the limits of their own community. There is no reason that a non-fictionalist atheist or agnostic cannot make common cause with those who are committed to developing virtues like humility and compassion. There is no reason that a non-fictionalist atheist or agnostic cannot make common cause with those who wish to develop heightened sensitivities through their engagement with the arts. There is no reason that a non-fictionalist atheist or agnostic who does make common cause in this way cannot develop the same kind of sense of self-worth and the same kind of sense of hope and optimism in decision and action. There is no reason that a non-fictionalist atheist or agnostic cannot engage in meditation or quiet reflection. There is no reason that a non-fictionalist agnostic, or even a less-than-certain non-fictionalist atheist, cannot engage in prayer. And so forth.

Moreover, there *are* costs to being a fictionalist atheist or agnostic that are not costs for mere atheists and agnostics. All else being equal, you should prefer that other people accept you for who you really are. If the commitment of the relevant religious community to the various things listed in the last paragraph is so thin that they are not prepared to make common cause with atheists and agnostics, then atheists and agnostics probably have good reason to reconsider whether the religious community is really one with which they should wish to make common cause. At the very least, there is a question here to which proponents of religious fictionalism might be encouraged to provide an answer: What are the goods that would be available to religious fictionalists but not to non-fictionalist atheists and agnostics who participate in a religious community in the way that I am now imagining? Non-fictionalist atheists and agnostics *may* eschew church attendance, observance of religious holidays, and the like. But, nonetheless, they can pursue effective altruism, volunteer for local charities, participate in the arts, teach, coach, embody a commitment to justice and equality, manifest virtues of humility and compassion, and be good neighbors and friends to all. Why be a religious fictionalist when you can be a non-fictionalist atheist or agnostic?

2. Even if you accept what I have just said about the value of non-fictionalist atheism and agnosticism, you might think that I have misidentified the values that are delivered by religious fictionalism. Rather than focus on either the anxiety-relieving goods that are unique to religion, or the social goods that are, at best, merely contingently related to religion, we should focus instead on the intrinsic goods of (a) accepting religious claims and evaluating them positively, and (b) participating fully in the prescribed practices and rituals of a religion. The thought here is that accepting religious claims and evaluating them positively and participating fully in the prescribed practices and rituals of a religion are goods in themselves; and, moreover, these goods outweigh the costs of being a fictionalist. Or, at any rate, we are to imagine that fictionalist atheists and agnostics might make this judgment: they might suppose that accepting religious claims and evaluating them positively and participating fully in the prescribed practices and rituals of a religion are goods in themselves that outweigh the costs that go along with being a fictionalist.

Perhaps some atheists and agnostics might swing this way. However, it strikes me that this would be a rather unusual judgment to make. Even those atheists and agnostics who were previously theists and who feel some kind of nostalgic regret about becoming atheists or agnostics should, I think, be suspicious of the claim that there is some positive intrinsic value that attaches to "accepting religious claims and evaluating them positively," when this is understood as the proponents of my third kind of parasitic religious fictionalism would have it understood.

Moreover, while it seems reasonable to suppose that such atheists and agnostics will continue to take pleasure in participating in some of the practices and rituals of religion—for example, perhaps attending a performance of Handel's *Messiah* in the lead up to Christmas—it seems to me that such atheists and agnostics should be suspicious of the claim that there is some positive intrinsic value that attaches to participating *fully* in the *prescribed* practices and rituals of the religion. Why would you judge that such participation is *intrinsically* good, given that you really are an atheist or agnostic?

3. A different line of criticism of the argument that I developed in the earlier sections of this chapter is that I seem to be imposing unnecessary conditions on religious fictionalists. In particular, it might be suggested that I am requiring that religious fictionalists must be self-conscious about their religious fictionalism: they must have a degree of intellectual sophistication that—we might suppose—many people whom we might otherwise take to be religious fictionalists do not have. The fundamental thought here is that there is a very wide spectrum of religious participants with very different kinds of attitudes towards the doctrinal claims of the religions to which they belong. Many people whom we might take to be rather full participants in particular religions have very low levels of belief in the principal doctrines of those religions. Moreover, if we ask those people why they participate in the practices and rituals of their religion, we get very little by way of an answer that indicates *belief*; rather, we get "This is what my family has always done," or the like. Why is it inappropriate to call these kinds of religious participants "religious fictionalists"?

Suppose that we are happy to risk patronizing "the folk." Suppose that it is true that many people cannot give an account of why they participate in the practices and rituals of their religion. Why would it be appropriate to call these kinds of religious participants "religious fictionalists"? On my third kind of parasitic religious fictionalism, it will be true that they are religious fictionalists only if they accept and positively esteem the doctrinal claims of their religion. What reason is there to suppose that they do this? Perhaps we might try saying that, were we to bring them to an understanding of what religious fictionalism is, they would then agree that they are religious fictionalists: they would then see that they do accept and positively esteem the doctrinal claims of their religion. But what reason is there to believe this? If you participate in the practices and rituals of your religion only "because this is what my family has always done," it is hard to see any justification for calling you a "religious fictionalist" (in the sense of the term that is captured in Brock's definition).

There is a wide range of motivations that people might have for participating in the practices and rituals of a given religion. Those motivations need not be clearly understood by the people in question. Consider George Orwell. He had a well-known disdain for Christianity, and was an atheist from his early teens. But he was a regular churchgoer who continued to take communion. In a letter to Eleanor Jacques, he wrote:

> It seems rather mean to go to H.C. [Holy Communion] when one does not believe, but I have passed myself off for pious, and there is nothing for it but to keep up the deception. (Quoted in Davison 2013: 21)

As far as I know, there is nowhere that Orwell clearly articulates why he persisted in churchgoing until the end of his life. But I think it is quite clear that Orwell was no religious fictionalist. Evelyn Waugh, in his review of *Critical Essays*, says of Orwell that "he seems never to have been touched at any point by a conception of religious thought and life." The remarks that Orwell makes about religion in his writing confirm Waugh's claim. It would just be a mistake to suppose that Orwell accepted and positively esteemed the doctrinal claims of Christianity. Why suppose that someone who participates in the practices and rituals of a given religion only "because this is what my family has always done" is importantly different from Orwell in their attitudes towards the religion in which they participate? In particular, why suppose that they accept and positively esteem the doctrinal claims of the religion in which they participate?

Of course, there are other cases that are importantly different from Orwell's. Imagine the case of an atheist in fourteenth-century Europe. Because this person does not have a death wish, they do not disclose their views about religion to others, and they strive to behave in all relevant respects as other members of their community do: they go to church, they display the typical level of enthusiasm for going to church, and so on. Their motivation is clear: they prefer living a lie to not living at all. It would be another kind of mistake to deem this kind of person to be a religious fictionalist. This person does not accept and positively esteem the doctrinal claims of Christianity. If there is something that they do positively esteem, it is success in deceiving others into thinking that they believe the doctrinal claims of Christianity.

The line of thought that we have just been pursuing raises an important question for those who think that there are religious fictionalists who would not recognize themselves in accounts of religious fictionalism. What evidence do we have that there could be religious fictionalists who do not recognize themselves in accounts of religious fictionalism? In the nature of the case, an inference from actuality to possibility looks problematic. It may well be that there are many participants in the practices and rituals of religion who have low levels of religious belief. But it is not obvious that this offers any succor to proponents of religious fictionalism.

4. Another criticism that you might think to make of the argument that I developed in the earlier sections of this chapter is that it fails to see religious

fictionalists who are in plain view. Perhaps it is true that there are no religious fictionalists among "the folk." But surely there are religious fictionalists among twentieth-century theologians and philosophers of religion. Consider mid-career Gordon Kaufman (1972) and mid-career John Hick (1989). While, in these works, Kaufmann and Hick are resolute realists about the existence of a focus of absolute concern ("the Real"), they also seem to maintain that we should self-consciously engage in what we take to be fictions that we, in some sense, "tell about" this focus of absolute concern.

The views of Kaufmann and Hick, in the works just mentioned, have an interesting affinity with those of religious believers who cleave either to apophaticism or to analogism. On apophatic approaches, we cannot say what are the intrinsic properties of the focus of absolute concern; we can say only what it (intrinsically) is not. On analogist approaches, we cannot say literally what are the intrinsic properties of the focus of absolute concern; we can only gesture towards its intrinsic properties using irreducibly analogical vocabulary. However, it is not the case, on either religious apophaticism or religious analogism, that religious doctrine is restricted to claims about the intrinsic properties of the focus of absolute concern. Religious fictionalism—as it is typically conceived—is a fictionalism about all of the religious doctrines of a given religion. Thus, in particular, religious fictionalism is also fictionalism about the extrinsic—relational—properties of the focus of absolute concern, fictionalism about the afterlife and salvation insofar as they fall under the provenance of the focus of absolute concern, and so forth. But, typically, apophaticists and analogists are not fictionalists about the relational properties of the focus of absolute concern, and nor are they fictionalists about afterlives and salvation, insofar as these are taken to fall under the provenance of the focus of absolute concern. (For more discussion of the relation between apophaticism and fictionalism, see Scott, Chapter 8 in this volume.)

Perhaps it will be said that Hick—like the later Kaufmann—was no realist about the afterlife, salvation, and so forth: for Hick—and the later Kaufmann—religion's sole concern is to get people to act morally. But, at least in Hick's case, there remained an ongoing commitment to the existence of "the Real," and—I think inconsistently—an ongoing commitment to the goodness of "the Real." In the later Kaufmann's case, when even the existence and goodness of the focus of absolute concern are treated as fictions, we are given a view that fails to offer any of the benefits that are unique to religion. I am happy to grant that the later Kaufmann is a religious fictionalist; but his religious fictionalism offers no more than Evans' Sunday Assembly or Comte's Religion of Humanity.

5. A fifth objection that some might wish to press is that there are clear cases in which religions exacerbate certain kinds of worries about death. In particular, it might be thought that religions that allow for eternal damnation do not ease

worries about death. I think that this objection overlooks the ways in which the goods essential to religion can be interrelated in complex ways. Recall that another of the goods essential to religion is managing worries about the injustices of this life that are not rectified in this life. For those who suppose that justice requires appropriate punishment and retribution, the combined package of survival of death and post-mortem justice will generate new fears. But this does not count at all against the claim that the religion overcomes direct worries about the fact of injustice and the fact of cessation of existence, particularly when survival of death and post-mortem justice are paired with a significant chance of eternal salvation.

6. A final objection that some might wish to press is that I ignore obvious cases of religious fictionalists outside the academy. Consider, for example, Jewish atheists. Surely they are a paradigm for religious fictionalists? I doubt it. To count as religious fictionalists, on the account of religious fictionalism that I have taken from Brock, we are required to have "propositional faith"—or, perhaps, "propositional hope"—in important doctrinal claims. But the Jewish atheists whom I know do not profess to have those things: their Jewish identification is entirely a matter of ancestry and culture.

Perhaps, though, the suggestion should have been to consider Jewish agnostics, rather than Jewish atheists. After all, it is hard to see how to square credence that is insufficient for agnosticism with a "positive evidence-sensitive attitude." But it is not clear that the case is any stronger, for it is also hard to see how to square credence that confers agnosticism with a "positive evidence-sensitive attitude." And, in any case, the Jewish agnostics whom I know do not profess to have either "propositional faith" or "propositional hope" in important doctrinal claims: it is a matter of indifference to them whether the doctrinal claims in question are true.

8. Concluding Remarks

The fundamental question that I have been addressing in this chapter might be formulated like this: Why move from non-fictionalist error theory to fictionalism in matters of religious belief? In order to approach this question, I have addressed two further questions: (1) What values are at stake in the decision about whether to move from non-fictionalist error theory to fictionalism in matters of religious belief? and (2) What reasons could there be for thinking that fictionalism is better placed than non-fictionalist error theory to deliver those values? In answering these questions, I have paid particular attention to the suggestion that there is value in having "propositional faith" in the teachings of religions that is available to religious fictionalists but not to religious non-fictionalist error theorists. I claim that "propositional faith" is unable to deliver anything of real benefit to those who are religious error theorists.[1]

References

Atran, S. 2002. *In Gods We Trust*. Oxford University Press.

Blackburn, S. 2007. "Religion and ontology." In A. Moore & M. Scott (eds.), *Realism and Religion: Philosophical and Theological Perspectives*. Ashgate. 47–59.

Braithwaite, R. 1955. *An Empiricist's View of the Nature of Religious Belief*. Cambridge University Press.

Brock, S. 2020. "Religious fictionalism and Pascal's Wager." In B. Armour-Garb & F. Kroon (eds.), *Fictionalism in Philosophy*. Oxford University Press. 207–34.

Cordry, B. 2010. "A critique of religious fictionalism." *Religious Studies* 46: 77–89.

Crane, T. 2017. *The Meaning of Belief: Religion from an Atheist's Point of View*. Harvard University Press.

Davison, P. 2013. *George Orwell: A Life in Letters*. Liveright.

Deng, N. 2015. "Religion for naturalists." *International Journal for Philosophy of Religion* 78: 195–214.

Deng, N. 2019. "Religion for naturalists and the meaning of belief." *European Journal for Philosophy of Religion* 11: 157–74.

Deng, N. 2020. "Agnosticism and fictionalism: A reply to Le Poidevin." *European Journal for Philosophy of Religion* 12: 183–8.

Dennett, D. 2016. "What to do while religions evolve before our very eyes." In M. Couch & J. Pfeifer (eds.), *The Philosophy of Philip Kitcher*. Oxford University Press. 273–82.

Đurković, N. 2016. "The psychological plausibility of religious fictionalism." *Belgrade Philosophical Annual* 29: 199–206.

Ekstrom, L. 2015. "Religion on the cheap." *Oxford Studies in Philosophy of Religion* 6: 87–113.

Eshleman, A. 2005. "Can an atheist believe in God?" *Religious Studies* 41: 183–99.

Eshleman, A. 2010. "Religious fictionalism defended: Reply to Cordry." *Religious Studies* 46: 91–6.

Eshleman, A. 2016. "The afterlife: Beyond belief." *International Journal for Philosophy of Religion* 80: 163–83.

---

[1] Thanks to Stuart Brock and Richard Joyce for their organization of the workshops, their oversight of this volume, and, in particular, their wise and generous feedback on earlier versions of this chapter. Thanks to everyone else who provided comments and encouragement. I remember, in particular: Tim Bayne, John Bigelow, Natalja Deng, Amber Griffioen, Victoria Harrison, Jessica Isserow, Seahwa Kim, Fred Kroon, Mary Leng, Jimmy Lenman, Bill Lycan, Robin Le Poidevin, and Rob Sparrow.

Field, H. 1980. *Science without Numbers*. Oxford University Press.

Gäb, S. 2020. "On behalf of Pascal: A reply to Le Poidevin." *European Journal for Philosophy of Religion* 12: 189–96.

Hesse, J. 2020. "Metalinguistic agnosticism, religious fictionalism, and the reasonable believer." *European Journal for Philosophy of Religion* 12: 197–202.

Hick, J. 1989. *An Interpretation of Religion*. Yale University Press.

Howard-Snyder, D. 2019. "Can fictionalists have faith? It all depends." *Religious Studies* 55: 1–22.

Jay, C. 2014. "The Kantian Moral Hazard Argument for religious fictionalism." *International Journal for Philosophy of Religion* 75: 207–32.

Jay, C. 2016. "Testimony, belief, and non-doxastic faith: The Humean argument for religious fictionalism." *Religious Studies* 52: 247–61.

Kaufman, G. 1972. *God the Problem*. Harvard University Press.

Kitcher, P. 2016. "Reply to Dennett." In M. Couch & J. Pfeifer (eds.), *The Philosophy of Philip Kitcher*. Oxford University Press. 283–7.

Klassen, C. 2012. "The metaphor of Goddess: Religious fictionalism and nature religion within feminist witchcraft." *Feminist Theology* 21: 91–100.

Le Poidevin, R. 1996. *Arguing for Atheism*. Routledge.

Le Poidevin, R. 2016. "Playing the God game: The perils of religious fictionalism." In A. Buckareff & Y. Nagasawa (eds.), *Alternative Concepts of God: Essays on the Metaphysics of the Divine*. Oxford University Press. 178–91.

Le Poidevin, R. 2019. *Religious Fictionalism*. Cambridge University Press.

Leng, M. 2010. *Mathematics and Reality*. Oxford University Press.

Lipton, P. 2007. "Science and religion: The immersion solution." In A. Moore & M. Scott (eds.), *Realism and Religion*. Ashgate. 31–46.

Malcolm, F. 2018. "Can fictionalists have faith?" *Religious Studies* 54: 215–32.

Malcolm, F. & Scott, M. 2017. "Faith, belief and fictionalism." *Pacific Philosophical Quarterly* 98: 257–74.

Palmqvist, C. 2019. "Forms of belief-less religion: Why non-doxasticism makes fictionalism redundant for the pro-religion agnostic." *Religious Studies* 55: 1–17.

Park, S. 2021. "In defense of religious practicalism." *European Journal of Science and Theology* 17: 27–38.

Pouivet, R. 2011. "Against theological fictionalism." *European Journal of Philosophy of Religion* 3: 427–37.

Robson, J. 2015. "Religious fictionalism and the problem of evil." *Religious Studies* 51: 353–60.

Sauchelli, A. 2018. "The will to make-believe: Religious fictionalism, religious beliefs, and the value of art." *Philosophy and Phenomenological Research* 96: 620–35.

Scott, M. 2020. "Faith, fictionalism and bullshit." *Thought* 9: 94–104.

Scott, M. & Malcolm, F. 2018. "Religious fictionalism." *Philosophy Compass* 13: 1–11.

Stone, A. 2012. "Spirituality for naturalists." *Zygon* 47: 481–500.

Vaihinger, H. 1924. *The Philosophy of As-If* (trans. by C. Ogden). Harcourt, Brace & Co.

Van Fraassen, B. 1980. *The Scientific Image*. Oxford University Press.

Van Leeuwen, N. 2014. "Religious credence is not factual belief." *Cognition* 133: 698–715.

Wettstein, H. 2012. *The Significance of Religious Experience*. Oxford University Press.

Yablo, S. 2005. "The myth of the seven." In M. Kalderon (ed.), *Fictionalism in Metaphysics*. Oxford University Press. 88–115.

6
The Pretensions of Religious Fictionalism

Bradley Armour-Garb and Frederick Kroon

1. Introduction

According to religious fictionalism on the standard sort of formulation given, for example, by Robin Le Poidevin (2019), Michael Scott and Finlay Malcolm (2018), and Stuart Brock (2020), it is morally and intellectually legitimate to affirm and to accept religious claims and to participate in religious practices without having religious beliefs. What can legitimate such religious engagement are important benefits that do not depend on believing the claims of a religion to be true. But despite this common ground among ways of understanding religious fictionalism (henceforth, "RF"), there are also important differences. Scott and Malcolm identify a variety of types of practitioners of religion who appear to fit their conditions; they hope to show thereby that RF is not only a conceptually coherent position, but the perspective of choice (implicit or explicit) of some *actual* practitioners. (We shall hereafter refer to Scott and Malcolm in relation to the views they express in their 2018 article as "S&M.") Le Poidevin takes a different route. There is no concern of any kind with trying to accommodate existing positions, as is clear from his understanding of "acceptance"—an attitude of pure make-believe—and his entirely secular understanding of the benefits of engaging with religion. Brock (2020) endorses a subtly different position: a "prescriptive" form of RF according to which, on pragmatic grounds and in light of certain goals, one might adopt a positive stance towards religious practice regardless of the actual credence one assigns to the truth of religious claims.

In this chapter we raise some problems for the kind of accommodationist approach that S&M and Brock seem to favor. We think that it is an instance of something that has worried some of the critics (and even proponents) of fictionalism in general: a tendency to let fictionalism become a procrustean bed for any view that allows the combination of a more or less uncritical participation in a discourse and its practices with resistance to a fully literal construal of its claims.

A useful way of articulating the problems we have in mind is to contrast these versions of RF with a more familiar kind of philosophical fictionalism: moral fictionalism, which is similarly focused on questions of how, practically speaking, we should act in the world. Like other paradigm varieties of philosophical fictionalism, moral fictionalism is usually characterized with a focus on discourse. By contrast,

S&M and, in a different way, Brock characterize RF in terms that center more on *users* of religious discourse, and we think that this is a feature that causes trouble for their accounts of RF. When RF is characterized in discourse-focused terms, as it seems to be for Le Poidevin, it is immune from such trouble. But we also think that this will not in the end save RF.

Describing RF and the challenges it faces on a user-focused approach will occupy the next section of this chapter. Section 3 will discuss our preferred discourse-focused approach to philosophical fictionalism. We show that a user-focused approach like that of S&M faces a problem of scope that is not faced by other familiar forms of fictionalism such as moral fictionalism. But despite the apparent advantages of a discourse-focused approach to RF, we suggest that discourse-focused RF doesn't have a future, unlike moral fictionalism. In particular, we argue in section 4 that it faces a collapse problem. Section 5 considers whether this worry also applies to Brock's account of RF. Section 6 draws the different threads of the chapter together.

2. Easy-Road RF?

RF has been described in a variety of ways, some stronger than others. Here are three representative formulations. The first is from S&M:

> Religious fictionalism is the theory that it is morally and intellectually legitimate to affirm religious sentences without believing the content of what is said. Additionally, religious fictionalists propose that it is similarly legitimate to engage in public and private religious practices, such as the observation of religious festivals, going to church, or prayer, without having religious beliefs. In general, fictionalists take the benefits of religious engagement to be available to those who do not believe that the claims of religion are true, or even to those that believe these claims are in error. (S&M 2018: 1)

Note the focus on individual practitioners and the benefits they might "legitimately" gain. (The significance of the classification will become apparent later.) Note also that, as stated, RF is a theory about the moral and intellectual status of ways of engaging with religion; on this way of understanding RF, even committed believers can be RF-ists (they might think it legitimate for others to engage with religion in this way, though without taking this path themselves). Like most writing on this topic, we will usually restrict the term to those who actually engage with religious discourse and its practices.

Here is Le Poidevin's formulation of RF:

> I shall take religious fictionalism to be the view that to immerse oneself in the religion, to employ its discourse to express that immersion, and to allow it to

influence (in part via the emotional responses it evokes) is to engage in a game of make-believe. In that (entirely serious) game, to utter religious statements is not to assert them, but to pretend to assert them. That is why neither the fictionalist's utterances, nor the attitudes they convey, are truth-normed.

(Le Poidevin 2019: 32)

Elsewhere he writes that he uses the term "religious fictionalism" to denote a theory of religious language that accepts that statements in the language are truth-apt and irreducible but denies that their purpose is to be objectively fact-stating (2019: 60).

At a glance, this suggests that for Le Poidevin religious fictionalism about some religion R is a view about the language or discourse of R and the way in which practitioners of R use the language to express their immersion in R. That can't be what Le Poidevin has in mind, however, since it would make RF a descriptive doctrine about how all practitioners actually understand the language of R—a surely implausible doctrine for most religions and one that Le Poidevin explicitly disavows (he classifies his version of RF as prescriptive or revolutionary in intent). But there are better ways to understand his account. On one such way, RF characterizes the way some practitioners of R might engage with the language of R; insofar as it is "a theory of religious language," it is a theory of an agent's or community's *use* of religious language. The reading of Le Poidevin that we prefer, however, takes it as denoting a theory about the language of R that accepts that statements in the language are truth-apt and irreducible, and endorses the continued use of the language in a make-believe spirit, not for the purpose of stating facts but for achieving other worthwhile goals. (As we suggest below, there is a crucial difference between this way of understanding Le Poidevin and the alternative user-focused way.)

Putting this difference aside for now, the most striking difference between Le Poidevin's and S&M's formulation is the central role Le Poidevin assigns to make-believe. S&M's formulation is consistent with letting RF-ists have some other kind of nondoxastic attitude to religious statements—e.g., acceptance (Alston 1996), acquiescence (Buchak 2012), or assumption (Howard-Snyder 2013). Some even take (propositional) *faith* to be such an attitude (indeed, it is at the forefront of Brock's account of RF, to be discussed below), although S&M themselves are dubious. They think that, at the very least, genuine faith that *s* requires that there is no outright disbelief in *s* (cf. Malcolm & Scott 2017: 269), so that some who count as adherents of RF by S&M's lights shouldn't, in their view, be credited with faith.[1]

The role of faith looms particularly large in Brock's recent discussion of RF (Brock 2020). Brock's version is a conjunction of five theses that by and large

---

[1] Malcolm (2018) considers an account that includes the "no disbelief" condition but thinks that it ultimately fails. More generally, Malcolm and Scott have provided a range of reasons for rejecting nondoxastic accounts of faith (Malcolm & Scott 2017; Malcolm 2018; Scott 2020).

agree with S&M's understanding of RF: the Truth-aptness thesis (religious statements are truth-apt), Nondoxasticism (a religious fictionalist does not (or need not) believe sincere religious claims; she *accepts* them), the Speech-act thesis (her religious utterances are not assertoric but perform some other function), the Immersion thesis (she fully engages in the practices and rituals prescribed by the religious community), and the Evaluative thesis (accepting religious claims and engaging in these practices and rituals has a certain utility independent of whether or not the claims are true or believed). Brock's account thus continues the focus on *users* of religious discourse and associated practices. But he adds a twist, viz., a nondoxastic notion of propositional faith—NDA-faith: An individual x has faith that p iff (1) x accepts that p and (2) x evaluates p positively. (Here "accepts" is a placeholder for a cognitive attitude that, unlike belief, does not aim at truth, is not sensitive to evidence in the same way as belief, and is voluntary in a way that belief is not.)

On Brock's preferred account of RF, acceptance is intimately related to NDA-faith. (We discuss Brock's position, together with some putative problems for it, in section 5.) Those who share S&M's doubts about calling a non-believing attitude of acceptance *faith* will, of course, reject this description, but there is one significant element to Brock's account that may explain the usage. Brock develops his account in large part to make room for a form of Pascal's Wager. He thinks the Wager adds pragmatic reasons to the moral reasons for people not already committed to accepting and immersing themselves in the religious way of life. It "introduces further benefits you might attain in the afterlife if you do so. Those benefits are selfish, but if you are lucky, and God exists, the benefits are infinite" (2020: 224). But this is beginning to sound familiar. As we point out below, it adds the element of hope to what can motivate acceptance, and hope is a significant element in anything deserving to be called *faith*.

It is important to emphasize another central feature of Brock's conception of RF. According to Brock, RF "is a stance you might adopt towards a particular religion R *no matter what credence you give R or the individual propositions that make it up*" (2020: 211, our italics). He goes on to explain that this is why "fictionalism, as stated, is compatible with theism (belief), with atheism (disbelief), and with agnosticism (neither belief nor disbelief)" (2020: 211). We return to this feature of Brock's conception below, as well as in section 4.

Despite their common features, these accounts exhibit some clear differences. Notably, for Le Poidevin the role of make-believe is central, whereas this is seen as an option rather than a compulsory element of S&M's and Brock's formulations. And Brock, but not the others, uses a nondoxastic notion of faith as the model for acceptance. Before saying more about these differences, we will note how a more familiar distinction—that between hermeneutic and revolutionary fictionalism—applies in the case of RF. This will allow us to see where these different versions fit along the hermeneutic/revolutionary divide.

In light of characterizations of hermeneutic and revolutionary fictionalism by Matti Eklund (2019) and S&M (2018: 1–2), we shall take hermeneutic RF (henceforth, "HRF") to be a species of RF according to which speakers who engage in religious discourse do not aim at the literal truth of what they are uttering, are not committed to the things the discourse purports to describe, and do not believe the religious claims that they and others make. We shall take the contrasting revolutionary version of RF (henceforth, "RRF") to hold that HRF is false, but that people *should* adopt RF. Note that this characterization should really be relativized to particular religions, since there is no reason to think that what goes for one religion also goes for another.

The following questions now arise. First, is RF coherent, and, second, assuming that it is, is there reason to think RF is a tenable view, whether as HRF or RRF or in some other guise? As S&M and Brock see it, the answer to both questions is yes—in fact, S&M think that we should recognize RF in some existing approaches to religion. (Le Poidevin also answers in the positive but does so more tentatively.)

S&M take their formulation to permit a particularly strong version of this answer. According to HRF, speakers of the target discourse do not in fact believe the content of what is said. But this raises the question of who the speakers are, since an answer is needed to determine whether or not HRF is an apt characterization of their practices. For Abrahamic religions, if *all* speakers of the target discourse (say, the discourse of Christianity) are included, the bewildering variety of attitudes and practices among this group surely shows without further ado that HRF is the wrong characterization.

S&M and Brock point to one way of resisting this conclusion. They remind us of the line taken by Georges Rey (2007) that inconsistencies in the discourse and practices of many religious people, particularly educated ones, suggests that they are self-deceived. The spin that S&M and Brock put on this is that the attitude of such people might be one of fictionalist acceptance rather than belief (S&M 2018: 7; Brock 2020: 213), and they think that in that case HRF is the appropriate characterization of the religious stance of such people. Although S&M don't explicitly say so, their account of the case requires that we restrict the domain of relevant speakers/participants to the ones who adopt this stance—if Rey is right, we should at least include all religious people with a basic scientific education. Call this way of defending HRF as the appropriate interpretation of the discourse and practices of some religious group *domain relativization*.[2]

---

[2] Brock's position on HRF is ambiguous. He writes: "Hermeneutic [religious] fictionalists think the five theses stated earlier accurately describe what many (if not all) of those engaged in religious discourse are doing. They argue that a close examination of the religious practices of some communities favors a fictionalist rather than a realist interpretation of those practices" (2020: 213). It is not clear whether Brock is claiming that HRF applies to a community if enough of the community subscribe to his five theses or that HRF applies only to the subgroup of the community who subscribe to these theses (domain relativization).

Domain relativization holds some surprises, for it is not hard to see that the way even some conservative Christians engage with the discourse of Christianity and its practices comes close (we think uncomfortably close) to satisfying the requirements for HRF. Some of the evidence is briefly described by S&M. Christians, even conservative ones, will often say that the central claims of their faith are to be construed as metaphorical or as pointing to a deep truth that language is ill-equipped to state. To accept the words attributed to Jesus, that "my father's house has many rooms," is (surely!) not to accept that God *literally* has a house with many rooms. Or, to take a more central theological tenet: "God is love" doesn't express the proposition that God is identical to the quality of love, nor does it merely express or convey that God loves all people (or all the *elect*, or ...). And the same will be true of many statements that are even more theologically loaded.[3] Just consider the way some conservative Christians may classify "God is three persons in one" as suggestive of a deep truth, rather than inviting them to believe one thing could literally be simultaneously three things. Indeed, given a tendency to regard the cornerstone of their faith as their trust in a *person* ("I trust the Lord Jesus Christ, not a book!"), it shouldn't be surprising to find many conservative religious believers open to the idea that the literal truth of statements about God is less important than a trust based on this personal relationship,[4] that their acceptance of such claims is to that extent not *truth-normed*, viz., not "answerable to the world." In principle, they might take this attitude to every important claim of Christianity.

Even if this is not enough for a full-blooded version of HRF, once we combine it with the fact that conservative Christians will often, or generally, describe their attitudes to their religious propositions as grounded in faith, it becomes difficult to escape the attractions of an HRF classification of the position. As S&M put it:

> [T]o the extent that religious discourse trades in the communication of faithful attitudes, it follows from [an NDA account of faith], since many (if not all) of the faithful do not believe the religious propositions they affirm, that the most charitable interpretation of religious discourse is that it does not conventionally express the beliefs of speakers. When speakers express their faith they are, in effect, quasi-asserting religious sentences. This appears to lend support to a (hermeneutic) variety of religious fictionalism. (2018: 6)

S&M don't say much about the supposed benefits of engaging with religious discourse and its practices on this picture, but presumably it will involve something like the way such engagement is thought to put its practitioners in touch with the

---

[3] Even a claim like "God exists" may, on reflection, be regarded as an inadequate form of words since "exists" is a category we understand in its application to the mundane, not anywhere else.

[4] We are indebted to Shirley Lamont-Grayson for her passionate defense of this view.

divine. In any case, it is clear that these observations are applicable only to *some* conservative Christians; for this target group, HRF may well seem the right classification.

Arguably there are radically different Christians who also fall under HRF on the domain-relativization approach, where these concerns equally apply. Thus, consider what S&M have to say about apophaticism, the view that we can't represent God's nature, except in purely negative terms:[5]

> [If apophaticism is true then] what we say in our attempts to describe God's nature is untrue. However, apophatic authors show no sign of preferring the elimination of religious discourse or withdrawal from religious practice. In part, this seems to be because even though what we say about God is untrue and should not be believed, the activity of attempting to represent God, and the recognition of its failure, may promote a closer relationship with God. The benefits of continued engagement outweigh the drawback that talk of God does not yield truths. (2018: 6)

Suppose that apophaticism can indeed be classified as a version of HRF. If so, we have two *opposing* versions of Christian discourse and its practices that can both be classified as actual instances of HRF on S&M's formulation.

Our final example involves the kind of nondoxastic account of NDA-faith preferred by a number of philosophers of religion, and explicitly used by Brock. Although he doesn't stress this point, Brock's talk of *faith*, understood as the kind of commitment and its relation to evidence that is instanced in Christianity, seems designed to make the combination of tenets, aims, and attitudes described in his conditions (1)–(6) look familiar to us, something that may be close to the views and attitudes of at least some religious people.

Are there actual "people of faith" who fit Brock's characterization of RF ("RFB," for short)? Many, it would seem. If the NDA-account of faith is a descriptively accurate account of what Christians and others call *faith*, then fully committed theists can be RFB-ists. Suppose they take themselves to have religious beliefs on the basis of strong evidence, but that they act out their religious commitments in a way that is quite independent of the available evidence. If presented with countervailing evidence, they might admit that they have no response—that, intellectually, their position may well be beyond the pale—but nevertheless insist that their faith remains strong. Or consider theists of a more familiar kind: the kind who undergo periods of deep doubt but don't see this as a reason to give up their

---

[5] For a more detailed and nuanced discussion of the issues, see Scott & Citron (2016). See also Scott, Chapter 8 of this volume.

faith.[6] (If we focus on the way religion sustains moral commitments, there may even be a kind of normative Kantian argument for privileging acceptance over belief as the appropriate attitude to the claims of religion. See Jay 2014; Joyce, Chapter 13 of this volume.)

But there are also agnostic and even atheistic RFB-ists. Take some of the people described in *Caught in the Pulpit: Leaving Belief Behind* (Dennett & LaScola 2015) who no longer believe but cannot leave the practices of their religion behind—not simply because they would miss the community of other people of faith, nor because they continue to recognize the value of what their religion has given them, but because they feel that their religion embodies a possible vision of the universe and their place in it that they still find awe-inspiring and now regard as a beautiful story, even hoping, perhaps against all hope, that it is true. (S&M too are likely to see this as a version of RF, perhaps even HRF despite its origins in unbelief.)

Or consider the seemingly self-deluded theist described by Rey (2007) and identified by Brock and S&M as a candidate religious fictionalist. Unlike Dennett's and LaScola's lapsed theist, such a "theist" does not own up to lack of belief; lack of belief is simply something that is evident from inconsistencies in her speech and practices. If S&M and Brock are right about this case,[7] it is we, as theorists, who think that what such a theist takes to be belief is best construed as mere acceptance, and it is we who go on to explain such variances in her speech and practices in terms of the hypothesis that she is a non-believing fictionalist. (This is arguably not so very different from the way hermeneutic mathematical fictionalists deal with the claim that people mostly believe that there are numbers, or moral noncognitivists with the claim that people mostly believe that there are moral truths.)

Finally, here is a philosophically more nuanced example of a version of theism that fits Brock's conditions for RFB. There has been a recent upsurge of interest in Jamesian fideism, a view that holds that religious belief need not be based on evidence but can be entered into when there is a choice to be made among "genuine" options—options that cannot by their nature be decided on intellectual grounds and are (as William James puts it) "forced, living, and momentous." On John Bishop's Jamesian account of a "'doxastic venture' model of faith" (Bishop 2007), it is morally permissible to make a "doxastic venture of religious faith" insofar as the truth or falsity of the relevant class of religious propositions is not adequately supported by one's total available evidence. Doing so "will not amount to inducing a state of belief (either directly or indirectly); rather it will be a direct act of *taking to be true* in one's practical reasoning what one already holds to be true from

---

[6] Cf. the sort of attitude epitomized in the cry from the father of the demon-possessed boy: "Lord, I believe; help my unbelief!" (Mark 9:24 NKJV). Doubt commonly sits alongside belief. If we want to give a name to this complex mix of attitudes that persists through periods of intellectual commitment and periods of doubt, *faith* seems as good a term as any.

[7] For a skeptical response, see, for example, Scott (2015).

passional, non-evidential, causes" (Bishop 2007: 12). (Bishop calls his account *doxastic*, but this merely reflects a semantic preference. If belief is taken to be a state that is sensitive to evidence, as Brock does, then the view counts as *nondoxastic*.)[8] The sort of theistic claims that count as passionally caused are ones "resulting from enculturation or from desires (perhaps deep-seated and unconscious)" (2007: 12). This ought to include the kind of motivations that are mentioned by Brock. It may well be the perceived attractiveness of the kind of moral virtues displayed in acts of communion, charity, humility, penance, atonement, and confession that leads someone to treat a certain class of theistic propositions as true, to accept them unconditionally, and to immerse herself in the rituals and practices that go with this theistic framework. Of course, there remains the hope that the propositions are indeed true, but that is also the case for the fictionalist who wagers on God in Brock's account of RF. The upshot, we think, is that such a Jamesian fideism can also be brought into the fold of RF as understood by Brock (and even S&M). Since the position can be thought of as a philosophical elucidation of the way many people of faith behave in relation to the faith-propositions they accept, this may even suggest that on a Jamesian fideist picture of faith these theists are implicitly committed to a form of HRF.

In presenting these various examples of a combination of theism and a rejection of full-fledged belief in God, we don't mean to imply that such a combination is a particularly easy one to maintain. For one thing, there is surely a tension. Take a theist to be someone who accepts that God exists, whether or not they believe that God exists. A claim like "God exists but I don't believe that God exists" seems to be a straightforward instance of Moore's paradox, and thus its reflective version "I am a theist but I don't believe God exists" will strike many as similarly paradoxical. RF, as understood by Brock and S&M, owes us an account of how it can be coherent to entertain such claims.[9] We think that all these various positions contain their own way of explaining, more or less well, how the trick is done, but the sheer variety of explanations discourages the thought that classifying them all as examples of RF adds much of value to the discussion.

We can now state our worries about Brock's and S&M's accounts in particular. Because they seem eager to show that RF and even HRF occupy a worthy niche in intellectual space, they have cast their net remarkably wide and thereby made it surprisingly easy to be counted an RF-ist. The resulting characterization allows a rather motley assortment of views to be labeled as instances of RF, and, assuming

---

[8] One reason for preferring "nondoxastic" is that, as Bishop agrees, there could be numerous such systems of belief, all "forced, living, and momentous," all vying to be chosen. But in that case, the probability that any particular one of them is true might well be negligible, and so a believer would have to say "I believe that p, but there is virtually no chance that p is true"—something that strikes us as close to being an instance of Moore's paradox.

[9] Above all, the coherence of such claims requires a strict acceptance–belief distinction. Brock (2020: 209, fn. 2) acknowledges the challenges to this distinction.

domain relativization, even as instances of HRF. This includes (i) views that we would be inclined to class as clearly religious (e.g., apophaticism); (ii) views where the motivating goals of engagement with religious discourse and rituals are affective in nature and not based on seeing the religion as true, but where the question of truth still matters to a larger or smaller degree (e.g., Jamesian fideism and the position taken by Dennett and LaScola's hopeful ex-believers); and (iii) views where the motivating goals of engagement with religious discourse and rituals are purely social and moral in character and where the possible truth of the religion is taken to be entirely irrelevant.

These accounts of RF have not merely made it easy to be counted an RF-ist—we think they have made it *too* easy. (This is the "it's-all-too-easy" problem.) One might wonder, though, what the worry is about an easy road to RF. (Don't many applaud rather than criticize forms of mathematical fictionalism for being easy-road?)[10] But the road here is "too easy" in the wrong way. Our main concern is that by casting its net so wide RF thereby offers too shallow a way of classifying views. It doesn't reveal much about the views the label classifies (especially views falling under (i) and (ii), above); in particular, it doesn't tell us what motivates such views, what distinguishes them from others, what characterizes the nature of acceptance on the different views, how we are to understand their relationship to other religious traditions, and so on. Call this the *shallowness concern*.

A related concern—call it the *breadth concern*—is the way that RF has been allowed to include views that we would classify as broadly religious (e.g., the views falling under (i) and (ii)), rather than secular. To the extent that the shallowness concern arises from the very diverse ways in which people continue to care about religious truth at some level even in the absence of belief, this concern about breadth does much to explain the shallowness concern.

Below, we say more about what is distinctive about the present easy-road approach. But, for now, we want to say more about what is concerning about the shallowness and breadth concerns that underlie this easy road. We agree, of course, that there is nothing inherently wrong with imposing a broad grid that hides much fine detail, but we think that to show the worth of philosophical fictionalism in philosophy the grid has to show appropriately deep and revealing patterns, something that has not been shown in the way RF is being understood.

Think of it this way. Religions and their languages and practices constitute an age-old and extraordinarily varied and complex phenomenon. In its many forms and manifestations, it runs the gamut from simple and rigid to extremely sophisticated. The history of religion is replete with debates and rivalries of the most intricate kind, often intellectual, often marked by deep philosophical differences, often in conjunction with sharply differing degrees of tolerance. While one could

---

[10] See Balaguer (2018) on easy-road versus hard-road mathematical fictionalism.

try to impose a grid on this swirl of doctrine, philosophy, and attitude, this is often best done in the context of the kind of theological, or theo-philosophical, discussion that is appropriately sensitive to the nature and dynamics of these differences. The sense in which one of Dennett and LaScola's lapsed but hopeful theists accepts Christian discourse, for example, is utterly different from the sense in which an apophatic Christian does so. For the lapsed theist, the vision and the faint hope of its realization has something close to literal truth as its focus. By contrast, apophaticists who reject literal truth seem leery of any univocal account of their attitude to statements of faith. Some statements are accepted because they are seen as a kind of analogical truth ("God is good," say), although the purpose of uttering such statements is not to say something close to the truth (finite humans can't do that) but to express devotion. Other statements may be accepted because they are seen as having a different purpose. For example, apophaticists may accept claims about God's hating sin and sinners because, as Gregory of Nyssa suggests, "the text informs us in every word of this kind...that the divine Providence deals with our feebleness by means of our own characteristics, so that those inclining to sin may restrain themselves from evils through fear of punishment" (2007: 154). If so, we accept and utter such statements because of their perceived regulative function rather than their expressive function.

In all of this, there is little reason to think that the philosophy of language and its deployment of the idea of fictionalism can have much to offer this discussion by way of enlightenment. But that is precisely what we seem to get from the way RF is being understood. The patterns that it lays across religion and its practices are indeed patterns (and so we don't accuse these accounts of some deep error), but they are patterns that hide the sophistication and nuances that characterize debates in these areas.

3. A Scope Problem

To see more clearly what distinguishes the present and (we think) problematic way of understanding RF from other types of philosophical fictionalism in the literature, consider again S&M's contention (2018: 7) that Rey's (2007) meta-atheism is a form of HRF. Rey's central thesis is the following: "Despite appearances, many Western adults who've been exposed to standard science and sincerely claim to believe in God are self-deceived; at some level they believe the claim is false" (Rey 2007: 245) Suppose we go along with the idea that such an attitude can be construed as a form of fictionalist acceptance. Importantly, Rey is not making a claim about *all* speakers who engage in this religious discourse; he is merely making a claim about *some* such speakers. Despite this, S&M contend that the view can be counted as a form of HRF, using the strategy of domain relativization to do so.

As HRF is standardly understood, however (even by S&M on a first reading of their account), the view that "claims of the disputed discourse are...accepted rather than believed" is not qualified. That is, it does not just apply to claims made by *some* or *many* agents; it applies to claims made by *all* such agents who are engaged in that discourse. If this is right, it follows that Rey's view is not a version of HRF, contrary to what S&M claim. Call the problem of the tension between the standard understanding of HRF and the way S&M relax the scope of the quantifier in their understanding of Rey's position *the scope problem* for their position.

This scope problem seems to infect other purported HRF positions. HRF is a view on which speakers in general do not aim at the literal truth but only appear or pretend to do so when they utter sentences from the discourse in question; the focus is squarely on the discourse, not on how some subset of the set of speakers understand the discourse. But it seems clear that at least some religious folk, when they are engaging in religious discourse, genuinely believe what they are uttering and are making sincere assertions. It is surely obvious that not all Christians, for example, would agree that because they trust Christ, they should agree that central claims of Christianity are to be construed nonliterally; it is equally obvious that not all are Jamesian fideists or apophaticists. Many are simply believers, on a pretty standard evidence-sensitive understanding of belief. If so, HRF is false for at least the discourse of Christianity on the standard conception of HRF.

We have seen that the scope problem arises for theorists whose versions of HRF take off from the actual attitudes and aims of ordinary speakers of the discourse in question, with the discourse relativized to its use by certain groups or communities. It might be thought that the scope problem can be resolved by simply opting for this more relaxed way of understanding the discourse-participants of the religion in question—that is, by allowing domain-relativization. This would make HRF very different from other types of hermeneutic fictionalism. In particular, it would radically change the *focus* of fictionalism. Traditionally, the focus of one or another variety of fictionalism has been taken to be on a certain discourse and how it is in *fact* understood by participants (hermeneutic fictionalism) or how it *should* be understood (revolutionary fictionalism). By contrast, S&M take the focus to be *users* or *participants* in the discourse, or perhaps communities of users. Users are also the focus in Brock's characterization of RF, since he thinks that it is a person's attitude of faith and the immersive nature of their engagement with the language and practices of a religion that makes them a fictionalist, not features of the discourse.

Should the scope problem be resolved in favor of a form of user-focus by letting domain-relativization determine the boundaries of a discourse? Our earlier discussion of the *it's-all-too-easy* problem shows the pitfalls of such an approach. Recall, in particular, the (shallowness) concern that the approach doesn't uncover appropriately deep and revealing patterns in the views it classifies. On the other hand, it might be thought that RF is very different from other fictionalisms and that it is peculiarly suited to a more user-focused understanding of a discourse. Like all the other major religions, Christianity contains numerous different branches, each practiced by people whose main partners in this practice belong to the same strand; why not count the discourses or languages of these different branches as being different? That would rationalize the categorization of at least some of the different ways of understanding Christianity as instances of HRF (although it wouldn't help with Rey's meta-atheism, for example). But such a response to our concerns would trivialize the notion of HRF. Since the various divisions within Christianity have all spawned their own micro-divisions on the basis of differences in doctrine and practice, it threatens to turn any distinctive use of the language of Christianity on the part of some subgroup into a separate discourse. Better, surely, to have a broad-based understanding of a religious discourse, however this is defined.

We have thus far raised two problems for RF as understood by S&M: the *it's-all-too-easy* problem (a problem for Brock as well) and the scope problem. We identified the source of these problems as the user-focused way in which theorists like S&M and Brock have understood RF. These problems suggest that we should return to a squarely discourse-focused way of understanding RF. On such an account, HRF is, we take it, out of the question. An advocate of RF should then opt for revolutionary, rather than hermeneutic, RF.

In fact, our putative examples of HRF have another feature that suggests the wisdom of opting for a revolutionary over a hermeneutic form of RF. Because S&M (and arguably Brock as well) wanted to show that RF was not just conceptually coherent but in some sense a recognizable view, their examples involved versions of RF in which the benefits of engaging in religious discourse and its practices were understood in terms that were themselves broadly religious or in sympathy with religious ends, and this might be thought not to jibe with the intent of RF. As a result, it seems reasonable to consider versions of RF where the benefits of embracing a particular religion are described in terms that are clearly secular or *areligious* (e.g., they are described as merely social or moral, but without the value of these social or moral ends being grounded in religion), and where those who accept the claims of the religion (possibly for the sake of these benefits) (i) do not believe the claims to be true and (ii) do not even believe that these benefits are enhanced by the possibility of their being true (which would presumably rule out Brock's version of RF). It is difficult but not impossible to imagine such versions as being hermeneutic (for this would involve people self-consciously inventing gods in order to get themselves to act in morally and socially responsible ways), but in any case that is not the right picture of existing religions and certainly not of the religions normally in focus when discussing fictionalism. In their case, a discourse-focused approach can yield only a revolutionary form of RF.

Since we take a discourse-focused approach to encapsulate what is best in the very idea of philosophical fictionalism, we begin our discussion of revolutionary forms of RF by saying more about the approach.

4. Revolutionary RF?

In our view, philosophical fictionalism is best seen as a view about the appropriate attitude to take towards some discourse in light of certain salient features that it possesses. An examination of extant versions of philosophical fictionalism reveals that what philosophical fictionalisms have in common is the view that there needs to be a change in our attitudes towards face-value discourse—that is, discourse that purports to state facts. Revolutionary philosophical fictionalists maintain that the face-value reading of some discourse is correct (i.e., the discourse indeed purports to state facts) but, for so being, the discourse is in error, viz., its distinctive statements are untrue, either false or without a truth-value at all.[11] But because they also see the need to retain the discourse—it is too useful to give up—such error theorists recommend a change in our attitudes towards that discourse. This is what makes the view *revolutionary*: Come the revolution, when people recognize the problems with this discourse, they should take on board the recommendation of these theorists. Such a view is *fictionalist* because it enlists one of the strategies, mechanisms, or approaches that have been deployed to show that genuine fictional discourse, or our attitude towards such discourse, is not ontologically committing.

A feature of philosophical fictionalism that needs particular emphasis is that all philosophical fictionalists maintain that there are good reasons for continuing to employ the relevant discourse. Take moral fictionalism. The usual way to defend moral fictionalism is to suggest, along with John Mackie, that the idea that certain actions are objectively categorically required of us is indefensible. But despite holding such an error theory, Mackie thought that moral discourse could continue with the status of a "useful fiction" (Mackie 1977: 239). But how can we be motivated to act if the beliefs are no longer in place, and all we have are beliefs that certain actions are required of us *according to a fiction*? The most fully worked out response to this motivational worry is contained in Richard Joyce's defense of moral fictionalism (Joyce 2001, 2005, Chapter 13 in this volume). He argues that an important practical benefit of having moral beliefs is that they diminish the possibilities for rationalization that we are all prone to. Adopting morality as a fiction yields some of the same benefits. Having rejected morality, but understanding the practical benefits of moral beliefs, we secure these practical benefits, or enough of them, by *accepting* morality rather than believing it.

---

[11] On a somewhat weaker understanding of revolutionary fictionalism, error theory is not necessary; agnosticism about whether the discourse is factual may be enough (Armour-Garb & Kroon 2020: 15–16).

This is a revolutionary form of moral fictionalism, since, like Mackie, Joyce thinks that at face-value the discourse purports to describe a realm of moral facts, but because there are no such facts and because the thought that there are such facts is needed to guide moral behavior, we need to reconstrue the thought: to avoid error, we should modify our attitude from belief to some form of nondoxastic acceptance (e.g., make-believe).[12]

Now consider *religious* revolutionary fictionalism, RRF—in the form, say, described by Le Poidevin. It is tempting to think that RRF not only escapes the *it's-all-too-easy* and scope problems, but that in its emphasis on moral and social goods it shares many of the virtues of a revolutionary moral fictionalism like Joyce's. But this is far from being the case, for other worries now arise. RRF-ists propose a revision to current practice. They think that commitments to the truth of the claims of the target religious discourse are misplaced and should be jettisoned, even though speakers should continue to engage with the discourse without believing what it purports to say. But now we encounter a converse problem: the "it's-all-too-hard" problem for RRF. The problem is that it is difficult to see how the religion can survive its practitioners taking up the advocated revolution. For suppose that everyone engaging in the discourse only *pretended* that its claims were true and entered into its rituals only in a make-believe spirit. Then the following question would arise. There is surely a large cost to such engagement (we are talking about a commitment that mimics full belief, not an occasional dipping into the religion when it suits), so in order to warrant this cost, the benefits of such engagement must then be correspondingly high. But what would these benefits be? Presumably not the kind of benefits we get from the far less demanding commitments of moral fictionalism. But if they involve the fostering of values and commitments that substantially exceed what secular interests could underwrite, why would one think that these would survive the extinction of religious belief itself (if not immediately then in due course) as the significance of the extinction sets in? (They needn't disappear entirely, of course, but could just be reconceptualized in other terms—precisely what happens in the case of scientific revolution where engagement with a viewpoint one rejects is maintained for a period because of the benefits of doing so, but where the search is underway for alternative ways of retaining what was valuable in the earlier view.)

In short, if Le Poidevin's RRF is a prescription for how thinkers should respond to the dictates of religious practice, it would seem to undermine the impetus for engaging in that practice. If there is resistance to the idea that the revolution is almost certain to fail, it may be because one imagines a sizable core of devotees who will maintain adherence to the religion come what may; for these people,

---

[12] See Joyce (2020) for further discussion of how such attitudes should be understood. Somewhat similar attitudes are said to be in play on the very different account of moral fictionalism advanced by Mark Kalderon (2005). Kalderon's is a hermeneutic form of moral fictionalism.

all attempts to argue for easier routes to the same ends will fall on deaf ears. The presence of such a core makes it seem like the revolution can be permanent. Attempts by revolutionaries to persuade this core that they need not keep attending church will be met with fervid religious arguments; since the revolutionaries know they can accept these arguments, even while not believing them to be cogent, the core is unlikely to change its ways. But the idea of such a core has a familiar ring about it. These are practitioners who genuinely believe in the truth of the religion's claims and the efficacy of its practices. They are the remaining religious realists, and thus the ones who intellectually resist the revolution, just like the scientists who hold out rather than change their beliefs during a scientific revolution. Revolution, at least when it is understood in these terms, is not *genuine* revolution. (Incidentally, this also helps to explain why the *it's-all-too-hard* problem for RRF does not apply to revolutionary *moral* fictionalism, such as that advocated by Joyce. His form of revolutionary moral fictionalism does not require that there be any moral realists, since a commitment to moral talk does not require the existence of a sustained community of moral realists to be efficacious.)

So much for the *it's-all-too-hard* problem for RRF. But there is kind of weakly prescriptive RF that may not be susceptible to this problem. This form doesn't say that the religion's practitioners *should* embrace the religion by nondoxastically accepting its claims and immersing themselves in its rituals, but merely that it is *permissible* to do so. Natalja Deng calls this "weak evaluative RF" (Deng 2015: 198; Chapter 9 of this volume). She rejects the view as it stands, on grounds that she finds the idea of nondoxastic acceptance problematic, but thinks that there is a version of the view that escapes her objections. In the version she prefers, nondoxastic acceptance is replaced by make-believe, as in Le Poidevin's account of RRF, but, unlike Le Poidevin, Deng allows considerable latitude in what to include in the content of the make-believe and the degree to which religious practices are adhered to:

> The make-believer can decide what to include in the fiction, and in principle he can include ideas from different religious traditions. His is a sui generis form of engagement with religious ideas and practices. (Deng 2015: 212)

We might call this "lightweight RF." Note that the label is not meant to denigrate the view. In fact, we think that lightweight RF clearly escapes the *it's-all-too-easy* and the *it's-all-too-hard* problems for the versions of RF we have discussed. But because Deng shares the ambition of other proponents of a secular form of RF, like Le Poidevin, that her RF-ists should feel part of a religious community, both of them worry that their versions of fictionalism might not allow practitioners to integrate properly into such a community. Both think that the problem is overstated: Deng counsels transparency and thinks that "the make-believer was always an unusual member of the community" (2015: 211), while Le Poidevin thinks that the problem is mitigated if the religious community defines itself primarily in terms of shared commitments (2019: 57).

We think that such responses underestimate the problem. No doubt self-confessed practitioners of prescriptive forms of RF will not be excluded from attending church or temple, but that can be for all kinds of reasons, including the hope that the fictionalist will come to his senses. If full rather than a kind of partial integration is what they care about, we suspect that the most that such RF-ists can in the end hope for is the *pretense* that they are fully integrated into their religious community. Given their views, perhaps that is all that they should care about, although it is not, we are confident, what properly integrated members of a religious community care about.

In the concluding section we briefly return to the place of Deng's lightweight version of RF in discussions about RF.

5. More on Brock on Religious Fictionalism

We have raised some general worries for certain aspects of HRF and of RRF. But suppose that there were a form of RF that falls under neither species of philosophical fictionalism: neither hermeneutic nor revolutionary (putting aside Deng's lightweight version of fictionalism). Would such a form evade the problems that we have raised for HRF and RRF? In this section we consider the question by looking closely at Brock's version of RF (abbreviated earlier as "RFB").

Recall that RFB is a combination of five theses (Truth-aptness, Nondoxasticism, the Speech-act thesis, the Immersion thesis, and the Evaluative thesis), together with a nondoxastic analysis of propositional faith. Recall too that for Brock "[RFB] is a stance you might adopt towards a particular religion R no matter what credence you give R or the individual propositions that make it up" (2020: 211). While RFB doesn't strike us as incoherent, we have already had occasion to worry about the *breadth* of RFB. Earlier we argued that there appears to be a bewildering variety of actual theistic, agnostic, and atheistic views that conform to RFB, and we saw this as a potential problem (the *it's-all-too-easy* problem): focusing on this would made it hard to see how interesting, and interestingly different, the trees are.

Assuming this is indeed a problem, we think the best way to deal with it is by deleting the theist option from the mix. Suppose, then, that we hold that someone can be an RFB-ist only if she is either an agnostic or an atheist and so doesn't have both acceptance and belief as attitudes to religious claims. This has consequences for one of Brock's other claims. Brock maintains that RFB is neither hermeneutic nor revolutionary. But Brock also maintains the Evaluative thesis:

> Accepting religious claims, and engaging in the associated religious practices and rituals, has a certain utility independent of whether or not the statements are true or believed.

At first glance, the Evaluative thesis looks out of place; unlike the other theses, it doesn't say that fictionalists accept, or do, such-and-such, but instead comments on a central feature of this doing and accepting. The connection is not hard to see, however. Brock presumably thinks that a fictionalist is involved in "accepting religious claims, and engaging in the associated religious practices and rituals" precisely because doing so has the utility proclaimed in the Evaluative thesis. But now we strike a problem. So interpreted, the thesis seems incomplete, since ascribing "a certain utility" to what a fictionalist does is not enough to explain why she does it—there could be all kinds of countervailing reasons for *not* adopting a fictionalist stance.[13] Brock's real view, we think, is that the fictionalist will see these benefits as an overriding reason for engaging with the religion, that the burden is well worth the cost. (For Brock, these benefits may even include the possibly infinite benefits that come from a kind of Pascalian Wagering for God, although it is hard to see the agnostic or atheist agreeing.)[14]

So, in the end, Brock's position seems to amount to this: for the agnostic or atheist fictionalist about some religion R, there are compelling reasons for accepting R's claims and engaging in R's practices and rituals, based on the secular (e.g., moral) benefits that accrue from doing so. If this is correct, however, then such a fictionalist must surely think that this attitude should be adopted by everyone, not just by herself.[15] If she thought that the benefits could also be obtained by some people in some other way—one that didn't require pretending things were other than they in fact are—why wouldn't she be an advocate for this less costly option, for both herself and others? It seems, then, that once we strip away theistic readings of RFB (because of the *it's-all-too-easy* problem), RFB amounts to a form of revolutionary religious fictionalism after all. If so, we suspect it is subject to the *it's-all-too-hard* problem that we earlier identified as a serious problem for RRF.

6. A Final Look at RF

Our chapter has taken a critical look at RF, contrasting it on a number of fronts with moral fictionalism. First, we looked at some more or less standard formulations of RF found in the current literature and argued that these made it too easy to be an RF-ist: these formulations suggest an easy road to RF that is beset by concerns about shallowness as well as breadth. We stressed that this *it's-all-too-easy* problem does not question the coherence of such formulations but rather the thought that

---

[13] Cf. Jay (2014: 212) on evaluative versus revolutionary fictionalism.

[14] After all, wagering for God has its risks. If there is a God, there might be a special place in Hell reserved for those who merely *pretend* to believe and who don't see the pretending as a hopeful first step to belief.

[15] Or perhaps by everyone who values these benefits, given the indispensable role the religion has in fostering them. (Such a [benign?] relativization also brings a view like Howard Wettstein's (2012) into the RRF camp.)

something important is discovered about religious traditions by categorizing them in this way. We further claimed that Scott and Malcolm's account in particular is subject to a distinctive kind of scope problem that does not seem to affect other cases of philosophical fictionalism.

Given these two problems, we then decided that the real place to look for a motivation for RF is elsewhere, in a desire to secularize the benefits of both religious belief and religious practice. But when we looked at secular ways of understanding the benefits of continued participation in religious discourse and practices mentioned by RF, we were struck by a converse problem: the *it's-all-too-hard* problem. Views that allege such benefits are prescriptive or revolutionary, rather than hermeneutic, but we argued that it is unlikely that views of this kind (RRF) can survive the revolution. We also saw that formulations of RF that try to steer a middle line, such as Brock's, may have trouble doing so.

These are strange troubles for a fictionalist to have. Even though it may be a matter of controversy just how to make the idea of fictionalism about this or that discourse precise, generally the locus of debate is on whether one *should* be a fictionalist of this stripe. It is usually easy to spell out the reasons, and often just as easy to find counterarguments. In the case of RF, however, all bets seem to be off. We have argued that RRF—which is RF's best and most exciting hope (so long as the alleged benefits are presented in appropriately secular form)—seems susceptible to collapse. By contrast, other sorts of revolutionary fictionalism, concerning different subject matters (e.g., mathematical talk, modal talk, and even moral talk) constitute a genuine option, even if unattractive for reasons not having to do with collapse.

In short, there is no corresponding *it's-all-too-hard* problem for revolutionary fictionalism per se. Similarly, there is no corresponding *it's-all-too-easy* problem for hermeneutic forms of fictionalism per se. Generally, the problem is the very different one of finding compelling reason to classify the attitude that ordinary participants in a discourse have as a nondoxastic form of acceptance rather than belief.

What is it about RF that makes it susceptible to both the *it's-all-too-easy* and the *it's-all-too-hard* problems—and where to go from here? We addressed the first question in section 2. In brief, the *it's-all-too-easy* problem is a reflection of the bewildering complexity of the phenomenon of religion, its discourses and its practices, and the time-tested sophistication of its debates; fictionalist patterns imposed will seem relatively shallow as a result. Our answer to the second question draws a slightly different connection to the phenomenon's complexity. Religions—the Abrahamic religions but, of course, not just these—have always been taken to provide guidance on questions of morality and justice. They have typically provided exemplars or models of morality and justice, and there is little doubt that these have provided, and can continue to provide, motivations for engaging in like behavior through story-telling and without requiring the beliefs that originally fueled the stories. But in the case of other forms of revolutionary fictionalism, theorists have provided sophisticated explanations for why the revolution should be made permanent. The very complexity of the phenomenon of religion—the debates occurring within and between the various religions and manifestations of the same religion, as well as the evolution of religious perspectives (sometimes in response to changes in moral perspectives)—discourages any thought of a simple connection between the stories they tell us and what we take morality and justice to require of us. While we don't doubt that an evolving mash-up of the stories of a whole range of incompatible religions will long continue to circulate and motivate should there be whole-sale abandonment of religious belief, none of this leaves us with a credible reason for supposing that the discourse and even practices of a *particular* religion will survive such an abandonment of religious belief.

If this is along the right path, where do we go from here? No doubt RF will continue to have its defenders, but we think that its best hope is something different, something more along the lines of Deng's weak conception of the way we might imaginatively use religious stories and religious models (or an evolving mash-up of these) to good purpose.[16] We doubt, however, that such engagement should be called a version of "fictionalism," not just because there is no recognizable single discourse that features in such imaginative episodes, but because there is no single community of users that participants belong to, communicate with, or learn from: as we suggested earlier, any sense of community will be illusory. To engage with religion in this limited manner is not to *participate* in religion in any sense deserving of the term. What we have is not religious fictionalism, but rather episodes of imaginative immersion in what might better be called (with a nod to Schiffer (1987)) *remnants of religion*.[17]

References

Alston, W. 1996. "Belief, acceptance, and religious faith." In J. Jordan & D. Howard-Snyder (eds.), *Faith, Freedom, and Rationality*. Rowman & Littlefield. 3–27.

Armour-Garb, B. & Kroon, F. (eds.). 2020. *Fictionalism in Philosophy*. Oxford University Press.

Balaguer, M. 2018. "Fictionalism in the philosophy of mathematics." In E. Zalta (ed.), *The Stanford Encyclopedia of Philosophy*. <https://plato.stanford.edu/entries/fictionalism-mathematics/>.

---

[16] See Deng (2015) and Chapter 9 of this volume.
[17] We wish to thank Stuart Brock and Richard Joyce for their very helpful comments and suggestions, and for organizing the meetings that led to this volume.

Bishop, J. 2007. *Believing by Faith: An Essay in the Epistemology and Ethics of Religious Belief*. Oxford University Press.

Brock, S. 2020. "Religious fictionalism and Pascal's Wager." In B. Armour-Garb & F. Kroon (eds.), *Fictionalism in Philosophy*. Oxford University Press. 207–33.

Buchak, L. 2012. "Can it be rational to have faith?" In J. Chandler & V. Harrison (eds.), *Probability in the Philosophy of Religion*. Oxford University Press. 225–46.

Deng, N. 2015. "Religion for naturalists." *International Journal for Philosophy of Religion* 78: 195–214.

Dennett, D. & LaScola, L. 2015. *Caught in the Pulpit: Leaving Belief Behind* (2nd edition). Pitchstone Publishing.

Eklund, M. 2019. "Fictionalism." In E. Zalta (ed.), *Stanford Encyclopedia of Philosophy*. <https://plato.stanford.edu/entries/fictionalism/>.

Gregory of Nyssa. 2007. *Gregory of Nyssa: Contra Eunomium II*. L. Karfíková, S. Douglass, & J. Zachhuber (eds.). Brill.

Howard-Snyder, D. 2013. "Propositional faith: What it is and what it is not." *American Philosophical Quarterly* 50: 357–72.

Jay, C. 2014. "The Kantian Moral Hazard Argument for religious fictionalism." *International Journal for Philosophy of Religion* 75: 207–23.

Joyce, R. 2001. *The Myth of Morality*. Cambridge University Press.

Joyce, R. 2005. "Moral fictionalism." In M. E. Kalderon (ed.), *Fictionalism in Metaphysics*. Oxford University Press. 287–313.

Joyce, R. 2020. "Fictionalism: Morality and metaphor." In B. Armour-Garb & F. Kroon (eds.), *Fictionalism in Philosophy*. Oxford University Press. 103–21.

Kalderon, M. 2005. *Moral Fictionalism*. Oxford University Press.

Le Poidevin, R. 2019. *Religious Fictionalism*. Cambridge University Press.

Mackie, J.L. 1977. *Ethics: Inventing Right and Wrong*. Penguin.

Malcolm, F. 2018. "Can fictionalists have faith?" *Religious Studies* 54: 215–32.

Malcolm, F. & Scott, M. 2017. "Faith, belief and fictionalism." *Pacific Philosophical Quarterly* 98: 257–74.

Rey, G. 2007. "Meta-atheism: Religious avowals as self-deception." In L. Antony (ed.), *Philosophers without Gods*. Oxford University Press. 243–65.

Schiffer, S. 1987. *Remnants of Meaning*. MIT Press.

Scott, M. 2020. "Faith, fictionalism and bullshit." *Thought* 9: 94–104.

Scott, M. 2015. "Realism and anti-realism." In G. Oppy (ed.), *The Routledge Handbook of Contemporary Philosophy of Religion*. Routledge. 205–18.

Scott, M. & Citron, G. 2016. "What is apophaticism? Ways of talking about an ineffable God." *European Journal for Philosophy of Religion* 8: 23–49.

Scott, M. & Malcolm, F. 2018. "Religious fictionalism." *Philosophy Compass* 13: 1–11.

Wettstein, H. 2012. *The Significance of Religious Experience*. Oxford University Press.

7
Is the Pope Catholic?
Religious Fictionalism and the Hazards of Belief

Mary Leng

1. Introduction

Religious participation can bring many advantages even to those who do not believe in God. Being part of a religious community can be a great comfort to people who might otherwise suffer from loneliness and isolation. For parents, attending a church and baptizing their children may be their children's entry ticket to a good local church school. Some enjoy the aesthetic experience of attending religious ceremonies—for example, via an appreciation of church music. Others may value the discipline involved in cultivating religious habits such as attending regular services, fasting, and prayers. And, for some, the promise of tea and cakes in the church hall after mass may be all they need to make their attendance worthwhile. In all these cases one might reasonably worry that there is something morally dubious involved in the individuals' decisions to behave "as if" they believe the central tenets of a religion when really they do not. There is at least a whiff of "free-loading" involved in someone's reaping the benefits of a religious life without actually believing the creed they so readily recite, and certainly a danger of hypocrisy. But can there be good *moral* reasons for behaving "as if" one believes in God even if one does not?

This chapter will consider some moral arguments for religious fictionalism. As such, it presupposes that there are moral facts, and indeed that adopting a religious fictionalist position might turn out to be the morally right thing to do. Quite how to construe those moral facts the chapter presupposes to exist (or indeed whether this presupposition could itself be understood in fictionalist terms) is not something that I will consider here. But a natural reading of the position developed in this chapter is that of Robin Le Poidevin's character "Moira" (in Chapter 10 of this volume), who advocates the combination of moral realism with theistic fictionalism.

One worry about adopting religious fictionalism on moral grounds is that, whatever moral reasons we might think we have for behaving *as if* one believes in God, they might all too easily spill over into moral reasons for overcoming our epistemic scruples and fully embracing religious *belief*. To bypass this problem, the chapter turns to an intriguingly different moral argument for religious fictionalism, due to Christopher Jay (2014). What is intriguing about Jay's Kant-inspired argument is that it aims to establish that "acceptance without belief" in God is the morally optimal attitude—better, that is, from a moral perspective, than full-blown belief.

My main aim in this chapter will be to consider whether the attitude Jay advocates, of fully immersed acceptance-without-belief in God, is possible. In particular I will consider a challenge raised to the idea of fully-immersed acceptance by Paul Horwich (1991), in the context of a discussion of Bas van Fraassen's constructive empiricism (1980). Horwich argues that, insofar as the constructive empiricist advocates full immersion in scientific practice, behaving exactly like the realist scientist does, there is nothing that distinguishes their proposed attitude of acceptance from full-blown belief. Drawing on a response to Horwich which I made previously on behalf of the mathematical fictionalist (Leng 2010), I will argue that there are some aspects of the behavior of self-professed religious believers, particularly in relation to their attitudes to grief and death, that suggest an attitude more indicative of fully immersed make-believe than fully fledged belief. As such, if the self-conscious fictionalist behaves in exactly the way that those believers do, then they both may well be better thought of as make-believing rather than genuinely believing in God.

2. Moral Motivations for Religious Fictionalism

Fictionalists about a discourse advocate immersed engagement in that discourse, while simultaneously professing not to believe the discourse's claims. Fictionalists advocate such a position because they think that there is some value served by speaking *as if* the claims of the discourse in question are true that does not depend on their actually being true. This means that, in order to support adopting a fictionalist attitude about X-talk, at a minimum, fictionalists need to answer two questions (cf. Leng 2020: 124–5):

Q1: What is it that X-discourse is useful for?
Q2: Why should we expect X-talk to be useful in this way if we do not believe our X-claims?

For example, Hartry Field's (1980) defense of mathematical fictionalism answers Q1 by saying that mathematical discourse is useful for enabling us efficiently to draw out the consequences of nominalistically-stated scientific theories. Q2 is answered by pointing to the conservativeness of mathematics over nominalistic theories. More recent so-called "easy road" defenses of mathematical fictionalism, including my own, disagree with Field on whether these answers point to the only important uses of mathematics, holding that in addition to enabling us to draw consequences of nominalistic theories, speaking as if there are mathematical objects as described in our mathematical theories also provides us with a rich—and potentially indispensable—descriptive apparatus for describing physical objects in our theoretical models. Q2 is then answered by noting that imagined, merely fictional, models can be as descriptively valuable as real ones (Leng 2010). In each case, though, the onus is on the fictionalist to identify the purposes to which they wish to put their X-discourse, and to explain why it is reasonable to expect participation in that discourse to serve those purposes if one does not believe that X-claims are true.

What might a religious fictionalist say in answer to Q1 and Q2? This will in part depend on one's motivations for fictionalism. One character, the "free-loader" religious fictionalist as described above, participates in religious discourse and practices for entirely prudential reasons, simply because of the personal benefits it brings to them in helping them to meet their ends. The free-loader fictionalist can answer Q1 and Q2 with relative ease. Suppose, for example, my aim is to get my children accepted into a top local state school, and the school in question is a Catholic one. Professing to believe in God, and supporting this by participating in the religious practices of the Catholic church, including baptizing my children and attending weekly masses, is a very useful way for me to ensure a school place. If motivated purely by non-moral reasons, such as my personal self-interest (or perhaps in this case, the interests of my children), engaging in a deceptive pretense is not going to undermine those motivations.

On the face of it, though, it is harder to see how a person motivated by *moral* reasons will be able to combine answers to Q1 and Q2 so easily. To the extent that one's answer to Q1 appeals to some moral end, one might worry that the apparent deception involved in "speaking as if" there is a God if one does not believe that there is one will undermine that moral purpose. One well known challenge to the mathematical fictionalist is, after all, effectively a moral one: Hilary Putnam (1971: 57) complains of the "intellectual dishonesty of denying the existence of what one daily presupposes." Can it ever be *morally* right to reap the benefits of engaging in a discourse if one does not believe the content of what one says?

How, then, might a religious fictionalist who is motivated by moral reasons rather than reasons of self-interest answer Q1 or Q2, given that Q1 must appeal to some moral motivation, thus raising the challenge (in Q2) of how the apparent dishonesty involved in fictional engagement could ever support such moral ends? Andrew Eshleman (2005) offers one plausible account. In Eshleman's view, religious discourse can be "a powerful vehicle through which we might realize fuller and less ego-centered lives" (2005: 188), so that "by engaging religion as a fiction one may foster growth in one's moral character" (2005: 190). If one's aim is to pursue a moral ideal, then to the extent that the symbols and ideas of one's chosen religion embody that ideal, participating in the religion can be a useful means to a moral end. One way that religious participation works in this regard is through enabling one to access the support of a religious community who share one's moral ideals. But Eshleman also points to another way in which religious participation may serve one's moral ends: by enabling us to formulate and represent those ends adequately. Thus Eshleman suggests the command to "Be imitators of God" as a way of pointing to moral perfection.[1] We have close to an *expressive indispensability argument* here: perhaps we cannot adequately characterize the moral ideal we think we ought to pursue except via engaging in religious imagery to form a conception of God. Nevertheless, though religious *immersion* may be necessary for us to form an adequate conception of the moral ideal, and may also be necessary to bolster us in pursuing that ideal (through the support of a like-minded community), if our aim is to flourish as moral beings, religious *belief* may not be necessary for achieving this aim.

Benjamin S. Cordry (2010) raises a number of challenges for Eshleman's religious fictionalism. The one I focus on here involves the effectiveness of fictional immersion in achieving our moral ends. If merely behaving *as if* you believe in God can help build moral character, wouldn't *actually believing* in God help even more? Cordry certainly thinks so: "If pretending to believe makes a person better and improves the world, then actually believing should do the same or more" (Cordry 2010: 86). But if this is so, then for those who are tempted by religious fictionalism for moral reasons, mightn't there likewise be good (moral) reasons to try to overcome their (epistemic) qualms about full-blown belief in the existence of God? After all, what evidence there is does not determine whether or not to believe in God: we may not think we have good evidence for the existence of God, but neither do we have conclusive evidence against. Faced with this evidential impasse, if there are moral reasons for believing in God (because doing so will better help us to commit to a morally valuable way of life), then those motivated to religious fictionalism for moral reasons should be equally motivated to give up their epistemic qualms and embrace theism.[2]

---

[1] Whether or not this is a good route to moral improvement may, of course, depend on which elements of which religious doctrine one adopts in forming a conception of God to aspire to. There are certainly aspects of, e.g., the depiction of God in the Old Testament, that, were we to focus on these as central, might result in a less than perfect moral outcome.

[2] In advocating believing without evidence, this line of thinking has similarities to Pascal's Wager as an argument for religious belief. In Pascal's case we have prudential, rather than moral, reasons to believe in God, but in both cases an argument is offered for adopting a belief even if there are not good *epistemic* reasons to do so. For a discussion of Pascal's Wager in the context of religious fictionalism, see Brock 2020. One interesting issue discussed there is Pascal's assumption that by behaving "as if" one believes in God, the non-believer might be able to put themselves into such a state as (eventually) to become a genuine believer: "You would like to attain faith, and do not know the way; you would like to cure yourself of unbelief, and ask the remedy for it. Learn of those who have been bound like you, and who now stake all their possessions.... Follow the way by which they began; by *acting as if* they believed, taking the holy water, having masses said, etc. Even this will naturally make you believe, and deaden your acuteness" (Pascal [1670] 1910: 68, quoted in Brock 2020: 217 [Brock's emphasis]). This raises the question, to be discussed below, of whether the fictionalist's proposed attitude, of immersed

I will not consider here whether Eshleman's version of religious fictionalism has the means to respond to this challenge, but instead will use Cordry's challenge as a springboard to consider another, rather intriguing, moral argument for a form of religious fictionalism. If successful, this argument is immune to the challenge that Cordry raises. The argument in question is Jay's (2014) Kantian "moral hazard" argument for religious fictionalism. What is particularly interesting about Jay's argument in the context of Cordry's challenge is that it is a moral argument for immersed acceptance of religious doctrine *without belief*. Indeed, the moral hazard of the argument is that, if acceptance tips over to full blown belief, the moral benefits of religious immersion are lost. So unlike Eshleman's moral argument for fictionalism (where it is arguable that whatever moral reasons there are to "pretend" that there is a God work equally well, if not better, as moral reasons to believe), if Jay is right, the moral reasons his Kantian appeals to in order to support immersed acceptance of religious doctrine are also simultaneously moral reasons *not* to believe in God.

3. The Kantian Moral Hazard Argument for Religious Fictionalism

Jay's argument is prompted by Kantian considerations. He notes that, in Kant's view, we have very good moral reasons for behaving *as if* we believe in the God of Christianity.[3] In particular, striving to be of good moral character is so demanding of us that, if we did not in at least some sense accept the immortality of the soul, it would be irrational of us to pursue the moral ends required of us. As Jay presents Kant's argument,

> since the gulf between our radical moral imperfection and moral perfection is *infinite*, Kant argues that we are rationally committed to the hope that we will be granted an infinite life in which to pursue the end of moral perfection.
>
> (Jay 2014: 213)

---

acceptance of religious doctrine without full belief, is one that can be stably held. If Pascal's proposed method for attaining faith is effective, then religious fictionalists might find themselves ending up as theists despite their best intentions.

[3] Jay's argument is extracted from Kant's writings, and Kant was brought up by Pietist parents (Pietism being a form of German Lutheranism), so Kant has in mind only the Christian God. As we'll see below, though, what is essential to Kant's picture is that belief in God involves belief in an infinite afterlife where sins are punished and virtues rewarded. This is a conception that is common to the Abrahamic religions; so the Kantian argument, if it works at all, should work to support acceptance of the God of Abraham, and could also be adapted to other religious systems involving an infinite afterlife and divine reward/punishment. Given the Christian context in which Kant's argument is presented, and given my own greater familiarity with the Christian tradition, I will focus on Christian doctrine and Christian conceptions of God in this chapter.

It is irrational for us to pursue ends that we know to be impossible. But given that the gulf between our moral imperfection and the moral perfection that Kant thinks we should strive to achieve is so large, if we were limited to a finite human lifetime, moral perfection would be unachievable. In order for our efforts at achieving moral perfection to be rational, we must have a rational commitment to the existence of an afterlife in which we may have time to achieve our moral ends after the death of the human body. Belief in the God of Christian theology would provide us with that commitment.

On the other hand, however, a different set of Kantian considerations suggest that religious belief is a hazard for those who wish to pursue a moral life. The argument on this side comes from the potential for religious belief—and specifically for belief in an afterlife—to undermine our moral motivations. It is important, Kant thinks, not only to act as the moral law requires, but also to do so *because the moral law demands it*. The moral person not only does the right thing, but does so for the right reasons. But suppose we come to believe the claims of Christian doctrine, and therefore believe that God exists, is watching what we are doing, and will reward or punish us in the afterlife on the basis of our actions. If we genuinely do hold those beliefs, Kant (as Jay presents him) thinks that it will be all too easy for our motivations to be corrupted, so that the reason on which we act is not because the moral law demands us, but because we wish to secure reward and avoid punishment in the afterlife.

We are left, then, in a sticky situation. It seems that if we truly believe in an afterlife and in a God who will reward or punish us in the afterlife, then our ability to act as fully moral agents—doing the right thing for the right reasons—is in grave danger of being undermined. But, on the other hand, if we *don't* believe in an afterlife and our ability to continue to strive for the kind of moral perfection displayed by God in that afterlife, the rationality of pursuing moral ends at all will be undermined, so we won't even try to act morality. Either way, the prospects for pursuing a moral life seem bleak.

Things, however, are not quite so bad, Kant thinks (according to Jay). Our having a rational *commitment* to the existence of an afterlife in which we will be able to continue to pursue moral perfection does not require full blown *belief* in the existence of an afterlife. After all, what is required of us is that we put ourselves in a position whereby the end we are pursuing—moral perfection—is not undermined by rational doubts about its very possibility. But in order to put ourselves in this situation, Kant thinks, all that is needed is that we engage in an immersed form of fictional (i.e., nondoxastic) acceptance of the Christian doctrine: we put ourselves in a position where we act as if we believe in God and an afterlife, without actually believing. The upshot of this, then, is that the moral hazard of full belief, alongside the essential moral importance of acting *as if* we believe, provides an argument in favor of religious fictionalism that does not spill over into an argument in favor of belief in God. What is required in order for us to be able to pursue a moral life is that we hit a religious fictionalist "sweet spot": just enough immersed acceptance of religious doctrine that we are able to act as if we believe in God and an afterlife, without tipping over into a state of full belief which, were it to occur, would jeopardize our moral motivations.[4]

4. Is Fully Immersed Acceptance without Belief Possible?

There are a number of objections that could be raised for Jay's picture. I will focus on just one. This concerns the very possibility of hitting the required "sweet spot" of fully immersed acceptance without belief. Consider the religious fictionalist who does not believe in God but resolves to be just "as if" they believe. Perhaps they go to church on Sundays, listen attentively to the readings, and spend time by themselves contemplating the Bible. But if they do not *really* believe in an afterlife, then how is all this religious practice going to help them to overcome the natural apathy that comes from realizing their moral imperfections as well as the finitude of human life? Faced with the enormity of the task of achieving moral perfection, one might ask oneself "I'm never going to be able to achieve my ends, so why even try?" The theist can respond to this worry straightforwardly: "Yes, you are, as you have an infinite life ahead of you in which to improve yourself," and thus find that any doubts are easily set aside. But what does the religious fictionalist say? As a fictionalist, speaking with the realist, they can also try to reassure themselves, in their internal monologue, about the infinite life that lies ahead. But they do not *believe* that there is such an infinite life, they only accept this claim nondoxastically. So how could such a response ever succeed in putting a stop to their internal doubts about the impossibility of achieving their moral ends?

An answer available to Jay in response to this worry would be to emphasize that the attitude that he is advising we cultivate is not one of simple "make-believe," where the thought that we don't believe in God and an after-life, but that we are make-believing that we do, is readily accessible to us (even if not quite at the forefront of our mind). Rather, the nondoxastic acceptance that Jay's Kant advocates is better thought of as something rather more immersive. If Jay's Kantian recommendation is going to succeed in doing its job of helping us avoid moral apathy, in nondoxastically "accepting" the Christian story we need to do

---

[4] Is this the only way of avoiding the moral hazard of belief? Richard Joyce (Chapter 13 of this volume) suggests another way out is available to the theist: "Believe that the afterlife exists, but distract yourself from that belief in everyday contexts—that is, nondoxastically accept that the afterlife does *not* exist." Presumably this combination will also face its own "sweet spot" challenge (see section 4): can we remain motivated by our belief in an infinite afterlife enough to continue to strive for moral perfection if we distract ourselves from this belief sufficiently to avoid its pernicious effects on our moral motivations?

more than simply make-believe that it is true. Like method actors preparing for a role, we are not meant simply to pretend, as and when the issue arises, that we believe in God, but rather we are required fully to inhabit the role of the believer, to transform our lives so that we live—and think—exactly as if we believe. If we adopt this attitude of fully immersed acceptance, doing so involves burying our sincerely held beliefs so that they are no longer easily accessible to us. For the fully immersed method-acting religious fictionalist, when wondering whether they'll have time to achieve moral perfection, the fully immersed answer that "you have an infinite life ahead of you in which to improve yourself" will be taken to heart just as much as it is by the true believer. After all, they have committed to act the role of the believer in a fully immersed manner, and as such, just like the believer, when faced with this question they will focus on the infinite life promised and answer without worry.

Unfortunately though, the solution of full immersion presents at least two further worries. The first concerns the reason Jay's Kantian fictionalist advocates that we merely make-believe but don't believe that there is a God. Recall that full belief is considered to be a moral hazard: if we really do believe that there is a God who will reward or punish us in the afterlife, then this is likely to taint our moral motivations, so that even if we do do the right thing, we do so for the wrong reasons. But if we are so fully immersed in a fiction that we unquestionably adopt the attitudes of the believer who thinks that they have an eternal afterlife in which to achieve moral perfection, then won't that level of full immersion also infect our moral motivations, just as much as it does for the believer? (See Joyce, Chapter 13 of this volume.) If a religious fictionalist is so immersed in the fiction that they behave entirely as if they believe that an infinite afterlife is coming to them, won't they likewise behave entirely as if they believe that an all-knowing God will reward their good deeds and punish their bad in this afterlife?—in which case their moral motivations will be just as much exposed to moral hazard as the true believer.

The second concern relates to the nature of belief vs. fully immersed make-believe, and owes its origin to an objection Paul Horwich (1991) raises in response to Bas van Fraassen's (1980) development of constructive empiricism. According to van Fraassen, the appropriate attitude to the claims of science is an immersed acceptance without belief. The constructive empiricist scientist should, for all practical purposes, behave exactly like the card-carrying realist scientist, the only difference being that the constructive empiricist doesn't actually believe what they say when doing science. Horwich (1991: 3) challenges whether this attitude of acceptance without belief is really possible:

> If we tried to formulate a psychological theory of the nature of belief, it would be plausible to treat beliefs as states with a particular kind of causal role. This would consist in such features as generating certain predictions, prompting certain

utterances, being caused by certain observations, entering in characteristic ways into inferential relation, playing a certain part in deliberation, and so on. But that is to define belief in exactly the way instrumentalists characterize acceptance.

The challenge to the fictionalist is that if what it is to accept a theory or doctrine is to be functionally just as if one believes, then there's nothing to distinguish this from actual belief. At best, the fictionalist suffers a form of false consciousness: they believe that they do not really believe the things that they say and act on, but their actions belie them.

One way of responding to Horwich's objection is to challenge his identification of beliefs with states with a particular kind of causal role. Another response points to behavioral differences between the immersed method actor and the person we take to be a true believer (e.g., their responses when the chips are down and they are forced into a context where they have to act on their genuine beliefs, which will see the method acting fictionalist snap out of role).[5] But I think a third response, one that I toy with in *Mathematics and Reality* (2010) on behalf of the mathematical fictionalist, has the benefit of speaking both to Horwich's challenge and also to the first worry I raised concerning the difficulty of immersing oneself in the fiction just enough for it to be effective in allowing one to rationalize the aspiration to act morally, but without its being so effective that one's moral motivations are undermined by the promise of divine reward/punishment. So I will develop this response on behalf of the religious fictionalist here.

In *Mathematics and Reality*, I consider the challenge that if the mathematical fictionalist, when doing mathematics and using mathematics in empirical science, behaves in exactly the same way that the ordinary (and therefore, presumably, realist) scientist does, then by Horwich's lights she just is a realist, despite her protests to the contrary. The response I suggest there is as follows:

> Rather...than accept Horwich's challenge to find something distinctive in the fictionalist's attitude to theories that shows it to be genuinely different from the attitude taken by self-avowed realists, the strategy I would like to take is to question Horwich's assumption that the attitude of self-avowed *realists* to their scientific theories should automatically be described as *belief* in the mathematical utterances of those theories. Horwich notes some behavioural features that might usually be taken to indicate that a person holds a particular belief, and notes that it is precisely *these* features that characterize the anti-realist's notion of immersed acceptance. In the light of this, it looks as though we will need to provide some positive argument for the claim that our *fictionalist* scientist does

---

[5] Chris Daly (2008) offers responses along these two lines.

not, in fact, believe the mathematical utterances of her theories. But it is easy to turn this argument on its head. The fictionalist scientist advocates that we merely *pretend* that the mathematical assumptions of our theories are true, treating our mathematically stated theoretical utterances as moves in a game of make-believe, which can be used to express, indirectly, hypotheses concerning what is fictional in the game of set theory with non-mathematical urelements. Why not, then, consider the behavioural features characteristic of uncontroversial cases of make-believe? If these features are also characteristic of the behaviour of immersed participants in scientific activity with regards to the mathematical assumptions of their theories, then the realist who holds that we ought to *believe* those assumptions might equally well be challenged to find some behavioural indicator that the attitude she does hold genuinely amounts to *believing* the mathematical hypotheses of her theories.   (Leng 2010: 210)

Horwich's assumption is that people who claim to believe our best scientific theories (and therefore to believe the mathematics used to formulate those theories) really do believe them to be true. If so, then to the extent to which the fully immersed fictionalist behaves just like the realist when doing mathematics and science, their attitude is (by Horwich's lights) also one of belief, and there is merely some "false consciousness" involved on behalf of the fictionalist who professes not to believe the claims that she utters and acts on. But turning things around, I ask, why assume that it is the *fictionalist* who suffers from false consciousness here? If we can find elements of the alleged realist scientist's behavior that look more characteristic of make-believe than belief, then the behavioral similarity between the knowingly immersed fictionalist and the self-described realist/Platonist suggests that, as I put it, "if Horwich's line of argument is right and attitudes such as belief are to be defined in purely behavioural terms, then there is a case to be made for questioning whether even the most dyed-in-the-wool self-proclaimed scientific realist/mathematical Platonist *really* believes the mathematical components of her theories" (Leng 2010: 215).

To motivate this case, I point to features of ordinary mathematical practice, including *tolerance of indeterminacy* and *stipulative freedom* that speak against the idea that, when push comes to shove, mathematicians *really* think they're dealing with abstract mathematical objects. For example, Frege, a *true* Platonist, famously worried about precisely which objects the numbers are, and sought a definition of number that pinned down these objects to the extent that all meaningful identity questions concerning them (including "Does 2 = Julius Caesar?") were provided with answers. But most mathematicians don't worry at all whether "2" really is this or that set (or whether it is a set at all), and instead seem happy to stipulate its identity as and when it suits them to do so. This kind of stipulative freedom is characteristic of make-believe engagement with fictions. Do we think there is a deep answer to whether Jean Rhys's first Mrs Rochester in *Wide Sargasso Sea* is the same person as the sketchily presented madwoman in the attic from Brontë's *Jane Eyre*? As neither really exists, at least from a metaphysical perspective, we can be happy to let Rhys stipulate that she is, so long as her story coheres with whatever Brontë does tell us about the first Mrs Rochester. (As Rhys put it: "She seemed such a poor ghost. I thought I'd try to write her a life" (Vreeland 1979: 235).) While Frege seems to behave as a true believing Platonist would in his engagement with mathematics and the questions he is willing to ask, for the most part the mathematicians whom the fictionalist wishes to emulate behave in ways that are, arguably, characteristic of immersed fictional engagement. So why not think that it is they who are suffering from false consciousness, rather than the fictionalist who advocates a self-conscious fictional immersion?[6]

Can this line of thought be taken further to respond to the worry that the fully immersed religious fictionalist might turn out to be a (self-deceived) theist after all? Are there features of the fully immersed practice that our fictionalist wishes to emulate that might suggest that even those who profess to believe are betrayed by their actions—that they too are really just carried away with an engaging make-believe? How would a true believer in religious doctrine, who really believed in an all-loving God and in divine reward (or punishment) in the afterlife behave, and do many people who self-describe as religious believers behave in that way? If we can show that self-professed believers actually behave in ways that are more suggestive of fictional immersion than full belief, then arguably it is they who are suffering from false consciousness, whereas religious fictionalists, who consciously immerse themselves in a fiction resulting in behavior that is indistinguishable from that of self-professed believers, are accurate in their self-understanding of their attitude.

5. Do Theists *Really* Believe in God?

Are there, then, cases where the behavior of self-professed believers looks more indicative of immersion in a fiction than of genuine belief? Georges Rey (2007) points to a number of features of theists' engagement with the content of Christian

---

[6] Relatedly, Stephen Yablo reminds us, in relation to the question of the existence of numbers, that "there is a certain cast of mind that has trouble taking questions like these seriously. Some would call it the *natural* cast of mind: it takes a good deal of training before one can bring oneself to believe in an undiscovered fact of the matter as to the existence of nineteen... And even after the training, one feels just a teensy bit ridiculous pondering the ontological status of these things" (1998: 230). If this is indeed the *natural* cast of mind, one might be wary of attributing enthusiastic *belief* in mathematical objects to the ordinary mathematician or scientist. Yablo thinks that this natural cast of mind is best described as *quizzical*, that of "one that doubts that there is anything to find" (231), questioning whether existence questions have answers at all. We need not follow Yablo so far as to attribute to the ordinary mathematical/scientist a form of meta-ontological skepticism in order to think that a willingness to shrug off ontological questions might be a sign of something less than full and sincere belief in the existence of mathematical objects.

faith that make it seem akin to fictional engagement, including, for example, the resistance to requests for detail about the content of the religious stories that they profess to believe:

> It seems as silly to ask the kind of detailed questions about God as to ask for details about fictional characters; for example, What did Hamlet have for breakfast? Just how did the tornado get Dorothy and Toto to Oz? These questions are obviously silly and have no real answers—the text pretty much exhausts what can be said about the issues. In keeping with the reliance on texts and appeals to non-literality that we've already noted, religious claims seem to be understood to be fiction from the start.   (Rey 2007: 256)

Rey also notes the oddness of those who profess to believe in the effectiveness of petitionary prayer not putting this belief to any serious tests (2007: 261). Why not engage in double blind studies of the effectiveness of different sorts of prayers, for example?

An interesting case study in this regard, also noted by Rey, concerns attitudes to death amongst self-professed religious believers. What should someone who believes in an afterlife involving divine reward and punishment think about the premature death of good people, and particularly of innocent children? Presumably this should be an occasion to rejoice, as God has hastened their path to their divine reward. And yet (and thankfully so, as to think otherwise would be monstrous) for most theists (perhaps members of the Westboro Baptist Church aside), lives cut short are a matter of great sadness, regret, and injustice. Indeed, our sense of injustice is often the greater the more convinced we are of someone's moral virtue ("Why do only the good die young?" we wistfully sigh), and is at its highest when contemplating the deaths of innocents. Pope Francis himself wrote (2016) "with a heavy heart" of the sound of "the lamentation of so many mothers, of so many families, for the death of their children, their innocent children." But if a loving God is waiting to reward virtue and punish sin in the afterlife, then it is the innocent and virtuous souls that stand most to gain from an early demise. Why regret those deaths, if we firmly believe they have gone to a better place?

Of course, there are many reasons why we might feel intense grief and sorrow at death even if we do believe fully in an afterlife and divine reward. When this involves loved ones, we grieve in part for what we will miss out on in this life, as the chance to enjoy their company during the worldly part of our lives is now gone. But what of strangers? Why should the true believer feel outrage and injustice at the deaths of those they would never have met and will never miss? Maybe our attention turns to their families and our sympathies are with *their* losses. And yet the sense of anger and injustice at the loss of an innocent life does not seem to reduce if we learn that anyone who might mourn them has died too. That the Lisbon earthquake took with it not only innocent children but their entire families seemingly did not temper the horror for 18th-century theists whose faith was shaken by the magnitude of this event; and neither did the loss of entire families make any less the horror of the Boxing Day Tsunami in 2004. The responses of self-described believers in the face of death—all death, not just the deaths of those they know personally and will miss, and particularly in the face of the deaths of innocents for whom the prospect of punishment in the afterlife is not to be feared—seem to speak against their self-avowed belief in divine reward.

If the suggestion that many who sincerely profess to believe do not *really* believe in an afterlife where the good are rewarded sounds outlandish—even offensive—it is perhaps of interest to note that it is one that has been made by at least one self-professed believer. In these passages from his 1961 essay on grief, C. S. Lewis wonders whether the faith he thought he had in an afterlife was ever real:

> You never know how much you really believe anything until its truth or falsehood becomes a matter of life and death to you. (1961: 22)
>
> Apparently the faith—I thought it faith—which enables me to pray for the other dead has seemed strong only because I have never really cared, not desperately, whether they existed or not. Yet I thought I did. (1961: 23)
>
> Of course it is different when the thing happens to oneself, not to others, and in reality, not in imagination. Yes; but should it, for a sane man, make quite such a difference as this? No. And it wouldn't for a man whose faith had been real faith and whose concern for other people's sorrows had been real concern. The case is too plain. If my house has collapsed at one blow, that is because it was a house of cards. The faith which "took these things into account" was not faith but imagination. The taking them into account was not real sympathy. If I had really cared, as I thought I did, about the sorrows of the world, I should not have been so overwhelmed when my own sorrow came. It has been an imaginary faith playing with innocuous counters labelled "Illness," "Pain," "Death," and "Loneliness." I thought I trusted the rope until it mattered to me whether it would bear me. Now it matters, and I find I didn't. (1961: 36–7)

Prior to his own personal loss, Lewis sincerely thought that he believed that the dead went to a better place. But in dealing with the death of his wife he wonders whether he ever really did.[7]

The phenomenon of self-professed belief in an afterlife being accompanied by behavior that seems to betray that faith is also recognizable outside of the

---

[7] Those familiar with Lewis's trajectory may protest that, while Lewis expressed these doubts in grief, he did recover his faith. But this too was predicted by Lewis in "A Grief Observed," where he expressed doubt about whether, even in believing his faith to have been restored, it really would have been: "Indeed it's likely enough that what I shall call, if it happens, a 'restoration of faith' will turn out to be only one more house of cards. And I shan't know whether it is or not until the next blow comes—when, say, fatal disease is diagnosed in my body too, or war breaks out, or I have ruined myself by some ghastly mistake in my work" (1961: 39).

Christian context, for example in the anthropologist Bronisław Malinowski's ethnographic observations of the Trobriand people of Papua New Guinea, in *Myth in Primitive Psychology* (1926). There Malinowski observes the contradictions in his subjects' attitude to death in light of their professed belief in the spirit world and eternal spiritual life. As in Lewis's case, his subjects' behavior in the face of the death of loved ones, or when contemplating their own imminent death, belies their self-professed belief in the afterlife:

> [I]t is perhaps well to realize that in his actual emotional attitude towards death, whether his own or that of his loved ones, the native is not completely guided by his belief and his mythological ideas. His intense fear of death, his strong desire to postpone it, and his deep sorrow at the departure of beloved relatives belie the optimistic creed and the easy reach of the beyond which is inherent in native customs, ideas, and ritual. After death had occurred, or at a time when death is threatening, there is no mistaking the dim division of shaking faith. In long conversations with several seriously ill natives, and especially with my consumptive friend Bagido'u, I felt, half-expressed and roughly formulated, but still unmistakable in them all, the same melancholy sorrow at the transience of life and all its good things, the same dread of the inevitable end, and the same questioning as to whether it could be staved off indefinitely or at least postponed for some little time. But again, the same people would clutch at the hope given to them by their beliefs. They would screen, with the vivid texture of their myths, stories, and beliefs about the spirit world, the vast emotional void gaping beyond them. (1926: 105–6)

However much Malinowski's "natives" profess to believe, their behavior in the face of death belies them as it does the rest of us.[8]

Suppose, then, that the predicament that Lewis felt that his grief uncovered is the predicament of very many self-professed believers in God. That is, they go through most of their life sincerely thinking that they believe in God and the afterlife, but in reality their faith in life after death and eternal reward is just a "house of cards," revealed as such in moments of clarity such as experiences of

---

[8] Indeed, as Malinowski hypothesizes elsewhere in his discussion, adopting the "myth" of an afterlife is plausibly a natural response to the realities of death: "Myth, warranting the belief in immortality, in eternal youth, in a life beyond the grave, is not an intellectual reaction upon a puzzle, but an explicit act of faith born from the innermost instinctive and emotional reaction to the most formidable and haunting idea" (1926: 42–3). This point is echoed in Philip Larkin's haunting meditation *Aubade* on the fear of death: "This is a special way of being afraid / No trick dispels. Religion used to try, / That vast moth-eaten musical brocade / Created to pretend we never die" (Larkin 1988). (I am grateful to Richard Joyce for drawing my attention to these discussions of the "myth" of the afterlife in face of the fear of death in Malinowski and Larkin.) Aside from being a natural response to our fears about death, the myth of divine reward in the afterlife is also extremely *convenient* to inculcate in an unequal society, for those who benefit from inequality. Think of Joe Hill's preachers' refrain to the starving masses: "You will eat, bye and bye, in that glorious land above the sky. Work and pray, live on hay, you'll get pie in the sky when you die."

grief. Mightn't we then best describe such people as (unknowingly) deeply immersed in a fiction, as thoroughly behaving *as if* they believe in God and the afterlife, but with their lack of belief revealed only in extreme circumstances? If so, then the self-conscious religious fictionalist whose behaviors mirror those of the "believers" is not the one who is suffering from false consciousness. If the identity of a mental state such as belief or acceptance is to be determined by its causal role, then the fact that the self-described "believer" behaves just like the immersed fictionalist does might, given the elements of their behavior that are more akin to the behavior of the immersed method actor than the true believer, suggest that, despite their self-avowals, many self-described believers do not really believe. And if fictional immersion is as widespread as attitudes to death might suggest, perhaps even the Pope, in lamenting the death of innocents, isn't really Catholic?

If even *the Pope* might not be Catholic, can we say that there *any* true believers? Are there any people whose behavior is compatible with genuine belief in an afterlife and divine reward? If Christopher Hitchens' (1995) complaints about Mother Teresa are to be believed, then perhaps she is someone who at least comes close. As Hitchens paints her, far from caring about alleviating the suffering of the poor and needy, Mother Teresa's focus was very much on converting souls to Christianity so that they would meet their rewards in the afterlife, with little regard to their earthly conditions. Thus Hitchens criticizes Mother Teresa for focusing on conversion and baptism of patients in her care, while contributing to their continued suffering through failure to provide adequate pain relief or basic comforts. In support of this picture, a Université de Montréal review of the literature on Mother Teresa described her as "caring for the sick by glorifying their suffering instead of relieving it" (Larivée et al. 2013), an attitude that is reinforced by her own comment that "I think it is very beautiful for the poor to accept their lot, to share it with the passion of Christ. I think the world is being much helped by the suffering of the poor people" (quoted in Hitchens 1995). If this picture of Mother Teresa as actually caring very little about alleviating suffering seems ill fitting for a Catholic saint, perhaps we can note that it is entirely consistent with a sincere belief that those who suffer most during their finite earthly existence will, if they accept God's grace, be rewarded most highly in their infinite afterlife. For a true believer in such an afterlife, the pursuit of religious conversion, even at the expense of alleviating worldly suffering, would seem the rational and indeed morally mandated course of action.

6. Achieving Kantian Immersed Acceptance

What does this all mean for the two objections I raised to Jay's moral hazard argument? In relation to the second (i.e., Horwich's objection) I have suggested that if the nature of one's propositional attitudes is to be determined by our behavior rather than our sincere self-descriptions, then arguably it is the self-described theist who is mistaken in thinking that they believe in the afterlife, rather than the self-conscious religious fictionalist who thinks that they are merely engaging in a make-believe. So in behaving just like the ordinary so-called "believer," and reaping the rewards of religious engagement that are available to them, the religious fictionalist need not be thought of as "really" engaged in belief at all. Both our fictionalist and the self-described theist display aspects in their engagement with religion that are more akin to nondoxastic acceptance than full belief, as evidenced by the horror shown by both to worldly suffering and premature death.

Furthermore, if I am right that the attitude displayed by both the self-confessed fictionalist and the self-deceived theist is one that holds back on full belief in divine reward and the afterlife, then it turns out that we also have the ingredients needed to solve the first worry that I raised. Recall that the concern was that the "sweet spot" of the exact amount of immersion-without-belief might not be achievable. That is, it might not be possible to immerse oneself just enough into the religious fiction to reap the benefits of being "as if" we believe in an infinite afterlife (and thus to be rationally motivated to aspire to a moral perfection that we will never meet in our finite earthly lives), while not tipping over so far to the point that we are also in all respects just "as if" we believe in divine reward/punishment, in such a way that our moral motivations will likely be undermined. Can this "sweet spot," essential for us to achieve full morality, really be found?

Well, what is actual is certainly possible, and if it is right that very many self-professed, sincere, theists do not *really* deep down believe in an afterlife in which the good will be rewarded, even though they behave in almost all respects as if they do, then it looks like the precise balance of immersed acceptance without belief that the Kantian religious fictionalist says is required in order to be able to be truly moral is something that very many people in fact *are* able to achieve.

7. Is Revolutionary Fictionalism Possible?

As a coda to this argument, it is interesting to consider how the proposal complicates the traditional revolutionary/hermeneutic divide for fictionalism. As this divide is standardly presented, the revolutionary fictionalist advocates fictionalism about a discourse as a *revision* to the attitude standardly taken by participants in the discourse, whereas the hermeneutic fictionalist holds that fictionalism is the attitude already actually taken by (many or most) participants. In *Mathematics and Reality* my aim was to argue for a revolutionary form of mathematical fictionalism: regardless of the attitude mathematicians and scientists actually take to their theories, I argued that they *ought* to adopt a fictionalist attitude. And yet in responding to Horwich's objection to the possibility of fictionalism of any sort, it seems that what is required is a defense of *hermeneutic* fictionalism, an argument to the effect that actual practitioners already do (albeit unbeknownst to them) adopt a nondoxastic attitude to their utterances. Does this mean that revolutionary fictionalism is unstable, that the only defensible form of fictionalism (in the face of Horwich's challenge) is hermeneutic?

Perhaps not. It's important to my response to Horwich that there are things that a true believer could do that would mark *their* engagement with the discourse in question out as genuinely realist. In the mathematical case, Frege as true believer differs from most ordinary users of mathematics in taking seriously the question of precisely *which* objects the numbers are. And in the theistic case I have suggested Mother Teresa (at least as Hitchens casts her) as someone who displays behaviors indicative of a genuine belief in an infinite afterlife with divine reward far outweighing any suffering that might be experienced in an embodied human lifetime. If most or all users of mathematics were like Frege, or if most or all religious practitioners were like Mother Teresa—such that hermeneutic fictionalism were false as an account of the attitude of ordinary practitioners—what would this mean for our fictionalist who wishes to advocate immersed acceptance without belief? If immersed acceptance involves behaving *just like* the masses, and if the masses are best understood as believing the claims of their discourse, then it appears that one cannot achieve the level of immersion that the fictionalist recommends without believing the claims of the discourse. On the other hand, if there remains a way of distinguishing the behaviors of individuals involved in immersed acceptance from those of the masses who genuinely believe, then, even if hermeneutic fictionalism fails, revolutionary fictionalism would appear to remain a live option. But our examples should speak in favor of this latter eventuality, even in a world where the masses do turn out to behave like true believers. The reason for this is that, in both the religious and the mathematical case, we have identified behavioral differences between true believers and immersed nondoxastic accepters, thus showing two genuinely distinct attitudes—even on Horwich's account according to which attitudes are identified via their behavioral consequences. The fact that many ordinary practitioners appear to behave more like fictionally-immersed accepters than true believers is helpful in confirming that someone who follows the fictionalist advice can reap the very same rewards as the masses while practicing nondoxastic acceptance; but perhaps what is most important is that we can distinguish between belief and immersed acceptance while showing that those whose behavior is indicative of the latter can benefit from participation in the discourse even without their attitudes spilling over into full belief.

8. Conclusion

In order to stand a chance of acting morally, Kant holds, we need to sustain a rather complex attitude to religious doctrine. We need to immerse ourselves deeply enough in the story of an infinite afterlife involving divine reward and punishment that we are able to rationalize our efforts to reach moral perfection (despite the certainty that, in a finite earthly lifetime, we will fail to do so). But we can't buy into that story so completely that we allow it to interfere with our moral motivations (so that we find ourselves doing all the right things but for all the wrong reasons). The required balance, the sweet spot of just enough immersion to support our efforts to act morally, but not enough so as to allow ourselves to focus on divine reward that would undermine our ability to act morally for the right reasons, may seem difficult to obtain.

Difficult though this may seem, I have argued that it is plausible that very many self-confessed theists have in fact achieved just the right amount of nondoxastic immersion. While they are so immersed in the religious story that they believe that they believe it, nevertheless aspects of their behavior—particularly in their laments for the deaths of innocents—suggest that they do not really believe in an afterlife of divine reward. Given that (if Jay's Kantian argument is right) our *only* chance at achieving full morality *requires* that we are psychologically able to hit the sweet spot that apparently many self-described theists do manage to hit, perhaps we are in the best of all possible worlds, after all. A perfect solution to the Kantian predicament that's almost enough to make one believe in the existence of God![9]

References

Brock, S. 2020. "Religious fictionalism and Pascal's Wager." In B. Armour-Garb & F. Kroon (eds.), *Fictionalism in Philosophy*. Oxford University Press. 207–33.

Cordry, B. 2010. "A critique of religious fictionalism." *Religious Studies* 46:77–89.

Daly, C. 2008. "Fictionalism and the attitudes." *Philosophical Studies* 139: 423–40.

Eshleman, A. 2005. "Can an atheist believe in God?" *Religious Studies* 41: 183–99.

Field, H. 1980. *Science without Numbers: A Defence of Numbers*. Oxford University Press.

Francis. 2016. "Letter of His Holiness Pope Francis to Bishops on the Feast of the Holy Innocents." Retrieved from: <https://www.vatican.va/content/francesco/en/letters/2016/documents/papa-francesco_20161228_santi-innocenti.html>.

Hitchens, C. 1995. *The Missionary Position: Mother Teresa in Theory and Practice*. Verso.

Horwich, P. 1991. "The nature and norms of theoretical commitment." *Philosophy of Science* 58: 1–14.

---

[9] I am grateful to participants in the 2021 Religious and Moral Fictionalism workshop for helpful comments and discussion of this chapter, and particularly to Richard Joyce for detailed comments on a draft. I am also grateful to Chris Jay and to other colleagues in the Department of Philosophy at the University of York for comments on an early version of this chapter, and to members of York's AHRC-funded "Grief" Project, including Louise Richardson and Matthew Ratcliffe, whose work drew my attention to discussions of grief and attitudes to death, including C. S. Lewis's essay on this topic.

Jay, C. 2014. "The Kantian Moral Hazard Argument for religious fictionalism." *International Journal for Philosophy of Religion* 75: 207–32.

Larivée, S., Sénéchal, C., & Chénard, G. 2013. "Les côtés ténébreux de Mère Teresa." *Studies in Religion/Sciences Religieuses* 42: 319–45.

Larkin, P. 1988. *Collected Poems*. Faber and Faber.

Leng, M. 2010. *Mathematics and Reality*. Oxford University Press.

Leng, M. 2020. "Should the mathematical fictionalist be a moral fictionalist too?" In B. Armour-Garb & F. Kroon (eds.), *Fictionalism in Philosophy*. Oxford University Press. 122–41.

Lewis, C. S. 1961. *A Grief Observed*. Faber and Faber.

Malinowski, B. 1926. *Myth in Primitive Psychology*. Kegan Paul.

Pascal, Blaise. [1670] 1910. *Pensées*, trans. by W. F. Trotter. J. W. Dent.

Putnam, H. 1971. *Philosophy of Logic*. Harper and Row.

Rey, G. 2007. "Meta-atheism: Religious avowal and self-deception." In L. Antony (ed.), *Philosophers without Gods: Meditations on Atheism and the Secular Life*. Oxford University Press. 243–65.

Van Fraassen, B. 1980. *The Scientific Image*. Clarendon.

Vreeland, E. 1979. "Jean Rhys: The art of fiction no. 64." *Paris Review* 76: 219–37.

Yablo, S. 1998. "Does ontology rest on a mistake?" *Proceedings of the Aristotelian Society suppl. vol.* 72: 229–61.

8
Religious Fictionalism
Strategies and Obstacles

Michael Scott

1. Fictionalism and Religious Fictionalism

Can one participate in the practices and language of a religious tradition without having religious beliefs? Recent debate has focused on prospects of a fictionalist answer: that such participation can be morally and intellectually respectable and also yield pragmatic benefits.[1] In the philosophy of religion, revolutionary varieties of fictionalism, which propose revisions to religious assertoric practices and doxastic commitments, have been at the forefront of discussion. In this chapter I will explore some of the strategies for developing and defending such an account and set out some of the difficulties that it faces. I will argue that the obstacles are substantial and that an alternative, non-revisionary, hermeneutic variety of religious fictionalism is a theoretically more appealing option. However, while I think that revolutionary religious fictionalist accounts of religious traditions should be abandoned, a localized version of the theory that targets a limited range of religious commitments and language may be defensible. As an example of this, I will propose a fictionalist interpretation of apophatic accounts of God-talk.

Section 1 will set out the religious fictionalist position in more detail. Section 2 will present three preliminary difficulties for the theory that focus on challenges to religious varieties of fictionalism. Sections 3 and 4 will turn to a discussion of the norms of religious discourse, which I think present a serious and underdiscussed problem for religious fictionalism, and strategies for responding to it. Section 5 will consider an apophatic variety of religious fictionalism.

Fictionalism about some field of discourse is typically seen as a salient option when the following conditions hold: (a) the sentences of the discourse posit the existence of properties that we should not believe exist, (b) continuing engagement with the discourse, including the affirmation of these suspect sentences, has pragmatic benefits that would be lost if the discourse were eliminated. Fictionalism, in its revolutionary form, proposes ways to alter the ways that speakers employ

---

[1] See Lipton 2007; Le Poidevin 2016, 2019; Cordry 2010; Deng 2015; Eshleman 2016.

Michael Scott, *Religious Fictionalism: Strategies and Obstacles* In: *Moral Fictionalism and Religious Fictionalism*. Edited by: Richard Joyce and Stuart Brock, Oxford University Press. © Michael Scott 2023.
DOI: 10.1093/oso/9780198881865.003.0009

the discourse and secure its pragmatic benefits so that speakers are no longer committed to the truth of the contentious claims. The discourse is often said to be usable as a fiction, though the details of how this works vary considerably. According to hermeneutic fictionalism, speakers are already uncommitted to the truth of the discourse sentences that they affirm. No revolution is needed. The prospects for the revolutionary variety of fictionalism in religion will be the main focus of this chapter.

In comparison with the extensive literature on revolutionary fictionalism about mathematics, ethics, possible worlds, and scientific theories, accounts of religious fictionalism are noticeably recent.[2] This is surprising because religious discourse looks like a particularly promising target for a fictionalist treatment. Atheists and agnostics, motivated by doubts about the existence of God or religious agents, will be inclined to agree with (a). And, even among critics of religion, there is often recognition of the psychological, social, and ethical benefits that can accrue from engagement with the language and practices of a religion.[3] So, the conditions that merit serious investigation of religious fictionalism appear already to have a significant constituency of supporters. Moreover, the viability of religious fictionalism will be a matter of pressing practical importance for individuals who are already participants in a religion but have lost their faith.

For the purposes of this chapter, I will take for granted two prerequisites for fictionalism: that we should not believe in the existence of the properties and agents that religious discourse appears to posit, and that engaging with religious discourse and practice does have significant pragmatic advantages that are sufficient to motivate consideration of a fictionalist rather than an abolitionist option.[4] I will take the principal pragmatic advantage to be the widely canvassed psychological, moral, cooperative, and social benefits that are said to come from participation in a religious community. I will call these *participatory benefits*.

The following three sections will consider some of the obstacles in the way of developing a successful revolutionary religious fictionalism. The responses available to the religious fictionalist will of course depend on the mechanics of the theory. The two most detailed (and interestingly different) defenses of religious fictionalism that I will focus on in this chapter are by Peter Lipton (2007) and Robin Le Poidevin (2016, 2019), each of which takes advantage of ideas that are familiar from accounts of fictionalism in other fields. On the one hand, the religious fictionalist might change her attitudes towards religious discourse by accepting and endorsing the claims of the discourse, rather than believing and asserting

---

[2] For a broad overview of writings on fictionalism, including religious fictionalism, see Liggins 2012.
[3] See, for example, J. S. Mill [1874] 2009. For a review of research into religious fictionalism see Scott & Malcolm 2018.
[4] Fictionalist theories are focused primarily on monotheistic and polytheistic religions that employ descriptive religious discourse, rather than other religious traditions—such as Buddhism or Daoism—where comparatively few (if any) metaphysical commitments appear to be made.

them. According to Lipton, someone who accepts a religious sentence is committed to using it as "a tool for thinking and for living" (2007: 45), and by endorsing a religious sentence she expresses that commitment rather than her belief in it. Acceptance goes along with the fictionalist imaginatively immersing herself in the stories and ideas that make up the chosen religious tradition (2007: 41–2). Alternatively, the religious fictionalist might be making assertoric religious claims about what is true according to the religious fiction in question. According to Le Poidevin, when the fictionalist says "God loves us," this is warranted by its being true in the given fiction that God loves us.[5] In general, "any given theological statement p is true if and only if it is true in the theological fiction that p" (2016: 178).

These two varieties of religious fictionalism are related to the *noncognitivist* and *cognitivist* types of fictionalism respectively (a distinction elaborated by Richard Joyce (2019) (see also Armour-Garb & Kroon 2020)). The former type of fictionalism recommends a change of attitude towards sentences of the discourse from belief to acceptance. To accept, as Lipton's account makes clear, is a practical decision rather than a truth-normed evaluation, and by affirming a religious sentence the fictionalist does not assert it or believe what it says. The latter is primarily a theory about the semantics of the discourse: a fictionalist may assert and believe sentences of the discourse but those sentences concern a fiction.[6] Both varieties of religious fictionalism take advantage of immersion tactics to engage with religious narrative and practice, to better integrate with religious communities and secure the proposed pragmatic advantages of religion.

2. Preliminary Issues: Scope, Error Containment, and the Oracle

While there are some general objections to fictionalism,[7] it's useful to begin by considering some of the obstacles in the way of implementing religious fictionalism that are not in play—or at least are much less prominent—in accounts of fictionalism in other fields. To be clear, I do not aim to press the following three issues as knockdown arguments against revolutionary religious fictionalism. However, these are ways in which religious fictionalism appears at a theoretical disadvantage to cognate fictionalist theories, and its implementation a significantly heavier lift. In the following section, I will consider a more direct argument against fictionalism.

---

[5] In more recent work, Le Poidevin has moved closer to Lipton's position, proposing that fictionalists pretend to assert the truth of religious sentences (2019: 35, 60).

[6] This cognitivist treatment of fictionalism is more prominent in Le Poidevin's earlier account: "When she asserts 'God loves us,' for example, she takes this to be true, but by virtue of the content of the relevant fiction. The general schema that she subscribes to is this: any given theological statement p is true if and only if it is true in the theological fiction that p" (2016: 178).

[7] For example, the phenomenological objection (Brock 2014).

A. The sentences of religious discourse that are typically at the forefront of discussion in treatments of religious language and fictionalism are ones with a clear religious subject matter, and in particular sentences about God or gods. For example,

1. God is good.
2. The Bible is the word of God.
3. God created the heavens and earth in six days.
4. Humans are created in God's image.

However, a fictionalist account that encompasses sentences with religious content will not be sufficient for participation in a religious community. For this, the fictionalist will need to engage with various additional commitments made by members of the community that do not have religious content—for example: (a) ethical demands concerning the manner and frequency of prayer, charitable giving, dietary laws, pilgrimage, and the pronouncements of religious authorities; (b) the wide-ranging statements made in religious scriptures, which may include historical claims, medical and psychological judgments, scientific theories, and various moral pronouncements; (c) the revelations of God or divine messengers.

According to some accounts, religious discourse extends beyond a religious subject matter to include utterances that satisfy contextual conditions about their use. For example, William Alston proposes that religious discourse includes "language (any language) in connection with the practice of religion—in prayer, worship, praise, thanksgiving, confession, ritual, preaching, instruction, exhortation, theological reflection, and so on" (Alston 2005: 220). Victoria Harrison concurs: religious discourse concerns language "that is used either to serve a religious purpose or in a religious context" (Harrison 2007: 128).

These points raise a preliminary question about the scope of the religious fictionalist's enterprise and how it should be implemented. If the religious fictionalist takes sentences with a religious subject matter as the target of what she considers for acceptance or for assessment as true in the fiction, this appears insufficient for more than a superficial engagement in a religious tradition and, therefore, is unlikely to secure the proposed participatory benefits. If, in contrast, the fictionalist stance is triggered by contextual factors, and extends to commitments that are not prima facie about a religious subject matter, this will make participation easier, but it is difficult to see how it would work in practice. For example, suppose the presiding minister makes claims about the suitability of one of the political candidates in an upcoming election or proposes a diagnosis of the medical condition of a member of the congregation. Should the fictionalist consider the merits of these claims for acceptance or their truth in the fiction, but discard these considerations once in a non-religious context, such as when she talks with others outside the church, or gets into the voting booth or considers medical treatments? This seems at odds with using religious ideas as "rules of thought and life."

B. A related issue concerns the inferential connections between religious and ostensibly non-religious sentences. For example, (3) might be taken to imply that the universe did not expand from an initial singularity; (2), combined with the assumption that the word of God is true, yields a wide range (take your pick!) of valid inferences from religious assumptions to false moral or historical conclusions. Moreover, similar patterns of reasoning in religious discourse can derive from a true non-religious assumption (such as that most contemporary cosmologists believe the Big Bang theory) an unsound non-religious conclusion (e.g., that most contemporary cosmologists are mistaken).

Religious fictionalists are not, of course, committed to defending a fictionalist account of these examples. They could select differently—a point I will discuss in more detail presently. The problem I want to raise here is not tied to these specific examples but centers on the fact that religious commitments seem to facilitate unsound reasoning that can leads to false conclusions on matters that extend beyond the characteristic bounds of religious discourse. If, therefore, the fictionalist seeks to endorse the claims of some pragmatically beneficial religion, will she also endorse the false non-religious claims that follow from them, or will she refuse to go along with those inferential connections, thereby putting at risk the participatory benefits of religious engagement? Will she, for example, affirm (without believing) a non-religious but false inference from religious premises when addressing a religious interlocutor, but assert its falsity when addressing a non-religious interlocutor?

In this respect, religious discourse looks different from other fields of discourse where fictionalism is in serious contention, such as mathematics or ethics. In these areas, fictionalists can argue, the systematic errors of these discourses do not lead us into further error in other areas of discourse. For example, mathematics is—or at least should be—consistent and is, arguably, conservative: "Good mathematics is conservative," as Hartry Field puts it (1980: 13). Using mathematics in inferences should not thereby lead us into error. Moral discourse stays within the terms of practical reasoning; participation in moral discourse and thinking seems possible without reaching extravagant and false non-moral conclusions. Religious discourse, in contrast, won't stay in its lane, permitting its users to intrude into the details of what are ostensibly non-religious matters. It is not clear how the fictionalist should contain this error. (See Joyce, Chapter 13, for a complementary argument.)

C. Another notable point of difference between religious discourse and mathematical or ethical discourse is the importance given by speakers to their metaphysical commitments. This is brought out by considering the Oracle thought experiment (Burgess & Rosen 1997; Yablo 2000). The Oracle is an infallible, omniscient being that tells us that there are no abstract objects. The Oracle's verdict, so the thought experiment goes, would not result in changes either to our use of mathematical discourse or to our attitudes towards it. A similar thought experiment could be applied to moral discourse, where the Oracle advises that no moral properties exist; speakers would carry on as before and not see this as a good reason to abandon ethical discourse. This thought experiment, even if not persuasive, helps motivate the idea that commitments to the existence of moral properties or abstract objects do not play a critical role for the participants in these discourses, suggesting that the revisions needed by revolutionary fictionalism will be modest and undemanding. Setting aside the awkward question of whether the Oracle is a religious entity, the same conclusion looks like a nonstarter in the religious case. One of the important points of difference is that whereas questions about the existence of ethical properties or abstract objects are largely confined to rarefied critical contexts such as philosophical seminars, abolitionism about religion is widely recognized as a live option. So, in advancing a religious claim, the existence of the religious properties or objects that it posits are a relevant point at issue. For many, the falsity of religious claims would render the discourse pointless and continuing engagement with it dishonest.

A related issue concerns the importance accorded by some religions to the possession of religious beliefs by its participants. Religious beliefs are reported in avowals of faith, either by an individual or collectively by a group. Moreover, such reports are sometimes explicitly formulated as a membership requirement for a religion or religious community. For example, the Nicene Creed begins: "We believe in one God, the Father Almighty, the maker of heaven and earth, of things visible and invisible." How should fictionalists deal with such explicit statements about religious belief? Le Poidevin proposes that these can be accommodated by fictionalists in a similar way to other religious sentences: "reciting the creed is part of the game of make-believe... what is going on here is pretense: the fictionalist does not actually believe, but is pretending to express belief" (2019: 38). But the problem with this strategy is that explicit statements of belief appear to be about the speaker's or community's own psychological attitudes; it is not clear why a religious fiction should provide any guidance on this matter. In the Christian religious fiction there is, for example, one God, the maker of heaven and earth, etc., but it is presumably not part of that fiction that a given speaker believe this. The fictionalist could take the position that in pretending that various religious propositions are true, she also thinks of herself as a believer and, in contexts where shared commitments are demanded or expressed, she could pretend that she has religious beliefs in common with others. This strategy points up some of the limits on the intellectual participation in a religious tradition (and the engagement with other religious believers) that is available to the fictionalist. A profession of faith will not, for the fictionalist, be the product of serious self-reflection on her commitments of the kind that may be expected from religious believers and in particular those who struggle with their faith. Instead, the avowal of faith will be part of the act of playing along with a religious fiction.

3. Discourse Norms

To get participatory benefits of religion, the fictionalist will need to conversationally engage on religious matters with other participants in a religious community. A concern sometimes raised is that this engagement will be in some way fraudulent. When the fictionalist affirms (1), she is (in noncognitivist mode) affirming a sentence that she does not believe to be true, while she is (in cognitivist mode) affirming a sentence about a fiction that appears to be about God, and her conversational audience—those, at least, who do not know the speaker to be a fictionalist—will presumably interpret what is said as an assertion and expression of belief. Why is this a problem? In the literature on religious fictionalism, the objection is usually expressed by pointing out the difficulties with distinguishing what the fictionalist is doing from what a liar is doing (Deng 2015; Cordry 2010).

Linking what the religious fictionalist is doing with the practice of lying, however, misplaces the worry about the fictionalist's conversational engagement. In lying, a speaker asserts a sentence that she (a) believes to be false, and typically does so with (b) the intention of deceiving the audience or, at least, (c) aims to present that sentence as being true.[8] Religious fictionalists are not trying to do any of those things. An intention to deceive is not part of the fictionalist's approach, a point made by Le Poidevin in response to the charge that the fictionalist is insincere: "sincerity is to be judged according to the intentions of the participant. If those intentions are to deceive, to enjoy the benefits of a society whose principles one secretly rejects, then this is indeed insincere. But if it is a means to moral and spiritual improvement, to the benefit of all, it is not" (2019: 38). Fictionalists, at least in the field of religion, do not appear to endorse the assertion of falsehoods. Instead, religious fictionalists (in cognitivist mode) are asserting sentences that they believe to be true in the religious fiction; religious fictionalists (in noncognitivist mode) affirm (or quasi-assert) religious sentences but do not intend to assert them. Additionally, fictionalists who are agnostic about the subject matter do not believe that the religious sentences that they affirm are false, even if they do not believe them to be true. So, it appears that the fictionalist may be able to engage in religious discourse without lying or being insincere. Moreover, to the extent that fictionalists appear to be lying, Stuart Brock suggests a straightforward way to correct this mistaken impression: "if the religious fictionalist's speech acts are misunderstood by her intended audience, the fictionalist can and will make

---

[8] The precise formulation of these conditions—and in particular whether lying requires the intention to deceive—is a matter of dispute. See Saul 2012.

explicit that she is not asserting what she says" (2020: 213). This would, of course, not only abruptly break the spell of make-believe but also put at risk the prospects of further participation with other religious believers.

If we set aside the comparison with lying, there is a more pressing worry suggested by the objections raised by Harry Frankfurt in his discussion of bullshitting: that, by bullshitting, the speaker misrepresents herself as believing something (2005: 54) and fails to pay due attention to telling the truth in a conversational context in which telling the truth is the norm (2005: 61).[9] Bullshitting is sometimes taken (not least by Frankfurt himself) to require the speaker to have certain characteristic attitudes—for example, a lack of interest in what the audience thinks about the subject matter of the bullshitting (2005: 15). But the salient issue when considering religious fictionalism, and the principal failing that Frankfurt's objections latch onto, does not concern the bullshitter's attitudes but instead her actions and specifically her conversational behavior. The bullshitter contributes to an ostensibly assertoric discourse but is not guided by the same rules as the other participants: when the bullshitter affirms an indicative sentence, she disregards the norm that she should say what she believes. This is not to say that the fictionalist, in affirming religious sentences, is intentionally bullshitting. Rather, the fictionalist exhibits similar shortcomings in failing to follow the belief-expressing and truth-telling norms of religious discourse.

The problem of discourse norms is in two respects more challenging than the objection about lying: first, it is concerned with the fictionalist's conversational interactions rather than questions about her motives; second, the problem is not addressed by the upfront honesty suggested by Brock.

To illustrate, consider a story A. J. Ayer relates about his marriage to Renée Lees. Although a lapsed Catholic, she was concerned that her family would be deeply upset if they did not have a Catholic wedding. Ayer was persuaded that he should go along with the ceremony "on utilitarian grounds." However, as part of the ensuing proceedings, he had to declare his agreement to bring up their children in the Catholic faith.

> Like a child keeping its fingers crossed, I muttered half audibly Euripides's line from the *Hippolytus*... "the tongue has sworn but the mind has not sworn." This is an action of which I have always been ashamed.   (1977: 127)

Ayer does not say exactly what it is about the event that led him to feel ashamed. But I take it that his concern was that engaging in this subterfuge not only failed to get him out of the commitment that he publicly made but also, in attempting it, led him to act in bad faith. Even if his intentions were good, by participating in

---

[9] For an elaboration of these issues in connection with expressions of faith, see Scott 2020.

this ceremony he misrepresented himself as having religious beliefs. If he had attempted to come clean on what he had done and made explicit that he had not asserted his agreement, this would not have had the effect of putting his actions on a good footing but instead would have pointed up the unsuitability of his participation in the ceremony.

I think that many cases in which religious sentences are affirmed in religious discourse—but certainly not all, as I will explain in the following section—occur in contexts where the kinds of maneuver proposed by religious fictionalists, such as employing a fictional operator or accepting rather than believing, are not recognized as legitimate. To follow up an affirmation by insisting that one had merely accepted rather than believed the utterance, or that one had thought of the utterance as saying something that is true only within a fiction, would—like crossing one's fingers—not convey respectability on this way of affirming a religious sentence. It would, instead, be seen as an attempt to *retract* what one had said, and likely as evidence of insincerity.

Perhaps the fictionalist could argue that while certain conversational contexts should be avoided, it's an exaggeration to see the norms of religious discourse as presenting an obstacle to fictionalist engagement in religious discourse more generally. Some interesting remarks by Alston on religion could be marshalled in support of this position. Alston—focusing on Protestant Christianity—argues that there are few if any explicit affirmations of propositional belief required by a participant in the religion. For example, he observes that while the Nicene Creed and Apostles' Creed talk of "belief," it is belief *in* various religious agents and institutions (God, the Holy Spirit, Jesus, the Church, etc.) that is demanded, rather than belief *that* some statement about these agents or institutions is true. "Belief in," Alston suggests, can be understood as a practical commitment rather than a commitment to the truth of a proposition.[10] The 1530 Augsburg Confession and 1647 Westminster Confession, he notes, "consist of doctrinal statements without any explicit injunction to believe them" (2007: 138). Additionally, the baptismal service in the Book of Common Prayer requires the faithful to say various things—to renounce Satan, to accept Jesus Christ as savior, to promise to follow Christ, and to affirm the Apostles' Creed—they do not require them to explicitly state their beliefs: "nowhere are they called on to make a statement of the form 'I believe that'" (2007: 138). Alston uses these and other examples to argue that engagement with the Protestant faith is available without "belief that" commitments. Could fictionalists exploit the same evidence to argue that (some) religious traditions will be largely hospitable to fictionalist engagement?

The problem with Alston's strategy is that a speaker's belief in a sentence that she affirms does not have to be explicitly stated for belief to be a normative

---

[10] This raises the complicated question of the relationship between objectual (or relational) belief and propositional belief. For a detailed discussion of this, see Malcolm & Scott 2022.

requirement. A speaker does not get out of the obligation to affirm what she judges to be true by not prefacing what is said by explicitly saying "I believe…". As an example of this problem, suppose that you are on a walking holiday in Wales. Your next stop on the route is Caernarvon Castle, but you have become lost. You see a passer-by and ask him the way. He says, "Take the next left and follow the pathway by the river for about a mile." This, it turns out, is the wrong route. However, on your way back you encounter him again and ask why he gave these directions. Consider the following responses:

5. I didn't tell you that I *believed* that that was the route.
6. I'm a visitor here myself. It seemed to fit with the landscape that a castle would be in that direction.
7. I did not believe it was the right way. But it's a beautiful pathway—wouldn't it be agreeable if that were the route?

These look like defective excuses: they don't identify suitable reasons for the misleading guidance. But even if the traveler did not reencounter the guide, it was inappropriate at the outset for the guide to say what he did if he did not believe that it was the right way. Why should the speaker's lack of belief be more appropriate if the discourse is religious?

4. Fictionalist Selection Strategies

There appears to be a straightforward way to escape the problem of discourse norms: if you are an aspiring religious fictionalist, don't try to be a Catholic! Instead, find some religion or limit oneself to suitable areas of religious conversation that will not put speakers into the kinds of predicament that Ayer found himself in.

The need for a fictionalist to engage in a selective process is already recognized and discussed by Lipton and Le Poidevin. However, they have a particular process of selection in mind: since the fictionalist is not limited in her selection of a religious tradition by her beliefs on religious matters, and since there appear to be many religions that can yield the prospective pragmatic benefits of engagement, a process is needed to narrow down the range of options from the panoply that are in principle available. For example, Le Poidevin recommends the benefits of a fictionalist keeping to just one religious tradition rather than trying to maximize beneficial outcomes by alternating through different religions or attempting to pursue more than one at the same time (2016: 184). Lipton prefers a religious tradition that minimizes the conflicts between its doctrines and one's existing moral and scientific beliefs, thereby reducing the demands of the immersion and pretense needed to engage with it (2007: 45).

A different kind of selection, however, will be needed to avoid the problem of discourse norms. The conversational contexts that the fictionalist will be looking for are not necessarily those where awkward questions about what one really believes are not pressed (as may be the case in some liberal religions), but rather those where such questions don't matter. Are there any religions and areas of religious language that are like this?

Religious fictionalists who are selective in this way may be able to take advantage of the long history of arguments and observations supporting the availability of (typically Protestant) religion and discourse without belief. There is a large literature on this (see Scott 2017 for an overview). Here, I will briefly mention just three kinds of consideration that could be relevant to making the selection:

1. An interesting observation made by George Orwell writing in 1944 is on the role of humor in religious discourse:

> Never, literally never in recent years, have I met anyone who gave me the impression of believing in the next world as firmly as he believed in the existence of, for instance, Australia. Belief in the next world does not influence conduct as it would if it were genuine. With that endless existence beyond death to look forward to, how trivial our lives here would seem! Most Christians profess to believe in Hell. Yet have you ever met a Christian who seemed as afraid of Hell as he was of cancer? Even very devout Christians will make jokes about Hell. They wouldn't make jokes about leprosy, or R.A.F. pilots with their faces burnt away: the subject is too painful. (1998: 152–3)

Notably, Joyce comments that joking is a familiar "commitment-nullifying practice" (2020: 105). In this case, the humor is presented as evidence that the kind of commitments expressed by (many) speakers in talk of hell—even an explicit statement of belief in hell—do not require a belief in its existence.

2. A question about religious faith that has recently become the focus of lively debate is whether propositional faith that *p* requires belief that *p*. Alston, for one, admits that he is "inclined to think that a sizable proportion of contemporary, sincere, devout Christians are accepters rather than believers" (2007: 136). Alston (1996) and Robert Audi (1991) were early supporters of a nondoxasticist theory of propositional faith, and related theories have subsequently proliferated. Now, to the extent that affirming the propositional content of one's religious faith—i.e., saying "God exists" if one has faith that God exists—is a normal part of religious discourse, then, if Alston is correct, such affirmations are routinely made without believing them. (For discussion, see Scott 2020.)

3. Some accounts of religious discourse question the importance of even *understanding* the propositional contents that are ostensibly the object of faith commitments, let alone believing them. Ronald Hepburn (1958) and Stephen Mulhall (2015) have suggested that some religious sentences express paradoxes or unsolvable riddles, the meaning of which speakers are unable to grasp fully, but which serve as imaginative devices that inform religious and moral thinking. When these sentences are affirmed, therefore, speakers do not believe what they say. George Berkeley, in his 1732 dialogue *Alciphron*, argues that speakers lack a comprehension of many of the key doctrinal claims of Christianity, including accounts of grace, original sin, the Trinity, and the afterlife. For instance, when we consider the idea of grace, he argues, we find a "perfect vacuity or privation of all ideas"; it is an "empty name" ([1732] 1950: 290). Faith in the doctrine of grace, however, does not require that one understand what grace is. Endorsing a sentence about grace may have a desirable practical effect "as a principle, destructive of evil habits, and productive of good ones, although we cannot attain a distinct idea of it" ([1732] 1950: 296). Speakers, therefore, do not believe the Christian doctrines that they affirm because they do not understand what these affirmations say. Rather, faith in these doctrines is exhibited by noncognitive commitments: they are "placed in the will and affections rather than in the understanding, and producing holy lives rather than subtle theories" ([1732] 1950: 301).[11]

A prospective candidate for selection by the fictionalist may be Anglicanism, or some branch of it. For example, many traditional Anglican churches have a formal, antiquated layout better suited to ceremonial events than the committed worship of God, with a calendar of events that are routinely attended by non-believers (including, sometimes, the presiding minister). The setting and the scripted language of religious events make it easy to see the church as akin to a stage with various supporting props that lend solemnity to an occasion in which no religious belief is required. So, for example, when an infant's prospective godparent agrees to "care for them and help them to take their place within the life and worship of Christ's Church," both speaker and hearers can understand the ethical obligation to care for the child to be the relevant subject matter that is being communicated.

Considerations of this sort could in principle be mustered to locate an area of religious discourse, or even a religious tradition or some branch of it, that lacks

---

[11] Georges Rey (2007) brings together elements of the first and third consideration in his comments on the "detail resistance" of religious beliefs. He argues that if asked for more specific details on the mechanics of how, say, God created black holes, religious believers not only have no further information to offer but tend to regard such questions as silly.

the assertoric norms discussed in Section 3. As such, they potentially offer a way of selecting a religion that provides an opening for fictionalist participation. The problem with the selection strategy for *revolutionary* fictionalism, however, is that the results of the selection will be the kinds of religious discourse and participation that are susceptible to a hermeneutic fictionalist interpretation. Similarly, the nondoxastic theory of faith along with other antirealist religious options look like grist to the mill of hermeneutic fictionalism (if not noncognitivism). So the religious fictionalist is faced with the following difficulty: the contexts in which the fictionalist's religious affirmations appear to escape the problem of discourse norms are ones where no revolutionary fictionalist work is needed.[12]

5. Apophaticism and Fictionalism

I have argued that revolutionary religious fictionalism faces a number of obstacles and that the problem of discourse norms, in particular, prevents its successful implementation for a wide range of religious participation. While there are ways of addressing this problem, the most promising ways of doing so result in a hermeneutic fictionalist account of religious discourse, rendering the revolutionary option redundant. I am, therefore, skeptical about the prospects for a defensible revolutionary religious fictionalist account of religious discourse characteristic of a religious tradition. Having said that, a type of fictionalism that is restricted to a limited domain of religious discourse—i.e., where religious believers identify systematic error in a significant part of religious discourse and, rather than eliminate it, adopt a fictionalist approach—may be better positioned to address the difficulties.

In the following, I will outline a theory of apophatic accounts of religious discourse about God as a working example of a restricted religious fictionalism. I intend this as a contemporary philosophical interpretation of the apophatic accounts of discourse about God, and in drawing attention to this area of common ground between apophatic authors, I don't intend to minimize their disagreements on other matters. There is also a large literature on apophaticism in theology and history that explores the varying positions taken by these writers and places their work in a broader intellectual context.[13]

---

[12] Notably, Lipton (2007) concludes his paper by recognizing that his approach is likely to be workable only for liberal forms of religion (his own being progressive Judaism). So, while his discussion of immersion and accepting parts of religious discourse that he thinks are untrue appear to be leading up to a defense revolutionary fictionalism, it may be that he has a different purpose in mind. That is, he is thinking through the ways in which he can become a better, more engaged participant in a community that he values, and take better advantage of the pragmatic benefits of a religious tradition that already makes few if any demands for religious belief upon its members.
[13] See, for example, Turner 1995. There is also a small but growing literature on apophaticism in analytic philosophy. See Jacobs 2015; Gäb 2020; Scott & Citron 2016 (for a recent review).

Apophaticism is a theological and philosophical tradition that was most widely supported from late antiquity through the medieval period. Its most influential early exponent was Dionysius, writing in the late 5th century CE. A common idea among apophatic writers is that God's nature cannot be truly represented in either thought or language. Here are some quotations to illustrate:

Dionysius: "It cannot be spoken of and it cannot be grasped by understanding… There is no speaking of it, nor name nor knowledge of it. Darkness and light, error and truth—it is none of these. It is beyond assertion and denial."

(1987: 141)

Maximus the Confessor: God is "beyond conception and being conceived."

(1985: 129)

Meister Eckhart: "Since God is inexpressible in and of his nature, what we say he is, surely is not him. Hence the Psalm text 'Every man is a liar.'"

(1986: 211)

Eriugena: "Nothing at all can properly be said or understood of God." (1987: 25)

While most apophatic writers have otherwise conventional positions on matters of doctrine, salvation, and the afterlife, they take the remarkable view that sentences of the form "God is p" are systematically untrue.[14] Accordingly, they propose that one should stop believing these sentences and, moreover, should cease having any such thoughts about God. Achieving this change is taken to be a somewhat arduous enterprise to be undertaken over months or years, and the metaphor of ascending a mountain is widely used to describe it. For example, the 14th-century text *The Cloud of Unknowing* (author unknown) proposes a series of intellectual exercises that the reader can undertake to set aside their beliefs about God's nature.

Apophatic writers are not, however, abolitionists about religious discourse that represents God. They recognize that talk of God's nature is indispensable (not least because the Bible is replete with it) and they identify various pragmatic benefits of talking about God's properties: it can be used to encourage virtuous behavior and leads religious believers away from even more serious errors (Dionysius 1987: 150; Gregory of Nyssa 2007: 154).

There is a great deal more that could be said on this topic but for the purposes of this chapter we are in a position to see why the apophatic account of sentences about God's nature make fictionalism a potentially promising way of understanding

---

[14] I should note that apophatic writers are keen to draw attention to the many things that God is *not*, and often provide lists of such properties. This is the "negative theology" for which apophatic writers are perhaps most famous. What they say is often interpreted as a metalinguistic negation—i.e., "God is not p" should be understood as voicing a disagreement with calling God "p" rather than asserting that God is not p. (See Scott & Citron 2016 for discussion.)

it. First, apophatic writers take sentences about God's nature to be systematically untrue and that such sentences should not be believed. Second, they allow for the continued use of sentences that represent God, despite their falsity, because such language is indispensable and in other ways pragmatically useful. This part of religious discourse should not be truth-normed. Instead, the target sentences should be affirmed because they are found in (or at least are compatible with) scripture and support the proposed moral, intellectual, and spiritual benefits.

Apophatic fictionalism, therefore, is a restricted variety of revolutionary religious fictionalism. In contrast with the kind of religious fictionalism envisaged by contemporary supporters of the position, the account is limited to a subclass of religious sentences. However, restricted religious fictionalism can meet some of the objections that I raised in Sections 2 and 3. To begin with, the scope of the apophatic fictionalist enterprise is clear: only sentences that represent God's nature are in question. Second, apophatic writers propose to implement their position by revising the attitudes of religious believers and reforming the linguistic norms for using sentences about God. Because apophatic fictionalists are part of a religious community with which they share many religious beliefs, they are in a position to promote change to religious attitudes and language from within the tradition.[15]

Restricted revolutionary religious fictionalism may, therefore, have the resources to respond to the objections raised earlier. I recognize, however, that apophatic fictionalism is not a position that most revolutionary religious fictionalists will find remotely appealing, and this is not least because it is a restricted account that does not dispense with all religious belief. The theory may, therefore, best be understood not as promising an alternative variety of fictionalism, but as an example of the kinds of maneuvers that would be needed, and the theorical costs that would be incurred, to get revolutionary fictionalism to work.

References

Alston, W. 1996. "Belief, acceptance, and religious faith." In J. Jordan & D. Howard-Snyder (eds.), *Faith, Freedom, and Rationality*. Rowman & Littlefield. 3–27.

Alston, W. 2005. "Religious language." In W. Wainwright (ed.), *The Oxford Handbook of Philosophy of Religion*. Oxford University Press. 234–42.

Alston, W. 2007. "Audi on nondoxastic faith." In J. Greco, A. Mele, & M. Timmons (eds.), *Rationality and the Good: Critical Essays on the Ethics and Epistemology of Robert Audi*. Oxford University Press. 123–38.

---

[15] Notably, Dionysius makes clear that this is unlikely to be an entirely successful endeavor: some religious believers will not understand the apophatic project and will continue to have false beliefs (1987: 149).

Armour-Garb, B. & Kroon, F. (eds.). 2020. *Fictionalism in Philosophy*. Oxford University Press.

Audi, R. 1991. "Faith, belief and rationality." *Philosophical Perspectives* 5: 213–39.

Ayer, A. J. 1977. *Part of My Life*. William Collins.

Berkeley, G. [1732] 1950. *Alciphron or the Minute Philosopher*. In A. Luce & T. Jessop (eds.), *The Works of George Berkeley*, volume 3. T. Nelson.

Brock, S. 2014. "The phenomenological objection to fictionalism." *Philosophy and Phenomenological Research* 88: 574–92.

Brock, S. 2020. "Religious fictionalism and Pascal's Wager." In Armour-Garb & Kroon (2020): 207–33.

Burgess, J. & Rosen, G. 1997. *A Subject with No Object*. Clarendon.

Cordry, B. 2010. "A critique of religious fictionalism." *Religious Studies* 46: 77–89.

Deng, N. 2015. "Religion for naturalists." *International Journal for the Philosophy of Religion* 78: 195–214.

Dionysius. 1987. *Pseudo-Dionysius: The Complete Works* (trans. by C. Luibheid & P. Rorem). Paulist Press.

Eckhart, M. 1986. *Meister Eckhart: Teacher and Preacher* (ed. by B. McGinn). Paulist Press.

Eriugena. 1987. *Periphyseon (Division of Nature)* (trans. by I. Sheldon-Williams). Ballarmin.

Eshleman, A. 2016. "The afterlife: Beyond belief." *International Journal for Philosophy of Religion* 80: 163–83.

Field, H. 1980. *Science without Numbers: A Defense of Nominalism*. Princeton University Press.

Gäb, S. 2020. "Languages of ineffability: The rediscovery of apophaticism in contemporary analytic philosophy of religion." In S. Hüsch (ed.), *Negative Knowledge*. Narr Francke. 191–206.

Gregory of Nyssa. 2007. *Gregory of Nyssa: Contra Eunomium II* (ed. by L. Karfíková, S. Douglass, & J. Zachhuber). Brill.

Harrison, V. 2007. "Metaphor, religious language, and religious experience." *Sophia* 46: 127–45.

Hepburn, R. 1958. *Christianity and Paradox: Critical Studies in Twentieth-Century Theology*. Watts.

Jacobs, J. 2015. "The ineffable, inconceivable, and incomprehensible God: Fundamentality and apophatic theology." *Oxford Studies in Philosophy of Religion* 6: 158–76.

Joyce, R. 2019. "Moral fictionalism: How to have your cake and eat it too." In R. Garner & R. Joyce (eds.), *The End of Morality: Taking Moral Abolitionism Seriously*. Routledge. 150–65.

Joyce, R. 2020. "Fictionalism: Morality and metaphor." In Armour-Garb & Kroon (2020): 103–21.

Le Poidevin, R. 2016. "Playing the God game: The perils of religious fictionalism." In A. Buckareff & Y. Nagasawa (eds.), *Alternative Concepts of God: Essays on the Metaphysics of the Divine*. Oxford University Press. 178–91.

Le Poidevin, R. 2019. *Religious Fictionalism*. Cambridge University Press.

Liggins, D. 2012. "Fictionalism." In *Oxford Bibliographies in Philosophy*: doi:10.1093/OBO/9780195396577-0034. Oxford University Press.

Lipton, P. 2007. "Science and religion: The immersion solution." In A. Moore & M. Scott (eds.), *Realism and Religion*. Ashgate. 31–46.

Malcolm, F. & Scott, M. 2022. *A Philosophy of Faith: Belief, Truth and Varieties of Commitment*. Routledge.

Maximus the Confessor. 1985. *Maximus Confessor: Selected Writings* (trans. by G. Berthold). Paulist Press.

Mill, J. S. [1874] 2009. *Three Essays on Religion*. Broadview Press.

Mulhall, S. 2015. *The Great Riddle: Wittgenstein and Nonsense, Theology and Philosophy*. Oxford University Press.

Orwell, G. 1998. *I Have Tried to Tell the Truth 1943–1944*. Secker and Warburg.

Rey, G. 2007. "Meta-atheism: Religious avowal as self-deception." In L. Anthony (ed.), *Philosophers without Gods: Meditations on Atheism and the Secular Life*. Oxford University Press. 243–65.

Saul, J. 2012. *Lying, Misleading, and What Is Said: An Exploration in Philosophy of Language and in Ethics*. Oxford University Press.

Scott, M. 2017. "Religious language." In E. Zalta (ed.), *The Stanford Encyclopedia of Philosophy*. < https://plato.stanford.edu/entries/religious-language/>.

Scott, M. 2020. "Faith, fictionalism and bullshit." *Thought* 9: 94–104.

Scott, M. & Citron, G. 2016. "What is apophaticism?" *European Journal for Philosophy of Religion* 8: 23–49.

Scott, M. & Malcolm, F. 2018. "Religious fictionalism." *Philosophy Compass* 13: 1–11.

Turner, D. 1995. *The Darkness of God: Negativity in Christian Mysticism*. Cambridge University Press.

Yablo, S. 2000. "A paradox of existence." In A. Everett & T. Hofweber (eds.), *Empty Names, Fiction and the Puzzles of Non-Existence*. CSLI Publications.

9
The Contours of Religious Fictionalism

Natalja Deng

1. Introduction

Religious fictionalism (RF), like moral fictionalism (MF), can seem to be caught in a dilemma. On the one horn there looms a stubborn conservatism threatened by incoherence, and on the other horn lies redundancy. It is instructive to compare the source and shape of this dilemma as it arises for RF with some of the challenges affecting MF. The comparison is instructive for a number of reasons. Quite apart from the central relevance of moral considerations to the feasibility and desirability of taking up a fictionalist stance about religion, there are interesting structural (dis)similarities regarding the scope and possibilities of fictionalism in the two domains. This chapter explores some of these parallels, with a view to illustrating how RF is particularly well placed to escape the dilemma.

Section 2 examines various forms of fictionalism that are potentially relevant to the discussion. Partly drawing on previous work, I argue that (what I call) "thoroughgoing" types of fictionalism, including both revolutionary fictionalism and weak evaluative fictionalism (WEF), are problematic. Section 3 then defends a more lightweight kind of fictionalism and shows how it applies in the religious domain. Section 4 compares some of the pressures on MF and RF to remain thoroughgoing, and provides some reason to think that RF can better negotiate these than MF. Section 5 considers the related objection that RF lacks a good answer to the question of why one should adopt a (particular) religious fiction and suggests that a comparison with MF points the way towards the right response. Finally, section 6 reflects on a peculiar difficulty faced by RF that is structurally similar to the difficulty thoroughgoing fictionalists have when attempting to demarcate acceptance from belief; the similarity highlights an additional reason to recognize RF as a *sui generis* stance on religion.

2. Varieties of Fictionalism

Revolutionary fictionalism about a domain of discourse combines a number of claims. It says that our current practice in the domain is truth-normed, and it adds that we should, all things considered, change this. Any practical costs involved in this step would be outweighed by the benefits involved in changing our attitudes from belief to nondoxastic acceptance.

Another variety of fictionalism that will be relevant to this discussion is weak evaluative fictionalism, which says that whether or not our attitudes in the domain are truth-normed, they need not be (see Jay 2014). WEF thus weakens revolutionary fictionalism in several ways. Not only does it make no descriptive claim about the discourse in question, nor say anything about what should be done or what would be best all things considered, but it also does not claim that there would be anything positively good about our attitudes in the domain not being truth-normed; it says only that there would be nothing bad about it. The claim is to be understood in the light of the prior assumption that there is some value gained from the practice. WEF says this value does not depend on our attitudes being truth-normed; our attitudes in the domain can permissibly be nondoxastic.

In fact, the position can be weakened further. Proponents of WEF (and indeed of revolutionary fictionalism) need not make their central claims about *all* of the values derived from the practice. A proponent of WEF might hold that only *some* of those values are independent of whether our attitudes are truth-normed or not.

I'll refer to both revolutionary fictionalism and WEF as examples of "thoroughgoing" types of fictionalism, to be contrasted in due course with a "lightweight" kind of fictionalism that I take to be key to making sense of fictionalism in the religious domain. What makes them *thoroughgoing* is that they both centrally rely on the notions of nondoxastic acceptance and of reasons disconnected from truth. Their thoroughgoingness hinges on the ambitiousness of these two notions.

To nondoxastically accept p is to accept p in all ordinary, non-critical contexts. It is to treat p as if it were true and assent to it in all ordinary, non-critical contexts, while being disposed to dissent from it in all non-ordinary, critical contexts. Thus, if I nondoxastically accept some set of religious doctrines (say), I'm living just as if those doctrines were true, except in critical contexts.[1]

The reason that this distinction between critical and non-critical contexts is needed is that the phenomenon of using some sentences one does not believe (even though they purport to describe reality) for some limited purpose is much more commonplace than the stance at issue; think of reductio ad absurdum as a form of proof, or of using any scientific theory that is strictly false but a good approximation in some domain of interest.

The notion of reasons disconnected from truth is needed because the thoroughgoing fictionalist still has to be able to make sense of the idea that some

---

[1] Further questions arise concerning what exactly assent involves, whether the speech acts this kind of fictionalist practitioner makes are to be understood as nonassertoric, and if so what it takes for them to in fact be nonassertoric. I touch on some of these questions in Section 3 below.

sentences in the domain are to be accepted (nondoxastically) while others are not. Since the norms governing acceptance have nothing to do with truth and falsity, this means that there have to be reasons to accept some particular sentences of the domain but not others that have nothing to do with their truth or the others' falsity. For instance, according to a religious form of WEF (say), it may well be important that the sentence "God loves us" be nondoxastically accepted, while "God hates us" or "God was born last Thursday" is not.

Why think that these notions are ambitious (cf. Deng 2015)? Zoltan Szabó (2011) provides a compelling presentation of the difficulties involved. Consider someone who has heard about a result in modern physics that sounds incredible to them. Suppose this person wishes to defer to physicists on matters of physics rather than dismiss a well-established scientific theory just because it seems incredible; but suppose that they also want to "give their pre-theoretical intuitions some weight" (Szabó 2011: 376). The fictionalist offers them a way out of their dilemma: the person should simply suspend belief in the theory but act in all ordinary circumstances as if they still believed it. Prima facie, the fictionalist's advice seems, to use Szabó's words, trivial and frivolous (and one might add, somewhat epistemically and socially irresponsible). In fact, prima facie, it seems like "an invitation to deceive" both themselves and others. However, Szabó recognizes that to do justice to the fictionalist's idea a key requirement has to be added to this, and this is that the right to follow this advice has to be *earned*.

> [T]he fictionalist does not issue a blanket proposal for any situations in which inclinations to believe clash.... You need to show that the virtues of the theory...are independent of its truth. You need to examine the reasons you and your [physicist] friends are attracted to this theory and see whether they would survive even if the theory turned out to be false. You need to throw out all the reasons that fail this test and then see whether the remaining ones still suffice to recommend the theory to you. Only then are you invited to accept the theory without believing it. (Szabó 2011: 376–7)

This nicely brings out the difficulties that a thoroughgoing fictionalist faces. The recommendation that looked "frivolous and trivial" before now looks "somber and paradoxical"; and it is in the space between these poles that thoroughgoing fictionalists have to make a home. This is not easy.

Consider the notion of reasons that are disconnected from truth. These would need to be specific reasons to accept particular sentences of the discourse rather than others that have nothing to do with truth. In familiar cases, a reason's being good has a lot to do with truth. Suppose I accept the hypothesis that there is a red laptop in front of me because of a certain visual appearance. And suppose I then learn that the kind of lighting illuminating the laptop makes red laptops appear black and black laptops appear red. The visual appearance in question would then constitute a much weaker reason to accept that there is a red laptop in front of me. It would still constitute *some* reason to accept this, because the visual appearance makes the hypothesis that there is a red laptop in front of me much more likely than some other hypotheses (e.g., that there is an elephant in front of me), even if it does not make it the most likely hypothesis (since the most likely one is that there is a black laptop in front of me). But it would have lost some of its force. And if I learned that I have in fact been given a drug that produces hallucinations of red laptops, presumably my reason for accepting the hypothesis that there is a red laptop in front of me would disappear altogether. In short, in familiar cases, reasons that support some sentences of a given discourse do not survive a disconnect from truth. "Fictionalism is committed to some extraordinary reasons" (Szabó 2011: 377).

Now consider the notion of nondoxastic acceptance. Recall that the attitude in question has to be a distinctive one. In particular, it can't just be the attitude we have with respect to claims we use for a reductio ad absurdum, or with respect to scientific theories that are strictly false but a good approximation in some domain of interest. The reason that nondoxastic acceptance has to be more distinctive than this is that in these more familiar cases we regard the falsity of the claim(s) in question as a defect, which the context (such as the appropriateness of certain approximations) allows us to ignore. The very familiarity of these cases makes them unsuitable as cases on which to model nondoxastic acceptance. After all, nondoxastic acceptance is an attitude one might take towards a claim one takes to be false that involves *no reservations whatsoever as long as one is not placed in a critical context*—that is, as long as one is not asked "Do you really believe this?," "Is this your considered philosophical view?," "Considering the philosophical objections against this claim, do you still accept it?," or something similar (where it is an excellent question exactly what kinds of questions count as sufficiently similar). This is what is peculiar.

Here is another way to put the point. In order to grasp this distinctive state of acceptance for all ordinary purposes, which is yet different from belief, thoroughgoing fictionalists make use of the distinction between critical and non-critical contexts. But can that distinction really bear that weight? Szabó compares the notion of a critical (philosophical context) with the Carnapian notion of an external question, such as "Are there numbers?"—understood as a question posed not from within the numbers framework but about that framework. The crucial difference is that Carnap thinks that any meaningful such external question is in fact a practical one about the fruitfulness, for certain practical interests, of adopting the numbers framework. In contrast, what the fictionalist needs is the notion of a kind of context that, unlike the non-critical kind, does not hang on practical considerations, but on the contrary brings non-practical, theoretical considerations suddenly back into the spotlight. As Szabó says:

In philosophical contexts we are supposed to open ourselves to different [non-practical] sorts of considerations, and acknowledge that despite its expediency, fruitfulness, or conduciveness to our purposes [the claim at issue] is false. But are philosophical considerations really different in kind from ordinary ones? Let me put all my cards on the table. The reason I worry whether we are sensitive to the ordinary/philosophical distinction is that I don't believe there are philosophical contexts, just as I don't believe there are astronomical contexts, sociological contexts, or stamp-collecting contexts. I think the distinction is a myth. We might retract or qualify some of our ontological commitments in the face of philosophical criticism but this isn't substantially different than retracting or qualifying other commitments in the face of other far-flung criticism we would like to bracket, at least for the time being. (Szabó 2011: 383)

Note that Szabó in effect acknowledges that there is such a thing as philosophical criticism. But what is at issue is whether giving weight to such criticism over other kinds is distinctive, such that one can think of that activity as creating, and/or being only done in, a particular kind of context. Without this, the supposed attribution of a distinctive mental state of nondoxastic acceptance collapses into a mere resigned description of certain users of the discourse who sometimes assent and sometimes dissent from the claim at issue. Perhaps this problem can in some way be addressed. But it seems sufficiently serious to throw some doubt on the notion of nondoxastic acceptance, and thus on the idea that it is possible to nondoxastically accept claims.

Perhaps the underlying problem for thoroughgoing fictionalism is that the reasons such a fictionalist envisions would have to be something like purely practical ones guiding action, separate from theoretical considerations that are brought to bear only in critical contexts. But this seems to presuppose a neater separation of life into practical versus theoretical situations than is plausible. A given situation is always both, in the sense that practical decisions are likely to serve their purposes better if they are based only on considerations that would survive critical scrutiny.

In his defense of revolutionary fictionalism about morality, Richard Joyce speaks of a spectrum of stances, at one end of which lies the stance we all take with respect to actual fiction, and at the other end of which lies what he calls "the more fully immersing kind of fictive judgment for which our disbelief will only be admitted in a very critical context, such as a philosophy classroom" (Joyce 2001: 194). This kind of fictive judgment seems equivalent to (or a form of) nondoxastic acceptance, and it is this kind of highly immersive fictive judgment that forms the basis of Joyce's fictionalism.

I find this a very helpful picture, but it seems to me as though the spectrum does not extend as far as the thoroughgoing fictionalist needs it to. The problems noted above tend to arise at the far end of the spectrum, where fictive judgments in Joyce's sense are called for. The near end of the spectrum, by contrast, does not suffer from these problems. We all can and do engage with fiction, and while there are many philosophically fascinating puzzles there too, the attitude we take towards fiction is at least familiar enough and, on the face of it, not that hard to make sense of.

Of course, there is a price to pay at the near end of the spectrum as well. Put simply, it's the far end of the spectrum where the (thoroughgoing) fictionalist action is. Is the near end able to sustain a meaningful, distinctive stance towards a given domain? Thus, fictionalists of all varieties have a dilemma to confront. On one horn of this dilemma looms incoherence and the inability to make sense of key notions, and on the other horn looms irrelevance and the lack of a distinctive, meaningful position. In the next section, I'll argue that RF can and should aim to wrestle with the second horn rather than the first.

3. Towards Lightweight RF

Religious claims often attribute supernatural features to aspects of reality. I call those who disbelieve all such claims "naturalists." (My focus here will be mostly on Western theistic religions, but RF is intended to be more widely applicable. "Theism" refers to the view that there is a God who is omniscient, omnipotent, and omnibenevolent, who created the world, and who is still actively involved in the world. Thus, naturalism implies atheism.) Suppose that there is such a thing as religious language (sentences with a religious subject matter) into whose meaning it makes sense to enquire. Suppose also that many religious sentences are truth-apt and ordinarily express beliefs, that many are not entirely figurative or metaphorical, and that many are really about what they seem to be about, including supernatural aspects of reality.

While there are many reasons that one might be interested in RF, I'll focus on RF as a basis for naturalist religious practice. Some naturalists feel an affinity with religion, for whatever reason. They may have been brought up in a certain religious tradition, or be close to people who are, or they may just resonate with its ideas and/or practices. The question then arises to what extent such naturalists can participate in the religious life associated with that/those religion(s) (without falling into deception, self-deception, mental fragmentation, periodic wavering, hypocrisy, or other pathologies).[2]

In focusing on this group, I am assuming that there is some value available in the religious domain, but, for my purposes, this can be understood fairly

---

[2] For brevity, I will use "RFist" as a shorthand for both "proponent of RF" and "religious fictionalist practitioner"—that is, someone engaged in religious practice in a fictionalist manner. Similar remarks apply to "MFist."

minimally: I am assuming that these naturalists think religious practice achieves something that they value and would like to achieve via religious means. This "something" may be inspiration, comfort, a sense of community and belonging, particular kinds of experiences, (perceived) spiritual or moral growth, a sense of purpose, or other things. These are the kinds of things that naturalists who feel an affinity with religion are, qua people who feel this affinity, most likely to seek in religion.

It is interesting to ask how these values relate to certain material gains, such as, for instance, the ability to get one's children into a good Catholic school (see Leng, Chapter 7 of this volume). One thing that comes to mind about this case is that it is not immediately clear that a wish for this particular good requires a fictionalist stance on religion at all, as opposed to merely the ability to perform convincingly— that is, to be good at deceiving relevant authorities and perhaps other parents into thinking that one espouses the relevant beliefs. Even in its thoroughgoing varieties, fictionalism at least *aims* to be something more than and/or something rather different from this. This is partly why thoroughgoing fictionalism is so hard to make sense of—because it is *not* intended merely as a flat-footed invitation to deceive. Another point about this case is that in real life RFists may well have a complex mixture of motivations. Perhaps someone could be partly seeking entry to the school for their kids, partly seeking harmony in conversation with local Catholics (including perhaps other parents and the school's principal), and partly seeking some of the sources of value I listed in the previous paragraph. While only the latter clearly require RF, some of these may well be closely intertwined with more instrumental values like conversational harmony. For instance, one of the values I listed is a sense of community and belonging. The satisfaction of this value may, in practice, require the maintenance of a harmonious relationship with local Catholics.

Note also that there are clearly better and worse choices a naturalist could make regarding which particular religious communities to approach. Some religious communities will be more hospitable to naturalists than others. This is especially clear when one keeps in mind that, in principle, having an affinity with elements of a religion is compatible with finding other elements of the religion and/or of its institutional realities morally objectionable.

Proponents of WEF (and of other forms of thoroughgoing fictionalism) claim that the value, or at least some of the value, inherent in religious practice can be retained by replacing belief with a distinctive form of commitment that is not truth-normed: namely, nondoxastic acceptance. But, as we have seen, this makes WEF problematic.

Recall that RF, like fictionalism in general, is prima facie caught between two horns of a dilemma. So far, I've focused on the first horn—that is, the threat of incoherence and the accompanying difficulty with making sense of central notions. In the case of religion, another way that this horn manifests is as a digging-your-heels-in kind of religious conservatism that leaves religious life largely unaltered no matter how little evidence supports these notions.

By contrast, lightweight RF is a position on the near end of Joyce's spectrum of stances: namely, the one that describes the stance we all take with respect to fiction or when engaging in the equivalent of children's games of make-believe.

Joyce considers a Sherlock Holmes fan creating an immersive experience as they walk through London and imagine thereby walking through the London of Sherlock Holmes. As Joyce points out, mere thoughts, not just beliefs, can elicit emotional reactions. In fact, the power of thought on our mental and (hence) bodily life may be familiar from domains as varied as sports, mental health, the performing arts, mindfulness meditation, positive thinking techniques, and so on.

These ideas carry over to the religious domain. Religious stories, religious rituals, participation in religious ceremonies and community life—all these are replete with opportunities for imaginative immersion and emotional engagement. There can be no generally applicable description of how this will look, for the simple reason that it is as open-ended and full of possibilities as is the religious imagination itself, which has produced a rich variety of religious ideas and practices in different times and places. Similarly, there is no limit to how often or how deeply a naturalist can delve into religion.

What makes lightweight RF lightweight, then, is not the extensiveness of the religious forms of life involved, but the nature of the underlying fictionalist stance and the scope of its ambition. People choose the stories they surround themselves with, and this will be the case for religion just as in other areas of life. Lightweight RF is a *sui generis* form of engagement with religious ideas, not one that copies the believer's religious life (though it may outwardly mimic it on occasion). Unlike Joyce's thoroughgoing MFist, this RFist will typically be aware of their make-believe, so that their fictionalist stance is phenomenologically introspectable. This lightweight RFist is not living *just as if* the religion were true in all "non-critical" contexts; rather, they are deliberately, and as often as they wish, using religious tools to create atmospheres which, for them, have the potential to instill a sense of something sacred.

One of the things a lightweight RFist may be after is a sense of community. This highlights that it's not just thoroughgoing fictionalists who have to confront the risk of deception. In particular, for lightweight RF too, the question arises how the RFist's speech acts are to be understood (cf. footnote 1). (This is a large topic, and the following remarks are only intended to sketch a response.)

Since lightweight RF is directed only at a certain small number of naturalists, Joyce's own solution, which emphasizes that MF is to be understood as a reform proposal for *groups*, does not straightforwardly apply here (except in religious communities that consist mostly of RFists). The RFist will often be an unusual language user among many more usual ones, and the RFist can't by themselves decide what kind of speech acts they'll make in uttering religious sentences.

While this problem is a genuine one, and while it arises equally for lightweight and thoroughgoing varieties of RF, the two are not equally well placed to address it. Admittedly, in the case of thoroughgoing RF, it is somewhat difficult to distinguish this problem from that of making sense of the notion of acceptance in the first place, and of understanding what it means to live "just as if the religion were true" except in critical contexts. But the solution that seems most natural does seem to fit somewhat better with lightweight RF, since lightweight RF does not aim at copying the believer's life, nor at losing oneself in the make-believe to the extent that one is unaware of it. The solution that seems most natural is that the RFist should make their naturalist commitments known, by uttering disclaimers (cf. Deng 2015; see also Brock 2020: 213)—perhaps not constantly but very openly, whenever this seems necessary and helpful for communication and connection. There is no need for concealment. Indeed, concealment is unlikely to bring about a greater sense of community, at least of the kind that is valuable and valued by the RFist.

The result of these disclaimers will be that the RFist's speech acts, when they occur, will not be best understood as assertions. Instead they may be best understood as nonassertoric affirmations along the lines of how Joyce envisions moral language would function once MF had been adopted by a group. If the RFist participates in a group prayer, for instance, then given an appropriate (most likely temporally prior) disclaimer, including perhaps a description of the RFist's motivation for being there and a brief explanation of RF, the RFist will likely be expressing religious thoughts rather than beliefs.

4. The Bearable Lightness

Even if lightweight fictionalism is a contender for the religious domain, it is unlikely to be workable for the moral domain. As we saw, Joyce's MF is thoroughgoing, located at the far end of the spectrum. This is so for good reason. In the case of morality, the relevant discourse is ubiquitous. Therefore, if we are going to make a fiction of morality, this will likely be a thoroughgoing affair. It will clearly go beyond the occasional reading of "moral stories," for instance. Joyce offers an analogy with Odysseus's decision to tie himself to the mast of his ship before being tempted by the sirens. Morality is to be adopted as a whole, in advance of any particular situation in which that point of view may be needed.

The comparison is instructive not least because many common objections to RF target its lightweight nature—that is, they emphasize, in one way or another, that RF would need to involve a wholesale commitment if it were to be workable at all (and then typically go on to argue against the possibility of such a commitment, on grounds similar to those I have endorsed).

So, what are some of the pressures on the RFist to embrace a more thoroughgoing kind of fictionalism? As we just saw, one potentially relevant consideration is whether or not the discourse in question is ubiquitous. I said that moral discourse is. There is a clear disanalogy with religion here. There are many corners of the globe where religious discourse is not ubiquitous; in some, it is almost absent. Many people never use, nor perhaps even frequently mention religious terms. Therefore, there is no source of pressure to be found here. (See Kim, Chapter 11 of this volume.)

But such pressure does arise from another feature of religion. This is the fact that it is natural for an RFist to feel that they ought to try to keep to the thoroughgoing end of the fictionalist spectrum *for religious reasons*. Another way to describe these would be as "moral" reasons—but they are moral reasons that arise conditionally on certain religious presuppositions, such as that there is a divine being who prescribes these particular moral precepts.

Seen from the standpoint *internal* to many religious fictions, perhaps especially ones based on certain Western theistic traditions, RF is blasphemous, or at least frivolous and morally misguided in the extreme. It is, absurdly, to attempt to place oneself in a position of making use of, and thereby treating as a mere means, the divine person who constitutes the ground of all being, and to whom, according to this story, each of us owes intense gratitude for their existence, not to mention for the possibility of their salvation.

The relevance of these remarks emerges when one recalls that the RFist feels an affinity with the religious story in question. This may well create a wish to mimic the unfragmented nature of the believer's commitment as closely as possible, and in particular to (attempt to) nondoxastically accept instead of merely picking and choosing when and how to immerse oneself in the religious story.

Consider, for instance, Peter Lipton's "immersion solution" (Lipton 2009). Lipton tries hard to accommodate the feature of thoroughgoing fictionalism that enables a *wholesale* adoption of the relevant theory, in analogy with constructive empiricism in philosophy of science. This is what then allows the subsequent struggle with fragments of which one may not approve. Arguably Lipton's position gains rather than loses plausibility when this element is dropped (Deng 2015). But he is hardly alone in wishing to retain it.

Moreover, this wish is not the result of any confusion—say, a confusion between what's true within the religious story and what's true of it. Rather, it is just that the religious life advocated by many religious institutions centrally involves a wholehearted, non-fragmented kind of commitment. This in turn forms part of the content of central religious doctrines. It's thus no easy psychological feat to manage the tension between an affinity for these ideas and the wish to make a fiction of them.

The following excerpt from John Cobb's *Becoming a Thinking Christian* provides a useful illustration here (though note that Lipton himself is writing from a Jewish perspective). After discussing a hypothetical Christian businessman conflicted about a pastor's interpretation of a biblical text regarding the pursuit of wealth, the author remarks:

> One of the great weaknesses of the mainline Christian churches today is that most of their members do not take their Christian identity as all-important or all-embracing. Our businessman may consider himself both a Christian and a committed member of the business community, and he may put these two ways of identifying himself on the same level. He will then understand his beliefs as a compromise between his two loyalties. Or he may think of his position as a personal synthesis that is not directly an expression of either identity. In either case, Christian identity loses its primacy. (Cobb 1993: 59)

But this problem does not undermine the feasibility of lightweight RF so much as it highlights the fact that typical religious fictions contain grounds for both inspiration and challenge for the RFist (just as they tend to contain grounds for both inspiration and challenge for the believer, though for different reasons). The real lesson here is that RF involves a delicate, deliberate creative effort, one that requires handling the products of the religious imagination with responsibility and care. RF is about developing the best aspects of what religious practice can achieve for human beings, from a first-person perspective, and in full awareness of the fact that the complexities encountered along the way arise both from the religious ideas themselves and from the nature of the human psyche.

5. Why Not Buddhism?

There is a closely related objection to RF that also contributes to the pressure to be thoroughgoing, where again a comparison with MF is instructive. The objection is, roughly, "Why adopt the religious fiction?" To be considered a fair objection, it needs to be understood a certain way. Given the lightweight nature of RF, the non-ubiquitous nature of religious discourse, and, perhaps most importantly, the fact that by no means every naturalist feels an affinity with religion, the question shouldn't be "Why be an RFist?" The answer to this has already been given: some people have reason to, because of their affinities. The more salient worry is, rather, that even if one is inclined to be an RFist, what reason does one have to adopt one religious fiction over another, or a religious fiction rather than a non-religious fiction that one finds equally satisfying? Another way to put the worry is this: on RF, what becomes of the binding and exclusive nature of religion? What could possibly ensure that a RFist chooses a religion and stays with it, and indeed what could ensure that they continue engaging with religion at all, as opposed to, say, gradually moving away from it towards other content and other practices? Whereas the objection considered in Section 4 focused more on the (perceived) fragmentation involved in RF, this objection focuses more on its optional, non-exclusive nature.

Keeping clearly in mind what exactly the objection is goes hand in hand with keeping in mind the irrelevance of certain controversial empirical claims.

These are claims to the effect that there are prudential benefits associated with religious beliefs that RF could preserve, such as subjective well-being and/or various social goods. Such claims have sometimes been explored in the RF literature (see Miller 2012), but they form no part of my motivation here. As mentioned, for my purposes we need not even assume that the effects that the naturalist seeks *have* value in any intersubjectively valid sense, only that they are valued by that naturalist.

Let's approach the answer via the comparison with MF. Consider the question of why, according to MF, anyone should adopt the fiction of morality. Joyce persuasively argues that a certain kind of expectation on behalf of the answer to this question would be entirely misplaced. Specifically, coherence dictates that there can be no overarching *moral* obligation to adopt a fictive stance towards morality. By Joyce's fictionalist and error-theoretic lights, the idea of inescapable reasons is itself an important part of the error. So, the idea had better not be that we all morally inescapably ought to adopt the fiction of morality. Actually, a slightly more fine-grained description of the view is that the moral fictionalist may well endorse a moral reason for adopting the moral fiction—it's just that this can't be their *grounding* reason. (Thanks to Joyce for pointing this out.) Once they're immersed in the moral fiction, they can then see being so immersed as a morally good thing.

What is the religious analog of this point? Note first that there is no coherence-related reason why someone couldn't in principle argue that we *morally* ought to be RFists, since religious error theory is about religious claims, not moral ones. (Of course, whether the idea that there could be such a moral obligation is plausible is another matter; this relates back to the point made two paragraphs back regarding certain empirical claims in the vicinity.) However, there is a coherence-related barrier to the real equivalent: namely, a *religious* motivation for adopting religion as a fiction. Reflecting on this point is salutary, because the objection we are considering can be interpreted in a way that makes it reminiscent of the expectation that the RFist provide such a motivation. Why utilize a religious fiction in particular, if one doesn't take oneself to be under moral obligations to behave a certain way towards God? What could keep the RFist on the divinely sanctioned straight and narrow, if not the sincere belief that no other path leads to salvation?

Andrew Eshleman considers something like this objection. His answer is that the RFist must understand religious discourse as a special kind of symbolic fiction, whose central symbol points to the ideal of being recreated in the image of God, where "[d]iscourse about such an ideal requires symbolic representation for the same reason realist theologians have stressed the need for symbolic, metaphorical, and/or analogical description when referring to God" (Eshleman 2005: 192).

Perhaps unsurprisingly, this answer has provoked critical responses from both RF supporters (e.g., Deng 2015) and RF detractors (e.g., Palmqvist 2019). But one thing that is intriguing about it is that it is an attempt to provide what is effectively a religious motivation for adopting the religious fiction. The thought is that the RFist needs to adopt the religious fiction in order to imitate God, who has "the kind of existence of which we may have some inkling but...that eludes full articulation" (Eshleman 2005: 192). The RFist is described as finding themselves in the same situation as, say, an apophatic theologian, humbled into silence before God's ineffability. Ideas about God's nature are temporarily lifted out of the fiction to provide the kind of reason for adopting the fiction that the RFist is perceived to be in need of. This is parallel to expecting a morally binding reason for why, according to revolutionary MF, we should adopt morality as a fiction.

In both cases, it is reasonable to question whether that kind of motivation is one that the fictionalist should be expected to provide. As Joyce points out, there certainly cannot be, and in fact there had better not be, a moral obligation to adopt morality as a fiction; but once the moral fiction is adopted, the MFist can endorse moral reasons for adopting it, in the sense that they can see being immersed in it as a morally good thing. Similarly, there certainly can't be, and in fact there had better not be, a reason deriving from our obligations towards God for adopting a theistic fiction; but once the theistic fiction is adopted, the RFist can endorse religious reasons for adopting it, in the sense that they can then see being immersed in the religious practices and discourses as a good way to develop their relationship with the fictional God. If this still isn't felt to be binding enough because it isn't as binding as the theist's commitment, that comes very close to begging the question against RF. After all, a reason to adopt the fiction that more closely parallels the theist's reason to interact with their God by being just as binding is precisely what is ruled out by naturalistic RF.

To do justice to lightweight RF, one has to take seriously the possibility that some people who disbelieve all religious doctrines are just as inclined to experience intense emotional reactions to religious rituals, to make-believe prayer, and to engagement with religious texts, as are believers. This kind of affinity will always be a product of the person's cultural proclivities (and usually, though not always, their cultural upbringing), which may well favor a particular religious fiction over others. There is such a thing as loving a particular story (and set of stories and texts and ways of thinking), just as there is such a thing as loving (what one thinks of as) a particular divine person. The psychological basis is real, and it is entirely unique, tied to that naturalist's religious resonances. If one loves a particular story, then one will find that story irreplaceable. And this is the case even if the story allows one to satisfy values that one wishes to satisfy for independent reasons.

Although a person's religious resonances may be tied to a single religion, they need not be. Indeed, one thing that makes RF interesting is its potential to loosen ties between culturally rich products of the religious imagination, on the one hand, and claims to exclusivity that are more likely to be associated with potential societal harms, on the other hand. RF by its very nature has the potential to lead away from exclusivist stances on what counts as *the* religious life, and towards thinking in terms of a plurality of forms of life that are engaged with religion to different degrees and in different ways.

Requests for clarification and elaboration of what RF looks like in practice are of course very reasonable (although there is a limit to how much of a general nature can be said about such an open-ended phenomenon). But we should be careful about which standards to apply. Michael Scott and Finlay Malcolm ask:

> If the sentences of religious discourse are not considered true, then according to what norm are they accepted or rejected by the fictionalist using the discourse?...This is particularly an issue when experiences or events require the speaker to go "off-piste" and say something that is not a routine or established part of the fictional narrative. If one can, in these cases, pursue pragmatically guided invention, then what preserves the integrity of the discourse? Why not, for instance, mix in a bit of Buddhism, or some choice lessons from the writings of Dostoevsky, if these are deemed to have potentially beneficial effects?
> (Scott & Malcolm 2018: 5)

Well, why not indeed? After all, there is nothing wrong with Buddhism, or with Dostoevsky for that matter. It seems quite possible that someone might find inspiration or comfort in texts drawn from all these sources, side by side with different religions' sacred texts, perhaps participating in rituals drawn from a variety of religious traditions. Again, it is interesting to explore the various religious forms of life that can result. But the idea that there is a non-negotiable imperative to preserve the integrity of any religious discourse, or that one needs to maintain a clear distinction between the authority accorded to, say, Dostoevsky, on the one hand, and that of say, biblical authors on the other hand, makes most sense from *within* a particular religious narrative. Suspending what is true *within* the story may shed a different light on what needs regulating regarding one's treatment and use *of* the story.

One could object that these exclusivist ideas will matter from the standpoint *within* the religious story, from which, as mentioned above, the RFist can endorse religious reasons to be immersed in the religious story. But since it is a story, nothing automatically gets included (such as an automatic move from "A religious authority or text says so" to "I must abide by it, whether I like it or not"). The RFist may of course choose to include claims about exclusivity and about a divine being with expectations of exclusive worship, and then it may end up true within the religious story that, say, Buddhism is wrong-headed and Dostoevsky is irrelevant. In this case, certain features will be automatically included as part of the fiction, but only because of a free (i.e., uncoerced, though not unconstrained) decision on the part of the RFist.

Of course, many religious communities are such that if one wishes to be a member, one had better choose a particular restricted religious discourse. But then this also constitutes another possible answer to the question of how and why one would in practice choose one particular religious narrative over another. The answer may simply be that one wants to belong to a particular religious community.

Robin Le Poidevin critically discusses an RFist "who simply moves at whim from one religion to another":

> It is hard to see how this involves anything other than a very provisional, and perhaps also superficial, commitment to the religious life. In contrast, a fictionalist who stays true to a particular religious fiction is in a better position to explore it more deeply, to let it guide them more thoroughly.
> (Le Poidevin 2019: 32)

Presumably "at whim" here doesn't mean "without meaningful engagement with any religion," since then the result follows trivially. Thus, the idea must rather be that choosing one religious narrative and sticking with it is preferable because it provides more of those perceived benefits that RFists are motivated by in the first place. But since those perceived benefits may vary, why not let a thousand flowers bloom? The detailed advice should probably simply vary according to which particular benefits a given RFist is after. However, constraints that are internal to particular religious narratives would seem to be out of place, and this includes the idea that the religious life involves a relationship with someone to whom one should stay true, perhaps in the sense of staying true to a friend. This last point may prompt the following thought. (Thanks to Joyce for this analogy.) Isn't the lightweight RFist's attitude comparable to that of someone who's dating another person for the first or second time, who hasn't committed to the other person and therefore still assesses their desirability in purely instrumental terms? And isn't there something at least temporarily lacking in the depth of this person's engagement with the person they're dating, as compared to someone who has fallen deeply in love, who is committed, who no longer assesses reasons for or against the relationship in that instrumental way? The theist may seem to be in a situation analogous to the latter person, while the RFist is in a situation analogous to that of the casual dater. Doesn't this illustrate the lack of depth available in RF?

This thought nicely illustrates how the objection I've considered in this section comes close to begging the question against RF, by being framed firmly from within the theist's worldview. What seems slightly frivolous about the casual dater is that they are not committing to the person they are actually dating, who exists. That is, theirs is an interaction of the same kind as, and with the same potential as, that of the committed life partner. If our topic were whether, in a world with many actually existing deities (say, from all the major world religions), someone who sometimes followed one deity and then another was missing out, compared to the committed theist, then this analogy would be apt. But since our topic is naturalistic RF, the analogy is not apt. And the reasons for which it is not apt are worth reflecting on, precisely because it is such a natural thought, for both theistic and naturalistic friends of theistic religions alike, since those religions often do involve claims of exclusivity. The question, from a standpoint outside of the religious fiction (where the fiction can be understood *as* a fiction) is not whether one is able to commit to the God depicted in the fiction; it's rather whether and to what extent one wishes to explore the relational possibilities that arise from (a) one's own religious capacities and resonances, and (b) the various stories, rituals, and ideas that humankind has produced with respect to that God, as well as, perhaps, other deities. This situation finds no analogy in the dating world.[3]

6. Recognizing RF

In this final section, I'd like to reflect on a peculiar difficulty RF faces, which seems structurally parallel to a difficulty faced by thoroughgoing fictionalists about various domains—whether about morality, religion, or some other domain of discourse.[4]

Fictionalists have sometimes been told that they are unable to distinguish non-doxastic acceptance from belief. If one is living just as if one believes, then one believes. When asked to provide a behavioral difference between acceptance and belief, fictionalists have pointed to dissent in critical contexts. To this, detractors of fictionalism have objected that the would-be-accepter is clearly confused: if they act just as if p, then they do believe p, and so they should assent to p even in critical contexts (e.g., Horwich 1991). Chris Daly makes the interesting point that this "would place the fictionalist in a no-win situation" (Daly 2008: 429). A behavioral difference was demanded and provided, but "then the fictionalist is told that that does not count." (I'll come back to this issue at the end of the section.)

Now consider the following difficulty a RFist faces. From the point of view of the religious believer (perhaps especially in Western theistic religions), if someone's experiential response to the religion takes on a meaningful appearance by leaving tangible traces on their perceived well-being or other aspects of their life,

---

[3] Perhaps one could fashion a modified analogy based on (projected or real) AI technologies enabling relationships with virtual beings. But even there, one would have to be careful not to import aversions that have to do specifically with one's reaction to the AI context (whether justified there or not); what we are dealing with here is more familiar. It's the power of the religious imagination and of religious ideas—quite simply, the human response to religion separated from any endorsement of a religious ontology.

[4] Note that in Section 2 I defended some closely related objections to thoroughgoing fictionalism. But this does not detract from the present point, which is just intended to draw attention to the parallel.

one rather salient interpretation of this is a religious one. On this interpretation, the reason the religion is bringing about meaningful experiences in the life of the would-be-RFist is that the person is opening themselves up to God's influence, whether they meant to or not and whether they realize it or not. Another way to put this is to say that from the perspective of the theist, it can be very tempting to interpret any practical success reaped by the RFist as evidence for theism, and, more to the point, as evidence that the RFist is in fact starting to believe, or at least to have faith in some sense. This kind of interpretation implies that the RFist is deceiving themselves, or perhaps more mildly, not aware of what is happening to them, and that therefore any practical success in reaping said benefits will not, from the theist's perspective, count as evidence that RF is viable in the sense of being capable of bringing about these benefits.

To an extent, this difficulty is faced by all fictionalists. For example, suppose someone is a priori convinced that MF is untenable, not because it can't be made sense of, but because they know a priori that an MFist could not, without belief, reap the benefits they were after (such as motivation, self-control, and so on). Then any apparent evidence that an MFist immersed in moral thought and language was reaping those benefits would be re-interpreted by this opponent to mean the MFist was actually believing moral claims.

But while such a dogmatic opponent to fictionalism is a distinct possibility in all domains, the unique feature of the religious domain (again, for certain religions) is that here the content of the discourse itself somewhat favors that opponent's stance. In the moral domain, there is nothing immoral about moving away from this opponent's stance by allowing that moral motivation may not require belief. By contrast, in the religious domain, the theist has some religious reason to think of all good things, including any meaningful experiences this RFist is having through religion, as brought about by God's involvement and (since this God wants to be known by human beings) by God's disclosing Godself to the RFist. The experiences would not be felt as so meaningful (thinks the theist) unless the RFist were starting to transparently sense God in them—that is, unless the make-believe were starting to shade over into belief.

Of course, a theist is not forced to interpret matters this way; nonetheless, the more meaningful the RFist's experience, the more salient this kind of interpretation becomes. After all, within the theist's belief system, insofar as the person is genuinely opening themselves up to the ideas and rituals involved, they are effectively opening themselves up to a loving God's influence who wants to answer precisely this kind of summons. Unfortunately, one side effect is that this can place the RFist in a no-win situation (at least when assessing the viability of RF in conversation with believers).

What I want to draw attention to, then, is a certain similarity between this peculiar difficulty faced by the RFist, and the problem thoroughgoing fictionalists in all domains face when distinguishing acceptance from belief. Admittedly, these are not the same by any means. After all, in the former case the disagreement is not over whether a conceptual distinction can be drawn, but about the plausibility of two competing hypotheses concerning the causes of the benefits in question. But there is a certain amount of dialectical similarity. In both cases, the fictionalist faces some in principle barrier to producing evidence in support of their view that will be recognized by their opponent.

This also demonstrates that the very communities RFists are likely to be drawn towards may have a tendency to systematically render fictionalist religious practice invisible. Perhaps this too can indirectly highlight the need to recognize RF as a distinctive stance on religion.

7. Conclusion

This chapter has explored the problems and possibilities of religious fictionalism through a comparison with moral fictionalism. I've argued that various varieties of thoroughgoing fictionalism are beset by problems affecting the notions of non-doxastic acceptance and of reasons disconnected from truth. While this spells trouble for moral fictionalism, and while there are some related sources of pressure on religious fictionalism to be thoroughgoing, these difficulties can be negotiated by religious fictionalism. I've also explored the question of why any (particular) religious fiction should be adopted over another. I've suggested that the temptation to demand a religiously grounded answer, just like the temptation to demand a morally grounded answer to the corresponding question regarding moral fictionalism, should be resisted. Thus, there is room for a lightweight fictionalist stance on religion. For naturalists so inclined, religious fictionalism paves the way to a plethora of different forms of life that are to various extents and in various ways religiously engaged. It is a distinctive philosophical basis of a *sui generis* and creative approach towards religion.[5]

References

Brock, S. 2020. "Religious fictionalism and Pascal's Wager." In B. Armour-Garb & F. Kroon (eds.), *Fictionalism in Philosophy*. Oxford University Press. 207–34.

Cobb, J. 1993. *Becoming a Thinking Christian: If We Want Church Renewal, We Will Have to Renew Thinking in the Church*. Abingdon Press.

Daly, C. 2008. "Fictionalism and the attitudes." *Philosophical Studies* 139: 423–40.

---

[5] Many thanks to all the participants of the Wellington workshop, and to Richard Joyce for very valuable comments on earlier drafts.

Deng, N. 2015. "Religion for naturalists." *International Journal for Philosophy of Religion* 78: 195–214.

Eshleman, A. 2005. "Can an atheist believe in God?" *Religious Studies* 41: 183–99.

Horwich, P. 1991. "On the nature and norms of theoretical commitment." *Philosophy of Science* 58: 1–14.

Jay, C. 2014. "The Kantian Moral Hazard Argument for religious fictionalism." *International Journal for Philosophy of Religion* 75: 207–32.

Joyce, R. 2001. *The Myth of Morality*. Cambridge University Press.

Le Poidevin, R. 2019. *Religious Fictionalism*. Cambridge University Press.

Lipton, P. 2009. "Science and religion: The immersion solution." In J. Cornwell & M. McGhee (eds.), *Philosophers and God: At the Frontiers of Faith and Reason*. Continuum. 31–46.

Miller, C. 2012. "Atheism and the benefits of theistic belief." In J. Kvanvig (ed.), *Oxford Studies in Philosophy of Religion*. Oxford University Press. 97–125.

Palmqvist, C.-J. 2019. "Forms of belief-less religion: Why non-doxasticism makes fictionalism redundant for the pro-religious agnostic." *Religious Studies* 57: 49–65.

Scott, M. & Malcolm, F. 2018. "Religious fictionalism." *Philosophy Compass* 13: 1–11.

Szabó, Z. G. 2011. "Critical study of Mark Eli Kalderon (ed.) *Fictionalism in Metaphysics*." *Noûs* 45: 375–85.

10
Should Moral Fictionalists be Religious Fictionalists (or Vice Versa)?

Robin Le Poidevin

1. A Natural Partnership?

Nobody, I imagine, would want to defend global fictionalism: fictionalism about everything under the (fictional) sun. Such a position would be self-defeating, for fictions have to be constructed out of real components. This reality base might be quite minimal. Perhaps even the subjects engaging in fictions, persons, are to some extent fictional constructions—"centers of narrative gravity," as Daniel Dennett puts it (1991: 418). There is no inconsistency, however, in being fictionalists about selves and realists about the attitudes towards fictions, and about the causal consequences of those attitudes. Perhaps it would be possible to extend one's fictionalism even to those. (Consider an ontological eliminativism about propositional attitudes which nevertheless concedes the usefulness of attitude talk.)[1] But the fictionalism has to stop somewhere, at the conditions, whatever they are, that make a certain kind of discourse appropriate.

So one can, indeed should, be selective about one's fictionalist stances. Fictionalism about domain *x* need not imply fictionalism about unrelated domain *y*. Mere structural parallelism is not enough to induce one to extend the domain of one's fictionalist commitment. But in some cases there is a close connection between different areas of discourse, and in these cases we might expect fictionalism about one to be accompanied by fictionalism about the other.

A plausible example of such a connection is that between religious discourse and moral discourse. A moral dimension is arguably an essential element of any religious outlook. Certainly, this is true of theistic religions. So a combined moral and religious fictionalism would not look entirely arbitrary, at least. But nor is it obviously obligatory. Moral fictionalism is a metaethical view, whereas it might be argued that the explicit moral content of theistic religion is purely normative.

---

[1] Richard Joyce explores a fictionalist position concerning mental states (Joyce 2013), and in particular the paradox that it seems to raise: of recommending the adoption of a certain attitude the existence of which it denies. The solution to the paradox requires realism about certain kinds of things (e.g., brain states). See also the other papers in the same issue, which is devoted to the topic of fictionalism about the mental.

Drawing a connection between theism and the ground of moral values would involve a further level of interpretation. It certainly can't be taken for granted, then, that religious fictionalism will be fictionalist with respect to the existence of moral values.

Nor does moral fictionalism in general entail religious fictionalism. Fictionalism with respect to discourse *x* implies some positive attitude towards employing *x*: it serves some useful purpose. But the moral fictionalist might not take a positive attitude, or indeed any determinate attitude, towards religion, and so not feel obliged to adopt an account of religion that makes sense of religious practice. However, in what follows, I will limit discussion to positions which do regard religion, and specifically *theistic* religion—religion in which the notion of God is the central animating feature—in a positive light, as something which can appropriately motivate moral behavior. In the context of those positions, the question is whether theistic fictionalism motivates (in some way that falls short of entailing) moral fictionalism, and vice versa.

I shall approach this question by looking at the stability—or otherwise—of two rival combinations:

(a) theistic realism and moral fictionalism
(b) theistic fictionalism and moral realism

Since the repetition of the full names of these combinations would become rather tiresome, I will employ the familiar device of pinning each combination of views onto a fictional character. The individual representing combination (a) I shall call "Theodore," and the individual representing combination (b) "Moira." I am interested in the state of mind of each of these two, including their motivation for adopting the position they do. Working with states of mind rather than abstract propositions may perhaps diminish the conceptual purity of the argument, but I am concerned with the psychological attraction of each position as well as its internal coherence.

In focusing on theism, I do not want to imply that religious realism/fictionalism is equivalent to theistic realism/fictionalism. There are non-theistic religions, and one could be realist or fictionalist with respect to the doctrines which characterize those religions (unless they are wholly non-doctrinal). But it is the potential metaethical content of theism that generates many of the issues discussed here.

I should concede at the outset that even if both (a) and (b) were to turn out to be unstable, it would not immediately follow that one had to choose between, on the one hand, realism concerning both domains and, on the other, fictionalism concerning both. One could reject both fictionalism *and* realism, for reasons which will become clearer once we offer characterizations of each stance in the next section. Nevertheless, if either position does turn out to be unstable, this will provide at least the beginnings of an argument that fictionalism in one domain naturally carries over to the other (though not necessarily in both directions).

On the face of it, combination (b) looks more promising than combination (a). Suppose we are already convinced by moral realism, that there are attitude-independent moral values. Then we may see theistic fiction as an effective means of making us both sensitive to, and motivated by, these values—or not. On the other hand, if we are already convinced that God objectively exists, then we are likely to view the authority of moral values as having its source beyond ourselves (though not necessarily in God). It looks, then, as if there is an asymmetry here: theistic fictionalism as neutral concerning the existence of moral values, but moral fictionalism as not neutral with respect to the existence of (at least a certain kind of) God. But does this asymmetry bear scrutiny? Is either of the above combinations viable—or neither?

I shall argue that, as we might suspect, combination (a) is unstable, but (b) also faces some challenges. The discussion will, I suggest, have consequences for what one might regard as the more natural combination of theistic and moral fictionalism, to which we turn at the end of the chapter.

To sound a cautionary note: the results presented in this chapter tend to rest on building quite a bit into both moral fictionalism and theistic fictionalism, as will become evident. Much more minimal conceptions of both would not generate the same results. But for those who like their fictions to be full of color and incident, I hope my final suggestion will be of interest.

2. Definitions

I take *realism* about a certain kind of discourse to be characterized by the following propositions concerning the core statements of that discourse:[2]

(1) *Truth-aptness:* they are truth-apt (capable of being true or false);
(2) *Irreducibility:* they are not reducible in terms of meaning to other kinds of statement;
(3) *Objectivity:* their truth-value is determined by some feature of the world, independently of any beliefs or attitudes towards those statements;
(4) *Truth:* they are (for most part) true.

Different shades of non-realism can then be defined, at least in part, in terms of which of these conditions they reject for the discourse in question. So, for instance,

---

[2] Compare the entity-centered characterization of realism offered by Brock and Mares (2006). I don't think, though, that the characterization above is incompatible with theirs. If the above conditions are met, then any entities postulated by the true statements of the discourse will exist. Brock and Mares also offer an important disambiguation of the notion of mind-independence which I would want to incorporate into a fuller account of realism than the sketch I gave here. Note the inclusion in the conditions above of a success condition: many of the statements of the discourse are in fact true. Elsewhere I have offered a characterization of realism which does not include this success condition, but am persuaded by one of the editors (Richard Joyce) that the inclusion of the success condition is more standard.

a positivist concerning scientific theoretical statements will (typically) accept (1), (3), and (4), but reject (2) on the basis that such statements are reducible to observation statements. (This does not, or need not, impugn (3), for what would or could be observed in certain circumstances need not depend on what we believe would be observed.) Such a position, historically, was motivated by epistemological doubts concerning unobservable entities and the meaningfulness of talking about them. A constructive empiricist, in contrast, will accept the first three conditions but reject the fourth. That is not a complete specification of constructive empiricism, however: the further feature is that theoretical statements are to be accepted on the basis of empirical adequacy: they permit inferences to observation statements which fit the appearances (van Fraassen 1981).

As I shall understand the term, a *fictionalist* concerning a certain kind of discourse retains (1) and (2) for that discourse but rejects (3) and (4). Moreover, the fictionalist views I am focusing on are not descriptive theses—not hypotheses about how moral and/or religious talk is actually and ordinarily understood, pre-theoretically, pre-philosophically, in the comfort of one's own home, etc.— but rather are normative theses, concerning how we *should* use the discourses in question. In what has become standard terminology, we are in the territory of "revolutionary," rather than "hermeneutic" fictionalism (Burgess 1983). Revolutionary moral fictionalism is a form of error theory (otherwise, what would need revolutionizing?). There is, in other words, an error in our ordinary understanding of the discourse. Different error theorists will have different views on what our ordinary understanding of the discourse involves and how much of it is mistaken. John Mackie, to take a particularly prominent example of a moral error theorist, takes our ordinary understanding to ascribe both objectivity and truth to moral judgments, and to be wrong on both counts (Mackie 1977). Compare Richard Joyce's characterization: "The moral error theorist thinks that although our moral judgments aim at the truth, they systematically fail to secure it: the world simply doesn't contain the relevant 'stuff' to render our moral judgments true" (Joyce 2021). So we aren't in error simply in asserting first-order judgments (e.g., "Stealing is wrong") but in taking them to be true in a substantial sense, to reflect some objective feature of the world. However, I don't intend to discuss the error-theoretical component of fictionalism(s) in this chapter, so can remain neutral on just how much metaethics is to be ascribed to the folk view of things. For this reason, I prefer to talk not of "revolutionary" fictionalism but of *normative* fictionalism: this is how we *ought* to understand the discourse, whatever the ordinary understanding might be.

My concern, then, is with the positive component of fictionalism: that, despite the fact that the realist truth-conditions of a certain discourse don't obtain, it is acceptable, indeed desirable, for us to employ that discourse as if realism were correct. Indeed, giving up the discourse may just not be viable. Conditions (1) and (2) do obtain, but conditions (3) and (4) are useful fictions. As Joyce points out, in construing the discourse as fictional, the fictionalist need not (and would be well advised not to) imply that any utterance from the discourse of the form "*p*" is elliptical for "It is fictional that *p*." Taking it that way would disrupt certain inferences that we take to be acceptable. Rather, the fictionalist recommendation is that we engage in *pretense* when we put forward statements of the discourse (Joyce 2005: 293). This pretense relieves anyone using the discourse of the obligation to be answerable to reality: acceptance of the discourse is not, in other words, "truth-normed" (Kalderon 2005: 2–3).

On the characterizations above, realism and fictionalism are incompatible positions. Anyone who thinks that one can somehow be a realist fictionalist has a different conception of at least one of these positions. But it is clear that a rejection of realism is not a commitment to fictionalism, or vice versa: there are other options. The progress of science provides a reason for rejecting realism concerning all sorts of discourse—of, for example, the four humors, phlogiston, vital force, the ether—without thereby recommending the subjects of these as *useful* fictions.

Let's now apply this scheme to a certain kind of religious case. *Theistic realism* accepts all four conditions with respect to theological statements. According to the theistic realist, a core statement such as "God exists" is true, true by virtue of mind-independent facts, not reducible to a non-theistic statement, and succeeds in picking out an object, namely God. An atheist of the traditional kind may well subscribe to (1)–(3), but will, of course, reject (4). Such an atheist is objectivist about God talk but not, in the sense I intend, a theistic realist (see Eshleman 2016). On the model above, a theistic fictionalist accepts the truth-aptness and irreducibility conditions, but rejects objectivity and truth for theistic discourse.[3] *Within the recommended fiction*, of course, all four conditions apply.

I will understand a *moral realist* to be the counterpart of the theistic realist, both with respect to first-order moral statements that such and such ought to be done, or is good, and with respect to the general metaethical statement that there are moral values. A *moral fictionalist* takes (3) and (4) to be false with respect to these same statements, but holds that adopting, or acquiescing in, the fiction that there are real moral values, and that in consequence (appropriate) first-order normative statements are true, helps us to choose what we think of as good.

Intriguingly, there is a significant divergence of metaethical views amongst theistic realists. What they have in common is the view that moral values are not wholly dependent on human attitudes. But this can be taken in two main directions. On the one hand, there is the view that moral values depend ontologically on God. For example, x is obligatory if and only if God commands x; x is good if and only if God approves of x. The right-hand side of each biconditional provides the fundamental ground of the left-hand side. An individual is good to the extent

---

[3] There is room for a fictionalist position which takes a more agnostic view, but I will not be considering it here. See, however, Le Poidevin 2020.

that they resemble God, and so on. I shall label the view (of which there may be a number of variants) that moral values depend on God, *theistic moral subjectivism*.[4] It is subjectivist in that it makes moral values mind-dependent, but unlike the kind of moral subjectivism defended by Mackie (1977), it takes the relevant mind to be divine, not human. But not all theistic realists are theological subjectivists. Richard Swinburne, for example, takes moral values to be independent of God (Swinburne 1977). But since for him such values exist as a matter of necessity, they pose no restriction on God's powers.

Both theistic moral subjectivism and moral realism hold that moral values have an authority that is beyond us. They therefore rule out moral fictionalism, which can deliver no such result. The question is whether theistic realism is committed to either theistic moral subjectivism or moral realism.

3. Real God, Fictional Value

So now let us consider Theodore, who takes God to be a real entity, existing independently of human minds. He is a theistic realist. However, he is neither a moral realist nor a theistic moral subjectivist. Why is this? Because he cannot see a satisfactory account of God's intrinsic moral properties that is not impaled on one or other of the horns of the Euthyphro dilemma (see, e.g., Kretzmann 1999). To rehearse the problem: suppose that what is good is constituted by God—that some version of theistic moral subjectivism is true, as spelled out in the previous section. If what is good depends on his will, then, given that God is free to will anything, what is good turns out to be entirely contingent. Worse, it is even arbitrary. For if God had reasons for willing what he does, it would be those reasons which would be the true ground of value. Further, it would seem that moral properties could not supervene on natural properties, for God is entirely free to judge x good and y bad, even if x and y are natural duplicates.

Apart from these issues of contingency, arbitrariness, and supervenience failure, there is the further worry that theistic moral subjectivism trivializes the divine property of omnibenevolence. If we say, for instance, that an action is good by virtue of God's willing that action, then the proposition "God wills what is good" is just the empty tautology that God wills what God wills. Or if we say that an individual is good by virtue of resembling God, then "God is good" just means that God resembles himself, which again is empty. If we say that an individual is good by virtue of God's approving of that individual, "God is good" just reduces to

---

[4] Norman Kretzmann (1999) calls it "theological subjectivism" in his discussion of the Euthyphro dilemma. Another name is "theological voluntarism." Divine Command Theory is one version of the general position. Confusingly, it is also often regarded as a species of moral objectivism, on the grounds that it makes moral values independent of *us*.

the proposition that God approves of himself. This, admittedly, is not tautologous, but it surely fails to convey much of significance. Can the goodness of God really amount to nothing more than his self-esteem? In response, the theological subjectivist is likely to propose that "God is good" has a different (though not completely unrelated) meaning to "*x* is good," and similarly for "God wills what is good" and "*x* wills what is good," where *x* stands for something or someone other than God. One possibility would be to interpret "God wills what is good" as "God wills whatever will promote our flourishing," and it is in virtue of his willing this that he is called "good." But what constitutes flourishing here? If the theistic subjectivist says that, however *we* may conceptualize our flourishing, what *genuine* flourishing consists of is surely determined by God, then the threat of triviality arises again, this time with respect to "God wills what will promote our flourishing." For if what constitutes genuine flourishing is what God wills for us, then, once again, "God is good" just reduces to tautology. It is considerations such as these, let us suppose, that drive Theodore away from theistic moral subjectivism.

But neither is Theodore a moral realist. He thinks that this would involve being impaled on the other half of the Euthyphro dilemma: that there is something that is independent of God, namely moral value, implying that God is not sovereign over all things. (Whether Theodore is being over-scrupulous on this matter might be suggested by the point made above concerning the compatibility of omnipotence and the necessity of moral truth. Later, we will return to the issue of divine sovereignty and the independence of moral value.) Moreover, such values would be "queer," in Mackie's sense (Mackie 1977: 38–9). They would be metaphysically queer: just what kind of thing could both exist independently of us and yet be tied specifically to behavior and character? They would also be epistemologically queer: how could we reconcile knowledge of these abstract, acausal things with any version of the causal theory of knowledge? Moral values, concludes Theodore, can be neither dependent on nor independent of God. So they have no grounding outside our own attitudes. He acknowledges, however, that we think and talk *as if* there were values existing independently of us. Moreover, he thinks that this way of thinking helps keep us on the straight and narrow. What vindicates such thought, then, is not correspondence to the facts, but rather its causal consequences. Theodore, in other words, is a moral fictionalist.

One question to put to Theodore is how much he is exercised by a third aspect of the alleged queerness of real moral values—namely, their psychological oddity. How can recognizing something as objectively, mind-independently good be intrinsically motivating? This is part of Mackie's argument against moral realism (Mackie 1977: 40). Moral fictionalists, apparently, do think that we are necessarily motivated to do things that we consider objectively good, and part of the source of this motivation (presumably) is the thought that it isn't just a matter of opinion what counts as good. Consider the relative power of the following considerations: "*x* is morally good" versus "*x* is conventionally considered the thing to do."

Isn't the first of these more motivating than the second? If Theodore thinks so, then although he may take moral values to be metaphysically and epistemologically queer, he does not take them to be psychologically queer. Still, this is really an issue for moral fictionalists in general: that one way of attacking a rival position (moral realism)—namely, through the arguments from queerness—is likely to cause difficulties for their own position. It isn't specifically a threat to Theodore's combination of theistic realism and moral fictionalism.

But the obvious question for Theodore is what view *he* takes of such commonplace, perhaps essential, theistic statements as "God is good," or "What God wills is good." He rejected theistic moral subjectivism on the grounds that it trivialized those statements. And his rejection of moral realism means that he cannot think God is good with respect to some objective, mind-independent standard. Does he hold that moral terms have no application to God, any more than they would have an application to a planet? No, he says; he applies moral terms to God in the same way that he applies them to human agents. But his moral attributions are made in both cases on the basis of affective responses to the individuals concerned. Like Mackie, he subscribes to a human subjectivist account of moral judgments. The natural properties of actions cause in us emotional responses, and as a result we project these onto the external situation, ascribing to it moral properties it does not, in reality, have. To describe God as good, explains Theodore, is a similar projection of our subjective responses onto God.

This may pay lip service to traditional theism, but it does not, surely, capture the divine attribute of omnibenevolence that is part of that tradition. Like omniscience and omnipotence, omnibenevolence is supposed to be an intrinsic, objective, and essential property of God. There are forms of theism which depart from this picture, no doubt, abandoning one or other of the traditional attributes, but they are not among the great monotheistic traditions of Christianity, Judaism, and Islam. For Theodore, God's omnibenevolence, considered as a moral attribute, is a merely extrinsic one, one which he has only by virtue of his relation to us. Indeed, it has less reality than other relational attributes such as being all-knowing, for goodness is something, on the subjectivist account, that we project onto God. In terms of intrinsic properties, all we can say on this view is that God has whatever intrinsic properties are sufficient (and perhaps also necessary) to cause us to project moral attributes onto him. Considered in himself, God is amoral. He does not project moral properties onto us, or make moral judgments, nor is he motivated by moral considerations, as (being omniscient) he sees things exactly as they are. He does not command or will or desire the good. It needn't follow that God is indifferent to us, however. He can still, it seems, be all-loving. It is this feature of Theodore's theism that arguably makes it a genuinely religious position, one which can be a guide to living, and not simply some quasi-scientific hypothesis concerning the origin of life and the universe. Given Theodore's views on the Euthyphro dilemma, he presumably has to see "loving" as a purely descriptive term, not an evaluative one. For if it ascribes some *value* to God, then some Euthyphro-like dilemma will arise here too. If what it is to be genuinely loving is relative to the standard set by God, then "God is loving" is trivially true. On the other hand, if it is relative to a standard independent of God, then God is not sovereign. It seems that Theodore's conception of God must, for the sake of consistency, be emptied of all evaluative content. The contrast with traditional theism becomes even sharper.

Theodore's moral fictionalism, then, robs his theism of moral content, and possibly (given his motivations) of any evaluative content whatsoever. In turn, his theistic realism threatens to make his moral fictionalism either intrinsically suspect or redundant. Take the redundancy threat first. The point of moral fictionalism is to provide a motivational source for moral behavior: immersed in the fiction of real moral values, we are motivated to act in accordance with them. Now, if Theodore's theistic realism is a genuinely *religious* theism, he has no need of this fictionalist prop. His non-evaluative vision of a loving (though intrinsically amoral) God may be sufficiently motivating in itself for him to have no need of fictional moral values. The more successful his theism, the more redundant his fictionalism. He may as well be just an old-fashioned moral error theorist.

But let us say that Theodore concedes that his theism, though an explanatory necessity, is religiously inadequate. Stripping all evaluative attributes away from God leaves him with a world view which is not, after all, the emotional and motivational force he would expect a religion to be. Perhaps, then, Theodore can offer a fictionalist twist on his theism: although God is real, not fictional, some of things we say about God *are* fictional, including the attribution to God of moral qualities, and perhaps personal ones. These fictions about God help to transform what would otherwise be a rather austere, even cold, quasi-scientific conception of the world into a genuine religion, something to comfort and guide us. He has now combined his theistic realism with a theistic fictionalism. Perhaps he is not fictionalist about *the existence* of a transcendent being, but rather about the elements which give this being its distinctively religious quality. This is not immediately suspect. A fiction can, of course, incorporate elements of the real world. For the moral fictionalist, this is important, since it is the real world which presents us with dilemmas (these being converted into moral, as opposed to merely practical, dilemmas within the fiction). The worry, however, about thus incorporating God into his moral fiction is that Euthyphro-type worries will once again arise concerning the content of the fiction. If God is good by virtue of moral standards that, within the fiction, exist independently of him, then he is not sovereign within the fiction.

Theodore faces a dilemma, then: either he renounces traditional, morally contentful theism in favor of morally empty theism, in which case he cannot claim to combine *theistic* realism, as it would generally be understood by his more traditional religious friends, with moral fictionalism, or he preserves morally contentful theistic elements by making them part of a fiction (a fiction in which theism and morality interact), in which case he cannot claim to combine unadulterated theistic *realism* with moral fictionalism. (The realist about God is, of course, free to regard *some* attributions to God as fictional, or metaphorical, or figurative, without undermining the realism. But God's *moral status* looks too central to be treated in this way.) Moreover, Theodore's fiction will then raise the kinds of Euthyphro-type worries which drove him into moral fictionalism in the first place.[5]

4. Fictional God, Real Value

What of Moira? Moira is Theodore's mirror image: she is a theistic fictionalist, but a moral realist. This certainly looks a less surprising position than Theodore's. Moral realism would appear to be neutral on the issue of God's existence, since it makes moral values independent of God. It is an open question, then, what view to take on theistic discourse, and fictionalism seems as available as any other approach. Still, difficulties may be lurking under the surface.

A question for Moira is what, within her theistic fiction, is the basis of moral value. She might reply that this is a metaethical question and so not something that the fiction has to take a stance on. After all, any given fiction will be indeterminate with respect to certain matters. There is no truth-within-the-fiction of the matter whether or not Jane Austen's Emma has ever played the French horn. Religious fictions will similarly be indeterminate as to a variety of metaphysical matters, such as the relationist/absolutist debate on the nature of space. However, the question of the ground of goodness is surely not so removed from the theistic fiction. Moira's religious fiction has as its central character a perfectly benevolent God. It is not out of order to ask in virtue of what God counts as benevolent in this fiction: is this being judged from some external standard, or does the fiction represent God as the source of moral value? Indeed, not addressing this

---

[5] A possible source of motivation for Theodore's amoral God, apart from the desire to avoid either horn of the Euthyphro, is that other staple of analytic philosophy of religion: the problem of evil. As far as his realist theism is concerned, Theodore sidesteps this problem, as he can simply deny one of the premises—namely, that God is omnibenevolent. But, depending on whether God appears in his moral fiction, Theodore may still confront the fictionalist version of the problem of evil. If, within the fiction, God not only has the traditional divine attributes of omniscience and omnipotence, but omnibenevolence as well, then whence fictional evil? (And the fiction had better contain evil, or it will fail to include enough of the conditions of life to be a useful guide. It will, in other words, be a morally impoverished fiction.) So, if Theodore's amoral theistic realism is motivated in part by a desire to escape the problem of evil, he may find any attempt to integrate God into the moral fiction in any meaningful way a destabilizing influence. This version of the problem of evil is not peculiar to Theodore's position, of course, and it may be that the tensions it raises are not ones of logical inconsistency, and such tensions can be tolerated within fiction. See Le Poidevin (2019) for a discussion of the fictionalist problem of evil.

question would be something of a missed opportunity, a failure to develop the theistic fiction adequately.

Moira turns out not to be neutral on this question. She acknowledges that a fully developed religious fiction will have some metaethical content. Since she is already committed to moral realism outside the fiction, it is no surprise to learn that she has imported this into the fiction. The fictional God counts as good by the standard of real moral values. This is simply another example of the familiar phenomenon, alluded to above, whereby real items are incorporated into fictions: we can tell stories about real places (Graham Green's "entertainment" *Stamboul Train* weaves its narrative around the real cities though which the Orient Express passed in 1930s) and about real persons and events (as in Phillipa Gregory's historical novels). The effect of allowing her moral realism and theistic fictionalism to interact in this way, points out Moira, is to overcome what might otherwise be seen as a shortcoming in moral realism. If real moral values are not intrinsically motivating (thinking again of the argument from psychological queerness), they can become at least extrinsically motivating by being pictured as what an all-loving God being would desire. Our contemplation of and relationship with this being helps us to realize these values in our own lives. (Of course, theistic fictionalism does nothing to alleviate the metaphysical and epistemological queerness of real moral values.)

However, if (within the fiction) God is good according to some external standard, does this not return us to one of the horns of the Euthyphro dilemma, that there is something independent of God? That old chestnut, says Moira. Whether or not the Euthyphro dilemma is a problem for theistic realists (she goes on to say), the real world is insulated from anything that goes on in fiction. After all, isn't theistic fictionalism largely motivated by the paradoxes and challenges that realist theism faces? Here, though, Moira overreaches herself. Fictionalism is not a panacea for paradox. Problems for the realist may have fictionalist counterparts, as we saw above when discussing Theodore's position. If it is a contradiction to say both that God is sovereign over everything and that moral values are independent of God, then it is also a contradiction within the fiction. (This observation need not depend on what looks like the more general and resistible principle that any actual contradiction would be a contradiction within a fiction, for some contradictions are buried deep, requiring several deductive steps for their exposure. Since fiction is not closed under deduction, some reductios will not go through. However, in the case under discussion here, the contradiction is too obvious to escape notice.) We do, admittedly, tolerate some contradictions within fiction—time-travel stories in which the past is changed can still be enjoyed. But the theistic fiction has a serious purpose, and that purpose would be compromised by the presence of a glaring fault in the narrative. It is not the kind of thing that we may be able to suppress while immersed in the fiction. (By contrast, we may well suppress the worry, whilst immersed in an enjoyable time-travel story, that it is logically impossible to change the past.)

Moira switches tack. I was a little hasty there, she concedes. *Of course* she doesn't want a contradiction at the heart of her theistic narrative. If it is fictionally the case that God is good by some external standard, then it is not fictionally the case that God is sovereign over everything, including moral value. But, she points out, there are theistic realists who simply embrace that particular horn of the Euthyphro dilemma—Swinburne, for example. If realists can make that strategy defensible, then surely fictionalists can avail themselves of it? Indeed they can, but *can* realists meet this challenge?

Here is a realist line of thought. Unless we are to have a rather odd conception of God's relation to the rest of reality, it is inevitable that some things will be independent of God. God may be a necessary being, but is it up to God what counts as necessary and what contingent? If we say "with God, nothing shall be impossible" (Luke 2.37), does this mean that God could falsify what we consider logically necessary? Isn't it more sensible to suppose God works within the boundaries of the possible, boundaries which are not fixed by him? However, this is only a partial response to this horn of the Euthyphro. One concern about the idea of an external moral standard is that it makes not only goodness, but also moral *authority*, independent of God. If God wills something which is obligatory anyway, then his willing it adds nothing to the obligation to do it. Admittedly, there may be certain things which would not otherwise be obligatory but are made so by God's command, but this does not make God unique. Being ordered by the company commander to reconnoiter some suspect enemy territory puts a solider under an obligation which would not exist but for the order. So what would give God unique moral authority?

Biting this bullet (that not even moral authority is grounded in God) does not make God morally *de trop*, it is true. He can still be the means by which we become acquainted with objective moral values (thus disposing of the epistemological queerness of objective moral values). And this is something that Moira can incorporate into her theistic fiction. But it does come at a cost. For if moral authority does not come from God, why would creating a *fiction* about what God wills be motivating? Isn't it just creating an unnecessary third party?

It is worth, then, contemplating the following curious combination of views, as a variant of Moira's position: moral realism, accompanied by a theistic fictionalism which incorporates theistic moral subjectivism into the fiction. So although, in reality, moral values exist independently of any mind (even God's, for he does not exist), *within the theistic fiction*, moral value is constituted by God's will. The point of this apparently rather strained stance is, first, to preserve the notion of God's unique moral authority, and second, to provide the motivational power which real moral values may lack. For the proponent of such a stance, moral realism may be the correct semantics for moral judgments, but it is psychologically feeble. To make moral values truly animate our lives is a work of the imagination. But doesn't this just invite the other horn of the Euthyphro? What if, within the fiction, God were to command something abhorrent? It would still be good within the fiction. However, here is where the theistic fictionalist may have an advantage over the realist. To the realist's riposte, "But God would never command anything abhorrent—it's not in his nature!," the objection will be that there is no non-circular way of guaranteeing this. It is no use saying, for example, that God would not command anything abhorrent because he is *good*. But fiction can be constrained in a way that reality cannot. It can simply be stipulated that within the fiction God does not, and would not, command or will anything abhorrent. This is anything but an arbitrary stipulation: the fictionalist will naturally choose a fiction which is a useful guide or prompt to behavior, and one in which God commanded abhorrent things could hardly be described in those terms.

There is a danger here, perhaps, of making the theistic fiction a little too comfortable. Naturally, a fiction in which God commanded one to commit atrocious acts would undermine the moral purpose of adopting the fiction. But theism can, and should, be morally challenging. We could imagine, for example, a situation in which a parent's love for their child causes them to conceal evidence of the child's wrong-doing (hiding their illegal drug haul before the police visit), an act which nevertheless results in a bad conscience occasioned by their religious faith. Would a theistic fiction have this same effect? Or, whenever there was a conflict of loyalties—to one's child on the one hand, and to God on the other, for instance—would the theistic fictionalists say, "Oh well, it is only a fiction, I can happily abandon my religious scruples for the sake of my child"?

There are other possible variants of Moira's position, of course. We have already mentioned one in which the theistic fiction has God as a communicator rather than the ground of moral values. And there are others in which God's sovereignty is further compromised: he cannot eliminate evil, for example. The theistic fictionalist does not have to buy into one particular account. What is on offer is a whole range of narratives, from the Anselmian perfect being to an amoral watchmaker. The advantages or shortcomings of these various conceptions of God, as the realist conceives of them, transmute into narrative strengths or weaknesses in the corresponding theistic fiction. And there is this further element: the extent to which the theistic fiction enhances or otherwise the motivational power of moral realism.

5. The Natural Partnership Revisited

Having looked at two alternatives, let us return to the "natural partnership" of moral fictionalism and theistic fictionalism. Is it better placed than either of the rival combinations? Theodore's position (theistic realism and moral fictionalism) we saw prevents him from aligning himself with traditional theistic religions: moral fictionalism threatens to rob realist theism of part of its, arguably essential, content. If Theodore tries to preserve a genuinely religious theism by appeal to a loving (though not intrinsically moral) God, his moral fictionalism is redundant. But Moira's position (theistic fictionalism and moral realism) looks much more stable, although Moira would be well advised at least to consider a revision in her outlook: combining moral realism with a theistic fiction that grounds moral values in God.

The encounter with Moira shows that there are in fact no fewer than three versions of her basic position, depending on whether or not the theistic fiction includes metaethical content and, if it does, whether that content is subjectivist or realist. A similar choice faces us if we are inclined to combine moral and theistic fictionalism. We have seen that there is reason to include metaethical content in the theistic fiction. A suitably rich narrative will tell us something about the relation between God and moral value. But if we do include metaethical content in the fiction, does this support or conflict with moral fictionalism? Perhaps it depends what that metaethical content is. Recall that moral fictionalism takes us to be motivated to act morally if we treat moral values as if they are real and not subjective, even though they are in fact fictional. What could be more natural, then, than incorporating moral realism into the theistic fiction? (That is, it is fictional that moral value is objectively real.) However, doing so threatens to diminish God's status vis-à-vis moral values: he is not the ultimate source of moral authority in the fiction. So moral fictionalism is somewhat in tension with this version of theistic fictionalism. This may not be disastrous by any means, but might it nevertheless reduce the power of the narrative? Suppose instead, then, that the theistic fiction incorporates theistic moral subjectivism. That is, according to the fiction, moral values are grounded in God. Then we have simultaneously to maintain *two* fictions: one, that moral values are completely independent of any mind, human or divine (this being the fiction we are invited by standard moral fictionalism to adopt), the other that they are dependent on the mind of God (this being the theistic fiction). So this version of theistic fictionalism is in tension with (standard) moral fictionalism. Not such a natural partnership after all?

How much simpler than any of the positions we have considered so far in this chapter would be this one: a moral fictionalism that incorporates as its central metaethical fiction theistic moral subjectivism! On this picture, there are, in reality, no moral values and no God. In the recommended fiction, however, moral values are constituted by the nature and will of God. What makes the fiction morally motivating is that it represents moral values as having a source outside us. But they are not queer, in any of the three senses. They are not metaphysically queer, since they are constituted by (divine) personal responses; they are not epistemologically queer, since God is the source of moral knowledge; and they are not psychologically queer, insofar as we are motivated to do what a loving being wills. The point of using a fictional God as our *focus imaginarius* is that it enables us to decentralize, as well as evoke, the kinds of emotional reaction (loyalty, love, shame, guilt) that are the psychological springs of our moral behavior. The fiction does not incorporate either horn of the Euthyphro dilemma, for God is (fictionally) sovereign and perfectly loving, and since we are the originators of the fiction, our conception of God is informed by our own sense of what it is to be loving. There is no danger, then, of the fictional God's will being either arbitrary or abhorrent (though it may be challenging: we are pretty good at beating ourselves up).

Standard moral fictionalism recommends a fiction in which moral value is independent of any attitude, human or divine. The revised moral fictionalism we have just been considering replaces this fiction with one in which God is the basis of moral value. The conclusion towards which we are heading seems to be that those attracted to both moral and religious (and specifically theistic) fictionalism would be well advised to accept this revision in how they conceive of the relevant metaethical fiction. The introduction of a divine source and sustainer of moral value might just be the best plot line for moral fictionalists.[6]

References

Brock, S. & Mares, E. 2006. *Realism and Anti-Realism*. Routledge.

Burgess, J. 1983. "Why I am not a nominalist." *Notre Dame Journal of Formal Logic* 24: 93–105.

Dennett, D. 1991. *Consciousness Explained*. Penguin.

Eshleman, A. 2016. "The afterlife: Beyond belief." *International Journal for Philosophy of Religion* 82: 163–83.

Joyce, R. 2005. "Moral fictionalism." In Kalderon 2005: 287–313.

Joyce, R. 2013. "Psychological fictionalism, and the threat of fictionalist suicide." *Monist* 96: 517–38.

Joyce, R. 2021. "Moral anti-realism." In E. Zalta (ed.), *Stanford Encyclopedia of Philosophy*. <https://plato.stanford.edu/entries/moral-anti-realism/>.

Kalderon, M. (ed.). 2005. *Fictionalism in Metaphysics*. Clarendon.

Kretzmann, N. 1999. "Abraham, Isaac and Euthyphro: God and the basis of morality." In E. Stump & M. Murray (eds.), *Philosophy of Religion: The Big Questions*. Blackwell: 417–27.

---

[6] Grateful thanks to the organizers and participants at the Religious and Moral Fictionalism workshop (Victoria University of Wellington, 2021), for their very helpful and constructive comments on an earlier version of this chapter, to the editors, for inviting me to be part of this project, and especially to Richard Joyce, for insightful comments on previous versions.

Le Poidevin, R. 2019. *Religious Fictionalism*. Cambridge University Press.

Le Poidevin, R. 2020. "Fiction and the agnostic." *European Journal for the Philosophy of Religion* 12: 163–81.

Mackie, J. L. 1977. *Ethics: Inventing Right and Wrong*. Penguin.

Swinburne, R. 1977. *The Coherence of Theism*. Clarendon.

Van Fraassen, B. 1981. *The Scientific Image*. Clarendon.

11
Do We Have Reason to Adopt Religious Fictionalism or Moral Fictionalism?

Seahwa Kim

1. Introduction

Consider a certain region of discourse D that we are engaged in, and consider claims Cs made widely within D that refer to or quantify over a certain kind of entity E. A standard version of revolutionary fictionalism about E consists of the following main claims:[1]

(A) Since Cs imply the existence of E but E does not exist, Cs are false. D is full of false claims.
(B) Since engagement in D and its associated set of practices P gives us benefits independent of Cs' truth, we should still engage in D and P.

There is an apparent tension between (A) and (B). It seems reasonable to assume that usually, when people engage in D, they believe Cs to be true. Given (A), and assuming that we wish to minimize holding false beliefs, it seems that the most natural step to take is to abolish D and P. So (A) seems to imply that we should stop engaging in D and P. This is in apparent conflict with (B) which says we should still engage in D and P. Proponents of revolutionary fictionalism claim that this apparent tension is avoided by accepting Cs in a way that does not require believing them to be true—that is, by taking the attitude of *nondoxastic acceptance* toward Cs.[2]

An important question still remains. In claiming (B), revolutionary fictionalists appeal to benefits specific to D and P. However, a useful fiction is still a fiction. We might be able to receive the same or similar benefits in some other way. We might be better off not even nondoxastically accepting any false claims. One might

---

[1] I will set aside hermeneutic fictionalism about E. For the distinction between revolutionary fictionalism and hermeneutic fictionalism, see, for example, Kim 2014: 321. See also Burgess & Rosen 1997: 6–7.
[2] "The claims you accept are the claims you regard as legitimate resources for justification, both theoretical and practical, within the context of a certain inquiry" (Rosen 2005: 15).

Seahwa Kim, *Do We Have Reason to Adopt Religious Fictionalism or Moral Fictionalism?* In: *Moral Fictionalism and Religious Fictionalism.* Edited by: Richard Joyce and Stuart Brock, Oxford University Press. © Seahwa Kim 2023.
DOI: 10.1093/oso/9780198881865.003.0012

still wonder why we should become fictionalists rather than abolitionists about E, given (A).

In this chapter, I argue that under certain conditions we (as individuals) have a *pro tanto* reason to adopt fictionalism rather than abolitionism.[3] I suggest that we focus on general benefits of continued engagement rather than benefits specific to D and P. I will identify certain specific conditions under which there would be general benefits of continued engagement. If at least one of these conditions is met with respect to D and P, then, as far as these conditions are concerned, we have a reason to adopt fictionalism instead of abolitionism with respect to D and P.[4]

Since the benefits of continued engagement are general, these conditions apply to all kinds of fictionalisms. After proposing three such conditions, I apply the result to two specific examples of fictionalism: religious fictionalism and moral fictionalism. One might think that since there is an affinity between their subject matters, we are justified in adopting fictionalism over abolitionism to similar degrees in both cases. I argue that this is mistaken. Religious discourse and its associated practices do not satisfy any of the three conditions whereas moral discourse and its associated practices satisfy two of them.

2. The Ubiquity Condition

Consider again a certain region of discourse D that we are engaged in, and claims Cs made within D that refer to or quantify over a certain kind of entity E. Let us suppose that we have discovered that E does not exist and therefore Cs are false.[5] For the sake of argument, I will make two important assumptions. First, let us assume that there are benefits specific to D and P. If there are no such benefits specific to D and P, then fictionalism about E should not be adopted. Second, let us assume that these benefits are still available to us even if our attitude is changed to nondoxastic acceptance. If none of these benefits specific to D and P are available to us when we stop believing Cs to be true, then fictionalism about E has no chance of success and therefore should not be adopted.

The question now arises: should we abandon D and P or should we still continue to engage in them by nondoxastically accepting Cs? That is, should we adopt abolitionism or fictionalism with respect to E? When we are faced with the choice between fictionalism and abolitionism in such a situation, we should examine whether there are any general benefits of continued engagement.

---

[3] In what follows, when I speak of there being "a reason to adopt fictionalism," I intend to refer to a *pro tanto* reason.

[4] In this chapter, I am only concerned with the choice between fictionalism and abolitionism. I will ignore other revisionary views such as conservationism.

[5] "We" does not have to denote many people. It can be just one individual.

I suggest that, firstly, we have to consider the extent to which people's engagement in *D* and *P* is widespread.

In general, the more people there are who are engaged in *D* and its associated set of practices *P*, the more strongly *D* and *P* are embedded in the society. In such a society, an individual who opts to abandon *D* and *P* is at risk of signaling that she refuses to be a part of the society. By rejecting such strongly embedded *D* and *P*, she might be considered or treated as a rebel, an outcast, or an outsider. This would cause her a considerable amount of practical cost since people in general are less willing to help rebels, outcasts, and outsiders. Unless she has some reason to accept such practical costs, she is better off continuing to engage in *D* and *P*. This means that the more people there are who are engaged in *D* and *P*, *ceteris paribus*, the more practical benefits people would receive by continuing to engage in them. If virtually everyone is engaged in *D* and *P*, then this fact gives us a reason to continue to engage in them. The fact that virtually everyone is engaged in *D* and *P* gives us a reason to adopt fictionalism rather than abolitionism when faced with the choice between them. Let us call this condition "the Ubiquity Condition." The satisfaction of the Ubiquity Condition gives us defeasible justification for adopting fictionalism.

One might object that just because everybody else does something, it does not give an individual any reason to do the same. The objection goes as follows. Suppose everyone in some society wears an enormously big hat and you find it strange. Does the fact that everyone else wears an enormously big hat give you any reason to wear the same kind of hat? No. It seems silly to follow their practice.[6]

The question of the choice between continued engagement and abandonment mainly arises for those individuals who used to engage in the practice as members of the society. I have argued that they have a reason to continue to engage in the practice if everyone else is engaged in it. However, the question of a similar choice between following the practice and rejecting it can arise for those individuals who are members of the society but have never engaged in the practice. It can also arise for those individuals who come from another society. Presumably the individual imagined in the above objection is one of these individuals. Suppose it is the individual of the first kind: the individual who is a member of the society but has never engaged in the practice. I maintain that the same reason applies to this individual. If she wants to avoid the kind of practical costs I have described for rebels, outcasts, or outsiders, then she does have a reason to follow the practice when everyone else is engaged in it. The fact that everyone else is engaged in a certain practice provides her defeasible justification for following the practice, at least until enough people in the society abandon the practice. In the above example, she has a reason to follow the practice of wearing an enormously big hat.

---

[6] I thank Richard Joyce and Jessica Isserow for pressing this point.

Suppose instead that it is the individual who comes from another society. Does she have a reason to follow the practice? It depends. Perhaps she does not intend to stay long in this society and does not mind the inconveniences caused by being treated as an outsider. In this case, then, she does not have a reason of this kind to follow the practice. However, if she wants to be successfully integrated into a new society, then she does have a reason to start engaging in the practice. If the latter is the case, then in the above example she has a reason to wear an enormously big hat.

Consider mathematics. Let us assume that there are benefits specific to mathematics and that these benefits are still available to us even if our attitude is changed to nondoxastic acceptance. Virtually everyone is engaged in mathematics. People are engaged in mathematics when they pay for groceries, calculate the arrival time of trains, measure the number of calories they consume, and so on. The fact that virtually everybody is engaged in mathematical discourse and its associated practices shows that there are practical benefits of continued engagement in mathematics. This gives us a reason to adopt fictionalism rather than abolitionism about mathematics when faced with the choice between them.[7]

3. The Indispensability Condition

The second consideration in examining whether there are any general benefits of continued engagement in D and P is the indispensability of D and P.

The indispensability in this discussion is different from that of the well-known Indispensability Argument. Some philosophers claim that the indispensability of a certain kind of entity in our best theory gives us reason to believe in the existence of this entity.[8] The indispensability that I consider is different from this. It is the indispensability to people who are engaged in D and P for relevant purposes. For example, if ordinary people are engaged in D and P for the purpose of U in their ordinary lives, then the indispensability I consider is the indispensability to ordinary people for the purpose of U in their ordinary lives. If a particular group of people are engaged in D and P for the purpose of U, then it is the indispensability to this particular group of people for the purpose of U.

If D and P are indispensable for the purpose of U, then abandoning them would mean that U cannot be successfully pursued until alternative ways are available. If U is something vital to one's life, then abandoning D and P makes one's life practically unlivable. Even if U is not so vital, abandoning D and P still makes one's life difficult and inconvenient. There would be a significant amount of practical costs for an individual if she abandons D and P. Unless she does not

---

[7] For discussion of mathematical fictionalism, see, for example, Field 1980.
[8] For recent discussion of the Indispensability Argument, see, for example, Baker 2009 and Saatsi 2016.

want to pursue U and is willing to embrace the consequences, she is better off continuing to engage in D and P and thereby avoid this kind of practical cost. This means that the more indispensable D and P are, *ceteris paribus*, the more practical benefits she receives from continued engagement in them. If D and P are indispensable, then this fact gives us a reason to continue to engage in them. The fact that D and P are indispensable gives us a reason to adopt fictionalism rather than abolitionism when faced with the choice between them. Let us call this condition "the Indispensability Condition." The satisfaction of the Indispensability Condition gives us defeasible justification for adopting fictionalism.

Consider mathematics again. Let us assume that there are benefits specific to mathematics and that these benefits are still available to us even if our attitude is changed to nondoxastic acceptance. People appeal to mathematics for a variety of purposes. For example, people use mathematics when they pay for groceries, calculate the grade point average (GPA), measure distance, and so on. Without it, even the most trivial activities in their daily lives would become nearly impossible to do. The fact that mathematics is indispensable to ordinary people for relevant purposes shows that there are practical benefits of continued engagement in mathematics. This gives us a reason to adopt fictionalism rather than abolitionism about mathematics when faced with the choice between them.

Consider the language of possible worlds. In contemporary philosophy, the language of possible worlds is almost indispensable. Even if there are no possible worlds and even if philosophers do not believe that possible worlds exist, it is very difficult for them to avoid appealing to possible worlds in discussion of modality and its related concepts. As Gideon Rosen says,

> [I]n discussion of modal subtleties—discussion which can hardly be avoided nowadays—the language of possible worlds has become a nearly indispensable tool. For it permits the articulation of modal views with a clarity and vividness that cannot be achieved by other means—so much so that even philosophers who officially renounce the idiom often find themselves talking about possible worlds anyway when it becomes important to make a modal claim precise or a modal argument rigorous. (1990: 327)

It would be nearly impossible for contemporary philosophers to abandon the language of possible worlds. Assuming that there are benefits specific to the language of possible worlds and that these benefits are still available to us even if our attitude is changed to nondoxastic acceptance, the fact that the language of possible worlds is indispensable to contemporary philosophy for relevant purposes shows that there are practical benefits of continued engagement. This gives contemporary philosophers a reason to continue to use the language of possible worlds and adopt fictionalism rather than abolitionism about possible worlds when faced with the choice between them.

In fact, fictionalism should be seen as accommodating two seemingly conflicting desiderata: indispensability and ontological parsimony. To show this more clearly, let me propose the following argument for fictionalism about musical works.

We engage in the discourse on musical works and its associated practices of creating, performing, and appreciating music. Claims made within this discourse refer to or quantify over musical works. It seems that musical works are not concrete objects. A musical work cannot be identified with any concrete object such as a particular copy of the score, the sum of all copies of the score, a particular performance, the sum of all performances, or the composer's thought. It seems that musical works are abstract objects.[9] However, it is difficult for us to believe that there are abstract objects. It seems that abstract objects, entities that lack a particular spatio-temporal location and are not the part of our ordinary causal nexus, do not exist. Therefore, it seems that we should abandon the discourse on musical works and its associated practices for the sake of ontological parsimony.

The problem is that we have an entrenched culture of creating, performing, and appreciating music. Within this culture, we engage in the discourse on musical works. For example, we analyze, evaluate, and compare various artists' musical works. It seems that unless we completely get rid of our culture of creating and appreciating art in general, it is practically impossible to abolish its sub-culture: the culture of composing, performing, and enjoying music. So long as we have the culture of music, it seems that it is unavoidable to engage in the discourse on musical works. Furthermore, it seems evident that there are benefits specific to the culture of creating, performing, and appreciating music. For one thing, we feel aesthetic pleasure in appreciating music. And when we appreciate music, we listen to particular performances that are concrete objects. For this reason, the benefits of appreciating music are still available to us, even if we do not believe in the existence of musical works as abstract objects.

The discourse on musical works and its associated practices are nearly indispensable to ordinary people for relevant purposes. This fact shows that there are practical benefits of continued engagement in the discourse on musical works and its associated practices. Thus, instead of abolishing the discourse on musical works and its associated practices, we should continue to engage in them without believing claims made within the discourse to be true. That is, we should adopt fictionalism about musical works by taking the attitude of nondoxastic acceptance.[10]

Fictionalism about musical works can accommodate two desiderata. The first desideratum is the indispensability of the discourse on musical works and its associated practices. This desideratum seems to require that we continue to engage in them. The second desideratum is ontological parsimony. The second desideratum seems to require that we stop engaging in the discourse on musical

---

[9] See Cameron 2008: 296.
[10] For discussion of fictionalism about musical works, see, for example, Killin 2018.

works and its associated practices. Fictionalism about musical works can accommodate these two seemingly conflicting desiderata by asking us to continue to engage in the discourse on musical works and its associated practices and accept claims made within the discourse without believing them to be true.

4. The Business as Usual Condition

Let us move to the third consideration. For illustration, let us imagine that people in a certain society are engaged in witch-hunting discourse and its associated practices. Now imagine how they would react when they have discovered that there are no such things as witches. After learning that there are no witches and that claims made within the discourse are false, reasonable people would abandon their beliefs about the existence of witches. They would not stop there. Reasonable people would also change their behaviors with respect to witches. For example, they would stop searching for witches. After all, there are no witches to hunt. This shows that we have a reason to adopt abolitionism about witches after learning that there are no witches. The non-existence of witches rationally requires us to change relevant behaviors as well as our relevant beliefs.

By contrast, in some other cases the non-existence of a certain kind of entity does not require us to change relevant behaviors although it does require us to change our relevant beliefs. If the non-existence of a certain kind of entity does not require us to change relevant behaviors with respect to the entity, then even if we realize their non-existence, it is not necessary to change our relevant behaviors.

In some of these cases, it is preferable not to change our relevant behaviors. They are cases where there are benefits specific to them. In such cases, an individual who opts to change her behaviors in question would effectively give up these benefits. If she still wants these benefits, then she must learn or devise some alternative ways to secure similar benefits. Learning or devising alternative ways would cause her a certain amount of practical cost. She has to exert unnecessary energy and effort. Unless she can easily come up with some alternative ways to secure similar benefits, she is better off not changing the relevant behaviors. This means that if the non-existence of a certain kind of entity does not require us to change relevant behaviors and there are benefits specific to them, then there are benefits of not changing the relevant behaviors. In this situation, there are benefits of continued engagement in D and P in question. This fact gives us a reason to adopt fictionalism rather than abolitionism when faced with the choice between them. Let us call this condition "the Business as Usual Condition." The satisfaction of the Business as Usual Condition gives us defeasible justification for adopting fictionalism.

Consider mathematics once more. Let us assume that there are benefits specific to mathematics and that these benefits are still available to us even if our attitude is changed to nondoxastic acceptance. Even if there are no mathematical entities and even if we realize this, would this fact require us to change our relevant behaviors with respect to mathematics? It does not seem so. We still have to pay the same amount of money at restaurants. Our college GPA does not change. The way we count the "number" of students in class will remain the same. The way we measure distance or the duration of time will remain the same. The non-existence of mathematical entities does not require us to change our relevant behaviors. After all, mathematical entities would be abstract entities if they existed. Even if they existed, we would not inquire into the abstract realm of mathematical entities in order to calculate, count, and measure. Stephen Yablo says "mathematics does not lose its point…if the *mathematical* realm disappears—or, indeed, if it turns out that that realm was empty all along" (2005: 88). The non-existence of mathematical entities does not require us to change our relevant behaviors. Since we are assuming that there are benefits specific to mathematics, this fact shows that there are benefits of continued engagement in mathematics. Therefore we have a reason to adopt fictionalism rather than abolitionism about mathematics when faced with the choice between them.

Consider the discourse on fictional characters and its associated set of practices. Let us assume that there are benefits specific to the discourse on fictional characters and its associated practices and that these benefits are still available to us even if our attitude is changed to nondoxastic acceptance. Even if there are no fictional characters and even if we realize this, it does not seem that this fact requires us to change our behaviors with respect to fictional characters. In discussing, for example, virtues and vices of fictional characters, we have to rely on the same kind of method as before. We still have to look into relevant novels, movies, or comic books. Even if fictional characters existed, whether they were abstract or concrete, ordinary people or professional critics would not inquire into the realm of fictional characters in order to discuss, compare, and analyze fictional characters. The way we discover "facts" about fictional characters will remain the same even if there are no fictional characters. The non-existence of fictional characters does not require us to change our relevant behaviors. Since we are assuming that there are benefits specific to the discourse on fictional characters and its associated practices, this fact shows that there are benefits of continued engagement in the discourse on fictional characters and its associated practices. Therefore we have a reason to adopt fictionalism rather than abolitionism about fictional characters when faced with the choice between them.[11]

5. Religious Fictionalism

I have proposed three conditions under which there are practical benefits of continued engagement in D and P. I have argued that under the three conditions,

---

[11] For discussion of fictionalism about fictional characters, see Brock 2002.

we have a reason to adopt fictionalism instead of abolitionism. They are the Ubiquity Condition, the Indispensability Condition, and the Business as Usual Condition. None of them are necessary conditions. They each provide defeasible justification for adopting fictionalism when faced with the choice between fictionalism and abolitionism. The more of the three are present, the stronger the reason in favor of fictionalism. I will leave it open whether there may be other conditions to adopt fictionalism instead of abolitionism.

Let us now examine whether religious discourse and its associated practices satisfy at least some of the three conditions. Let us assume that there are benefits specific to religious discourse and religious practices and that these benefits are still available to us even if our attitude is changed to nondoxastic acceptance. Let us suppose that people who have been engaged in religious discourse and its associated practices have discovered that supernatural entities such as gods do not exist and therefore that religious claims are false. The question now arises for them: should they abandon religious discourse and religious practices or should they continue to engage in them without believing the truth of religious claims? Should they adopt abolitionism or fictionalism about religious entities?[12]

Religious discourse and its associated practices do not satisfy the Ubiquity Condition. There are considerable numbers of non-religious people. They do not engage in religious discourse and religious practices. More and more people become non-religious as the society becomes more developed and civilized. Furthermore, even those people who claim themselves to be "religious" do not regularly engage in religious discourse and its associated practices. This shows that in typical contemporary societies we do not have a reason of this kind to adopt fictionalism rather than abolitionism about religious entities when faced with the choice between them.

One might object that there are societies where nearly everyone engages in religious discourse and its associated practices. I admit that in these societies, people may have a reason to continue to engage in them even if they have realized that religious entities do not exist and religious claims are false. My claim is that in many contemporary societies, where fewer and fewer people engage in religious discourse and religious practices, people do not have a reason of this kind to adopt fictionalism rather than abolitionism about religious entities.

Nor do religious discourse and religious practices satisfy the Indispensability Condition. It does not seem that they are indispensable to ordinary people for relevant purposes. Usually people seek for answers in religion: they seek answers about the origins of the universe and humanity, answers to the existential question about the meaning of life, and answers to questions about morality. In contemporary society, there are obvious and reasonable alternatives. One can scientifically

---

[12] For discussion of religious fictionalism, see, for example, Brock 2020; Deng 2019; Eshleman 2005; Le Poidevin 1996.

inquire into the origins of the universe and humankind. The meaning of life can be examined by philosophical investigation. Secular ethics provides answers about moral questions. In the past, almost every aspect of a person's life was governed by religion. Nowadays, religion is not indispensable even to religious people.

One might object as follows. Although religious discourse and religious practices are not indispensable to ordinary people, they are indispensable to those who professionally engage in them. They are theologians, priests, ministers, and so on. Just as the indispensability to philosophers matters in the case of the language of possible worlds, the indispensability to these professional people matters in the case of religion. In response to this, I maintain that, firstly, there is an important disanalogy between the language of possible worlds and the language of religion. "Possible worlds" is a technical term in philosophy. By contrast, "god" and its related terms are not technical terms. These terms are available to ordinary people. Therefore, the indispensability to ordinary people must matter as well in the case of religion. Secondly, even if we ignore the fact that religious terms are not technical terms, the indispensability of religious discourse and its associated practices to professional people can show only that these professional people have a reason to adopt fictionalism when faced with the choice between fictionalism and abolitionism.[13] It does not show that ordinary people have a reason to adopt fictionalism when faced with the choice. I conclude that religious discourse and religious practices do not satisfy the Indispensability Condition with respect to ordinary people.

Let us see whether religious discourse and religious practices satisfy the Business as Usual Condition. Does the non-existence of religious entities require changes in relevant behaviors with respect to religion? I think so. God is supposed to have influences on almost every aspect of people's lives. People lead their lives under the guidance of god. God reveals truths about the world and displays moral ideals that people aspire to pursue. In the past, many of our behaviors reflected such influences. However, after realizing that there is no god, the reasonable reaction would be to change not only relevant beliefs but also relevant behaviors with respect to god. After all, there is no god that can have any influence on anything. The non-existence of religious entities requires us to change relevant behaviors such as prayer and church or temple attendance.

One might object that there may be some religions that have little influence on people's lives. With respect to these religions, people would not need to change relevant behaviors so much even if they realized that supernatural entities do not exist. I admit that such religions may satisfy the Business as Usual Condition.

---

[13] I admit that these professional people have a reason to adopt fictionalism rather than abolitionism when faced with the choice because religious discourse and religious practices are indispensable to them for relevant purposes.

However, my point stands with respect to familiar religions. With respect to familiar religions, the Business as Usual Condition is not satisfied.

Religious discourse and its associated practices satisfy none of the three conditions. I conclude that as far as the three conditions are concerned, we do not have a reason to adopt religious fictionalism rather than abolitionism when faced with the choice.

I would like to make three notes. First, as I have mentioned above, my argument does not exclude the possibility that there may be some societies where some of the three conditions are satisfied. In such societies, people have a reason to adopt fictionalism rather than abolitionism about religious entities when faced with the choice.

Second, as I have said above, I do not deny that there might be other reasons to adopt religious fictionalism rather than abolitionism. For example, one might claim that we have a reason to adopt religious fictionalism because adopting religious fictionalism can help in providing a solution to some important philosophical problem. For example, when Peter Lipton says that religious fictionalism may help in dealing with "the cognitive tension between science and religion" (2007: 31), he can be taken as making such a claim.[14] In any case, the burden of showing that there are such conditions and some of them are satisfied in the case of religion is on those who want to defend religious fictionalism.

Third, in examining whether there are general benefits of continued engagement in religion, I have assumed that there are benefits specific to religious discourse and its associated practices. However, there are many people who raise concerns about "the dangerousness of religion" (Sauchelli 2018: 633)[15] and this can be taken as claiming that any benefits brought by religion are outweighed by costs. Against this concern, those who wish to defend religious fictionalism must accomplish three tasks. Firstly, benefits specific to religion must be identified.[16] Secondly, these benefits must be shown to be independent of the truth of religious claims.[17] Finally and most importantly, it must be demonstrated that these benefits remain as benefits even from a broader perspective. For example, although one might claim that religion brings the benefits of promoting such virtues as bonding and trust, it might be objected that a broader perspective will reveal that religion promotes these virtues "only between members of a particular group" and "often encourages the opposite sort of attitude to members outside the group"

---

[14] It seems to me that lessening the cognitive tension between science and religion is hardly a solution to any important philosophical problem or puzzle. Fictionalism about astrology as a way of lessening the cognitive tension between science and astrology does not seem to be a solution to any important philosophical problem at all.
[15] See also Grzymala-Busse 2012: 424.   [16] See, for example, Scott & Malcolm 2018: 3–4.
[17] See, for example, Le Poidevin 1996: 111–12.

(Chambers and Kopstein 2001: 841)—which ultimately counts as a cost.[18] Again, the burden is on those who seek to defend religious fictionalism.

6. Moral Fictionalism

Compared to religious fictionalism, moral fictionalism is in a significantly better position.[19] It is easy to see that moral discourse and its associated practices satisfy the Ubiquity Condition and the Indispensability Condition and that therefore we have a reason to adopt moral fictionalism rather than abolitionism when faced with the choice between them.[20]

As with the discussion on religious discourse and its associated practices, let us assume that there are benefits specific to moral discourse and its associated practices and that these benefits are still available to us even if we change our attitude to nondoxastic acceptance. Let us suppose that people who have been engaged in moral discourse and its associated practices have discovered that moral properties do not exist (or, at least, are not instantiated) and therefore that moral claims are false. Should they abandon moral discourse and its associated practices or should they continue to engage in them without believing the truth of moral claims? Should they adopt abolitionism or fictionalism about morality?

Moral discourse and its associated practices satisfy the Ubiquity Condition. Virtually everyone is engaged in moral discourse and its associated practices. People discuss moral rightness and wrongness. People debate about moral responsibilities, moral duties, and moral rights. People criticize morally wrong actions and praise morally right actions. The satisfaction of the Ubiquity Condition gives us defeasible justification for adopting moral fictionalism.

Moral discourse and its associated practices also satisfy the Indispensability Condition. People appeal to morality for a variety of purposes. People appeal to morality when deliberating on and choosing a course of action. People blame or praise other people based on moral evaluations. People even talk about moral virtues of fictional characters when discussing novels or movies. It seems unavoidable to use moral predicates such as "right," "wrong," "fair," "unjust," and so on, in our daily lives. Moral discourse and moral practices are nearly indispensable to ordinary people for many purposes. The satisfaction of the Indispensability Condition gives us defeasible justification for adopting moral fictionalism.

---

[18] I thank Jennifer Sejin Oh for helpful discussion on the political scientists' view on religion.
[19] For discussion of moral fictionalism, see, for example, Jay 2020; Joyce 2001, 2017; Nolan, Restall, & West 2005.
[20] My claim is only that when faced with the choice between fictionalism and abolitionism about morality, we have a reason to adopt fictionalism. My argument does not cover whether we have a reason to favor moral fictionalism over other revisionary views. For discussion of conservationism as an example of an alternative option for the moral error theorist, see Olson 2014; Moberger & Olson, Chapter 3 of this volume.

How about the Business as Usual Condition? It may seem that moral discourse and its associated practices satisfy this condition. Moral properties are not ordinary observational properties like colors. Even if moral properties existed, we would not be able to detect them with our ordinary physical senses. So, it seems that even if there are no moral properties and even if we realize this, our relevant behaviors with respect to morality will remain the same. The way we discover "facts" about morality seems to remain the same even if there are no moral properties. However, more careful reflection reveals that this is not the case.

If there are no moral properties, then there are no such things as morally right actions and morally wrong actions. If moral properties do not exist, then there is no moral fact that can settle issues related to morality such as moral responsibilities, moral duties, and moral values. If this is the case, then there will be no ground for moral evaluations. I maintain that this has an important ramification on our customary practices of blame and praise based on moral evaluations. If there are no moral properties, then, in particular, our practices of morally blaming and praising certain actions or people will lose their ground. After all, there are no morally wrong actions to blame and no morally right actions to praise. People who are morally blamed or praised do not deserve these reactions. Just as reasonable people would not give prizes or punishments to those who do not deserve them, reasonable people would not blame or praise those who do not deserve it.

This shows that if there are no moral properties and if we realize that moral claims are false because there are no moral properties, then there will be pressure to change our relevant beliefs with respect to morality. Also, until some alternative ground is found, there will be pressure to change a substantial number of relevant behaviors with respect to morality, namely our behaviors of moral blame and moral praise. The non-existence of moral properties requires changes in at least some relevant behaviors with respect to morality. This shows that moral discourse and moral practices do not satisfy the Business as Usual Condition.

However, the Business as Usual Condition is not a necessary condition. Moral discourse and moral practices seem to satisfy at least two other conditions, the Ubiquity Condition and the Indispensability Condition. Therefore, it still stands that we have a reason to adopt moral fictionalism when faced with the choice between fictionalism and abolitionism.

I would like to make one note. Some philosophers claim that we should adopt abolitionism rather than fictionalism about morality because there is harm specific to moral discourse and its associated practices. For example, Richard Garner says "there are more problems with morality than moralists and moral fictionalists usually admit" (2007: 511) and "the death of moralizing might be good for the individual and for society, and...moral abolitionism may be more useful than moral fictionalism in helping us reach the goals that most compassionate moralists seek" (500). As I have said in section 2, I agree to the following conditional statement: *if* there is more harm than benefit specific to a certain *D* and *P*, then no matter how difficult it is to abolish *D* and *P*, we should not adopt fictionalism with respect to *D* and *P*.

7. Conclusion

In this chapter, I have examined whether there is a reason to favor religious or moral fictionalism rather than abolitionism when faced with the choice between fictionalism and abolitionism. Assuming that there are benefits specific to *D* and *P* and that these benefits are available even if we change our attitude to nondoxastic acceptance, I argued that if there are general and practical benefits of continued engagement in *D* and *P*, then we have a reason to adopt fictionalism rather than abolitionism. I further argued that there are three conditions—the Ubiquity Condition, the Indispensability Condition, and the Business as Usual Condition—under which there would be such benefits. Satisfaction of at least one of these conditions provides defeasible justification for adopting fictionalism when faced with the choice between fictionalism and abolitionism. I showed that religious discourse and its associated set of practices do not satisfy any of the three conditions, whereas moral discourse and its associated set of practices satisfy two of them. I conclude that as far as the three conditions are concerned, we do not have a reason to adopt religious fictionalism whereas we do have a reason to adopt moral fictionalism.[21]

References

Baker, A. 2009. "Mathematical explanation in science." *British Journal for the Philosophy of Science* 60: 611–33.

Brock, S. 2002. "Fictionalism about fictional characters." *Noûs* 36: 1–21.

Brock, S. 2020. "Religious fictionalism and Pascal's Wager." In B. Armour-Garb & F. Kroon (eds.), *Fictionalism in Philosophy*. Oxford University Press. 207–34.

Burgess J. & Rosen, G. 1997. *A Subject with No Object*. Oxford University Press.

Cameron, R. 2008. "There are no things that are musical works." *British Journal of Aesthetics* 48: 295–314.

Chambers, S. & Kopstein, J. 2001. "Bad civil society." *Political Theory* 29: 837–65.

Deng, N. 2019. "Religion for naturalists." *International Journal for the Philosophy of Religion* 78: 195–214.

---

[21] I thank participants of the Moral and Religious Fictionalism Workshop (2021) for their helpful comments and discussions.

Eshleman, A. 2005. "Can an atheist believe in God?" *Religious Studies* 41: 183–99.

Field, H. 1980. *Science without Numbers*. Princeton University Press.

Garner, R. 2007. "Abolishing morality." *Ethical Theory and Moral Practice* 10: 499–513.

Grzymala-Busse, A. 2012. "Why comparative politics should take religion (more) seriously." *The Annual Review of Political Science* 15: 421–42.

Jay, C. 2020. "A realist-friendly argument for moral fictionalism: Perhaps you'd better not believe it." In J. Falguera & C. Martínez-Vidal (eds.), *Abstract Objects*. Synthese Library 422: 339–56. Springer.

Joyce, R. 2001. *The Myth of Morality*. Cambridge University Press.

Joyce, R. 2017. "Fictionalism in metaethics." In T. McPherson & D. Plunkett (eds.), *The Routledge Handbook of Metaethics*. Routledge. 72–86.

Killin, A. 2018. "Fictionalism about musical works." *Canadian Journal of Philosophy* 48: 266–91.

Kim, S. 2014. "A defence of semantic pretence hermeneutic fictionalism against the autism objection." *Australasian Journal of Philosophy* 92: 321–33.

Le Poidevin, R. 1996. *Arguing for Atheism*. Routledge.

Lipton, P. 2007. "Science and religion: The immersion solution." In A. Moore & M. Scott (eds.), *Realism and Religion*. Ashgate. 31–46.

Nolan, D., Restall, G., & West, C. 2005. "Moral fictionalism versus the rest." *Australasian Journal of Philosophy* 83: 307–30.

Olson, J. 2014. *Moral Error Theory: History, Critique, Defence*. Oxford University Press.

Rosen, G. 1990. "Modal fictionalism." *Mind* 99: 327–54.

Rosen, G. 2005. "Problems in the history of fictionalism." In M. Kalderon (ed.), *Fictionalism in Metaphysics*. Clarendon Press. 14–64.

Saatsi, J. 2016. "On the 'indispensable explanatory role' of mathematics." *Mind* 125: 1045–70.

Sauchelli, A. 2018. "The will to make-believe: Religious fictionalism, religious beliefs, and the value of art." *Philosophy and Phenomenological Research* 96: 620–35.

Scott, M. & Malcolm, F. 2018. "Religious fictionalism." *Philosophy Compass* 13: 1–11.

Yablo, S. 2005. "The myth of the seven." In M. Kalderon (ed.), *Fictionalism in Metaphysics*. Clarendon Press. 88–115.

12
Revolutionary Moral Fictionalism and the Problem of Imaginative Failure

Stuart Brock

1. Introduction

This chapter is an exercise in connecting the dots. I want to draw attention to two debates in the philosophical literature that are importantly related; I hope to draw out the connection. Specifically, I wish to discuss the literature on revolutionary moral fictionalism, on the one hand, and the literature on the puzzle of imaginative failure (often deceptively referred to as "the puzzle of imaginative *resistance*"), on the other. By doing so, I hope to tease out a previously unnoticed problem for the revolutionary moral fictionalist.

The problem, very roughly, is this: revolutionary moral fictionalists seem to be committed to the claim that it is possible to imagine moral propositions being true when we know they are in fact false; however, the philosophical and empirical literature on the puzzle of imaginative failure seems to demonstrate that we cannot easily do that. The problem is not a decisive consideration against fictionalism, but it presents a challenge that the moral fictionalist must answer before we can properly evaluate the view.

In §2, I outline what I take to be the main tenets of moral fictionalism and the considerations in its favor. In §3, I explain the puzzle of imaginative failure. In §4–§6, I outline various positions one might take on the puzzle and explain why I believe none of them offer succor to the fictionalist. In the concluding section, §7, I consider various responses to the challenge that might be offered on behalf of the fictionalist and articulate what I take to be fruitful directions for future research.

2. Revolutionary Moral Fictionalism

Moral fictionalism can be characterized as the conjunction of the following four theses.

Anti-Realist Thesis. No basic moral statement is true. (Basic moral claims, and associated thoughts, ascribe moral properties to actions; such claims are atomic sentences of the form "φ-ing is M," where "φ-ing" denotes an action, and "M" expresses a moral property such as being good, bad, right, wrong, permissible, obligatory, etc.)

Truth-Aptness Thesis. Moral discourse aims at the truth in the sense that the statements we utter when engaging in moral discourse—normally, basic moral statements—are propositions, and so are truth-apt; that is, they are capable of having a truth value.

In opposition to the moral realist, then, the Anti-Realist Thesis tells us that basic moral claims are not true. Against the non-factualist, the Truth-Aptness Thesis tells us that moral claims have a truth value. On the plausible assumption that there are only two truth values—True and False—these two theses together entail that the basic moral claims we make when engaging in moral discourse are systematically false, perhaps necessarily so.

These two theses need to be supplemented in order to capture what's distinctive about the moral fictionalist's view.[1] Anti-Realism and the Truth-Aptness Thesis are accepted by the abolitionist (e.g., Garner 1994, 2007) and the revisionist (e.g., Husi 2014). Unlike the abolitionist and revisionist, however, the fictionalist denies that sincere moral utterances are assertions and denies that they express beliefs—instead moral utterances involve another kind of speech act to express what we are merely imagining to be the case. Consequently, the fictionalist maintains that we can coherently engage in moral discourse despite accepting the Anti-Realist and Truth-Aptness Theses; to do so does not require us to be insincere or mistaken in any way. We might articulate the remaining two related theses as follows:

Speech-Act Thesis. A fictionalist who utters a positive moral statement doesn't *assert* what she says. Instead, she uses moral statements to perform some other speech act: *nonassertoric affirmation*.

Nondoxasticism. A fictionalist who sincerely utters a positive moral statement doesn't *believe* what she says. Instead, she merely *make-believes* what she says.

These second two theses are importantly related. Just as assertions express the beliefs of the speaker, nonassertoric affirmations express the content of the

---

[1] What follows is just one way to capture the essence of moral fictionalism. Moral fictionalists will always accept the Anti-Realist and Truth-Aptness theses, but in contrast to the view articulated in this chapter, an alternative kind of moral fictionalist view maintains that what appear to be basic moral claims should not be taken at face value. Instead, such claims should be interpreted as containing a silent story prefix, such as "According to the moral realist's theory..." On this kind of view, apparently basic moral claims might be asserted and believed, but when they are, they are always about the content of a theory. This kind of prefix or story-operator fictionalism is not the target of this chapter (see Joyce 2005 for an illuminating contrast between these two views). Moreover, there are subtly different ways one might explicate Nondoxasticism and the Speech-Act Theses. (See the Introduction to this volume for an extended discussion of these alternatives.)

speaker's make-believe or act of imagining. Consequently, the fictionalist must distinguish clearly between the two kinds of attitude (to avoid the charge that she is making a distinction without a difference). For the fictionalist, the difference between the two attitudes is not one of degree; make-believing and believing are qualitatively distinct cognitive states. Make-believe is the kind of attitude we adopt when reading fiction or watching a play. It is an immersive attitude. It is also an imaginative act, and is something we are aware we are engaging in. Finally, make-believe is not truth-normed or constrained by the available evidence. Engaging in acts of make-believe does not presuppose that what we make-believe is true, even if we're fully rational. Beliefs, on the other hand, are dispositional states, and so we do not need to be conscious of them or imaginatively engage with them. Our beliefs, though, are constrained by the evidence, and as such we have no direct control over them.[2]

A distinction is often made in the literature between two kinds of fictionalism: *hermeneutic* fictionalism and *revolutionary* fictionalism.[3] In the moral domain, hermeneutic fictionalists think the four theses stated above accurately *describe* what many (if not all) of those engaged in moral discourse are doing. They argue that a close examination of the discourse and practices of some communities favors a fictionalist rather than a realist or alternative anti-realist interpretation of that discourse and practice (see, e.g., Kalderon 2005; see the Introduction to this volume). Hermeneutic moral fictionalism is justified by an inference to the best explanation. Moral fictionalism, it is alleged, best explains the phenomenological and linguistic data.

Revolutionary fictionalists, by contrast, claim that most of us are *not* currently moral fictionalists—we are instead misguided moral *realists*.[4] However, because the basic moral claims we tend to make turn out to be systematically false, we are in error and are guilty of making a mistake about the moral domain. Consequently, once we become aware of this error on our part, we face the following pressing question: *what should be done in light of this discovery*? We could, like the abolitionist, stop speaking and thinking the way that we do. Or we could, like the revisionist, engage in a project of conceptual re-engineering, by *repairing* our moral concepts (see Burgess, Cappelen, & Plunkett 2020 for an exploration of

---

[2] In saying this, I concede that the distinction requires further elaboration (cf. Isserow, Chapter 2 of this volume). I have not tried to make the distinctions precise here in part because different fictionalists say such different things about how to make out the distinction precisely. I also note that Richard Joyce, in a number of publications, explicitly claims that the nondoxastic attitude employed by the fictionalist is distinct from make-believe. The challenge for Joyce, then, is to explain the attitude in such a way to make it clear how this distinctive nondoxastic attitude is different not only from belief, but also from make-believe and supposition (see §7 for an elaboration of this challenge).

[3] The distinction was first made in Burgess 1983.

[4] Of course, revolutionary moral fictionalists aren't required to make this last claim—they just tend to. There is conceptual space available for the revolutionary moral fictionalist to claim, for example, that moral discourse is amenable to a constructivist (non-realist) interpretation, but is nevertheless systematically false.

this idea). Revolutionary moral fictionalists, however, advise us to do something very different: continue to talk as we have all along, but with a different force and a different attitude towards what we say—that is, we *should* become moral fictionalists, even if we are not already (see, for example, Joyce 2001).

Revolutionary fictionalists, then, face a challenge that hermeneutic fictionalists don't: they must explain why we *should* engage in this pretense. What could justify such a prescription? The answer must appeal to some kind of *non-moral* value associated with moral discourse in its current form, lost to those who abandon it. This idea will be captured in something like the following thesis:

> **Utility Thesis.** There is non-moral value associated with moral discourse and associated thought. Moreover, the comparative value of engaging in moral thought and talk is greater than the value of abandoning it.

Moral fictionalists, then, claim that there are benefits associated with the use of moral concepts and moral language. The relevant benefits may be personal benefits (e.g., facilitating self-control when we might otherwise succumb to temptation) or social benefits (e.g., facilitating the peaceful resolution of conflicts). Moreover, fictionalists also claim that these benefits are not available to those who abandon the discourse. Indeed, it is crucial for moral fictionalists that the cost–benefit analysis comparing abolitionism with fictionalism comes out in the fictionalist's favor.

Revolutionary moral fictionalism, as articulated, holds much promise. Before evaluating its prospects, though, let us consider a puzzle, introduced in a different context by David Hume over 250 years ago.

3. The Problem of Imaginative Failure

Towards the end of his essay "Of the standard of taste," David Hume makes the following insightful observation:

> Whatever speculative errors may be found in the polite writings of any age or country, they detract but little from the value of those compositions. There needs but a certain turn of thought or imagination to make us enter into all the opinions, which then prevailed, and relish the sentiments or conclusions derived from them. But a very violent effort is requisite to change our judgment of manners, and excite sentiments of approbation or blame, love or hatred, different from those to which the mind from long custom has been familiarized. And where a man is confident of the rectitude of that moral standard, by which he judges, he is justly jealous of it, and will not pervert the sentiments of his heart for a moment, in complaisance to any writer whatsoever. ([1757] 1987: 246–7)

The relevance of the passage to our current concerns should be obvious. Hume is considering what "turn of thought or *imagination*" is possible for us when considering the "errors [that] may be found in the polite writings of any age or country." Moreover, he is concerned explicitly with the *moral* errors made by others. He is struck by our failure to imagine, even for a moment, what it would be like for a different moral standard to apply when we are confident that those who apply the standard are mistaken. In this respect, our imaginative tendencies are very different to the non-moral case. When invited to imaginatively engage with the "speculative errors" of the past, we do so with relative ease.

Influenced by Kendall Walton's (1990) work on imagination and make-believe, philosophers have recently seen the relevance of Hume's observations to fiction. Extending Hume's point, Brian Weatherson asks us to entertain the following story:

> *Death on a Freeway.* Jack and Jill were arguing again. This was not in itself unusual, but this time they were standing in the fast lane of I-95 having their argument. This was causing traffic to bank up a bit. It wasn't significantly worse than normally happened around Providence, not that you could have told from the reactions of passing motorists. They were convinced that Jack and Jill, and not the volume of traffic, were the primary causes of the slowdown. They all forgot how bad traffic normally is along there. When Craig saw that the cause of the bankup had been Jack and Jill, he took his gun out of the glovebox and shot them. People then started driving over their bodies, and while the new speed hump caused some people to slow down a bit, mostly traffic returned to its normal speed. So Craig did the right thing, because Jack and Jill should have taken their argument somewhere else, where they wouldn't get in anyone's way. (Weatherson 2004: 1)

Walton, Weatherson, and others think that Hume's puzzle is even more striking than Hume himself realized. In cases like these, where readers are invited to imagine something without any implication that they should also believe it, something goes interestingly wrong. When the author's explicit moral evaluations within a fiction conflict with the evaluations we would naturally make in such cases, readers fall short of imagining what they're invited to imagine. For whatever reason, we just cannot bring ourselves to imagine that Craig did the right thing, even in this fictional context. Generalizing, then, the puzzle as Hume conceived it is to explain *why* we fail to imagine moral claims we believe to be false when confronted with them in a story, whether fictional or non-fictional.

Hence, Hume's puzzle of imaginative failure—sometimes misleadingly called "the puzzle of imaginative *resistance*"[5]—is the problem of accounting for the apparent asymmetry between the following two propositions:

---

[5] As many authors have noted, this name for the puzzle—coined in Gendler 2000—presupposes what I later call a "wontian solution" to the puzzle (see footnote 6). In order not to beg any questions about the solution to the puzzle, I prefer the label "the puzzle of imaginative *failure*" (cf. also Stock 2005: 608).

1. We easily comply with an invitation to imagine or make-believe that a *speculative* (i.e., descriptive) claim is true even if we know or believe the claim is actually false.
2. We do *not* easily comply with an invitation to imagine or make-believe that a *moral* claim is true if we know or believe the claim is actually false.

Philosophers who write in this area tend to take statements (1) and (2) as basic data that need to be explained. They find each thesis pretheoretically plausible and assume their truth, without citing any independent evidence in support of either of them. After making their intuitions explicit, they take their task to be one of explaining this apparent asymmetry in our imaginative tendencies.

Derek Matravers and Walton each make this point explicitly before addressing the puzzle:

> I shall not be providing arguments that this asymmetry exists. *There seems to be enough agreement that it does exist for it to be worth considering.*
> (Matravers 2003: 92, my emphasis)

> We easily accept that princes become frogs or that people travel in time, in the world of a story, even, sometimes that blatant contradictions are fictional. But we balk—*I do anyway, in some instances, and it is evident from the literature that I am not alone*—at... [any invitation to imagine] that female infanticide is right and proper. (Walton 2006: 140, my emphasis)

What is interesting is that there is close to a consensus in the philosophical community about the existence of the asymmetry, and the consensus has been stable for the last 250 years, since Hume first made these observations. This is somewhat surprising given that it is extremely difficult to find philosophical consensus on any matter in philosophy (see Chalmers 2015). No doubt, this is in part because the philosophical method requires us to challenge our pre-theoretic intuitions, to put pressure on them where we can (see Brock 2017). And so, if intuitions count as evidence in philosophy, and intuitions that the asymmetry exists are widely shared in the philosophical community, stable across time and place, then this is strong evidence that the asymmetry is genuine.

This is not to suggest that there has been widespread agreement about the scope and nature of the asymmetry. To be clear, there has not. Some philosophers think the puzzle is strictly limited to explaining a mysterious difference between how we treat deviant moral claims in fiction as opposed to other claims made in the work. Others think the puzzle arises in other contexts, and we can learn valuable lessons by drawing the boundaries in the right place. Moreover, there are disagreements about the nature of the puzzle. Walton (1994) noticed that Hume conflates at least three different puzzles—and Weatherson (2004) notes a fourth. Ever since, there has been a growing interest in disentangling the different asymmetries that Hume alludes to in this passage to determine how they are related to one another, which of them are genuine, and which of the asymmetries (if any) is fundamental. Some philosophers focus on an asymmetry in an author's control over the content of her story, some on an asymmetry in the phenomenology of our engagement with fiction, some on differences in the aesthetic value of works of literature that make such claims, and some focus primarily—as I do in this chapter—on an asymmetry in our imaginative tendencies.

Nor is this to say that there have been no philosophers who have challenged the claim that there is a genuine asymmetry crying out for an explanation. Michael Tanner (1994), Mary Mothersill (2003), and Cain Todd (2009) have all come close to doing just that. But in each of these cases, the authors in question have either focused on a puzzle other than the imaginative puzzle that we're interested in here or they have suggested that an explanation of the asymmetry is so obvious and easy to provide that there is no puzzle to be worked through. None of these philosophers, though, directly challenges the existence of the asymmetry in our imaginative tendencies identified above.

There have been a series of different and interesting empirical studies supporting the philosophical consensus. Barnes & Black (2016); Black & Barnes (2017); Barnes & Black (2020); Brock (2021); Campbell et al. (2021); Liao et al. (2014) all confirm, in different ways, that there is a genuine asymmetry here that cries out for explanation. Moreover, Hu et al. (2017) have shown that the basic effect for morality in the most famous of these studies—Liao et al. (2014)—could be replicated, further validating the findings.

Why, then, does this asymmetry in our imaginative tendencies give rise to a problem for the moral fictionalist? To understand the problem, we don't merely need to appreciate that we are comparatively less likely to take up invitations to imagine or make-believe *moral* (as opposed to descriptive or speculative) claims that we know or believe to be false; we need to get an appreciation of *why* this is the case. While there are many proposed explanations to be found in the literature, they tend to fall into one of three kinds: cantian solutions, wontian solutions, and hardian solutions.[6] I'll briefly explain each proposal in the following sections and explain either why I think the kind of explanation is fatally flawed (in the case of wontianism) or why I think the explanation presents a *prima facie* challenge for the moral fictionalist (in the case of cantianism and hardianism).[7]

---

[6] This terminology is coined by Tamar Gendler (2006: 157)—from the terms "can't," "won't," and "it's-hard." I owe a great debt to the insights presented in Gendler's paper—far more than may be conveyed in the main text of this chapter.

[7] The alert reader will recognize that there is a problem in the same vicinity for the hermeneutic moral fictionalist: The hermeneutic fictionalist interprets us as make-believing basic moral claims when we don't believe them to be true; but if, in fact, we cannot do this, then the hermeneutic fictionalist's interpretation cannot be accurate. However, because arguments in support of hermeneutic fictionalism tend to take the form of an argument to the best explanation, rather than appealing to pragmatic considerations or cost-benefit analyses of the alternatives, a hardian solution to the problem that I outline above is open to the hermeneutic fictionalist and is not touched by the critique in §6.

4. Cantian Solutions

According to the cantian, we fail to take up an author's invitation to imagine moral propositions that we know to be false because of an *inability* to do so. Our lack of imaginative engagement is due to the fact that we, the readers, are *unable* to imagine what we are invited to imagine. While we may well want to imagine what the author invites us to imagine, it is simply not possible for us to do so, perhaps because we simply do not understand or comprehend the content of the fiction, or perhaps because we face a psychological barrier of a different kind that prevents us from imagining what we're being invited to imagine.

Walton tentatively endorses a cantian solution of this kind. He suggests that perhaps we fail to take up an author's invitation in such contexts because we cannot comprehend what it would mean for morally deviant propositions to be true. He expresses the idea as follows:

> We still need an explanation of why we should resist allowing fictional worlds to differ from the real world with respect to the relevant kind of dependence relations. My best suspicion, at the moment, is that it has something to do with an...inability to understand fully what it would be like for them to be different.
> (Walton 1994: 45–6)

This, of course, is not an *explanation* of our comparative difficulty imagining deviant moral claims; at best it is an elaboration of the phenomenon. We still need an explanation as to *why* we can't—*why* we are unable to—imagine deviant moral statements when invited to do so. Cantians suggest that the underlying reason for our inability lies in the fact that we can't imagine impossible propositions of a certain kind. Just as I can't imagine something being visually appealing and also invisible because what I am invited to imagine is obviously impossible, likewise I can't imagine that killing people for arguing and holding up traffic is the morally right thing to do because what I am asked to imagine in such cases is also impossible. Both invitations require us to imagine something impossible—and the impossibility is salient enough for us to be at a loss to know what to imagine in such cases.

The challenge for the cantian lies in explaining what it is about the impossible content of deviant moral claims that prevents our imaginative engagement with them when we have no trouble imagining other impossibilities that are just as obvious and just as salient. We have no difficulty taking up invitations to imagine metaphysical impossibilities in which snowmen sing and playing cards talk; we enjoy make-believing time travel stories in which characters go back in time and successfully kill their parents before they have children; and if the author is clever enough, perhaps we can even imagine blatant contradictions being true (cf. Gendler 2000: §4). What (at least some of) these cases seem to show is that it is not the mere impossibility of the scenario described—even if the impossibility is striking—that prevents us from imagining it. The explanation therefore must be supplemented, perhaps by identifying a *special kind* of impossibility that is responsible for our failure to take up the author's invitation. Thus, Walton, for example, suggests the following in reply to this kind of challenge:

> I hold neither that conceptual impossibilities in general are unimaginable, nor that what is unimaginable cannot in general be fictional. What seems to me to be important is a very particular kind of imaginative inability, one that attaches to propositions expressing certain sorts of supervenience relations, which the imaginer rejects.
> (Walton 2006: 145–6; cf. also Weatherson 2004 and Yablo 2009)

Cantians tempted by this sort of response might elaborate further, suggesting that in such cases one won't be able, in one's imagination, to hold the naturalistic base facts fixed while also imagining that the moral properties that supervene on the naturalistic facts are different. This would be like trying to hold fixed in one's imagination that a shape is a square while also imagining that it has five sides. Imagining that agents can change the past or that animals can talk, on the other hand, is simply not an imaginative task of the same kind.

If we assume that something like this sort of answer to the challenge is correct, we can articulate the cantian objection to moral fictionalism as follows:

1. Cantian thesis: We *cannot* make-believe moral claims that we believe are false.
2. But if moral fictionalism (of either the hermeneutic or revolutionary variety) is true, we *can* (and should) make-believe basic moral claims are true when we believe that they are false.
3. Therefore, moral fictionalism is false.

5. Wontian Solutions

The moral fictionalist, therefore, will hope there is an alternative to the cantian resolution of the puzzle of imaginative failure—a solution that does not commit one to the cantian thesis. The most popular solution of this kind has fittingly been coined *wontianism*, and can be stated as follows:

> **Wontianism.** Readers fail to take up the author's invitation to imagine a deviant moral claim because of an *unwillingness* to do so.

According to wontians, imaginative failure occurs because we, the readers, *choose* not to imagine what the author asks us to imagine; our lack of imaginative engagement is the result of a *desire* not to imagine what we're invited to imagine. This kind of solution was first defended by Gendler (2000).

Of course, in order to get a full explanation of the asymmetry, we still need an explanation as to *why* we won't—*why* we choose not to—imagine alternative, merely fictional, moral claims when invited to do so. Imagining, after all, is not the same as believing. Gendler traces "the source of this unwillingness to a general desire not to be manipulated into taking on points of view that we would not reflectively endorse as authentically our own" (2000: 56). Later, she tells us "that cases that evoke genuine imaginative resistance will be cases where the reader feels that she is being asked to *export* a way of looking at the actual world which she does not wish to add to her conceptual repertoire" (2000: 77). This is not the only answer that a wontian might give to this question. To be sure, slightly different wontian answers to this question have been defended by Currie (2002), Gendler (2006), Stokes (2006), and Driver (2008).

It should be obvious why this alternative kind of explanation of Hume's asymmetry will appeal to the moral fictionalist. If the wontian is right, we do in fact have the ability to make-believe alternative moralities—we just choose not to. Moreover, the moral fictionalist will be able to supplement the wontian's explanation of why we resist an author's invitation to imagine moral claims we believe to be false. Gendler may be right to suggest that when authors issue such invitations, readers feel they are being asked to export a way of looking at the world. But readers don't resist simply because they don't wish to add to their "conceptual repertoire" in this way. The moral fictionalist will have something substantive to say about why *her* moral fiction is useful. This will be captured by her elaboration of the Utility Thesis, which enumerates the personal and social benefits of imagining her specific moral fiction. Consequently, we should want to make-believe that this fiction is true. But to take up an invitation to make-believe an alternative moral fiction would likely be to give up on these benefits. No wonder we resist!

Despite the initial plausibility of wontianism, the view is misguided—for two related reasons. First, the phenomenon of imaginative failure persists even for those who want to take up the author's invitation to imagine the morally deviant scenario. Perhaps many of us don't want to imagine that Craig did the right thing by shooting Jack and Jill because they were getting in the way of traffic. But the fictional nature of the scenario will be enough to encourage many of us to *try* to imagine it (without thinking that we need to export this way of thinking about the world). When we attempt to do this, we fall short—still failing to imagine what the author invites us to imagine.

Second, there are *speculative* (non-moral) propositions we are invited to imagine that we don't want to imagine. In such cases, the invitations to make-believe tend to be taken up *against our will*. It's not as though we read or hear the invitation, process it, and intentionally decide not to take it up. To the contrary, merely hearing or reading the invitation prompts our imagining, and sometimes triggers a negative response. To illustrate, consider the transgressive fiction of Chuck Palahniuk, certain passages of which many people find unbearably unpleasant and quickly stop reading. In contexts where it is not possible to stop reading or listening, though, we are unable to resist imagining what Palahniuk is inviting us to imagine. Consequently, public readings of Palahniuk's short story "Guts" (2005) would commonly cause audience members to faint (or so it is reputed). This phenomenon is familiar enough, explaining the widespread use of trigger/content warnings. Such warnings are essential when the content of what could be read or heard contains potentially distressing material.

The wontian observes correctly that many people who begin reading "Guts" fall short of imagining all of it. And the reason is, quite rightly, that they simply don't want to. But notice that our desire not to imagine what's described in such cases results in us ceasing to read further. Against the wontian, then, it seems that *had we continued reading*, we *couldn't help* but imagine what's described. We stop reading at the point we find it too offensive because we know that once we become aware of what's being described we will instinctively make-believe the scenario depicted (and that's something we don't want to do). The same is not true of morally deviant propositions. We read "Death on a Freeway" to the very end—perhaps multiple times—but we do not take up the invitation to imagine the final statement. Wontianism, then, does not provide us with the resources to explain our imaginative failure in such cases.

6. Hardian Solutions

An alternative and more plausible kind of resolution to the puzzle of imaginative failure, distinct from both wontianism and cantianism, has been suggested by Tyler Doggett and Andy Egan.[8] They call the resolution *hardianism*, and it might be articulated thus:

> **Hardianism.** Readers fail to take up the author's invitation to imagine a deviant moral claim because it is *difficult* to do so.

According to hardians, imaginative failure occurs because an imaginative barrier of some kind prevents the reader from imagining what the author invites them to imagine. But the imaginative barrier is not conative in nature; that is, the difficulty of the imaginative task is not merely the result of a lack of will power. Moreover, hardians leave room for the possibility that these barriers may be overcome by the reader. The imaginative task is a difficult one—it requires some effort to ensure

---

[8] The attribution to Doggett and Egan is given in the last footnote of Gendler (2000).

success—but it is not an impossible one. Were our desire strong enough, our mental capacities great enough, and the assistance from the author skillful enough, we would imagine the deviant moral claims made in fiction. For most of us, these antecedent conditions are missing and so we fall short of imagining such content, even when we desire to imagine it.

This kind of solution is supported by much of the empirical literature on the puzzle. Perhaps the most striking support can be found in Barnes and Black (2016). They presented 102 participants with scenarios that were categorized as either Morally Deviant, Factually Unlikely, or Conceptually Contradictory. Participants were presented with two scenarios in each category. The morally deviant scenarios were adapted from thought experiments in Walton (1994) and Weatherson (2004). The (so-called) conceptually contradictory scenarios were adapted from vignettes or mathematically impossible propositions in Gendler (2000) and Yablo (2009). After each scenario, participants were asked, *inter alia*, to rate how difficult it was for them to imagine a fictional world in which the scenario is true. Their findings confirmed the philosophical orthodoxy regarding the apparent asymmetry between invitations to imagine morally deviant as opposed to descriptively deviant propositions. Moreover, their findings support a hardian explanation of the asymmetry. Morally deviant worlds turn out to be significantly harder to imagine than worlds containing unlikely events (though interestingly a large number of participants found it fairly easy to imagine the stated scenarios). Most important in the present context, however, is the finding that comparatively few participants found it impossible to imagine the morally deviant scenarios presented. Participants represented the degree of imaginative difficulty associated with each scenario by pulling a bar from 0 ("I absolutely cannot imagine such a world") to 100 ("I can easily imagine such a world"). After calculating the mean imaginability across the two scenarios in each category, it was found that over 85% of participants self-reported that they *could* imagine the morally deviant scenarios even if it was difficult to do so—less than 15% claimed that they "absolutely could not" imagine these worlds. And even for those who did so, it is unclear whether this was because they thought the morally deviant scenarios were impossible to imagine, or merely because they failed to imagine the scenarios after trying hard to do so (in the same way it might be natural for me to claim that "I absolutely cannot understand quantum mechanics no matter how hard I have tried").[9]

It should be obvious why this third explanation of the asymmetry might seem attractive to the moral fictionalist. Recall the embarrassment for the revolutionary moral fictionalist. According to her, we *ought to* make-believe moral claims

---

[9] Further empirical research needs to be undertaken to confirm hardianism and eliminate alternative explanations of the asymmetry. And, even if confirmed, further research would be needed to understand the nature of the psychological barriers.

are true once we come to believe that they are false. And so plausibly, because ought implies can, she will be committed to the view that we *can* make-believe moral claims that we don't in fact believe. The view would be refuted if it could be demonstrated that we *cannot* make-believe moral claims that we believe are false. The hardian explanation of the asymmetry does no such thing. According to the hardian, we can all *make-believe* moral claims are true even when we believe that they are false, it's just that it can be comparatively difficult to do so. Hardianism, then, is entirely consistent with moral fictionalism.

If the fictionalist is tempted by this response, though, she needs to concede that there are psychological barriers that need to be overcome if we are to successfully make-believe an alternative set of moral facts holds true. Our choice under these circumstances is not a straightforward choice between make-believing and not make-believing a set of basic moral statements. Because the response presupposes some kind of psychological impediment to our imaginative abilities when it comes to our contemplation of moral propositions that we don't believe, our choice must instead be between *trying* to make-believe the relevant claims or not trying; there is no guarantee of success if we do try, though, due to the psychological barriers in place that will prevent us from imaginative engagement unless they are overcome.[10] Moreover, if Hume's postulated asymmetry is genuine, the probability of imaginative success must be significantly lower than it would be if we were instead trying to imagine a speculative or descriptive claim (even if the probability of that claim being true is very low indeed). Making this clear allows us to bring to the surface a problem for the view.

The case in favor of revolutionary moral fictionalism assumes falsely that the moral error theorist has only three options once she becomes aware of her error:

1. Continue to believe the moral claims that we now know are false
2. Make-believe moral claims that we now know are false
3. Abolish thought (and talk) about morality altogether

The first option is unavailable to her. If she is an epistemically rational agent, she will be unable to bring herself to believe what she knows is false. But she does have the choice to continue to make-believe what others believe, and perhaps what she herself once believed. Revolutionary moral fictionalists suggest that this choice is preferable to the third option of abolishing thought and talk about morality. Why is it preferable? Because engaging in moral make-believe has benefits that you forsake by giving up on moral thought altogether (cf. the Utility Thesis). What could such benefits be? It seems to me that a lot hangs on this

---

[10] Moreover, the degree of difficulty may be higher in some cases than in others. Barnes and Black (2016), for example, suggest that their results provide evidence that the degree of difficulty associated with imagining morally deviant worlds may be influenced by the magnitude of the moral violation.

answer. But few philosophers have attempted to answer it in any detail. There are, however, two notable exceptions.

Richard Joyce famously argues that, by comparison with the alternative of abolishing moral thought altogether, it would be more beneficial to make-believe (or, more precisely, to nondoxastically accept) morality without believing it. By doing so, we can fend off temptation and weakness of will, thus enabling us to promote our own long-term interests, in a way we could not do otherwise. Joyce puts the idea as follows: "the instrumental value of moral beliefs lies in their combatting of weakness of will, the blocking of temporarily revaluing of outcomes that is characteristic of short-sighted rationalizations, their silencing of certain kinds of calculation... these desiderata can be satisfied, to some extent, even if the moral claims are not believed" (Joyce 2001: 215; see also Joyce, Chapter 13 of this volume). Daniel Nolan, Greg Restall, and Caroline West argue that moral thought and talk has additional social benefits. They suggest, for example, that morality can help "coordinating attitudes and regulating interpersonal conflict in cases where people disagree about what they are to do, especially where collective action is needed or the proposed actions of different people interfere with each other" (Nolan, Restall, & West 2005: 312).

Philosophers have sometimes questioned whether moral fictionalists can attain these kinds of benefits, and likewise have sometimes challenged the assumption that abolitionists cannot. Let us, however, grant these assumptions for the sake of argument. It is still an open question as to whether these benefits can be attained in some other, more reliable way—a way that doesn't require us to engage in a kind of make-believe that is psychologically difficult and may lead only to frustration. This question isn't really considered in any detail by moral fictionalists, but interestingly the suggestion is hinted at by Hume, in a less well-cited passage immediately following his short discussion of the puzzle of imaginative failure. He says:

> Of all speculative errors, those, which regard religion, are the most excusable in compositions of genius; nor is it ever permitted to judge of the civility or wisdom of any people, or even of single persons, by the grossness or refinement of their theological principles. The same good sense, that directs men in the ordinary occurrences of life, is not harkened to in religious matters, which are supposed to be placed altogether above the cognizance of human reason. On this account, all the absurdities of the pagan system of theology must be overlooked by every critic, who would pretend to form a just notion of ancient poetry; and our postcrity, in their turn, must have the same indulgence to their forefathers. No religious principles can ever be imputed as a fault to any poet, while they remain merely principles, and take not such strong possession of his heart, as to lay him under the imputation of bigotry or superstition. Where that happens, they confound the sentiments of morality, and alter the natural boundaries of vice and virtue.   (Hume [1757] 1987: 247)

Here Hume is drawing attention to the fact that religion often plays a similar role to morality in guiding human action, but religious claims *should be* viewed as purely speculative or descriptive in nature. Hume concedes that the poet often can't help conflating religion and morality, when religion takes "strong possession of his heart." But so long as we retain our "good sense" we will not "confound the sentiments of morality" when reading of "all the absurdities of the pagan system of theology"—or any other religion, for that matter. Religious claims, therefore, do not (and should not) present an imaginative challenge for rational agents; it will be comparatively easy to imaginatively engage with a theology that we reject, no matter how preposterous we may find it.

But now here's the rub. The supposed benefits of imaginative engagement with morality include that it helps us "to combat weakness of will" (a personal benefit) and helps us "regulate conflict" (a social benefit). On the basis of a cost-benefit analysis comparing just abolitionism with fictionalism, it might seem that fictionalism is the preferable option, but this is only on the assumption that we don't put something else in its place. The suggestion I am recommending here is something rather different. Specifically, the suggestion is to abolish thought and talk about morality *and adopt a form of religious fictionalism instead*. Imagining that there is a god who will punish defectors with an eternity in hell and reward cooperators with an eternity in heaven seems, on its face, a much better motivator than merely imagining that by cooperating I am doing the morally right thing, and that by defecting I am doing the morally wrong thing.[11] But more importantly, our attempt to engage in this imaginative activity is much more likely to be successful. If the hardian is right, moral pretense is hard, but religious pretense is comparatively easy. So religious fictionalism is preferable to moral fictionalism in at least two ways.

7. The Prospects for Moral Fictionalism

This seems to exhaust the possible space for solutions to Hume's puzzle of imaginative failure. Cantianism, wontianism, and hardianism all present *prima facie* problems for the revolutionary moral fictionalist that seem difficult to overcome. That's not to say that there are no prospects for a solution open to the fictionalist. I can see at least five:

---

[11] Joyce does consider something like this alternative to moral fictionalism. He says, "akrasia may be fended off to some degree by the tempted subject picturing as vividly as she can herself punished and vilified. But the chastisement may also lead her to reflect more carefully on the possibilities of evading it. She does better if such images are supplemented by the thought that the action in question is just wrong" (Joyce 2001: 217). The suggestion here is that the imaginative activity is one in which the agent make-believes that she can't evade punishment—god, it is supposed, is omnipotent, omniscient, and shows no mercy.

believed. If I can remember what it was like to believe a certain way, I may well be able to make-believe myself into that frame of mind.

If this is right, then revolutionary moral fictionalists may have an easier time with their recommendations. Insofar as a revolutionary fictionalist advises the error theorist to make-believe the basic moral claims that *they formerly believed to be true*, she is asking us to make-believe something that is not at all alien to us. Such claims should be much easier to imagine being true than claims to the effect that one is morally obliged to kill innocent babies for fun, for example, or any of the other strange and shocking examples people cite in the literature to illustrate the imaginative barriers that give rise to the puzzle of imaginative failure.

Let me conclude by considering a rather different line of response open to the fictionalist. I have argued that when a moral error theorist contemplates whether to embrace abolitionism or fictionalism about morality, she should consider not merely the costs and benefits of each option, but also the *probability* of achieving one's aims. If we aspire to retain as many of the benefits associated with moral belief as possible, fictionalism looks like the preferred option—it's hard to see how we could attain many of those benefits if we give up thought and talk about morality entirely, replacing it with nothing else; the moral fictionalist, though, can potentially attain some benefits of this kind (e.g., an antidote to problematic cases of akrasia) that remain out of reach for the literally-minded abolitionist, who intends all of her claims to be taken at face value. The point I stressed in the previous section was that this is a false dichotomy: the error theorist is not forced to choose between moral fictionalism on the one hand and literally-minded abolitionism on the other. Taking my cue from Hume, I suggested that the option of a moral abolitionism combined with a form of religious fictionalism looks like a strikingly attractive option for those who are skeptics about both domains— much more attractive than the option of moral fictionalism and theological abolitionism. The reason is two-fold: first, the prospect of an omnipotent and omniscient God who is likely to punish me severely for my transgressions seems to be a better motivator than imagining that my transgressions have attached to them some esoteric and metaphysically weird property of "being-morally-wrong." As such, I am more likely to achieve the individual and social benefits I aspire to if I am a religious fictionalist rather than a moral fictionalist. Second, and more importantly, while I might try to become a moral fictionalist, there are (supposedly) psychological barriers that need to be overcome before I can do that. But no such psychological barriers stand in the way of my becoming a religious fictionalist: I can do that at will—or so it seems.

Religious fictionalists must specify which religion we are to engage with in imagination. A *religion*, let us suppose, is constituted at least in part by a set of statements about a supernatural or sacred realm. Moreover, a religion, as understood in this context, postulates a god or gods that interact with the natural world by controlling it in certain ways. There are many actual and possible religions that fit this description. While the fictionalist is free to choose from amongst them, she will favor religions that posit a god most likely to detect and punish/reward behavior that is in our best interest. (An omnipotent, omniscient, and jealous god, perhaps?) Claims about such a god would appear to be entirely speculative in nature and will not (or at least need not) imply anything at all about morality; as such, they present no obstacle to our imaginative engagement with them.

The moral fictionalist might put pressure on this line of thought by pointing out that the Abrahamic religions (Judaism, Christianity, and Islam) make important moral claims that seem to be essential components of the religion—including claims about our obligations and duties to God, as well as claims about God's goodness and moral nature. So, a fictionalist about the Abrahamic religions who is also a moral skeptic seems forced to embrace a kind of moral fictionalism alongside her religious fictionalism. This might, of course, require her religious fiction to be tweaked a little to make it coherent (cf. the final section of Le Poidevin, Chapter 10 of this volume, for some suggestions about how this might be done). But, if this line of thought is correct, rather than presenting an *alternative* to moral fictionalism, a religious fictionalism of this kind seems to *require* it. Consequently, any imaginative impediment associated with our moral fiction will be inherited with equal measure by our religious fiction.

Of course, we can generalize still further. To the extent that the criticism of moral fictionalism outlined in this chapter is sound, it will spell trouble for *any* religious fictionalism where morality is subsumed by the religion. Religious fictionalism will be a viable alternative to moral fictionalism only if it is entirely divorced from morality. Is this possible? Hume certainly thought it was. With such considerations in mind he directed us to consider not the Abrahamic religions, but the more ancient Roman and Greek religions. He says explicitly that "the absurdities of the pagan system of theology [can and] must be overlooked by every critic," but whatever absurdities we associate with these religions, their concomitant morality is not among them—moral principles are simply not an essential part of them. Pagan religions postulate amoral but powerful and jealous gods with the capability of detecting and punishing transgressions as required. Engaging with this sort of religion is more likely to deliver the social and personal benefits we aspire to than engaging with either the Abrahamic religions or any kind of moral fiction.

So, for religious fictionalism to be a genuine competitor to moral fictionalism, a constraint must be placed on the kind of religion appealed to by the religious fictionalist. It cannot be an essential part of the religion that God is the source of moral values, or that it is part of God's nature to be morally good, or that we have a moral duty, or that we are morally obliged, to do as God commands. It should be obvious that there are actual and possible religions that could fit the bill. What is less clear, though, is that we can imaginatively engage with these alien religions *in the right way*. My culture, education, and upbringing have ensured that I can imagine vividly what it is like for the Abrahamic God to exist, and it still brings "the fear of God" in me when I do so, despite being an atheist. But even if I can imagine in some detail what it would be like for Zeus, Poseidon, Hera, Demeter, Aphrodite, Athena, Artemis, Apollo, Ares, Hephaestus, Hermes, Hestia, and Dionysus to exist, this imaginative engagement doesn't tap into my emotions in the same way, and perhaps not sufficiently to ensure that I don't succumb to temptation, for example, or to stop potential social conflicts.

The religious fictionalist, then, will advise us to imaginatively engage with one of the myriad religions we might choose from. If the religion is one we are familiar with, it will include substantial moral components that are essential to it, and so, for the error theorist, embracing religious fictionalism will also require her to embrace a kind of moral fictionalism. If, on the other hand, the religion does not presuppose anything at all about morality, the religion will likely be unfamiliar to us, in which case it is unclear that we can imaginatively engage with it appropriately. Either way, religious fictionalism cannot be touted as a superior alternative to moral fictionalism.

Like many others, I believe there are few knockdown arguments in philosophy. The argument presented in this chapter is no exception. The main claim of this chapter is that the puzzle of imaginative failure presents a *prima facie* challenge that the revolutionary moral fictionalist must answer. I have closed by sketching a number of fruitful defensive maneuvers on the moral fictionalist's behalf. The next step will be to test each defense empirically. Once done, we will be in a much better position to evaluate the view.[13]

References

Barnes, J. & Black, J. 2016. "Impossible or improbable: The difficulty of imagining morally deviant worlds." *Imagination, Cognition and Personality: Consciousness in Theory, Research and Clinical Practice* 36: 27–40.

Barnes, J. & Black, J. 2020. "Morality and the imagination: Real-world moral beliefs interfere with imagining fictional content." *Philosophical Psychology* 33: 1018–44.

Black, J. & Barnes, J. 2017. "Measuring the unimaginable: Imaginative resistance to fiction and related constructs." *Personality and Individual Differences* 111: 71–9.

Brock, S. 2012. "The puzzle of imaginative failure." *Philosophical Quarterly* 62: 443–63.

---

[13] I am grateful for helpful discussions and comments on earlier iterations of this chapter from audiences at Waikato University and the Australian Catholic University. I am especially thankful to Richard Joyce and Daniel Nolan for detailed comments and helpful suggestions on the final draft of the chapter.

Brock, S. 2017. "Is philosophy progressing fast enough?" In D. Broderick & R. Blackford (eds.), *Philosophy's Future: The Problem of Philosophical Progress*. Wiley Blackwell. 119–31.

Brock, S. 2021. "The puzzle of fictional morality." In S. Sedivy (ed.), *Art, Representation and Make-Believe: Essays on the Philosophy of Kendall L. Walton*. Routledge. 127–44.

Burgess, A., Cappelen, H., & Plunkett, D. 2020. *Conceptual Engineering and Conceptual Ethics*. Oxford University Press.

Burgess, J. 1983. "Why I am not a nominalist." *Notre Dame Journal of Formal Logic* 24: 93–105.

Campbell, D., Kidder, W., D'Cruz, J., & Gaesser, B. 2021. "Emotion in imaginative resistance." *Philosophical Psychology* 34: 895–937.

Chalmers, D. 2015. "Why isn't there more progress in philosophy?" *Philosophy* 90: 3–31.

Currie, G. 2002. "Desire in imagination." In T. Gendler & J. Hawthorne (eds.), *Conceivability and Possibility*. Oxford University Press. 201–21.

Driver, J. 2008. "Imaginative resistance and psychological necessity." *Social Philosophy and Policy* 25: 301–13.

Garner, R. 1994. *Beyond Morality*. Temple University Press.

Garner, R. 2007. "Abolishing morality." *Ethical Theory and Moral Practice* 10: 499–513.

Gendler, T. 2000. "The puzzle of imaginative resistance." *Journal of Philosophy* 97: 55–81.

Gendler, T. 2006. "Imaginative resistance revisited." In S. Nichols (ed.), *The Architecture of Imagination: New Essays on Pretence, Possibility, and Fiction*. Oxford University Press. 149–73.

Hu, W., Rambharose, N., & Phelan, M. 2017. "XPhi replicability project: Replication of Liao, Strohminger and Sripada 2014." *Open Science Framework*. <https://osf.io/7e8hz/>.

Hume, D. [1757] 1987. "On the standard of taste." In E. Miller (ed.), *Essays: Moral, Political and Legal*. Liberty Fund. 226–49.

Husi, S. 2014. "Against moral fictionalism." *Journal of Moral Philosophy* 11: 80–96.

Joyce, R. 2001. *The Myth of Morality*. Cambridge University Press.

Joyce, R. 2005. "Moral fictionalism." In M. Kalderon (ed.), *Fictionalism in Metaphysics*. Oxford University Press. 287–313.

Kalderon, M. 2005. *Moral Fictionalism*. Clarendon Press.

Liao, S., Strohminger, N., & Sripada, C. 2014. "Empirically investigating imaginative resistance." *British Journal of Aesthetics* 54: 339–55.

Matravers, D. 2003. "Fictional assent and the (so-called) 'puzzle of imaginative resistance.'" In M. Kieran & D. Lopes (eds.), *Imagination, Philosophy, and the Arts*. Routledge. 91–106.

Mothersill, M. 2003. "Make-believe morality and fictional worlds." In J. Bermudez & S. Gardener (eds.), *Art and Morality*. Routledge. 74–94.

Nolan, D., Restall, G., & West, C. 2005. "Moral fictionalism versus the rest." *Australasian Journal of Philosophy* 83: 307–30.

Palahniuk, C. 2005. "Guts." In his *Haunted*. Anchor Press.

Stock, K. 2005. "Resisting imaginative resistance." *Philosophical Quarterly* 55: 607–24.

Stokes, D. 2006. "The evaluative character of imaginative resistance." *British Journal of Aesthetics* 46: 387–405.

Tanner, M. 1994. "Morals in fiction and fictional morality II." *Proceedings of the Aristotelian Society* supp. vol. 68: 51–66.

Todd, C. 2009. "Imaginability, morality, and fictional truth: Dissolving the puzzle of 'imaginative resistance.'" *Philosophical Studies* 143: 187–211.

Walton, K. 1990. *Mimesis as Make Believe*. Harvard University Press.

Walton, K. 1994. "Morals in fiction and fictional morality I." *Proceedings of the Aristotelian Society* supp. vol. 68: 27–50.

Walton, K. 2006. "On the (so-called) puzzle of imaginative resistance." In S. Nichols (ed.), *The Architecture of Imagination: New Essays on Pretence, Possibility, and Fiction*. Oxford University Press. 137–48.

Weatherson, B. 2004. "Morality, fiction, and possibility." *Philosopher's Imprint* 4: 1–27.

Yablo, S. 2009. "Coulda, woulda, shoulda." In his *Thoughts: Papers on Mind, Meaning, and Modality*. Oxford University Press. 103–150.

13
Yes to Moral Fictionalism; No to Religious Fictionalism

Richard Joyce

1. Introduction

Atheism and moral error theory are types of skepticism. The former is familiar and reasonably popular (in certain demographics, at least); the latter is less well known outside academic circles and, even within those circles, not a terribly widespread view. The atheist denies the existence of such things as gods, cosmic karma, the afterlife, prophesy, etc., and thus holds that many central claims of religious discourse are simply false. The moral error theorist denies the existence of such properties as moral wrongness, praiseworthiness, moral permissibility, evil, moral rights, etc., and thus holds that many central claims of moral discourse are simply false.

It seems fair to say that many people who embrace religious skepticism remain *appalled* at the prospect of moral skepticism. This strikes me as somewhat surprising, given the plausibility of the claim that most moral concepts were born in a theistic framework, outside of which it's far from clear that they can sensibly survive. An action's being *morally forbidden*, say, might make sense when there is a divine being doing the forbidding, but once that forbidder is removed from the ontological scene, it's not obvious that a secularized notion of *being morally forbidden* remains there for the taking—any more than a secularized notion of *an eternal soul* remains.[1] The last few centuries of moral philosophy can be read largely as an attempt to tether these originally-non-naturalistic moral concepts to the natural world, but the success of this project has been, to put it charitably, disputable. The moral error theorist is in all likelihood an ontological naturalist, generally speaking, but one who thinks that moral normativity has features that render it unsuitable for accommodation within the naturalistic worldview— features like a special kind of *practical authority*, a kind of *autonomy*, and/or a kind of *agency*. "So much the worse for the naturalistic worldview," say some philosophers—but then they face a nagging worry that this relaxation of

---

[1] See Anscombe 1958; MacIntyre 1984: 2.

Richard Joyce, *Yes to Moral Fictionalism; No to Religious Fictionalism* In: *Moral Fictionalism and Religious Fictionalism*. Edited by: Richard Joyce and Stuart Brock, Oxford University Press. © Richard Joyce 2023.
DOI: 10.1093/oso/9780198881865.003.0014

naturalistic scruples might sit uncomfortably with their grounds for confidently rejecting religious ontology. "So much the worse for moral concepts," say moral error theorists.

Both the atheist and the moral error theorist face what might be called the *"what next?" question*: given that a widespread way of talking and thinking has turned out to be erroneous, what should we do with it? The most obvious answer, in both cases, is the abolitionist's response: we should just do away with the subject, much as we previously did away with talk of mermaids, phlogiston, and bodily humors. Of course, not even the abolitionist claims that we must never *utter* such non-denoting words. Even the religious abolitionist, for example, thinks it's fine to tell a joke about Satan, or assert something like "In the past, people believed in gods." But the religious abolitionist thinks that religious discourse should be relegated to a small and harmless corner of language—it should not play the central role that it currently occupies in a great many people's lives. The religious fictionalist disagrees and offers a less obvious answer. The religious fictionalist notes that engaging with religious language and thought has been quite useful in various ways—for all its error—and proposes that we could retain some of this usefulness by preserving religious language and thought in our lives. The fictionalist remains opposed to *believing* falsehoods, and so recommends the adoption of a kind of positive attitude toward religion that is not belief: let's call it "nondoxastic acceptance." Regarding religious language, the fictionalist is typically opposed to *asserting* falsehoods, and so recommends the adoption of a kind of positive speech act that is not assertion: let's call it "nonassertoric affirmation."

The moral fictionalist makes the analogous claim about morality. Even though a proposition like "Stealing is morally wrong" is, strictly speaking, false—since there's no such property as moral wrongness—it is a useful kind of falsehood, and thus we should (pragmatically speaking) carry on endorsing it but without believing or asserting it.[2]

An ambitious fictionalist will claim that the benefits of nondoxastic acceptance and nonassertoric affirmation will come close to matching the benefits of sincere belief. A less ambitious fictionalist accepts that the benefits might fall well short of those of sincere belief and assertion, but thinks that the former at least offers *some* benefit—enough to make it a preferable option to abolitionism.

My goal in this chapter is to sketch out a plausible version of ambitious moral fictionalism, but then argue that this sketch does not transfer over to lend plausibility to ambitious religious fictionalism. In other words, someone who is both an atheist and a moral error theorist might have good reason to retain *morality* as a

---

[2] I have in mind only revolutionary fictionalism. Hermeneutic forms of fictionalism—whether moral or religious—are not under consideration in this chapter. See the Introduction to this volume for this distinction explained.

kind of useful fiction, but should be an abolitionist about *religion*. Yes to moral fictionalism; no to religious fictionalism.[3]

2. The "What Next?" Question

There is not really a single "what next?" question; there is an open-ended plurality. Consider the atheist's version of the question as it pertains to religion. For a start, we must decide whether we're asking what should be done with religious *language* or done with religious *thought*. Then we must decide who it is that we imagine asking the question. Are we picturing the question asked by an individual atheist—and, if so, are we imagining them surrounded by theists—and, if so, are these theists inclined to burn non-believers at the stake? A sequence of "yes" answers should make it clear that it would be a good idea, practically speaking, for this individual to maintain a pretense of religion—and not just sporadically, but 24/7. Alternatively, perhaps we're picturing the question being posed by a *group* of atheists. But, if so, then what kind of practical question is the group asking when it inquires what it "should" do? What it should do to maximize preference satisfaction among its members? Or to maximize overall pleasure? Or to ensure that the worst off member couldn't be better off? Or what? There is not a single correct understanding here; rather, there are different reasonable ways of taking the question, and the person asking it needs to specify. (This is not to say, though, that the decision is an inherently moral one.)[4]

This indeterminacy isn't a problem for the skeptic per se; it permeates the way we talk about practical recommendations in general. If I steal your wallet, then presumably I harm your interests—but in what sense? By frustrating your preferences? By making you unhappy? By detracting from a list of your objective goods? Or what? It would be unreasonable to maintain that all advice-giving must be held in abeyance until we settle these thorny questions. Presumably, my stealing your wallet harms you on any reasonable account. But other cases may be less clear cut: an action may harm you in one legitimate sense of "harm" and not harm you in another legitimate sense of "harm," and that's all there is to it. Someone who wonders whether such an action harms you has to specify which sense they mean.

If we are talking about an individual atheist surrounded by non-atheists, then it isn't hard to imagine circumstances in which this person should definitely "play along." These circumstances needn't be so dramatic as involving stakes and burning; they may simply involve social distrust and being labeled an oddball. Let's imagine an atheist in such a situation; we'll call him *Brad*. Brad "plays along"

---

[3] Large portions of the first half of this chapter are a condensed version of some chapters of my book *Morality: From Error to Fiction* (forthcoming, Oxford University Press).

[4] *Pace* Lenman, Chapter 1 of this volume.

with religion at the level of language and social practices, and we'll assume that he has good pragmatic reasons for doing so—he stands to gain the benefits of participation—or, at least, avoid the harms of non-participation. We'll assume, though, that Brad's "playing along" does not extend to his own mental life: he doesn't engage in anything deserving the name "nondoxastic acceptance"; rather, his mental attitude toward religious claims is fairly straightforward disbelief. It's reasonable to suppose, though, that Brad's securing of participatory benefits might depend on his staying quiet about his disbelief, so although he doesn't believe in God, he allows everyone else to believe that he *does* believe in God. Thus when Brad makes religious utterances he does not do so with a nudge or a wink, nor with any accompanying explanation, and therefore his audience will, naturally, take him to be making assertions. It is important to note that a speaker cannot determine unilaterally which speech acts they perform: from the fact that Brad doesn't believe that p it doesn't follow that, when he says "p," he is merely "quasi-asserting" or "pretending to assert"—this depends in part on how his audience takes his speech. Thus if all of Brad's audience take him to be asserting religious claims, then he *is* asserting them (whether he intends to or not)—his utterances are in no sense a form of nonassertoric affirmation—in which case Brad's *language* (in contrast to his mental states) remains ontologically committed to gods, etc. It is clear, then, that Brad's "playing along" with religion for pragmatic purposes is a long way from being an exemplar of what the fictionalist has in mind. The problem is not that the deception of Brad's interactions is distasteful or dishonest; it is, rather, that he practices neither nondoxastic acceptance nor nonassertoric affirmation, and, moreover, his language remains ontologically committed to the existence of problematic entities.

Ideally, the fictionalist recommendation would cover both language and thought, recommending for each a kind of assent *sans* ontological commitment. We have already seen, however, that the former is problematic if fictionalism is advice directed at an individual, since which type of speech act is performed is not up to the speaker alone—it depends in part on how the audience takes the speech. If, however, the religious fictionalist recommendation is aimed at a *group* of atheists, rather than an individual, then the suggestion can be that the group should develop conventions such that, when the topic of religion is entered into, everyone knows that assertoric force, and thus ontological commitment, is lifted. (Compare, say, our conventions surrounding sarcasm—another commitment-nullifying linguistic device.)

In this chapter I will focus on the fictionalist recommendation more as it pertains to thought than language; I am, in other words, more interested here in nondoxastic acceptance than nonassertoric affirmation. Accepting something *in one's mind* suggests that the benefits of acceptance must come from within (so to speak), not just from the reactions of others—and this, I think, is the more challenging kind of case to attempt to establish. The crucial questions are, first, what kind of benefits might these be, and, second, can these benefits be gained from "mere acceptance" rather than belief? In what follows I shall offer answers to these questions for the case of *moral* fictionalism; we will return to religious fictionalism later.

3. The Usefulness of Moral Beliefs

The dispute between the moral fictionalist and the abolitionist concerns whether morality is, on balance, useful. The fictionalist says yes; the abolitionist says no. But the question of the usefulness of morality is not confined to a squabble among the error theorists. We could also ask a moral *realist* whether morality is useful. Most will probably say yes, but we can certainly imagine a moral realist claiming that the practice of constantly referring to moral facts in our deliberations is, on balance, harmful and that it would be better if we stopped. So *abolitionist moral realism* is a possible (albeit sparsely populated) category (see Ingram 2015). In any case, anyone who thinks that the question "Is morality useful?" is *coherent*—even if they complain that the question requires some disambiguation before it can be addressed—is allowing two kinds of normativity into the picture: the normativity of morality and the normativity of usefulness.[5]

The error theorist thinks that the former kind of normativity is bankrupt—there's no such thing. John Mackie (1977) famously argues that moral normativity requires a kind of *objectivity*, whereas the only kinds of normativity that actually exist are "subjective." According to Mackie, we "objectify" our preferences and values: we see our moral assessments as responding to (or, at least, as attempting to respond to) moral demands that are already there, in the nature of things, whereas in fact there are no demands that are "there" independently of our valuing activity. We think that there are things that we must do, or must not do, regardless of our desires, and that these rules of conduct are not simply made up by humans. According to Mackie, then, a view that might be called "Kantian realism" captures the *content* of our moral claims. But this view does not capture the *reality* of what's really going on when we make moral judgments. Hence the error at the heart of morality.

There is no obvious reason, however, for the error theorist to think that the second kind of normativity—that which pertains to *usefulness*—is also bankrupt. What makes something useful is *us*: something is useful, one might claim, if it satisfies our desires or preferences. And we know this; there is no tendency to

---

[5] This isn't strictly true. One could have some kind of *moral* understanding of "usefulness," in which case the question would concern whether morality is self-validating (which, I guess, it is). I suggest, however, that most parties who find the question "Is morality useful?" coherent (even if indeterminate) do not have in mind the question of self-validation.

objectify the values of usefulness, or to endorse a Kantian realist interpretation of the content of utility judgments. Rather, a view that might be called "Humean subjectivism" captures both the content of our utility judgments and the reality of what is going on when we make these judgments. Hence there is no error at the heart of what makes things useful—including the matter of what makes morality useful.

(A few quick qualifications. First, I am using the terms "Kantian" and "Humean" more as gestures of convenience than as scholarly claims about what these historical philosophers really argued for. Second, Mackie's is just one way of arguing for moral error theory; the truth of error theory does not live or die with the soundness of his argument—any more than the plausibility of atheism depends on, say, the success of the argument from evil. Third, I have no space on this occasion to attempt to support the premises of this view. It is outlined and assumed in order to devote energies to other discussions.)

What has been the practical benefit of having such a system of Kantian realist norms? Why do we have this tendency to objectify certain preferences and values?

Daniel Dennett (1995) argues that one benefit of having moral considerations in our conceptual repertoire is that they can serve as *conversation-stoppers*: their value is to bring deliberations to a close. We are rational creatures, always able to ask for justification, and in many contexts this is a trait that has served us well. The problem is that upon receiving a perfectly good answer we can always sensibly respond, "Okay, but what justifies *that*?"—and we can potentially do so ad infinitum, never coming to a decision, forever hesitant and doubting, undone by our own rational prowess. This is potentially as much a problem for our own private deliberations as for our public interpersonal ones. Dennett suggests that it is useful to have "consideration-generator-squelchers" (1995: 506): items that, once introduced, stop any further deliberation in its tracks. "That would be morally wrong!" would appear to work in this manner. Once this claim is accepted then there is no need or room for further consideration: the action mustn't be done, even if it is tempting, and that's all there is to it.

In saying this I am, of necessity, considering matters at a highly general level. The claim certainly isn't that using a moral judgment as a conversation-stopper is always going to be useful. If the content of the judgment were that it is morally obligatory for me to eat broken glass (regardless of whether I want to)—and if this functioned as an emphatic end-point to my deliberations, blocking me from even raising the natural objection "But why would I want to do that?"—then we could safely file this under the heading of "when good conversation-stoppers go bad."

It is worth noting that if Dennett is correct then the benefits of moral judgment need not be seen in terms of its contribution to cooperation or to social cohesion or to the solution of coordination problems—all of which are commonly assumed to be the basic "point" of human morality. Even Robinson Crusoe, alone on his island, might conceivably benefit from internal conversation-stoppers—if he is prone to over-thinking and second-guessing his daily plans, for example. That said, it is clear that conversation-stoppers are also terribly useful in public interpersonal relations. Debates and discussions about social policy and the justification of interpersonal interactions are just as likely to spiral endlessly unless we have a shared bedrock of unquestioned values: "We won't do that because *it's morally wrong*" has a finality to it. By contrast, "We won't do that because *we don't want to*" remains open to negotiation: desires can be interrogated; they can be bargained with; they can be altered. For this reason, values with a Kantian flavor stop conversations more effectively than those with a Humean flavor. Values that are treated as objective can stop conversations more effectively than those that are taken to depend on some agent's or agents' attitudes. The latter are likely simply to throw up further calls for justification ("But why should we care about that agent's attitudes?"), while the former enjoy the realist's table-thumping conclusiveness: "That's just the way the world is!"

Conversation-stoppers that gain general currency within a group can be predicted to serve the group's collective ends. Sometimes values might do this *directly*. It should be no surprise, for instance, to find moral values requiring individuals to restrain the unbridled pursuit of their own personal gratification. But sometimes values might accomplish this *indirectly*. The value in question may, on the face of it, have little to do with cooperative projects (it might concern, e.g., dietary prohibitions), but nevertheless the fact that members of the group all share and commit to this value can contribute to social cohesion. Having a range of values that are imbued with this kind of no-questions-asked finality allows one to signal to others where one draws the line between, on the one hand, those practical matters that might be up for negotiation and for which diversity will be tolerated, and, on the other hand, those matters for which any concession or softening is emphatically off the table. The willingness of an individual to draw this line in the same place as their fellows can be a powerful indicator of group solidarity.

In many contexts it will remain in an individual's interests to cultivate a no-questions-asked approach to these prosocial values and rules. If I am constantly publicly questioning why I should follow the rules, what justifies the rules, whether I can get away with breaking the rules, etc., then this will likely go against my own practical purposes by creating mistrust and the possibility of ostracization. If various important goods are available to me only if I wholeheartedly embrace a range of prosocial values, then it will be in my interests to loudly advertise that I have those values—and, indeed, simply to *have* those values. As before, taking a Kantian and realist attitude toward those values is likely to serve me better than taking a Humean and non-realist one. If my fellows are seeking a companion who doesn't break promises (say), and they are faced with a choice between someone who values promise-keeping *come what may*, and someone who values promise-keeping because she believes that keeping promises contributes to the satisfaction of her desires, then the former looks by far the better bet. My fellows want a companion who will, upon realizing that a prospective course of action requires the breaking of a promise, immediately reject that action with no further queries about justification and no weighing of the strengths of competing desires. Richard Whately hit this nail on its head when he declared: "Honesty is the best policy; but he who acts on that principle is not an honest man" (1856: 106).

A background assumption of the hypothesis outlined in this section has been the idea that, in order to furnish such benefits, moral judgments must be *beliefs*. If one is to stop a conversation or a deliberative process with the thought "No, that would be morally wrong!", the natural assumption is that in order to play this role effectively the thought must be a *belief*. However, in order for us to accept this hypothesis about the kinds of benefits that moral judgments bring, there's no need for us to assume that the beliefs are *true*. The hypothesis just outlined is one that the moral error theorist should have no problem endorsing.

The next question to ask is whether these practical benefits could still be secured if the attitude were not a belief but rather an act of nondoxastic acceptance. I will come at this question obliquely, which (as we shall see) is often the best route.

4. The Suspension of Disbelief

Samuel Taylor Coleridge introduced the phrase "the suspension of disbelief" (1817: 2) to describe how the enjoyment of a romantic or Gothic work will require the reader to suppress the urge to respond skeptically to the supernatural elements of the narrative. One will not enjoy *The Rime of the Ancient Mariner* if constantly thinking "Well, *that* couldn't happen!" Just as the appreciation of the work might require one to silence one's *dis*belief, so too it requires the stifling of one's beliefs. One will not enjoy any movie at the cinema if constantly thinking "I am surrounded by strangers in a large, dark room." Crucially for our purposes, the "*suspension*" of belief/disbelief must not be confused with the *cessation* of belief/disbelief. One never ceases to believe that one is in a cinema, but one ceases to think about this fact; the belief goes on the back burner once the movie starts.

The suspension of belief that characterizes a person's reading a poem or watching a movie is short-lived. Can there be a more "all-encompassing" suspension of belief that someone might implement in many or most everyday situations? We don't need to search anywhere terribly unfamiliar in order to locate such a case. Consider what J. S. Mill said (in his autobiography) about the pursuit of happiness:

> Those only are happy (I thought) who have their minds fixed on some object other than their own happiness; on the happiness of others, on the improvement of mankind, even on some art or pursuit, followed not as a means, but as itself

an ideal end. Aiming thus at something else, they find happiness by the way. The enjoyments of life (such was now my theory) are sufficient to make it a pleasant thing, when they are taken *en passant*, without being made a principal object.... The only chance is to treat, not happiness, but some end external to it, as the purpose of life. Let your self-consciousness, your scrutiny, your self-interrogation, exhaust themselves on that; and if otherwise fortunately circumstanced you will inhale happiness with the air you breathe, without dwelling on it or thinking about it, without either forestalling it in imagination, or putting it to flight by fatal questioning. ([1873] 1924: 100)

Henry Sidgwick later called this a "paradox"—though it's really more an ironic twist of human psychology than it is a paradox. According to Sidgwick, certain pleasures are such that "in order to get them, one must forget them" (1907: 51). And this seems a fairly widespread phenomenon: we often achieve things best by aiming at them not directly, but obliquely. Someone who asks how to get the most out of a personal relationship, for example, might receive the excellent advice "Don't constantly calculate how much you are getting from the relationship." Someone who asks how to come across to others as "cool" might receive the excellent advice "Don't try so hard to be cool." Later we will discuss the version of this called "the paradox of self-interest" (also not really a paradox), but for now let's stick with the happiness version.[6]

Suppose that Janet strives for happiness but finds it elusive. If she seeks advice from Mill, then the recommendation will be that she should forget about the fact that happiness is her ultimate goal—even though it *is* her ultimate goal—and instead she should focus her attention on achieving other ends: loving relationships, publishing scholarly articles, stamp-collecting, whatever. All along, Janet's ultimate goal remains her own happiness, and at no point does she cease to believe this. But she puts this belief on the back burner most of the time, since experience has taught her that if it is in the forefront of her mind then it simply gets in the way of her achieving happiness. When absorbed in her favorite hobby of stamp-collecting, for example, Janet thinks of the activity as valuable for its own sake; she does not constantly contemplate or calculate the contribution that her hobby makes to her happiness. Doing so takes all the fun out of the activity, and (ironically) makes her less happy.

This is not to say, though, that Janet cannot be brought to admit explicitly that happiness is her ultimate goal and that the only kind of value that stamp-collecting has is instrumental. When in a reflective mood—when thinking overtly about

---

[6] Under some understandings of what *happiness* is, the paradox of happiness and the paradox of self-interest might turn out to be the same thing. For a useful catalog of many different "paradoxes of happiness" that are often lumped together under that single heading, see Martin (2008). Ethical theories that have this quality (and many of them, arguably, do) are usually referred to as "self-effacing."

the paradox of happiness and the advice that Mill offers her—Janet frankly acknowledges exactly what's going on: namely, that in order for her to achieve her ultimate goal, most of her everyday life is an exercise in distracting her mind from what that goal really is. Indeed, it is the fact that she is prepared to admit this when she sits down in a cool hour that indicates that she believes it all along and has simply "suspended" that belief rather than ceased to believe it. All along, she *has* the disposition to acknowledge the facts, but most of the time she is unaware that she has this disposition, and even actively encourages this lack of awareness in herself in everyday situations. She may well even be reluctant to enter into this "critical mode" too frequently, since doing so dampens the effectiveness of the distraction, thus interfering with her pursuit of happiness. Still, it's not as if once she learns of the paradox of happiness then all hope of her attaining happiness is lost. Mill did not tell us about the paradox of happiness with the cruel expectation that doing so would crush our capacity to achieve happiness!

Moreover, it's not as if in moments of transparency Janet will lose all motivation to continue stamp-collecting. Even when she becomes aware that stamp-collecting lacks the inherent value with which she usually imbues it, she can still acknowledge its instrumental value for her; it's just that things go better for her (and she knows it) if she's not constantly in this state of transparency. Janet can, effectively, get the cat back into the bag by focusing her attention in the right way. Doing so might not even take much effort on her part—it may be habituated and natural, requiring nothing more complicated than perusing through her stamp albums. (Hume mentions playing backgammon as a means of driving away skeptical ruminations.)

Is Janet engaged in *make-believe*? Possibly, but describing her attitude in this manner might be misleading. If asked independently to think of episodes of make-believe, one's mind is likely to alight on paradigms where a person can easily and voluntarily slip in and out of the pretense, and is perfectly aware the whole time that they are engaged in make-believe. But these are not necessarily features of Janet's attitude toward the value of stamp-collecting, so I prefer to stick with the label "nondoxastic acceptance."

Is Janet *self-deceived*? She is not self-deceived in the manner of someone who sticks with a falsehood come what may—who is unable to give it up. Such a person would *not* have the disposition to admit the truth if asked in all seriousness, which indicates that this person would *believe* the falsehood. If Janet's attitude does count as a form of "self-deception," then (if Mill is to be believed) it's a kind that we should all strive to cultivate—something on which nothing less than human happiness depends. I suggest that it is more fruitful to think of Mill (and Coleridge) as counseling "self-distraction" than self-deception.

This notion of "self-distraction" lies at the heart of the kind of moral fictionalism that I find plausible. According to this view, Humean values exist and Kantian values do not, and a smart person knows this. But a smart person also realizes that something similar in its irony to the paradox of happiness is in play: that the practice of deliberating explicitly in terms of Humean values tends to be self-defeating, whereas deliberating in terms of realist Kantian values can further important personal and social goals (goals, that is, which are understood in Humean terms). The moral fictionalist, thus, prescribes a course of self-distraction and suspension of disbelief: in your day-to-day activities, forget about the Humean truth; let your thoughts, speech, and actions be guided by Kantian normativity. In other words, when it comes to Humean values, "in order to get them, one must forget them."

This is not to say that in moments of transparency you would lose all motivation to act in accordance with your moral fiction. Even when you enter "critical mode" and realize that, say, breaking promises is not really morally wrong, you are still in a position to acknowledge that promise-breaking will likely frustrate your Humean values. (After all, if this weren't true—if your moral fiction were urging you to do something that goes against your Humean values—then clearly that is not a useful moral system: you have embraced the wrong moral fiction.) It's just that things go better for you, and you should know it, if you're not constantly in this state of transparency.

So long as you retain the disposition to sincerely deny the Kantian foundations if asked about them in all seriousness, then you do not really believe in them, and we can classify your attitude toward morality as one of "nondoxastic acceptance." If you follow this advice studiously, then in your day-to-day life you won't even be particularly aware that your attitude toward morality is not one of sincere belief—indeed, you won't be conscious that you are "following advice studiously" at all. In everyday contexts, your attitude toward morality will have the phenomenology of belief—all the emotional, motivational, and practical advantages of moral belief—without being moral belief.

5. A Fictionalized Morality Is *Better* than a Believed Morality

Ambitious moral fictionalism attempts to show that the practical benefits of taking a nondoxastic attitude toward morality are not much different from those of having sincere moral beliefs. An even more ambitious project is to attempt to show that the benefits of the former are *greater* than those of the latter. In order to see that the latter is plausible, let's return to Janet and the paradox of happiness.

Janet seeks happiness and has taken on board Mill's advice that the best way (perhaps the only way) to achieve it is obliquely, by seeking something else. For Janet I've imagined that this activity is stamp-collecting. Janet does not really *believe* that stamp-collecting is a worthwhile activity in itself, but she thinks and acts and talks as if it is—she nondoxastically accepts that stamp-collecting has a kind of value that it does not have (and that she knows it does not have). Suppose, though, that over time the pleasures of stamp-collecting begin to fade for Janet. She is able to step back and acknowledge that stamp-collecting is not inherently valuable, that it never really was (even though it was useful for her to think that it was), and that the only kind of value that stamp-collecting ever had was as an instrument to her happiness. Nondoxastic acceptance, unlike belief, does not have to wait upon evidence in order for rejection to be rational. When, therefore, Janet realizes that her hobby no longer makes her happy, there is nothing to stand in the way of her simply stopping this activity; she can instead throw herself into a new hobby that brings her renewed happiness. If, by contrast, Janet had sincerely *believed* stamp-collecting to be inherently valuable, then she might have felt the need to persist with the activity, albeit stoically and unhappily.

The moral fictionalist is in a comparable position. It may well be useful to have moral values as conversation-stoppers—both personally and publicly—but we don't want to be so committed to moral values that we refuse to recognize any context wherein they can be critically examined. Our situation may change over time: what was once a useful conversation-stopper might become a destructive conversation-stopper. The individual or group who can periodically reflect on how well their conversation-stoppers are serving their ends will (*ceteris paribus*) do better than an individual or group who cannot. If one of the benefits of moral judgment is that it allows an individual to signal their normative commitments to others in the community as a way of marking group solidarity, then if the community's values shift (for whatever reason), then the individual's commitments had better shift with them if they are going to continue to play this role. That's not to say that the individual was never really *committed* in the first place. There is a great deal of space between not being committed in the slightest to something and being willing to die for it.

The benefits of morality may require a kind of steadfast and inflexible commitment, but a moral system that is *utterly* steadfast and inflexible—that will crash and burn rather than adapt—is very probably less beneficial overall than a moral system that is able, *in extremis*, to adjust and evolve. This holds whether considering matters at the level of the group or the individual. It is here, then, that an attitude of nondoxastic acceptance toward morality may serve us better than sincere moral belief.

6. Kant's Moral Hazard Argument

It is time to return our attention to religious fictionalism. Might it also be that an attitude of nondoxastic acceptance of religion is better than belief? My point of departure will be Kant's argument for a positive answer to this question (with my views on this matter being heavily influenced by Christopher Jay's 2014 article).

Kant certainly seems to be a religious fictionalist. In the *Critique of Pure Reason*, he argues that we have good reason for postulating God and an immortal soul—but these reasons are practical rather than epistemic. It is reasonable (Kant thinks) for us to hope that our actions will be appropriately rewarded or punished, and in order for this hope to be rational we must allow the possibility of its being satisfied. Kant rejects the proposal that there is an analytic connection between being moral and the attainment of happiness (a view he associates with Stoicism and Epicureanism), and so concludes that this connection could only be synthetic.[7] But since we pretty clearly cannot rely on the natural world to satisfy the expectation that acting morally will be rewarded with happiness, we must postulate an eternal afterlife and a "wise Author" who can act as guarantor of the connection. "Such a Ruler, together with life in such a world [i.e., an afterlife], which we must regard as a future world, reason finds itself constrained to assume; otherwise it would have to regard the moral laws as empty figments of the brain."[8]

Kant's "moral hazard argument" is that taking an attitude of (what Jay calls) "nondoxastic acceptance" toward the existence of God is actually *better* than belief, since belief would encourage the wrong kind of motivation for our actions. If we really believed that virtue will be rewarded in heaven, then this would risk becoming our motivation for acting, in which case we'd become like Kant's shopkeeper who's honest with customers only because it's profitable to be so: acting in accordance with duty but not acting *from* duty. In other words, though it's fine and necessary to expect that good actions will be rewarded, in order for those actions to *be* good (i.e., morally praiseworthy) they'd better not be performed for the sake of that reward. According to Jay's interpretation of Kant, this risk is absent (or at least reduced) if one's attitude is one of nondoxastic acceptance rather than belief.

I don't propose to go any further into the intricacies of Kant's views than this, and it is certainly not an argument I intend to advocate. I want to point out one plausible thing about the argument—which will be the basis of further discussion—and one implausible thing which, I think, sinks the moral hazard argument.

The component of the argument that has an intuitive ring is Kant's concern about the tension between the undesirability of selfish motivations and the belief in postmortem rewards. If we consider someone deeply religious and also morally admired—someone like Mother Teresa, perhaps—although we presume both (1) that she believes that she is acting in a morally right way, and (2) that she believes that acting in a morally right way will receive some kind of divine reward, we would surely be troubled to also discover (3) that she is *motivated by the anticipation* of that reward. We would think less of her, morally, if we knew that

---

[7] This rejection is found in the *Critique of Practical Reason* (5.111 ff.).

[8] *Critique of Pure Reason* A811 (trans. Kemp Smith). A moral error theorist, reading this passage, is likely to be reminded of the adage that one person's *ponens* is another's *tollens*.

she was always dreaming of her own future eternal bliss as she ministered to the needs of the poor.

This is reminiscent of the paradox of happiness. A religious person might much prefer the prospect of receiving posthumous rewards over posthumous punishments, but in order to secure those rewards they must take an oblique approach: they must cultivate concerns for, and interests in, other things (e.g., genuine sympathy for others' suffering). What is surprising, however, is that this intuitively acceptable component of Kant's argument speaks in favor of a kind of fictionalism that is directly opposed to that which he actually supports. Simplifying things dramatically: the Kantian religious fictionalist (persuaded by the moral hazard argument) might recommend "Nondoxastically accept that the afterlife exists, but do not really believe it"; but the viewpoint we have just been discussing—the advice for Mother Teresa et al.—is "Believe that the afterlife exists, but distract yourself from that belief in everyday contexts—that is, nondoxastically accept that the afterlife does *not* exist." (More on this in a moment.)

The less intuitively acceptable component of Kant's argument is the assumption that taking a nondoxastic attitude toward God and an afterlife will make one immune to the corrupting effect upon motivation that sincere belief in God and the afterlife would (allegedly) have. This is an instance of a generic challenge for fictionalism—whether moral or religious. The fictionalist might hope to recoup the *benefits* of belief by recommending a nondoxastic attitude that "feels" a lot like belief, but this attitude is likely also to bring the *costs* of belief. Finding an attitude that allows one to cherry-pick the benefits while avoiding the costs is tricky. And so it is with Kant's moral hazard argument. If *believing* in the promise of posthumous rewards risks corrupting one's motivation by fostering selfishness, then *nondoxastically accepting* the promise of posthumous rewards is likely to have exactly the same corrupting influence—that is, so long as this attitude of acceptance has enough of an impact on one's other psychological states to supply the touted practical benefits. There are, then, serious doubts to be raised about the capacity of the Kantian "moral hazard argument" to show that an attitude of nondoxastic acceptance of the existence of God and an afterlife is better than one of sincere belief.[9]

7. Postmortem Rewards and the Paradox of Self-Interest

The discussion of Kant has succeeded in bringing into the light a general complication for religious belief systems, centered on the issue of selfish versus altruistic motivation. Most major religions endorse values or requirements that are opposed

---

[9] See also Leng, Chapter 7 of this volume.

to flat-out selfishness. All the major religions, for example, prize love, kindness, and generosity—and not just in the realm of *action*, but motivation. (The first hadith of Islam, for instance, could hardly be more explicit on this last point: "Actions are judged according to intentions.") But, at the same time, all major moralizing religions include an elaborate ontology of postmortem rewards and punishments.[10] So before the possibility of atheism even raises its skeptical head, there is already something psychologically complicated going on with most religious belief systems. "If you're good you'll get into paradise, but if your motivation is to get into paradise then you're not good!" There is a straightforward solution to this complication, but, I will argue, it is not a solution for the religious fictionalist.

The challenge here is an instance of the paradox of self-interest—a close cousin to the paradox of happiness. Robert Frank presents the former as "a simple paradox, namely, that in many situations the conscious pursuit of self-interest is incompatible with its attainment" (1988: ix). The key word here is "conscious." How do you advance your long-term best interests? Answer: By not constantly deliberating about those interests as you act; by not always taking those ends as your motivating reasons. Similarly: How can you get into heaven? Answer: By not thinking about heavenly rewards as you minister to the needs of the poor; by being genuinely loving, kind, and generous. There is no incoherence to any of this, just sensible advice for complicated creatures. One can see such advice to practice "self-distraction" as a kind of fictionalist recommendation; ultimately what you are being counseled to do is imbue things with a kind of value that they do not have, and that you know they do not have. (Think back to Janet and her stamp-collecting.) The possibility of following such advice is what allows one to navigate the obvious tension inherent in those religions that promise glorious rewards (or threaten terrible punishments) while also decrying ubiquitous selfishness.

It's important to note here that the undesirability of egoism need not come from values of the religion itself. Even if the religion is silent on what our motivations should be, one might independently deem it morally undesirable to be always motivated by thoughts of self-gain. Indeed, the undesirability of egoism need not be prompted by *moral* considerations at all. Even a moral error theorist, if asked a straightforward practical question about, say, what will generally best advance a person's interests, will likely give an answer that encourages one to cultivate genuine friendships, to sympathize with others, to fall in love, to be generous with no thought of compensation, and so on. Basically, if someone is wondering how to advance their own interests, then even the moral error theorist should recognize that any response that includes "always keep your own interests in the forefront of your mind" is almost certainly *terrible* advice; it amounts

---

[10] See Johnson & Krüger 2004; Bernstein & Katz 2010; Baumard & Boyer 2013.

to counseling the cultivation of sociopathy, which is not a good recipe for happy humans.

Once we distinguish between what ends a person is pursuing, on the one hand, and what ends the person is *thinking about* while engaged in the pursuit, on the other, then the solutions to a lot of these seemingly-tense situations fall into place. We should seek happiness, sure, but we should not *think about* the pursuit of happiness while acting—doing so actually makes us less happy. We should seek our Humean ends, sure, but we should not *think about* those ends while acting—doing so actually prevents our attaining those ends. We should seek heavenly rewards, sure, but we should not *think about* those rewards while acting—doing so makes us unworthy to receive those rewards.

The point to which I'm keen to draw attention is that the last solution, pertaining to the attitude one might take toward a religion's promise of postmortem reward, is a solution for those who *believe* in those rewards; it's sensible advice for a theist. If, however, we picture a religious *fictionalist* trying to follow this advice, then things get weird.

Consider an atheist, Brad, who resolves to embrace a certain religion with a kind of nondoxastic acceptance: he's going to accept that God exists, that God created all life, that the virtuous are rewarded in the afterlife, etc.—all the while believing none of these things. Remember that we're assuming that Brad's "acceptance" is not just a matter of his playing along with religious language and practices (attending church, etc.); we're assuming that he benefits from adopting a positive psychological attitude toward religion even in private. We might describe this as Brad's cultivating a habit of holding religious thoughts in his mind, of being guided by them, of allowing them a role in his deliberations—all the while remaining disposed to deny these religious propositions if probed in a sufficiently critical manner.

Now let's introduce into the picture another piece of advice for Brad: that it goes against his interests to be *motivated* by thoughts of self-gain in many interpersonal contexts. This is not to deny that self-gain should be Brad's ultimate end; it's a claim about what kind of thoughts and concerns he should have in mind when deliberating and acting, if he is to pursue that end successfully.

Brad, then, appears to be subject to competing pieces of advice about which thoughts he should attend to and which he should suspend when acting in everyday contexts: that he should hold religious thoughts in mind—including, presumably, thoughts of the postmortem rewards—and that he should at the same time endeavor to banish thoughts of postmortem rewards from his mind. Combining these pieces of advice, we seem to have the recommendation that Brad should keep in his thoughts some thoughts that he should keep out of his thoughts. This does not sound like a coherent recommendation.

One might respond that this is simply a case of a fiction within a fiction, and there's nothing incoherent about *that*. The play *Hamlet*, for example, contains the play *The Murder of Gonzago*. But upon consideration the comparison is not an apt one.

Let's consider a contemporary actor whose part, in a performance of *Hamlet*, is to be one of the players whose part (in *The Murder of Gonzago*) is to be the King. The actor pretends to be someone who is pretending to be someone. More specifically, the actor pretends to be not a contemporary actor but rather a Medieval player; and the player (the character in *Hamlet*) pretends to be not a player but rather a King (and the King doesn't pretend to be anyone; he just dies). At first glance, one might think that the actor is expected to both pretend to be a player and pretend not to be a player. But if we keep our eye on the ball then we can see that this is mistaken. There *are* two acts of pretense here—one nested in the other—but only one of them is real. The actor pretends to be someone who is pretending something, but the second pretense is no more a real act of pretense for the actor, psychologically speaking, than the pretended death is a real death.

An actor can certainly pretend to be someone who believes in postmortem rewards and who is distracting themselves from their belief. But the actor would not thereby be *actually* distracting themselves from thoughts of postmortem rewards, only pretending to. However, the practical advice that one should not be always motivated by thoughts of self-gain is that one should *really* not be always motivated by thoughts of self-gain, not that one should pretend to not be always motivated by thoughts of self-gain. We would be no less disappointed in our discovery that Mother Teresa was always gleefully anticipating heavenly rewards if we learned that she was convincingly pretending otherwise.

8. Religious Fictionalism versus Moral Fictionalism

I have raised an awkward problem for religious fictionalism. Moral fictionalism does not face this problem.

The obvious escape route for the religious fictionalist is to protest that I have focused far too much on postmortem rewards and punishments—a focus that, it might be complained, reflects an old-fashioned view of religion. The contemporary religious fictionalist might prefer to recommend the nondoxastic acceptance of a much more contemporary vision of religion—one that's indiscriminately loving and forgiving, for example, and where nobody's soul is treated differently on the basis of their worldly behavior. After all, if (1) nondoxastic acceptance of religion is recommended on pragmatic grounds, and (2) the religion that one has embraced involves postmortem rewards and punishments, and (3) reflecting on these rewards and punishments encourages selfishness in one's attitudes, but (4) selfish attitudes are ultimately a poor strategy, pragmatically speaking—then the religious fictionalist can simply retort that this shows that one has chosen the wrong religion. If you'd be better off nondoxastically accepting a religion that does not include postmortem rewards and punishments, then that's the religion for you!

While I would not argue that having a system of postmortem rewards and punishments is a necessary feature of religion, I'm doubtful that it's a feature that is as easily separated from religion as one might think. A system of rewards and punishments that involves beatific angels among the clouds and gruesome Boschian hellscapes is one that, I'm sure, many modern theists will dismiss as florid excess; but, nevertheless, the general idea that there is a divine being who *cares* about how we act, and that this will somehow be differentially reflected in one's ultimate fate, may be, though vaguer and less tangible, a fairly important component of many theists' worldview. This is an empirical claim upon which I won't speculate further.

Even if one countenances embracing a religion that lacks any system of postmortem rewards and punishments, it seems safe to assume is that this religion will still involve a fairly elaborate ontology. The ontological commitments of morality, by contrast, are less extravagant. Indeed, the ontological commitments of morality are so modest that the error theorist is sometimes criticized for thinking that there are any at all (see Lenman, Chapter 1 of this volume). As a moral error theorist sympathetic to Mackie-style arguments (of the kind touched on earlier), I think that this criticism is mistaken—but, still, if a sensible philosopher can reasonably suspect that a discourse carries no ontological burden, then the ontological burden that it does in fact carry must be fairly unassuming.

When I talk here about ontological commitments being "extravagant" or "unassuming," I am not talking so much about the modality of the ontology as about the difficulty of the psychological task of entertaining the thought. For example, pretending that my dog understands most of what I say to her (when in fact I know that she understands very little) is an easy act of pretense: it comes naturally and I'm not constantly encountering counter-evidence. (When she fails to respond to my reasonable requests, I just roll my eyes and interpret her as willful.) By contrast, pretending that I have a leopard for a pet would require a constant cognitive effort on my part. Nevertheless, the possible world at which the former is true is a lot further from actuality than that at which the latter is true—and so in that sense the former involves "more ontology" than the latter.

The moral fictionalist recommendation outlined earlier sees our actual Humean reasons and values painted with a Kantian veneer. The Kantian overlay renders the reasons and values *false*, but also makes them more attainable. Some critics of moral fictionalism argue that it would require a strenuous level of self-surveillance to maintain this kind of fiction.[11] If this were true, then one should accept it as a mark against moral fictionalism. After all, if the fictionalist stance is recommended on

---

[11] See Cuneo & Christy 2011; Eriksson & Olson 2019.

pragmatic grounds, then, when we perform the cost-benefit analysis of comparing it with other options, one of the things that must be taken into account is whether the adoption of the type of psychological attitude has generic running costs. If nondoxastic acceptance required cognitive effort that is exhausting and distracts from other mental activities, then this would need to be taken into consideration.

However, I find the claim that the nondoxastic acceptance of morality would have heavy "upkeep costs" quite unconvincing. Such critics, I suspect, simply have the wrong paradigm of nondoxastic acceptance in mind: they're thinking of an act of make-believe that takes effort to maintain and of which one is constantly transparently aware. I have endeavored in this chapter to focus on a different kind of paradigm. With this correction made, we should see that adding the Kantian veneer to one's practical deliberations is, far from requiring strenuous effort, a very natural and easy act of self-distraction to undertake; there is very little to it. Instead of thinking "Promise-keeping will serve my long-term preferences" (say), one thinks, "I must keep promises regardless of my preferences." This is no more taxing than Janet's thinking of stamp-collecting as being a worthwhile goal in its own right rather than as something she pursues only because it is an instrument to her happiness. Despite neither example's requiring any great feat of psychological maneuvering, in both cases the shift from deliberating in terms of true beliefs to nondoxastically accepting something false may be of the utmost practical significance. One's happiness may depend on it.

Here, I think, is another place where religious fictionalism suffers in comparison to moral fictionalism. The ontology of a religion is invariably a more elaborate affair than the ontology of morality. First of all, the former typically has a much broader range: covering all that morality covers, but in addition purporting to explain what happens when we die, where humans came from, the origin of the universe, etc. Second, the ontology of religion is more "substantial" than that of morality alone. Morality involves positing properties and relations (e.g., values and reasons), while religion tends, in addition, to be centrally oriented toward objects (e.g., gods), places (e.g., paradise), and events (e.g., the Last Judgment). Morality still *has* ontological commitments, but they seem nebulous in comparison with the ontology that religion wears boldly on its sleeve.

For this reason, the falsity of religion is going to intrude more frequently on the fictionalist's experience. (See Scott, Chapter 8 of this volume.) Imagine, for example, a religious fictionalist attempting to nondoxastically accept a religious account of the origin of life. The fictionalist doesn't *believe* the account—they know very well that life evolved through Darwinian selection—but they attempt to distract themselves from their scientific beliefs by encouraging in themselves thoughts of life being produced in a single act of divine creation. The problem is that this project of self-distraction looks vulnerable. Every time this would-be fictionalist reads an article on biology, every time they watch a David Attenborough nature documentary, every time they encounter a fossil in the museum, the falsity of their religious fiction is going to slap them in the face. It will not be viable to maintain a fictionalist attitude if the fact that one has the disposition to deny the content of the fiction is something of which one is made constantly aware. It's like trying to enjoy a movie but the phone keeps ringing, jolting one from the fictional world and back to reality. For the *moral* fictionalist, by contrast, the phone rarely rings.

9. Conclusion

I have outlined the case for an ambitious yet plausible kind of moral fictionalism, modeled roughly on a solution to the paradox of happiness that is focused on our capacity to distract ourselves from what we really believe, without ceasing to believe it. I have argued, however, that this model is unlikely to provide any matching plausibility for religious fictionalism.

This is not to deny that an alternative kind of religious fictionalism might be reasonable—one that understands "nondoxastic acceptance" in a different fashion, or one that focuses on the benefits of "playing along" with religion in a manner that doesn't require any substantial acceptance at the psychological level. I have also aimed to establish an ambitious form of fictionalism for which the net benefits of acceptance aspire to rival, or even surpass, those of sincere belief. A less ambitious form would require the net benefits of acceptance to outstrip only those offered by abolitionism (and perhaps only marginally so), while allowing that they may fall well short of the net benefits secured by sincere belief.

The proposal that it might be a good idea, pragmatically speaking, for an atheist to "play along" with religion at the level of language and social practices is something I am willing to label a minimal form of "fictionalism"; and I think that it is so easily established as a sensible recommendation for some people in certain circumstances that it probably doesn't warrant a great deal of discussion. But this just shows, in my opinion, that there are easy wins available for the religious fictionalist (and, indeed, the moral fictionalist) when ambitions are kept modest. As for more interesting and ambitious forms of religious fictionalism, however— especially when the focus is on the cultivation of a kind of psychological nondoxastic acceptance—I have argued that it's a very different story.

References

Anscombe, G. E. M. 1958. "Modern moral philosophy." *Philosophy* 33: 1–19.

Baumard, N. & Boyer, P. 2013. "Explaining moral religions." *Trends in Cognitive Sciences* 17: 272–80.

Bernstein, A. & Katz, P. 2010. "The rise of postmortem retribution in China and the West." *Medieval History Journal* 13: 199–215.

Coleridge, S. T. 1817. *Biographia Literaria*, Vol. 2. R. Fenner.

Cuneo, T. & Christy, S. 2011. "The myth of moral fictionalism." In M. Brady (ed.), *New Waves in Metaethics*. Palgrave Macmillan. 85–102.

Dennett, D. 1995. *Darwin's Dangerous Idea*. Penguin.

Eriksson, B. & Olson, J. 2019. "Moral practice after error theory: Negotiationism." In R. Garner & R. Joyce (eds.), *The End of Morality: Taking Moral Abolitionism Seriously*. Routledge. 113–30.

Frank, R. 1988. *Passions within Reason: The Strategic Role of the Emotions*. W.W. Norton & Company.

Ingram, S. 2015. "After moral error theory, after moral realism." *Southern Journal of Philosophy* 53: 227–48.

Jay, C. 2014. "The Kantian Moral Hazard Argument for religious fictionalism." *International Journal for Philosophy of Religion* 75: 207–32.

Johnson, D. & Krüger, O. 2004. "The good of wrath: Supernatural punishment and the evolution of cooperation." *Political Theology* 5: 159–76.

MacIntyre, A. 1984. *After Virtue*. University of Notre Dame Press.

Mackie, J. L. 1977. *Ethics: Inventing Right and Wrong*. Penguin.

Martin, M. 2008. "Paradoxes of happiness." *Journal of Happiness Studies* 9: 171–84.

Mill, J. S. [1873] 1924. *Autobiography of John Stuart Mill*. Columbia University Press.

Sidgwick, H. 1907. *The Methods of Ethics* (7th edition). Macmillan.

Whately, R. 1856. *Thoughts and Apophthegms*. Lindsay & Blakiston.

Index

For the benefit of digital users, indexed terms that span two pages (e.g., 52–53) may, on occasion, appear on only one of those pages.

Abolitionism 12–13, 29–30, 33–5, 41–2, 59–60, 66, 168, 171–2, 180, 219–32, 235–7, 247–8, 251, 257–8, 260, 275
Akrasia *See* Weakness of will
Alston, W. 170, 175–7
Apophaticism 122, 133, 135–8, 167, 179–81, 195–6
Ayer, A. J. 4, 174–6

Barnes, J. *see* Barnes & Black (2016)
Barnes & Black (2016) 245, 246n.10
Berkeley, G. 178
Bishop, J. 134–5
Black, J. *see* Barnes & Black (2016)
Blackburn, S. 29, 31
Brock, S. 109–10, 120, 123, 127–31, 133–6, 138–9, 143–5, 173–4

Cobb, J. 193–4
Coleridge, S. T. 263, 265
Consequentialism (/Utilitarianism) 35–7, 44–5, 67, 82–3, 94, 97–104
Conservationism 12–13, 29–30, 33–5, 41–2, 59–60, 64–6, 70–2, 78–84, 92, 102–4
Constructive empiricism 109, 149, 155, 193, 205–6
Conversation-stoppers 44, 70, 77, 82–3, 261–3, 267
Cordry, B. 151–2
Critical contexts 45, 51, 90–4, 97, 100–4, 116–17, 171–2, 185, 187–8, 191–2, 199, 264–5

Daly, C. 199
Demetriou, D. *See* Oddie & Demetriou (2007)
Dennett, D. 134–7, 203, 261–2
 (*See also* Conversation-stoppers)
Deng, N. 116, 142–3, 146

Eshleman, A. 150–2, 195–6
Evil, Problem of 212n.5

Faith 110–11, 117, 123–4, 129–30, 132–8, 143, 160–2, 172–3, 175, 177–8
Fictionalism, types of
 Cognitivist fictionalism 169
 (*See also* Prefix fictionalism)

Distraction fictionalism 44–5, 55, 265–6, 270
Hermeneutic fictionalism 5–11, 43, 65n.1, 111, 130–2, 138–41, 143, 145, 167–8, 178–9, 206, 236–7, 240n.7
Lightweight fictionalism 142–3, 185, 189–94, 196, 198, 201
Make-Believe fictionalism 4–5, 29–30, 41, 45, 67, 89–104, 129, 142, 154–5, 191, 206–7, 235–6, 265
Mathematical fictionalism 109, 134, 136, 149–50, 156–8, 163–4, 171–2, 222–3, 225–6
Metaphorist fictionalism 45, 68–70, 72–8, 84
Modal fictionalism 223, 228
Narrationist fictionalism 67, 70–2, 84
Noncognitivist (/Force) fictionalism 89–90, 169
Original fictionalism 110–11, 113–15
Parasitic fictionalism 111, 115–17
Prefix (/Story Operator/Content) Fictionalism 14, 44, 55, 89–90, 206–7, 235n.1
Revolutionary fictionalism 6, 11–15, 43, 65n.1, 86–7, 111, 131, 139–43, 145–6, 163–4, 167–8, 179–81, 184–5, 206, 219–20, 236–7, 251, 257n.2
Thoroughgoing fictionalism 184–93, 199–201
Weak Evaluative Fictionalism (WEF) 142, 184–6, 190
Fideism, Jamesian 134–6, 138
Field, H. 149–50, 171
 (*See also* Mathematical fictionalism)
Frank, R. 270
Frankfurt, H. 174
Frege, G. 95, 157–8, 164

Garner, R. 47n.11, 231–2
Gendler, T. 96–7, 242–3
Gibbard, A. 29

Hare, R. 67n.5
Harman, G. 10
Harrison, V. 170
Hick, J. 121–2
Hitchens, C. 162

Horwich, P. 149, 155–7, 163–4
Howard-Snyder, D. 110, 117
Hume, D. 68–9, 72, 74–7, 80–1, 237–40, 243, 246–8, 251–2, 260–3, 265–6

Irrationality 12–13, 64–5, 78, 80–2, 87, 91–2, 102–4, 152–3, 268
Isserow, J. 92–3

James, W. 134–5
(*See also* Fideism, Jamesian)
Jay, C. 148–9, 152–5, 162–3, 165, 267–8
Joyce, R. 23–6, 29–30, 34–7, 43–6, 51, 56–7, 65–70, 72–84, 88, 90, 140–2, 177, 188–9, 191–2, 195–6, 206–7, 247, 249

Kalderon, M. 7–9, 206–7
Kant, I. 23–4, 133–4, 148–9, 152–5, 163–5, 260–3, 265–70, 273–4
Kasselstrand, I. 49
Kaufman, W. 121–2

Le Poidevin, R. 127–31, 141–3, 168–9, 172–4, 176, 198
Lenman, J. 96
Lewis, C. S. 23n.1, 160–2
Lewis, D. 40
Lillehammer, H. 56
Lipton, P. 168–9, 176, 179n.12, 193, 229

Mackie, J. 24, 29–34, 64–5, 74, 140–1, 206, 209–10, 260–1
Malcolm, F. 127, 197
(*See also* Scott & Malcolm (2018))
Malinowski, B. 160–1
Matravers, D. 239
Metaphor 45, 68–70, 72–8, 84, 94n.4, 132
Mill, J. S. 67n.5, 263–5
Moral Hazard Argument 152–5, 162–3, 267–9

Nichols, S. 53–4
Nolan, D. *See* Nolan, Restall, & West (2005)
Nolan, Restall, & West (2005) 33–5, 50, 247

Oddie, G. *See* Oddie & Demetriou (2007)
Oddie & Demetriou (2007) 52, 54–5
Olson, J. 32–4, 41–2, 46–50, 54–5, 96, 98, 101–4
Orwell, G. 120–1, 177

Palahniuk, C. 243–4
Paradox of Happiness (/Hedonism) 94, 263–6, 269–70, 275
Pascal's Wager 130, 144, 151n.2
Priest, G. 96–7

Relativism, moral 10
Restall, G. *See* Nolan, Restall, & West (2005)
Rey, G. 7–9, 131, 134, 137–8, 158–9, 178n.11
Rosen, G. 223

Scanlon, T. 26, 35–6
Scott, M. 127
(*See also* Scott & Malcolm (2018))
Scott & Malcolm (2018) ("S&M") 127–39, 197
Sidgwick, H. 264
Stich, S. 54
Street, S. 28
Szabó, Z. 186–8

Walton, K. 238–42
Weakness of will (/Akrasia) 11–12, 43–4, 69, 75–6, 91–2, 99, 247–8, 251
Weatherson, B. 238–40
West, C. *See* Nolan, Restall, & West (2005)
Whately, R. 262–3
Williams, B. 23, 25–8

Yablo, S. 158n.6, 225–6